CFROI™ Valuation
A Total System Approach to Valuing the Firm

To Maricela, Gregory, Jeffrey, Miranda and Lucinda

CFROI™ Valuation
A Total System Approach to Valuing the Firm

Bartley J. Madden

CFROI is a trademark of HOLT Value Associates, L.P.

OXFORD AMSTERDAM BOSTON LONDON NEW YORK PARIS
SAN DIEGO SAN FRANCISCO SINGAPORE SYDNEY TOKYO

Butterworth-Heinemann
An imprint of Elsevier Science
Linacre House, Jordan Hill, Oxford OX2 8DP
200 Wheeler Road, Burlington MA 01803

First published 1999
Reprinted 1999, (twice), 2000 (twice), 2002, 2003

British Library Cataloguing in Publication Data
A catalogue record for this book is available from the British Library

ISBN   0 7506 3865 6

For information on all Butterworth-Heinemann
publications visit our website at www.bh.com

Typeset by Laser Words, Madras, India
Printed and bound in Great Britain by Biddles Ltd, *www.biddles.co.uk*

Contents

Preface

The main topic of this book is HOLT's CFROI (cash flow return on investment) valuation model. HOLT Value Associates is an ideal place for me to work because my research instincts are closely aligned with the core beliefs that drive HOLT's business. Those beliefs center on empirically demonstrating advancements in the CFROI valuation model that bring better understanding of the link between firms' performance and stock market valuations. HOLT's primary business is providing software, data, and consulting to help money managers make better investment decisions on buying and selling stocks on a global basis.

Bob Hendricks, HOLT's president, and I have had a particularly beneficial association over the past 30 years. Bob has a unique ability to understand client needs, to communicate complex issues, and to coordinate research, product development, and marketing. Some years ago Bob made a major commitment to expand HOLT's coverage of firms to include all major countries. This has substantially benefited the research reported in this book.

HOLT's portfolio manager clients provide an endless stream of useful problems concerning firms' performance and valuation, on a global basis. Consequently, HOLT's research is directed by the needs of knowledgeable and tough-to-please portfolio managers and security analysts. Improvements that satisfy clients and increase the knowledge-base lead to another round of deeper problems which are subsequently addressed. The end result is an unusual combination of pushing the state of the art while simultaneously improving practical tools for valuation analysis.

In my opinion, the most important role of this book is in providing:

(1) a sharpened way of thinking about relationships among financial variables that drive a firm's warranted value; and
(2) a focus on managerial skill and related business processes that produce the results recorded in financial statements;
(3) an explanation and demonstration of the unique benefits of HOLT's CFROI valuation model.

Some readers might be curious as to how this all began.

In the late 1960s, as part of a finance course at the University of California–Berkeley, I studied an article, 'Dividend policy, growth, and the valuation of shares,' by Merton H. Miller and Franco Modigliani. I was attracted by their total asset approach, which avoided an earnings on common equity orientation. Particularly appealing was their focus on valuing a firm as the sum of two parts — that due to existing assets and that due to future investments. The implementation of this approach to valuation hinges crucially on estimating returns on future investments.

During the 1970s at Callard, Madden & Associates, I was involved full-time in developing a valuation model rooted in the existing asset/future investment approach. Attention was given to developing track records of firms' *economic* performance from reported financial statements and measuring expected returns on future investments implied by stock prices.

The CFROI measure was developed to minimize accounting distortions in measuring firms' economic performance; particularly distortions related to inflation. A time series display of CFROIs helps in forecasting a firm's likely returns on future investments. The CFROI is best understood not as stand-alone performance metric, but as part of a valuation model.

On a technical level connected with measuring firms' economic performance and calculating warranted values, Sam Eddins has made enormous contributions to the material presented in this book. At HOLT, Sam is the 'primary source' for across-the-board technical expertise. Other members of HOLT's research team whose work I have used include Steve Bock, Allan Chhay, Lauren Hackett, Andy Jakes, Tom Hillman, Todd Leigh, John Montgomery, Craig Sterling, and Raymond Stokes. None of the research could have been done without the skill of HOLT's computer staff, especially Hon Ying Chan, George Ching, Joe Cursio, Gaurang Dave, Donn DeMuro, James Gordon, Paul Hackett, and Liza Ylagen.

Some early ideas have proven useful. Charles Callard made the case that equity discount rates could be analysed in terms of the combined effects of anticipated inflation with personal tax rates for dividends and capital gains. Marvin Lipson emphasized the graphical analysis of time series, comparing actual stock prices to warranted values. Rawley Thomas argued that CFROI fade rates (i.e., regress to the average) needed to be applied to both existing assets and future investments.

Over many years, substantial improvements in HOLT's model and software evolved from extensive client relationships maintained by John Birkhold, Tim Bixler, Chris Faber, and George Wedemeyer.

Frank Bock and Matt Halkyard keep HOLT's fax machine busy with European valuation issues. US company problems and solutions have been ably orchestrated in recent years by John Bordes, Mark Giambrone, Brian Graves, Bruce MacFadyen, Rob McClure, and Jim Ostry.

Charles Lee of Cornell University and James Darazsdi of Washington College provided detailed criticisms of every chapter, and that clearly improved the final product. Useful criticisms were also provided by corporate consulting colleagues Gary Bergland, John Carroll, Joel Litman, Mike McConnell, John Penrose, and Bob Rebitz. Major sections of the book were improved from organizational guidelines and detailed comments provided by Lee Glasner.

I feel fortunate in having received particularly high standards of quality in typing from Paige Ayo-Puc and in graphical design from Noel Rupprecht.

Finally, I owe a large debt to Ernie Welker for editing the manuscript and contributing important thinking to every chapter. My wife, Maricela, cooperated admirably with me in dealing with the extended time I needed for writing while sharing the joy of adopting two girls from Guatemala during the time the book was being written.

Author biography

Bartley J. Madden is a partner of HOLT Value Associates, the premier developer and provider of CFROI valuation methods, data, and insights to portfolio managers worldwide. He focuses on basic research to improve the usefulness of the CFROI valuation model for portfolio applications and corporate applications.

Bartley J. Madden has a BS in mechanical engineering from the University of Southern California and an MBA from the University of California-Berkeley. He has been published in economic, finance, and engineering journals, and in the *Wall Street Journal* and other business publications.

The author's work on the CFROI valuation model dates back to the late 1960s. *The Journal of Investing* has published two of his recent articles. Appearing in the Summer 1996 issue, 'The CFROI life cycle' is an empirical study that underpins the CFROI-model's *fade rates*. 'The CFROI valuation model,' published in the Spring 1998 issue, presents empirical support and argument for the CFROI-model's *market-derived discount rate* as superior to the conventional CAPM/beta approach used for estimating firms' costs of capital.

Endorsements

Bart Madden's path-breaking study of CFROI is one of the most important works on corporate finance to appear in the past three decades. His unique systemic approach to valuing the firm, by giving explicit attention to managerial competence and to how work is done, frees valuation from bondage to narrow accounting considerations. This book provides a welcome bridge that offers hope for healing the chasm between concerns of socially-responsible managers and the necessities of market valuation.

> H. Thomas Johnson
> Retzlaff Professor of Business Administration
> Portland State University, Oregon

This is a well-thought-out and splendidly written handbook of the CFROI (Cash Flow Return on Investment) Valuation method. The manuscript is richly endowed with hands-on examples and practical applications. I, as an academic, especially took delight in Chapter 8 in which Madden disposes of two of the most asinine products of academic thinking: the use of the CAPM in capital budgeting and the Free Cash Flow Hypothesis. I would expect to find this book on the desk of every corporate and investment financial analyst and manager.

> George M. Frankfurter
> Lloyd F. Collette Professor of Financial Services
> Louisiana State University

Bart Madden has presented us with a thoughtful blend of economic intuition and practical insights, gleaned from years of careful empirical observation. The CFROI model presented here is a conceptually rigorous, yet eminently practical, approach to measuring firm performance and investment value. Written from a practitioner's perspective, this book nevertheless brings striking insights to academic debates on the cost-of-capital, the handling of accounting items, and cross-sectional differences in ROI fade rates.

Charles M.C. Lee
Henrietta Johnson Louis Professor of Management
Director, Parker Center for Investment Research
Cornell University

Overview

Summary

- Principal objectives of the book are: (1) to explain in detail HOLT Value Associates' CFROI valuation model, (2) to show the CFROI model's unique benefits, and (3) to encourage more productive thinking about issues involving the management of business firms and shareholder value.
- Because the need has never been greater for a useful description of the connections between the performance of firms and the prices of their common stock, valuation models deserve hard-nosed, critical examination.
- Feedback is crucially important to correcting erroneous knowledge and raising the reliability of knowledge, so that actions taken based on what we think we know do in fact have their intended results.
- The CFROI valuation model, with its CFROI performance metric, constitutes an exceptionally useful model for investors, business-firm managements, and corporate boards to gain a *total system perspective* on business firms' internal operations, GAAP financial statements, and the stock market's valuation of expected economic performance.
- By minimizing accounting distortions and adjusting for inflation, CFROIs create a level playing field for measuring firms' economic performance and gauging managerial skill.

Valuation foundation

The need

What is a stock worth and why? The answer to this question is critically important to investors' net worth, to the management of business firms, and to the economic advancement of society generally.

This book answers this question in the form of a comprehensive valuation model increasingly used by professional portfolio managers worldwide to make buy, sell, or hold decisions on specific stocks and by senior corporate managements to take corporate actions to enhance the value of the firm over the long term. In this book we explain in detail the CFROI (cash flow return on investment) valuation model of HOLT Value Associates. Our purpose is to help readers understand the model and have a basis for judging its usefulness.

The author was instrumental in the development of the generic CFROI model during the 1970s and has spent considerable time since then working on detailed components of the HOLT Value Associates' version of the model. The book's sub-title, 'A Total System Approach to Valuing the Firm' conveys a crucially important and differentiating characteristic of the model: '*Total system*' has to do with knowledge generally, what it is, and how it improves. In particular, total system stresses the need to understand how variables affect each other and to avoid analyses that treat parts as independent of the whole. This is a cornerstone for why the CFROI model is more useful than competing models.

The need for reliable knowledge about valuation has never been greater. In recent years increasing pressure has been applied to boards of directors and top corporate officers to implement shareholder-value-based management systems, yet rarely are these individuals knowledgeable about the linkages of corporate performance and stock price. They often admit having little understanding of how the stock market works; worse, they often express erroneous thinking on this topic. The key point is that a valuation model is a critically important part of one's knowledge-base and deserves the same hard-nosed, skeptical scrutiny given to other types of make-or-break knowledge.

Process for learning what works

We have chosen to begin this book by discussing connections among knowledge beliefs, actions based on them, their results, and improvement of knowledge beliefs. Actions informed by erroneous beliefs tend to produce unwanted results—that is, mistakes. Constructive skepticism combined with a process for organizing feedback are crucial to developing more-reliable knowledge.

False knowledge in the form of severely flawed valuation models are behind many costly mistakes, such as investment losses, under-performing businesses, misallocation of resources, retardation of economic advancement, and harmful public policies. The CFROI valuation model is a major improvement to the valuation knowledge-base in large part because it directs attention to *results*, to what 'works' and 'doesn't work' in firm-specific applications. Integral to the CFROI model is a process for its continual improvement.

The style of presentation in this book reflects a strong belief that *processes*, and in particular those rooted in the learning process of the knowledge and action system, are key to outcomes. Thus, our discussion of the model's calculation details emphasizes relationships among variables in order to discourage mindless number crunching and, instead, to promote awareness of processes for improving calculations.

Process underpins our criticism of mainstream finance and our replacement of the CAPM/beta method for estimating cost-of-capital rates for firm-specific valuation. Our method for determining firm-specific costs of capital, or discount rates, is integral to the CFROI model and its approach to net-cash-receipts forecasts, which logic demands. This is one example of how concentration on process nurtures insights, many of which are *obvious* once they are pointed out.

A focus on process led to development of the CFROI metric as an inflation-adjusted measure of economic performance with comparability across firms with disparate asset compositions, across national borders, and across time. The inflation-adjustment process was maintained for calculating investors' discount rates. This led to better observations of relationships between returns on capital and the market's demanded cost for using that capital.

One final reason for our attention to what constitutes knowledge is the ongoing debates about a host of critical issues concerning the management of business firm and shareholder value. These include, among others, stakeholder interests versus maximizing shareholder value; internal performance measurement and non-accounting variables; and the development of financial statements suitable for the Information Age. These critical issues are addressed in the final chapter. Because of their importance, these issues demand a clarity in how we think about them and a critical examination of how others think about them.

Knowledge and action

Knowledge as assumptions

Every day each of us acts to accomplish myriad purposes. For many purposes of daily life, we know with effective certainty what actions to take to achieve our desired outcomes. We know, for example, how to translate what we see into actions required to drive a car to get to work, a highly complex set of knowledge and actions. This 'assumptive world' of highly reliable expected relationships between actions and results is part of our knowledge-base.

For many other purposes we are unsure, to varying degrees, of what to do in order to achieve our purposes. Examples abound in life, whether family or work. Yet, we have to act in order to solve the problem, to meet the objective, to deal with what needs to be done. When we are not sure what to do, the knowledge we draw on is more readily recognized as assumptions: we are forced to assume, to some degree, a relationship in the form, if this, then that: if I do this, then the result will be ... what I want it to be ... I hope.

From time to time when we have been highly confident of what we know, all of us have had the experience of subsequently learning that it was not so. This suggests that even those relationships of which we have a high degree of confidence should be held with some doubt. Indeed, all our knowledge-base might usefully be thought of as assumptions, not just those things we question. Labeling knowledge 'assumptions' has the benefit of reminding us of the tentativeness of the current state of knowledge and to be skeptical of what we think we know. The connotation definitely is *not* that all knowledge is equal in its prediction-and-control usefulness. There are generally accepted ways of establishing degrees of reliability and usefulness.[1]

Critical role of feedback

Figure 1.1 diagrams the knowledge-action relationship as a total system. While knowledge informs actions, actions also inform knowledge. What makes this common-sense knowledge-action system so useful is a feedback loop by which our assumptive knowledge is tested via comparison of the actual results of actions to the expected results. Our assumptive knowledge is either reinforced and taken to be more reliable or is doubted if results were not as expected. The feedback loop is a mechanism for improvement of our knowledge-base, so that the success rate in achieving desired results from action taken goes up.[2]

In view of the importance of feedback for correcting erroneous assumptions and improving the knowledge-base generally, it deserves much attention. Notice that the 'Results' box of Figure 1.1 has two sub-points to the 'Feedback' bullet-point: (a) data selected and (b) measurement tools. What is considered important and relevant (data selected) and how those are recorded (measurement tools) inform the feedback; indeed, they *are* the lens that determines what is perceived.

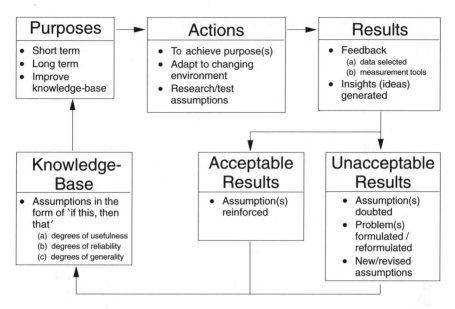

Figure 1.1 Knowledge and action system. Adapted from Bartley J. Madden, 'A transactional approach to economic research,' *Journal of Socio-Economics*, Vol. 20, No. 1, 1991, Figure 2.

Problem recognition

Past experiences influence what we observe

Data selected and measurement tools are the products of the present knowledge-base. Consequently, feedback has a bias in favor of the present knowledge-base, and tends to reinforce it. Shortcomings and problems with the present knowledge-base often go unrecognized because feedback inconsistent with the present knowledge-base is filtered out. This is a major obstacle to detecting erroneous knowledge and correcting it.

In the realm of valuation for example, many managements believe that stock prices are driven by accounting earnings per share (EPS). This assumption has been reinforced by observations of stock price movements shortly after announcements of quarterly EPS surprises, positive or negative. This assumption that EPS drives share price apparently was strongly held by AT&T's top management, which reportedly offered to pay a very substantial amount to NCR for the express purpose of using pooling instead of purchase accounting when they combined.[3] Pooling accounting would increase accounting EPS for the firm, although after-tax cash flows would not be affected by the accounting treatment of the combined firms.

Results observed through the lens of the CFROI model reflect different data selected as important as well as different measurement tools. As we shall demonstrate, feedback in the form of firms' historical track records of CFROI are far superior to a firm's EPS in explaining levels of and changes in stock prices. If stock-price expectations of AT&T's top decision makers were based on the CFROI model rather than the EPS model, no favorable result for the firm's stock price would have been expected solely from the use of pooling accounting rather than purchase accounting. More generally, expected stock-price reactions to various actions can be improved by getting feedback from types of data and measurement tools other than accounting EPS and ranges of P/E (price/earnings) multiples.

Nurturing clearer observations

Progress in improving the knowledge-base often flows from challenging well-accepted assumptions.[4] If a major obstacle to improving knowledge is the bias of feedback, and if knowledge is improved by the identification/formulation of problems arising in the context of the current knowledge-base, then an important aspect of the usefulness of models is their effectiveness for nurturing feedback, insights, and problem identification.

Analyzing the firm as a total system

Feedback

As displayed in Figure 1.2, the CFROI valuation model is part of a total system. In its presentation of the HOLT CFROI valuation model, this book devotes considerable space to the narrow problem of calculating a warranted value of business firms.[5] This CFROI model is a set of assumptions about how the stock market values business firms. Not a lot of thought is required for one to have an appreciation for the wide scope and enormous complexity of the processes and the relationships involved with business operations. So, when we write favorably about the level of detail of the CFROI model, we are not referring so much to the model's detail of the causal relationships among the many important variables *inside* the firm that determine performance as we are referring to the model's detail for measuring performance, forecasting future cash flows, and valuing them. In setting stock prices, investors value the total firm including intangible

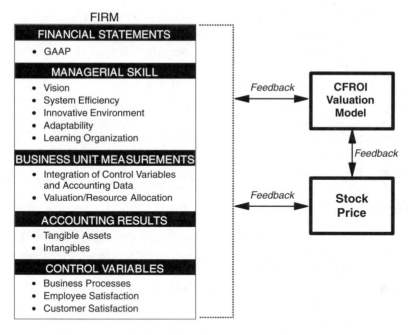

Figure 1.2 Analyzing the firm as a total system.

assets not reflected in GAAP financial statements. Feedback from comparing warranted values calculated from the CFROI model to actual stock prices is a key ingredient for learning how to treat difficult performance/valuation issues within the model.

Figure 1.2 suggests that the CFROI model can also orchestrate feedback from the stock market to managements. This can play a vital role as a check on management's view of the firm's basic mission, what Peter Drucker has called 'the theory of business.'[6] Both corporate managers and portfolio managers tend to blunder most seriously when structural change is counter to their most strongly held assumptions — assumptions which have become articles of faith not to be questioned. Regular analyses of peer performance and stock market expectations can provide feedback useful for early recognition that fundamental change external to the firm is occurring.

Accounting statements measure results

Financial statements, by and large, can be made useful for measuring business firms' longer term *results*. It is a grave mistake, however, to assume that, internal to the firm, accounting variables are causal variables in the creation of wealth.[7] Figure 1.2 separates accounting results from control variables that deal with business processes, employee satisfaction, and customer satisfaction. This is to emphasize

firm-wide operating efficiency as opposed to local accounting efficiencies in the wealth creation process.

Consider, as an illustration, the question, Should employee training
be treated solely as a cost or as an asset integral to the process of
providing value to customers? If the former, the goal is easy to
quantify: near term, net income will rise if these costs are lowered.
On the other hand, if the firm strives to be a learning organization,
the longer-term value of a current expenditure on training must be
considered, and managers must focus on how non-GAAP intangible
assets affect performance and market valuation.

Benefits of approach

Stock prices incorporate the likely future benefits from R&D expenditures and other intangibles.[8] As managements and board members
improve their knowledge of the link between firms' economic performance and share price, they will increasingly look beyond accounting
earnings. They will gain conviction that large investments in core
competencies and long-lived, viable projects in which the firm has
demonstrated skill can raise the company's stock price, even if near-
term accounting results suffer from it.

Once one adopts a total system perspective, it becomes eminently
sensible that the stock market should be used as a tool for learning
about the valuation effects of firms' operations not adequately
reflected in GAAP financial statements. Research can then be focused
on what kinds of information appear to be important, without
necessarily seeking to promote a particular accounting rule as the
best treatment. For example, reporting considerable detail on outlays
for R&D, patents, employee training, and the like may be more
useful than capitalizing and amortizing them over some arbitrary
time period. From a CFROI valuation perspective, investors can
assimilate this information and use it to forecast future CFROI levels
and expected fade rates, i.e., the rate at which abnormally high or
low CFROIs regress towards the competitive average.

With a better valuation lens, directors and top executives can use
the stock market as a source of intelligence gathering. Corporate
staffs and investors can continually improve their understanding of
what determines levels of and changes in stock prices over time. They
also can make better resource allocation and investment decisions.
Among such decisions are acquisition pricing, warranted values for
each of the firm's business units, buy/hold/sell decisions on individual stocks, and the like. The accounting profession and regulatory
bodies can better focus on the benefits of providing relevant detailed
information that does not neatly fit into the accounting-earnings

paradigm but does fit the paradigm of analyzing the firm as a total system.

CFROI valuation model

Rooted in discounted cash flow (DCF)

The foundation for valuation is the concept of a net present value based on discounted *expected* cash flows. The CFROI valuation model is rooted in DCF principles: (a) more cash is preferred to less; (b) cash has a time value, sooner is preferred to later; and (c) less uncertainty is better.

The firm's warranted value is driven by a forecast *net cash receipt* (NCR) stream which is translated into a present value by use of the investors' *discount rate*. At this fundamental level, the CFROI valuation model always 'works.' In applying DCF, the CFROI model illuminates variables ignored in many valuation models, and this makes it more complex than other popular models. In practice, however, the CFROI model's completeness enables users to more easily and effectively work out complex performance/valuation problems.

CFROI economic performance metric

Before the mechanics of DCF valuation are explored, readers are presented with the CFROI approach to displaying the track records of firms. Company examples reveal benefits of the model's use of inflation-adjusted, or *real* magnitudes. All valuation drivers in the CFROI model are calibrated as 'real' values. This gives consistency to time series and makes different time series directly comparable. It also facilitates global research dealing with CFROIs and discount rates in country environments with sharply different accounting conventions and inflation rates. Readers will quickly see that economic performance, displayed in the CFROI framework, provides company-specific insights and helpful comparability of performance over time and across companies, both domestic and foreign.

Managerial skill and competition are the fundamental determinants of the path of a firm's economic performance through time. The CFROI valuation model incorporates these in the form of a competitive life-cycle framework for analyzing firms' past performance and forecasting future performance. The life-cycle framework postulates that over the long term there is competitive pressure for above-average CFROI firms to *fade downward* toward the average economic return and for below-average firms to *fade upward*. This tie-in between the past and the future serves as the solid foundation on which to judge the plausibility of a CFROI forecast in terms of both the firm's (or the business unit's) own track record and the performance of relevant competitors.

As for the model's net cash receipt forecast, the primary focus is on the fade patterns for forecasted CFROIs and for reinvestment rates (asset growth), with particular attention given to the next five years. Guidelines for linking managerial skill to these competitive fade rates and some useful empirical relationships are presented. As a practical matter, common stockholders substantially outperform or underperform the general market over a particular time period when the firm delivers CFROIs which are much higher or lower than expected at the beginning of the period. Consequently, investment decisions are crucially dependent on the difference between the market's revealed expected CFROI fade rate and the investor's forecasted CFROI fade rate.

A new approach to discount rates

Regarding the discount rate component of DCF valuation, we reject conventional CAPM (Capital Asset Pricing Model) and beta procedures for estimating firms' discount rates (cost of capital), because they are rooted in a backward-looking estimate of a premium for the general equity market over a risk-free rate coupled to a dubious volatility measure of risk (beta). Currently popular valuation models other than CFROI treat these discount rates as independent of the models' procedure for forecasting net cash receipts. In practice, there is no described feedback loop by which to judge the plausibility of these discount rates. The employment of CAPM/beta and related procedures has become a ritual due not to empirical usefulness, but to its mathematical elegance — the touchstone of mainstream academic corporate finance.

In contrast to CAPM/beta, the CFROI valuation model does not import a discount rate determined without regard to the model's forecasting procedures. In HOLT's model, a firm's discount rate is determined by the market rate plus a company-specific risk differential. The market's discount rate is derived using monitored forecast data for an aggregate of firms with known market values. This makes it a *forward-looking* rate, derived much in the manner that a bond's yield-to-maturity is calculated from a known price and a forecast of future cash receipts from interest and principal. A firm's risk differential is a function of the firm's size and financial leverage. The empirical foundation of these risk differentials is consistent with HOLT's CFROI-model procedures for forecasting a firm's net cash receipt stream.

Portfolio manager perspective

At year-end 1997, HOLT's CFROI valuation model was in worldwide use by approximately 250 money management organizations. Why? First, they gain the efficiency of analyzing firms' track records with data that are directly comparable and have the same meaning regardless of the firm's asset composition, or whether the chronological period is 1970 or 1997, or whether the country is Japan, Germany, the United Kingdom, the United States, or any other country. Second, HOLT's model has proven useful to these managers in improving their buy/hold/sell decisions. Accuracy does count. Winners (losers) in the stock market deliver performance substantially greater (less) than market expectations. HOLT's model is especially well-suited to gauge market expectations of performance reflected in a stock price and to calibrate probable stock prices for different levels of forecasted performance.

The usefulness of the model to explain levels of and changes in stock prices over time is continually challenged. HOLT's CFROI valuation model is currently applied to publicly traded firms in all major countries. By focusing on significant *deviations* between warranted and actual stock prices over time for individual firms, problems are recognized. Resolution takes the form of both understanding the reasons for the deviation and empirical confirmation that a proposed fix does in fact significantly reduce this deviation. In this way, the model continually and actively raises questions as part of an ongoing process of improvement. The completeness of the CFROI model also greatly helps in dealing with difficult issues and diverse accounting conventions: for example, plant revaluations in the United Kingdom; large cross-holdings in Japan; substantial investments in non-operating assets in France; the blending of pensions and operating assets in Germany; and the treatment of post-retirement health benefits (FASB 106) in the United States.

There is a growing academic interest in residual income valuation models. One version of residual income is Stern Stewart & Co.'s EVA® (Economic Value Added). Salient differences between HOLT's CFROI model and residual income/EVA® are addressed.

Rankings of firms by various financial measures are widely reported. HOLT has developed a DualGrade® Performance Scorecard grounded in the CFROI model. The 'dual grade' system comprises an A through E grade based on near-term forecasted CFROI and another A through E grade based on the percentage of a firm's current market value attributable to future investments. The second grade is called '%

Future', and is interpreted as the market's assessment of management's ability to position and operate the firm to create wealth in the future, arguably the primary task of top management. The usefulness of HOLT's DualGrade® Performance Scorecard is demonstrated with actual dual grades for firms grouped by industry, and its advantages over some widely reported ranking measures are explained.

2

CFROI^{TM} *lifecycle*

Summary

- Twenty example companies' performance records in terms of some key CFROI-model variables are displayed as time series to enable readers to see some of the CFROI model's advantages.
- First, highly summarized descriptions of the CFROI-model components relevant to the displayed time series are presented so that readers will have the basic understanding needed to interpret the charts.
- *Economic* performance can be understood as a *real* rate of return earned on a completed project where all cash outlays and receipts are expressed in monetary units of equivalent purchasing power.
- The CFROI economic performance metric can be understood as an estimate of the real rate of return earned by a firm on all its assets, which can be thought of as a portfolio of projects.
- Managerial skill and competition are the fundamental determinants of a firm's economic performance over time.
- There is a competitive life cycle, wherein competition tends to force high CFROI firms downward over time toward the average. Below-average CFROIs for a number of years set the stage for restructuring, whether voluntary or forced upon management by outside shareholders. Significant improvement toward earning the cost of capital typically necessitates shrinking the firm.
- The amount of wealth a firm creates is related to both the rate of return it earns on its assets and the amount of its assets. Consequently, all else equal, the increase in wealth creation is higher when high CFROI firms also grow fast.

Economic performance

Those experienced in the use of valuation models realize that calculating a warranted value is not an exact science. Slightly varied
assumptions about a firm's forecasted economic performance can
produce enormous changes in warranted values. Therefore, a key
component of a valuation model's usefulness is its ability to facilitate
plausibility judgements concerning the forecast. Plausibility judgements entail benchmarks. Benchmarks regarding a firm's *future*
performance are obtained from analysis of the firm's *past* performance and the performance of competitors. So, rather than beginning
with a description of handling forecast data and making warranted
value calculations, our first topic is how best to display firms' track
records of past economic performance.

At a basic level, *economic* performance can be described in terms of
a completed project. Consider a project that the firm had undertaken
and has completed. All cash outflows and inflows have been recorded
for each time period covering the project life.[1] Relevant time periods
could be annual or more frequent (e.g. quarterly). Figure 2.1 represents project economics as an initial cost for assets (down arrow)
followed by net cash receipts (up arrows), the last of which includes
salvage value, if any.

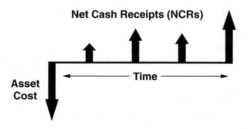

Figure 2.1   Generic product cash flows.

Economic performance is measured by the firm's achieved ROI
(return on investment) adjusted for any changes in the purchasing
power of the monetary unit. The ROI is the internal rate of return
that equates the project's net cash receipt (NCR) stream to its cost.
Cash outflows and inflows are expressed in monetary units of the
same purchasing power (e.g., constant dollars) by adjusting for
period-to-period changes in the general price level. The measurement
of economic performance requires inflation adjustments; otherwise,
the cash amounts reflect a combination of economic performance
and monetary unit changes. In final form, the firm's economic
performance for this project can be expressed as a *real, achieved ROI*.

Now let us focus on projects not yet undertaken. As we emphasize in later chapters, stock prices of individual firms change nearly continually in part due to investor changes in forecasts of likely ROIs from the individual firm's future projects. How might investors make these forecasts? Ideally, investors would prefer detailed information on ROIs achieved by the firm historically. But ROIs on individual projects (or business units) are not available to investors. Financial statements are all that is available, and they represent *aggregate* results.

In working with aggregate financial statements, investors need to assess likely ROIs on future projects in relation to the firm's cost of capital. This is the language of discounted cash flow: internal rates of return and discount rates. This is *not* the language of accounting-based ratios derived from financial statements and often loosely referred to as 'ROIs'.

HOLT's CFROI valuation model is particularly rigorous in its inflation-adjustment procedures, i.e., in calculating 'real' magnitudes. This added *complexity* is necessary in order to better observe patterns and important relationships in time-series data and to better judge the plausibility of forecast data. An intuitive grasp of the CFROI concept might be quickly achieved from a review of its original development.

CFROI as a return measure

During the early 1970s, this author worked on modeling the economic ROIs on a firm's projects and the resulting accounting statements. This led to an inflation-adjusted cross-sectional measure of ROI that became known as CFROI. In an environment of varying inflation rates, as-reported accounting data can be translated into CFROIs that more accurately measure the economic returns actually achieved on the model firm's portfolio of projects. The original work developed out of this research question:

> Suppose a model firm has always made annual *incremental* investments in similar projects that achieve the same *real* ROI. The firm operates in an environment with changing price levels and varying nominal interest rates. How should *aggregate* data, as reflected in the accounting statements, be translated into a time series of cross-sectional annual return measures that accurately reproduce the ROIs being achieved on incremental projects?

In constant-dollar terms, each year's capital expenditures were invested in a project as represented in Figure 2.2. The model firm can be constructed as an ongoing portfolio of projects with a portion

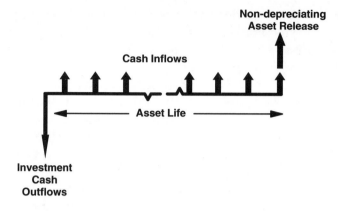

Figure 2.2   Model firm's project cash flows.

of gross plant retired each year and new plant added, along with associated working capital. A spreadsheet can be created where a specified series of known real project ROIs are translated into real cash outflows and inflows.

These real cash flows can be converted into conventional accounting statements that take account of the complex effects of a specified time series of inflation rates and nominal interest rates. The actual US inflation rates and long-term corporate bond yields over the last century shown in Figure 2.3 were used for illustrative purposes.

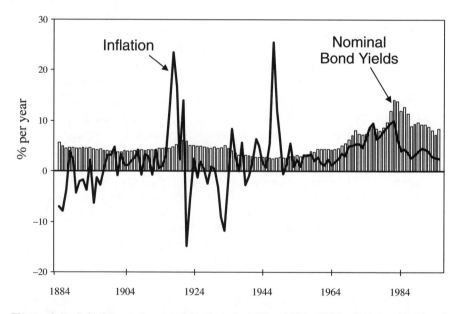

Figure 2.3   Inflation and corporate bond yields, 1884–1994. Source: Bartley J. Madden, 'The CFROI life cycle,' *Journal of Investing*, Vol. 5, No. 2, 1996, exhibit 3.

Conventional annual earnings/book ratios can be calculated and compared with the known economic performance, i.e. the originally specified series of real project ROIs. CFROIs can be calculated and compared with these project ROIs.

After incorporating asset composition, financial leverage, and dividend payouts similar to the S&P Industrial Index of the last two decades, and after using a 6.5 per cent real project ROI, the model firm's earnings/book ratio displays the roller coaster time series shown in Figure 2.4.[2]

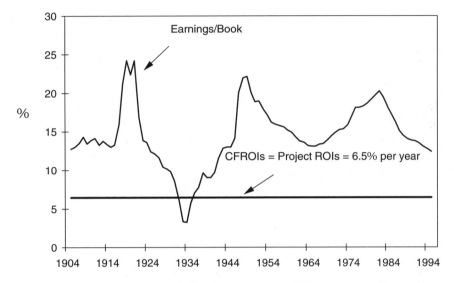

Figure 2.4 Model firm's earnings/book ratios and CFROIs corresponding to 6.5 per cent real project ROIs. Source: Bartley J. Madden, 'The CFROI life cycle,' *Journal of Investing*, Vol. 5, No. 2, 1996, exhibit 4.

The horizontal line at 6.5 per cent reflects not only the ongoing real project ROIs, but also the annual CFROIs, calculated from the built-up, as-reported accounting data.

This exercise convincingly demonstrates the need to avoid the distortions that are intrinsic to all historical-cost accounting proxies for ROI, such as earnings/book. Who, referring to Figure 2.4, would not be misinformed about a firm's performance by relying on the gyrating earnings/book series while economic performance did not vary? Yet, the earnings/book ratio is used by many investment professionals and corporate managements as a gauge of performance.

The CFROI is a much more informative performance measure. CFROI is a real *cross-sectional* return measure derived at a point in time from *aggregate* data contained in conventional financial statements. 'ROI', in CFROI lexicon, denotes an internal rate of return

(IRR) for a *project*. Displayed as a time-series track record, the CFROI is an excellent measure with which to judge levels of and trends in a firm's economic performance, which then can be used to help forecast ROIs on future projects.

Managerial skill and the competitive life cycle

This basic introduction to the competitive life cycle is essential for readers to appreciate the content of the company examples that follow. As mentioned in Chapter 1, managerial skill and competition are the fundamental determinants of a firm's economic performance over time.

A firm's level of *managerial skill* is gauged, over the longer term, by the extent that:

(1) customers believe they have received high value from the firm's products/services;
(2) the average competitor in the industry is unable to reproduce what the firm delivers, and/or to achieve its level of resource efficiency; and
(3) larger investments are made while still earning returns on its investments well above the cost of capital.

Managerial skill involves five critical tasks highlighted in Figure 2.5:

(1) setting a vision that elicits a personal commitment from employees and addresses a substantial economic need;
(2) aligning business processes in a system designed to efficiently deliver value to the customer;
(3) organizing feedback within the firm so that change is not threatening and innovation is commonplace;
(4) continually integrating strategies, opportunities, and core competencies so that adaptability is a way of life; and
(5) creating and transmitting knowledge throughout the firm.

Figure 2.6 depicts the stylized competitive life cycle of businesses. During this life cycle, businesses continually strive to earn high CFROIs by efficiently using resources in providing value to customers. This can take the form of creating new products and services, and/or improving an existing design, production, distribution or servicing process.

When businesses succeed in achieving above-average returns, competitors are attracted by above-average returns and try to serve

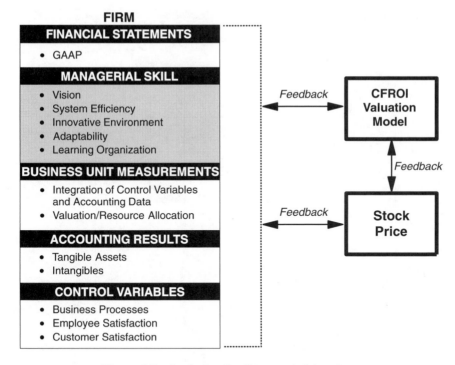

Figure 2.5 Analyzing the firm as a total system.

the customer even more effectively. The competitive process tends to force high-CFROI firms down toward the average. Competition here refers to any and all types: direct, indirect, pricing, quality, convenience, reputation, and the like. Businesses earning CFROIs below the cost of capital are eventually compelled to restructure and/or downsize in order to earn at least the cost of capital, or eventually they cease operations.

George Stigler authored a classic study of how long-term competition diminishes any spread, positive or negative, between return on capital and the cost of capital. His findings were encapsulated in two sentences[3]:

> There is no more important proposition in economic theory than that, under competition, the rate of return on investment tends toward equality in all industries. Entrepreneurs will seek to leave relatively unprofitable industries and enter relatively profitable industries.

For an established business, the time series of CFROIs communicates a great deal about the level of managerial skill. The stock market places considerable weight on managerial skill in forecasting future economic performance. The crucial forecast is for ROIs on incremental investments, and past levels of and trends in CFROIs are useful for gauging future ROIs.

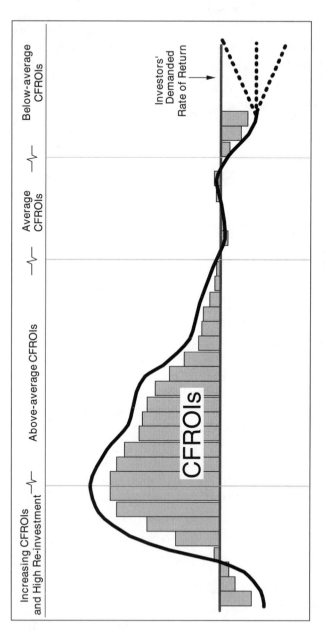

Figure 2.6   Stylized competitive life cycle.

All else equal, more wealth is created when CFROIs above the cost of capital are coupled with larger asset bases. But as a tendency, a higher rate of asset growth drives down CFROIs. So, the complete display of a firm's life cycle includes both CFROIs and real asset growth rates.

A significant advantage of the CFROI valuation model is that firms' track records of CFROIs and real asset growth rates provide a visual display of past performance which corresponds exactly with the key drivers of forecasted future performance. This is not to say that the future must be much like the past. Rather, the point is that if performance for established firms is forecasted to be substantially improved, the business plans for doing it would be expected to break with business-as-usual. The better one understands the past, the better equipped one is to deal with the future.

Life-cycle examples

The stylized competitive life cycle depicts a business having experienced a period of successful innovation, followed by CFROIs fading downward due to competitive pressure, which in turn is followed by returns approximately equal to the cost of capital, and finally a period of wealth-dissipating returns. Firms do not mechanistically follow this stylized life cycle. As the forthcoming examples demonstrate, many firms deviate from the stylized stages.

The stock market continually assesses a firm's future life cycle. It is when firms deliver economic performance that deviates from market expectations that investors receive excess positive or negative shareholder returns. Such deviations can be described as *unexpected* CFROI and/or asset-growth patterns. The example company track records that follow provide an introduction to the usefulness of these visual displays in the context of the life-cycle framework.

The company examples are displayed in two charts, with data covering 1960 (or when first available after that) to 1996. The left-side chart shows, at the top, the annual high-low range of the firm's stock price (vertical line) and the closing price for the year (horizontal line). The other two lines show the firm's annual gross assets and gross cash flow. For US firms, both series are in millions of current dollars—i.e., the assets are expressed in dollars with purchasing power of the plotted year, instead of the historical dollars of balance-sheet amounts which have mixed purchasing power. Non-US firms are treated similarly with data expressed in the monetary units of the particular country.

These time series are plotted on logarithmic scale to better reveal rates of change and trends in them. In order to plot on the same scale a variety of data for the same firm and have minimum intersection of the different series, base data have been multiplied by suitable factors (e.g. 0.1, 10, 100, etc.). For example, a $20 stock price is typically plotted at the 200 position, thereby keeping the stock price series at the top of the chart.

The conventional time series plots of asset amounts and cash flow amounts provide only a crude indication of a firm's economic performance. However, they are important inputs to the CFROI calculation. The firm's track record of CFROIs is shown in the top panel of the right-side chart. The track record of CFROIs is in the language of real, internal rates of return and is useful for assessing a firm's probable ROIs on future investments.

Shown below the CFROI panel is the real asset growth rate chart, which is highly volatile for many firms, often due to acquisitions and divestitures.

The 'Relative Wealth Index,' in the bottom panel, has a beginning value of 1.0. For a firm with data beginning from 1960, the starting point is the firm's closing stock price for 1959. The index is constructed in the following manner. Suppose that in 1960, a US firm's stock price appreciation plus dividends provided a 10 per cent return while the S&P 500 provided a total return of 5 per cent. In this illustration, the firm's shareholders outperformed the S&P 500 by 5 per cent and the Relative Wealth Index would plot as 1.00 for 1959 and 1.05 for 1960.[4] The Relative Wealth Index is a cumulative measure which reflects the total return to the firm's shareholders in relation to the total return provided by the S&P 500.

This procedure is continued each year through 1996. If a firm's return to its shareholders through 1996 exactly matched that of the S&P 500, the value of the index for 1996 would be 1.00. An ending value of 2.00 indicates that the shareholders' wealth grew at twice the rate of the S&P 500. Similarly, an ending value of 0.50 indicates that shareholders fared poorly, with their ending wealth being only one-half of the wealth that could have been earned by owning the S&P 500 index.

Whatever the ending index value, periods of upward trends indicate returns exceeding the S&P 500 and downward indicate the opposite. Shareholder returns approximately match the S&P 500 when the trend is horizontal. For non-US firms, the local country stock market index replaced the S&P 500.

Two benchmarks might be helpful. The long-term average CFROI for all US industrial/service companies has been around 6 per cent, with relatively small annual deviations from the average. Because CFROIs have eliminated the effects of inflation, they can meaningfully be compared across time. The long-term average real asset growth rate for the same sample of companies has ranged between two and three per cent.

Our commentaries appearing with the example charts call attention to revealing patterns. *The charts provide a rough sense of the relationship between CFROI performance that deviates from expected patterns and the related trends in the Relative Wealth Index.* As noted earlier, differences between market expectations and subsequent actual performance ultimately determine excess positive or negative shareholder returns.

Table 2.1 Twenty example firms (Figures 2.7 through 2.26) were selected to illustrate a wide variety of life-cycle performance.

Firm	Country	Equity Market $US Billions (1996)	CFROI (1996)
International Business Machines	United States	77.0	7.2
Wal-Mart Stores	United States	52.0	11.3
Hewlett-Packard	United States	51.0	12.4
Abbott Laboratories	United States	39.3	16.3
Emerson Electric	United States	21.7	10.0
Mannesmann	Germany	15.9	4.2
Nintendo	Japan	10.1	11.6
Air Products & Chemicals	United States	7.6	4.7
Hershey Foods	United States	6.7	9.5
Whitbread Plc	United Kingdom	6.5	5.5
Wrigley	United States	6.5	16.7
Atlas Copco	Sweden	4.4	11.2
Analog Devices	United States	4.0	10.4
Advanced Micro Devices	United States	3.5	−3.9
Dana	United States	3.4	8.1
Apple Computer	United States	2.6	−18.8
Cooper Tire & Rubber	United States	1.6	8.2
Briggs & Stratton	United States	1.3	8.3
Bethlehem Steel	United States	1.0	0.6
Coors	United States	0.8	2.2

A final note concerns data sources for the company charts in this chapter and similar data throughout the book. The data are contained in the *ValueSearch* database of HOLT Value Associates. This database uses a variety of original source data files which are translated into variables used in the CFROI valuation model. For fundamental financial statement data, the original source provider for US firms was Standard & Poor's *Compustat*; for Japanese firms, *Pacific Data*; and for all other non-US firms, *World 'Vest Base*.

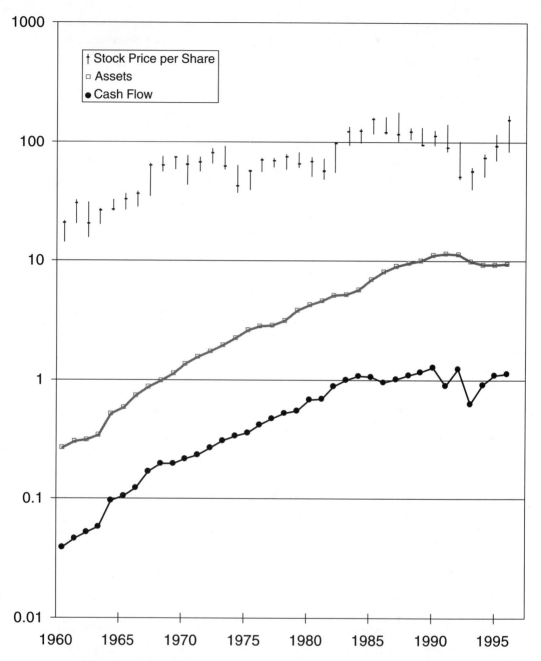

Figure 2.7A International Business Machines. The IBM story is well known. From 1960 to the mid-1980s, IBM earned well above-average CFROIs while dominating the mainframe computer industry. From the mid-1980s to the early 1990s, IBM's relative wealth index sharply declined due to rapidly falling CFROIs. In recent years new management has restructured IBM. Negative real asset growth and improving CFROIs with upward trending relative wealth suggest that past managerial mistakes have been adequately addressed.

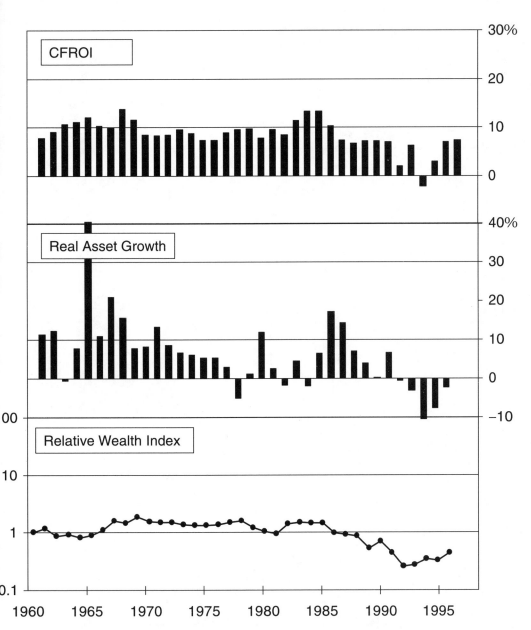

Figure 2.7B   International Business Machines.
Source: Compustat and HOLT/*ValueSearch*™

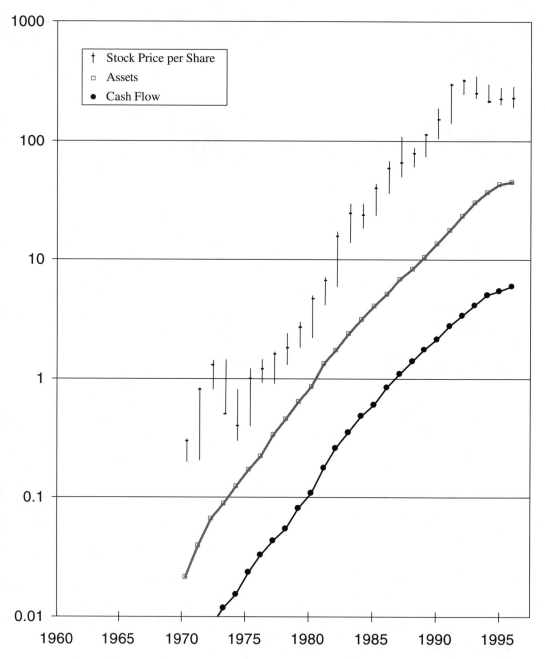

Figure 2.8A Wal-Mart Stores. Until the early 1990s, long-term shareholders in Wal-Mart, the world's largest retailer, achieved a truly extraordinary string of positive excess returns. Not only did Wal-Mart earn high CFROIs, but this was combined with *exceptionally high* asset growth year after year. Expectations at the beginning of the 1990s were subsequently not met as CFROIs declined somewhat and asset growth sharply declined. Note the declining Relative Wealth line in recent years.

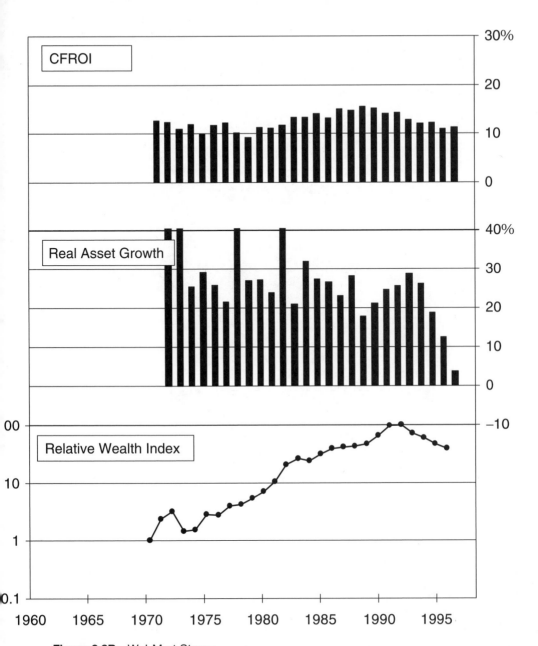

Figure 2.8B Wal-Mart Stores.
Source: Compustat and HOLT/*ValueSearch*™

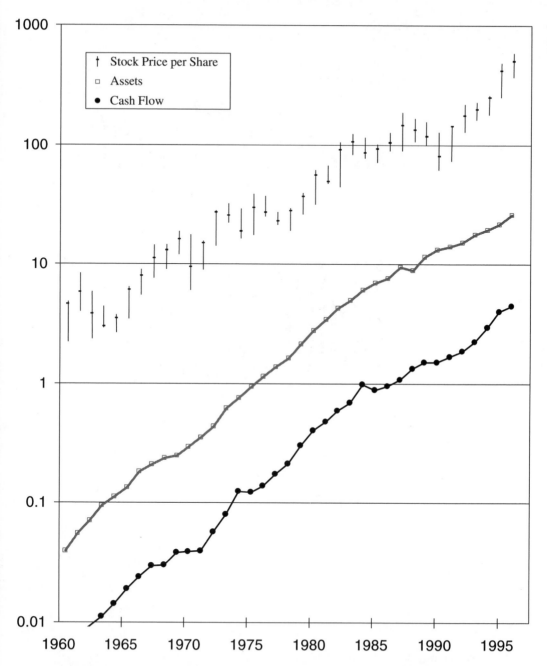

Figure 2.9A Hewlett-Packard. For much of the 1980s, Hewlett-Packard's CFROIs weakened and the stock underperformed. The 1990s showed increasing CFROIs and a rising Relative Wealth line. HP is a well-managed firm that grows at a rapid rate and over the long term, 1960 to 1996, has "beat the fade." That is, its above-average CFROI in the early 1960s is still maintained in the mid-1990s.

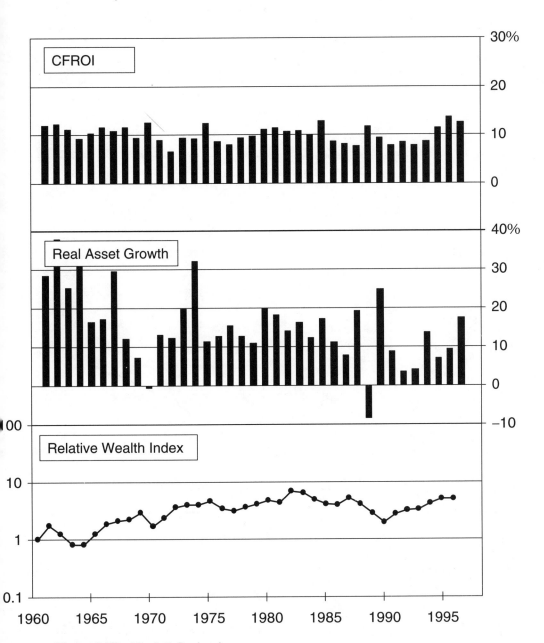

Figure 2.9B Hewlett-Packard.
Source: Compustat and HOLT/*ValueSearch*™

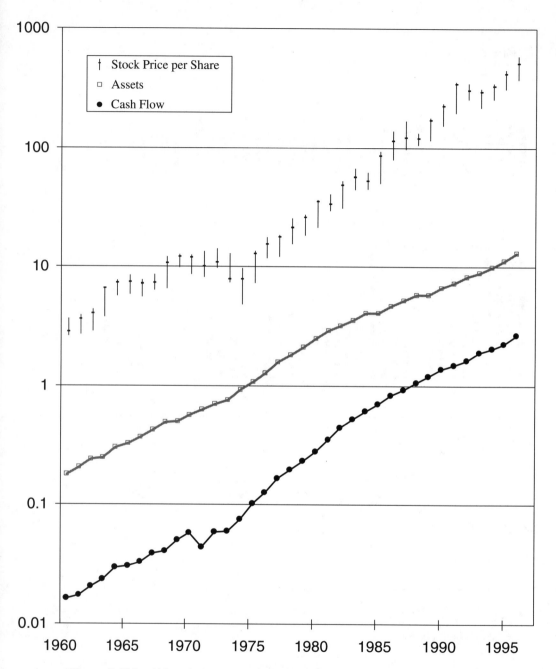

Figure 2.10A   Abbott Laboratories. Abbott Laboratories is a diversified health-care products company. Its stock substantially outperformed the market for many years as the firm's increasing CFROIs surprised investors.

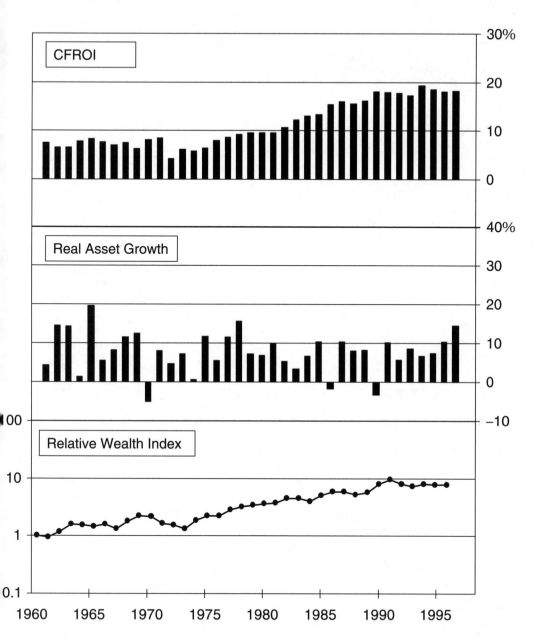

Figure 2.10B   Abbott Laboratories.
Source: Compustat and HOLT/*ValueSearch*™

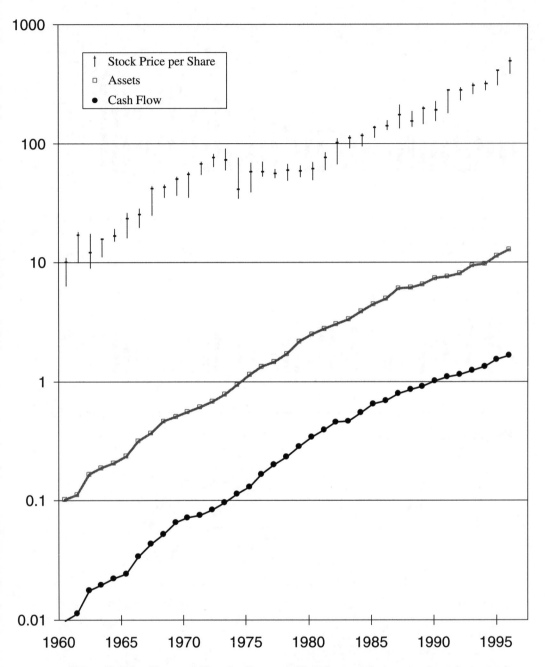

Figure 2.11A   Emerson Electric. Emerson Electric manufacturers a broad range of electrical and electronic products. For many years, the firm has delivered excellent perfomance, as seen in the CFROI track record, yet shareholders did not earn returns greater than the general market (flat Relative Wealth line). The market evidently has long recognized management's high skill level and has priced the firm's stock with appropriate expectations of excellent performance.

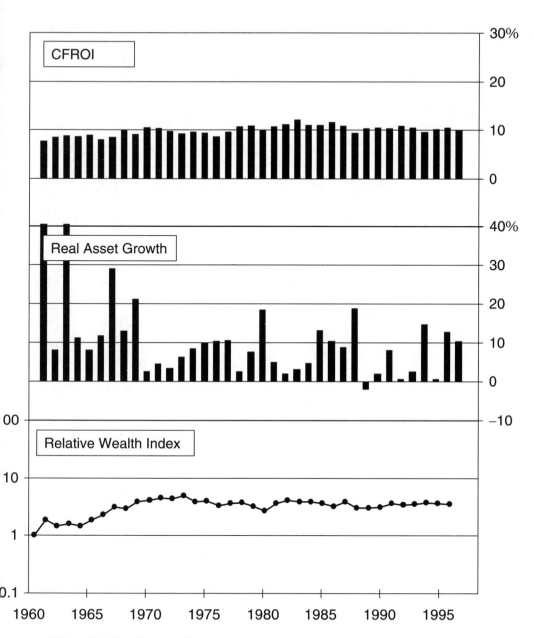

Figure 2.11B   Emerson Electric.
Source: Compustat and HOLT/*ValueSearch*™

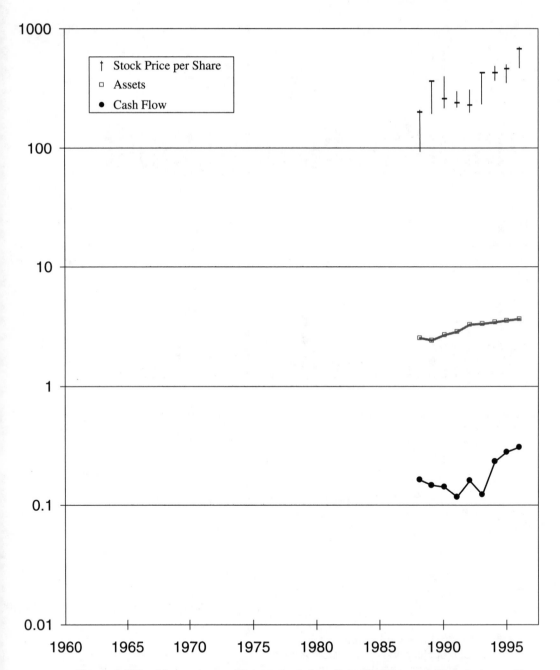

Figure 2.12A Mannesmann. Mannesmann is a diversified German manufacturer of highly-engineered machinery and control systems. Earlier in the 1990s, it grew its assets while CFROIs were abysmally low, and its stock underperformed the market. Over the past few years, its CFROIs have improved as management emphasized new investment in its telecommunication services business. Its stock has outperformed the market during this period.

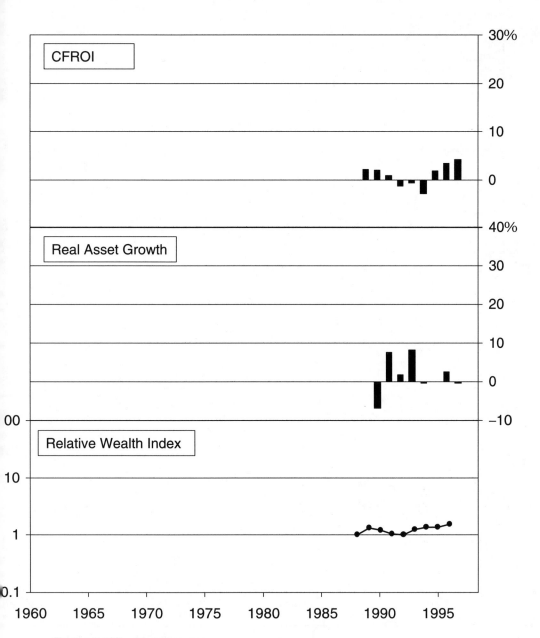

Figure 2.12B   Mannesmann.
Source: World 'Vest Base and HOLT/*ValueSearch*™

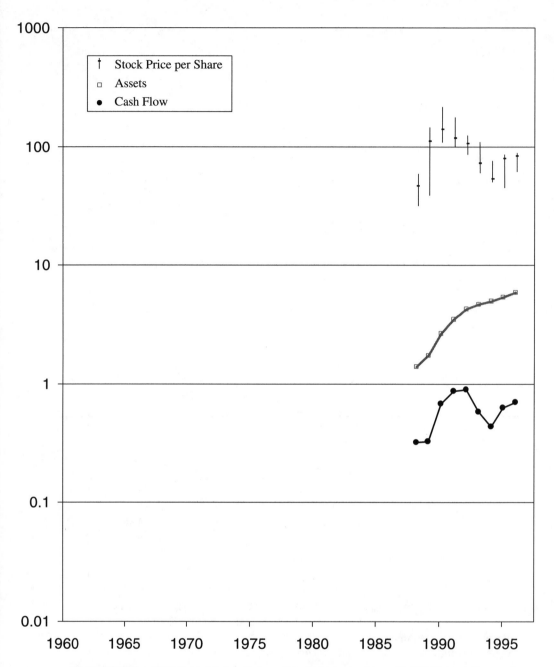

Figure 2.13A Nintendo. Nintendo is a Japanese company with the largest share of the home video game market. Very high CFROIs and asset growth near the turn of the decade first raised market expectations (upward Relative Wealth line) and then disappointed (downward Relative Wealth line) when both CFROIs and asset growth dropped off.

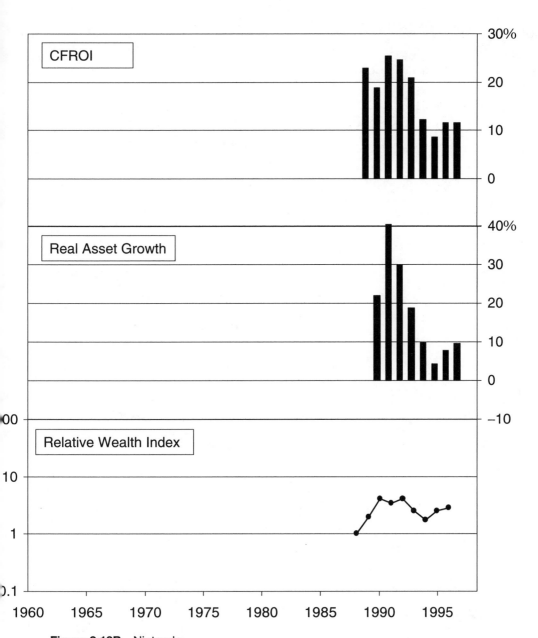

Figure 2.13B Nintendo.
Source: Pacific Data and HOLT/*ValueSearch*™

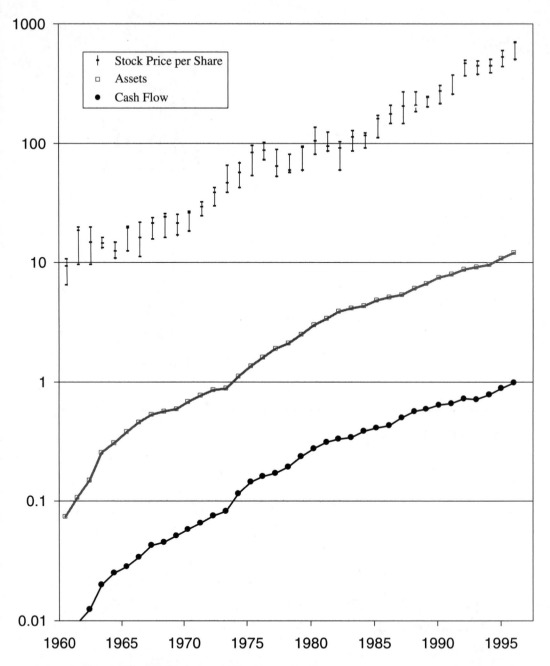

Figure 2.14A Air Products & Chemicals. Air Products & Chemicals has achieved a steady level of CFROIs, like Emerson Electric, but at a much lower level. It produces a variety of gases and chemicals. The flat Relative Wealth line suggests the market has come to expect what the firm delivers. For Air Products to outperform the general market, CFROIs need to sharply improve, since continued capital expenditure at the cost of capital creates zero wealth.

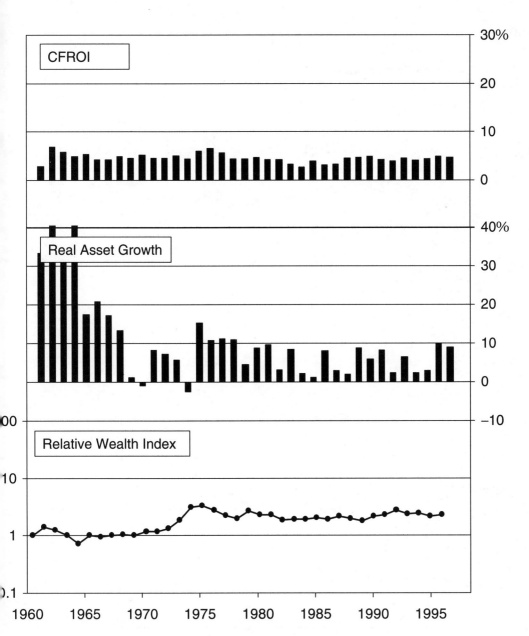

Figure 2.14B Air Products & Chemicals.
Source: Compustat and HOLT/*ValueSearch*™

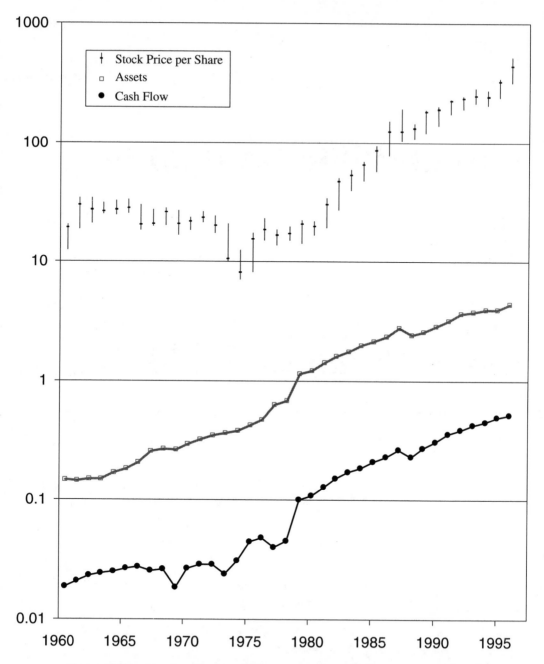

Figure 2.15A   Hershey Foods. Hershey Foods Corporation (see Chapter 5) manufactures and distributes consumer food products. Its CFROIs gradually improved
during the 1980s and into the 1990s. The flat Relative Wealth line since 1987 indicates
that Hershey's economic performance has matched market expectations.

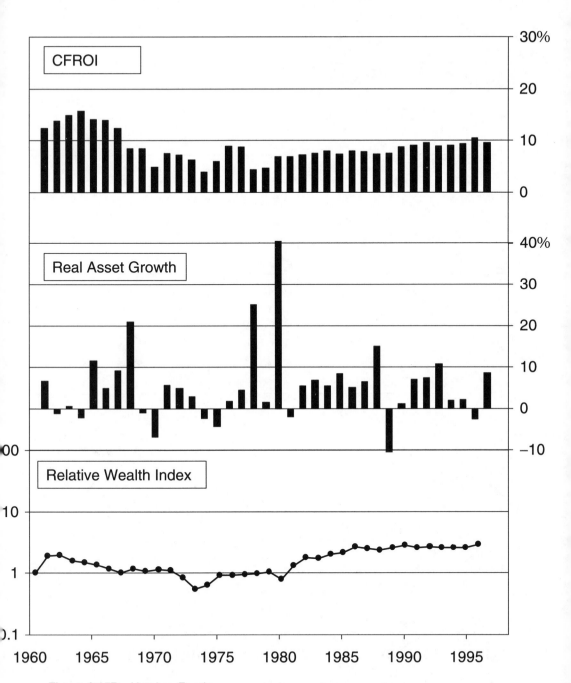

Figure 2.15B   Hershey Foods.
Source: Compustat and HOLT/*ValueSearch*™

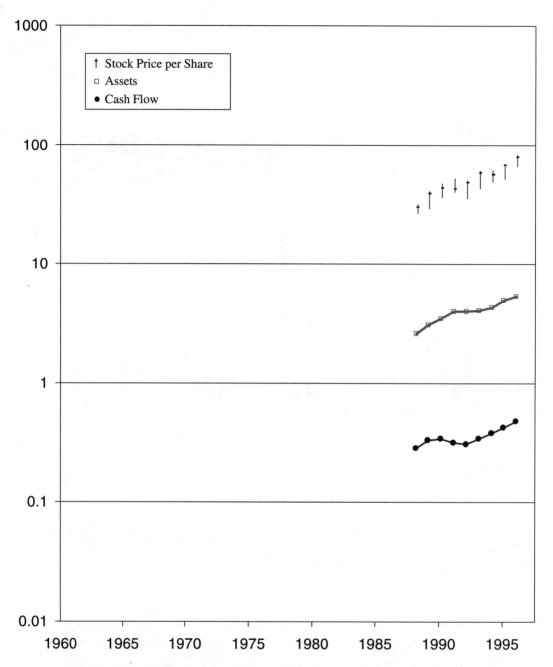

Figure 2.16A   Whitbread PLC. Whitbread's announced goal is to become the United Kingdom's leading retailer in beverages, eating out, hospitality, and leisure. Mediocre performance to date has been in line with market expectations. The firm needs to improve its CFROIs in order to favorably surprise the market and produce excess positive shareholder returns. Merely growing the asset base when CFROIs are near the cost of capital creates little or no shareholder wealth.

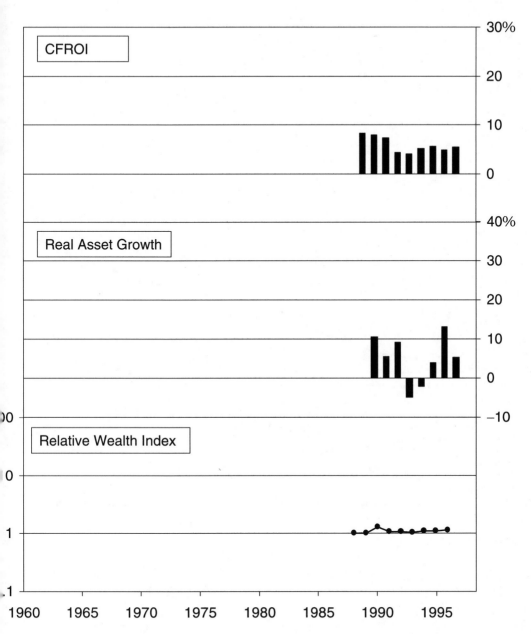

Figure 2.16B   Whitbread PLC.
Source: World 'Vest Base and HOLT/*ValueSearch*™

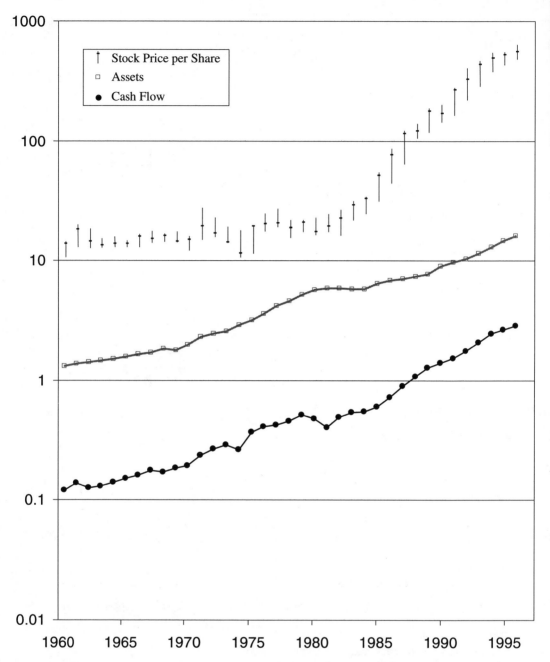

Figure 2.17A Wrigley. Glamour industries are not a prerequisite for superior economic performance. Wrigley is the world's largest manufacturer of chewing gum. After a period of declining CFROIs during the latter 1970s, Wrigley's management set a clear path of improvement beginning in the early 1980s. First CFROIs were raised to above average by the late 1980s and then asset growth was raised. The market was repeatedly favorably surprised (upward Relative Wealth line) until recently, when CFROIs declined in 1995 and 1996.

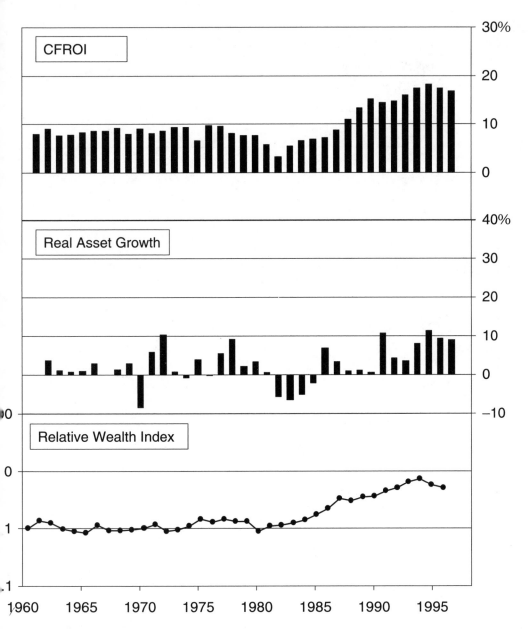

Figure 2.17B Wrigley.
Source: Compustat and HOLT/*ValueSearch*™

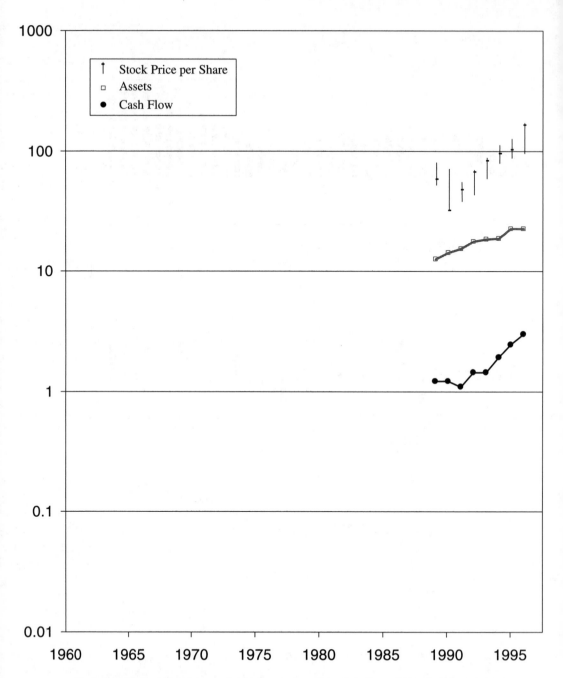

Figure 2.18A   Atlas Copco. Atlas Copco is a Swedish firm with international operations in the manufacturing of compressors, construction equipment, and industrial
tools. CFROIs have recently been improving accompanied by erratic asset growth.

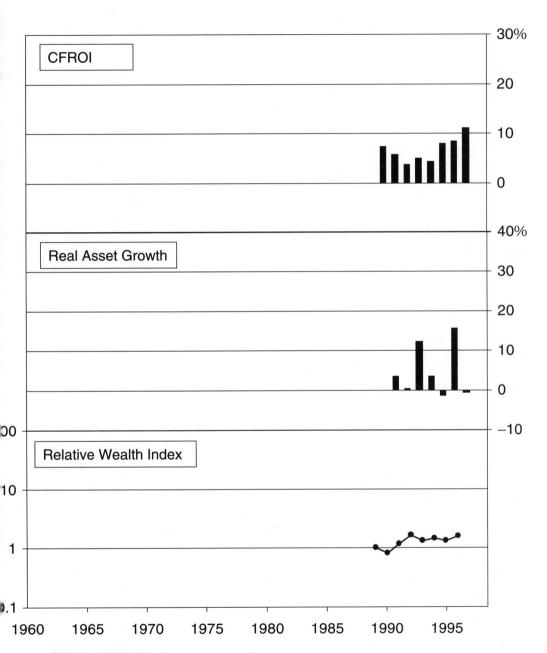

Figure 2.18B   Atlas Copco.
Source: World 'Vest Base and HOLT/*ValueSearch*™

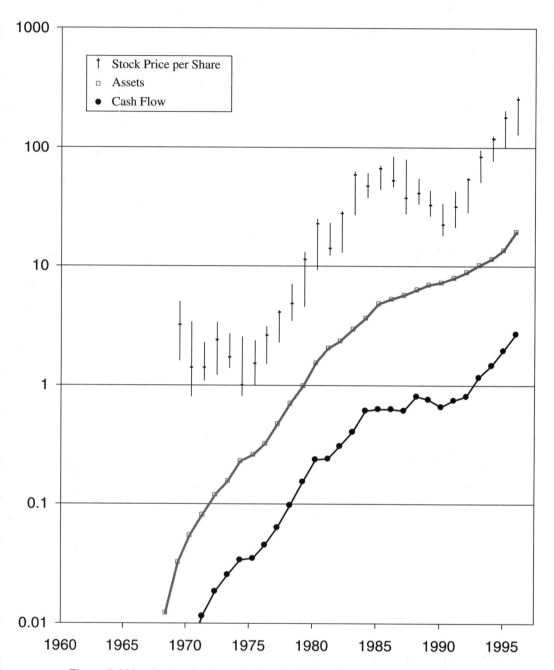

Figure 2.19A Analog Devices. Analog Devices is a semiconductor company that develops, manufactures, and markets high-performance integrated circuits. A short-fall in corporate performance during the latter 1980s prompted management to fundamentally challenge their organizational structure. As described in Chapter 9, the firm dramatically improved its learning capabilities and operating efficiencies. CFROIs and growth surged during the 1990s, and Analog's stock substantially outperformed the market during this time.

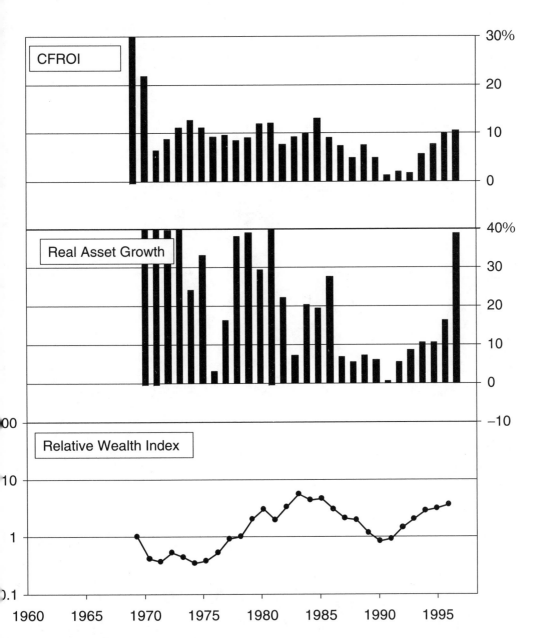

Figure 2.19B Analog Devices.
Source: Compustat and HOLT/*ValueSearch*™

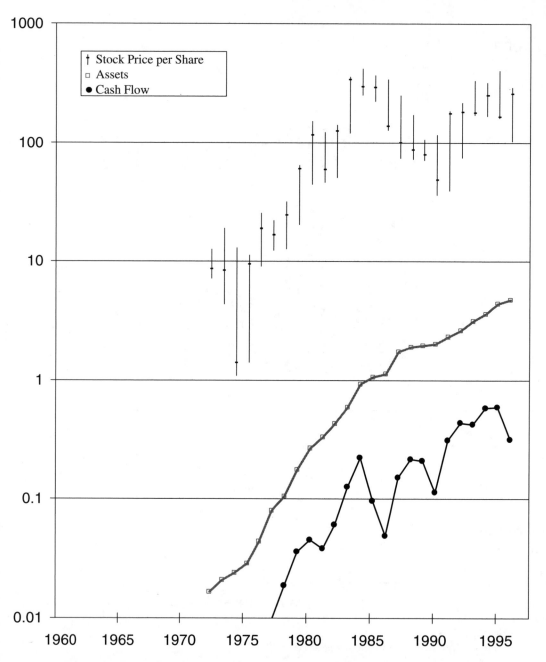

Figure 2.20A   Advanced Micro Devices. Advanced Micro Devices is a leading maker of integrated circuits and faces the difficult task of competing against Intel. The firm has not demonstrated an ability to consistently earn above-average returns. Its high CFROI volatility makes it difficult for the market to have confidence in valuing existing assets, let alone future investments.

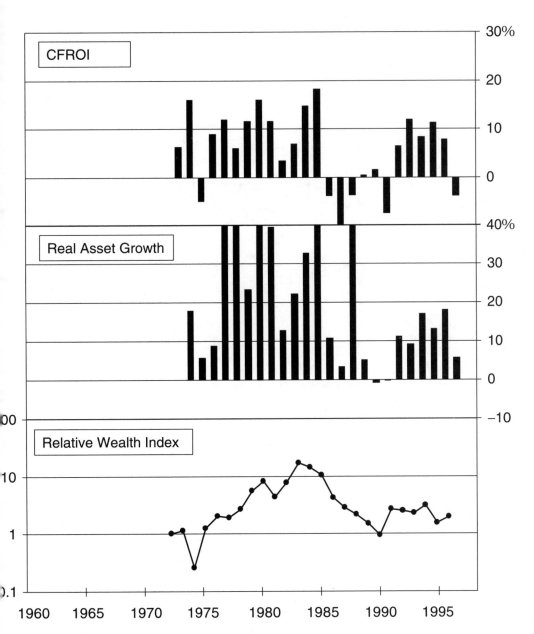

Figure 2.20B Advanced Micro Devices.
Source: Compustat and HOLT/*ValueSearch*™

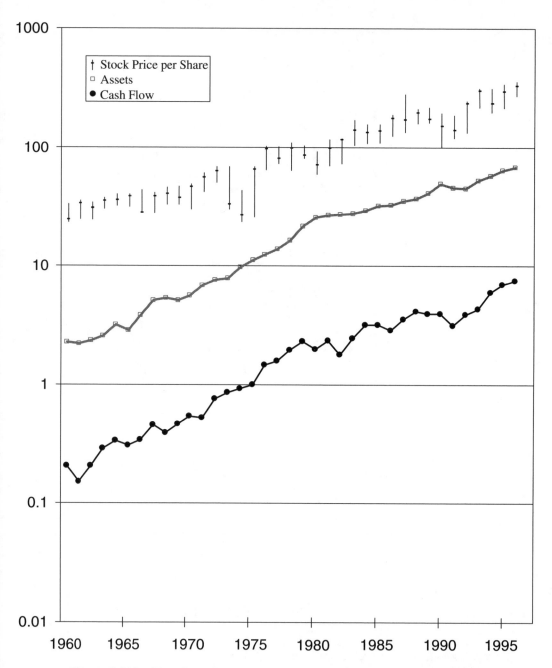

Figure 2.21A Dana Corp. Dana manufactures parts for the automotive industry and historically has earned CFROIs near the industrial average CFROI. The firm has not demonstrated an ability to maintain above-average CFROIs and to grow significantly while doing so.

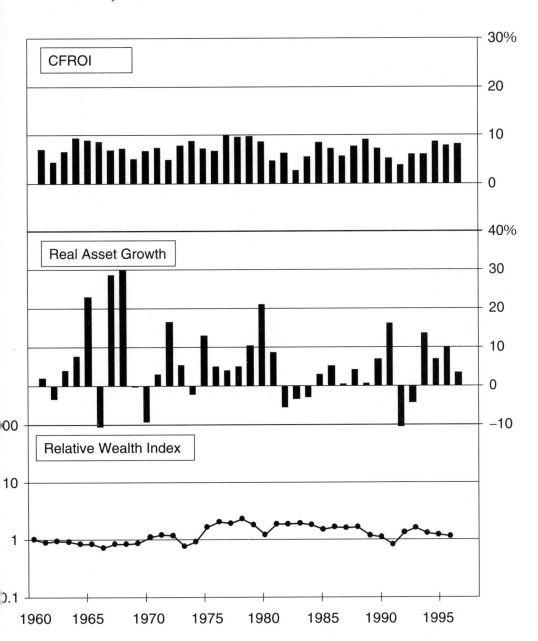

Figure 2.21B Dana Corp.
Source: Compustat and HOLT/*ValueSearch*™

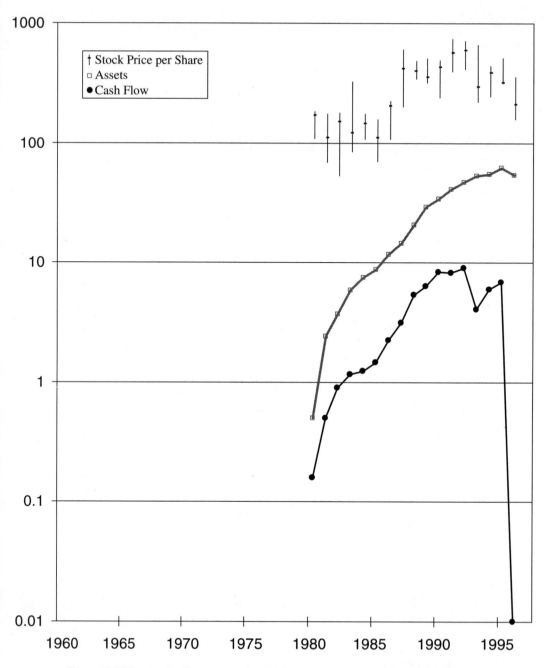

Figure 2.22A Apple Computer. Apple Computer started the personal computer industry and initially earned very high CFROIs. The early competitive advantage of Apple was squandered by poor management. Competitors ate Apple's lunch.

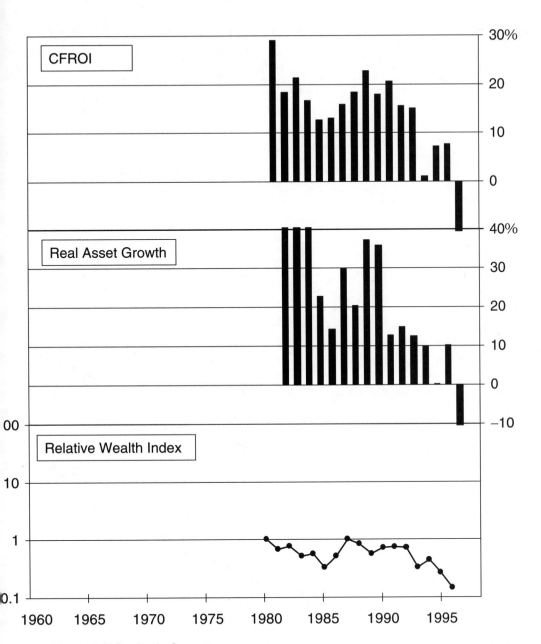

Figure 2.22B   Apple Computer.
Source: Compustat and HOLT/*ValueSearch*™

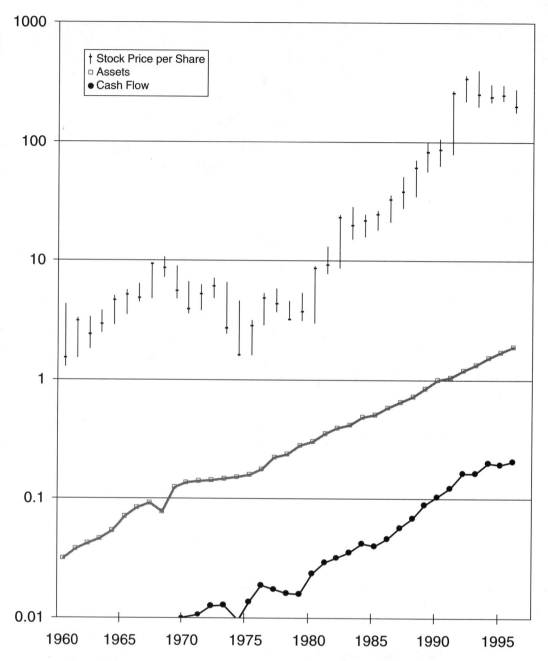

Figure 2.23A Cooper Tire & Rubber. Cooper Tire & Rubber is an example of a below-average performer that successfully restructured. The rise in CFROIs from the early 1980s to the early 1990s was matched by a rising Relative Wealth line, a very typical pattern. Recent declines in CFROIs have caused investors to lower their expectations.

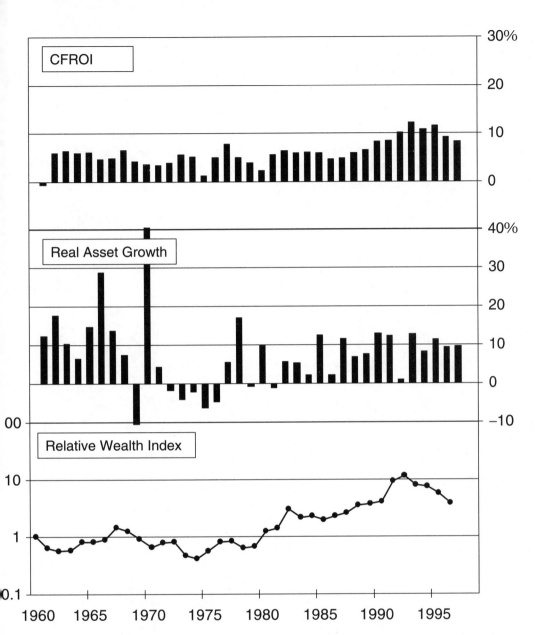

Figure 2.23B   Cooper Tire & Rubber.
Source: Compustat and HOLT/*ValueSearch*™

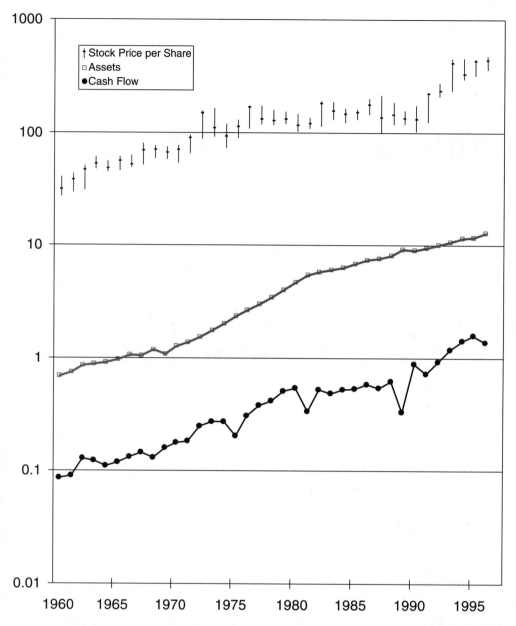

Figure 2.24A Briggs & Stratton. Briggs & Stratton is the world's largest manufacturer of air-cooled gasoline engines for outdoor power equipment. From 1960 to
the mid 1970s, CFROIs held around 13 percent compared to the corporate average
of 6 percent and the stock outperformed the market. Since the mid 1970s, mass
merchandisers have grown to dominate the retailing of lawn and garden equipment
while emphasizing low price. Coupled with increasing competition from Japanese
manufacturers, the result was a downward trend of CFROIs reaching sub-par levels
in the 1980s. Since that time, Briggs & Stratton has improved its competitive position. Its stock has outperformed and underperformed roughly in line with CFROI
performance trends.

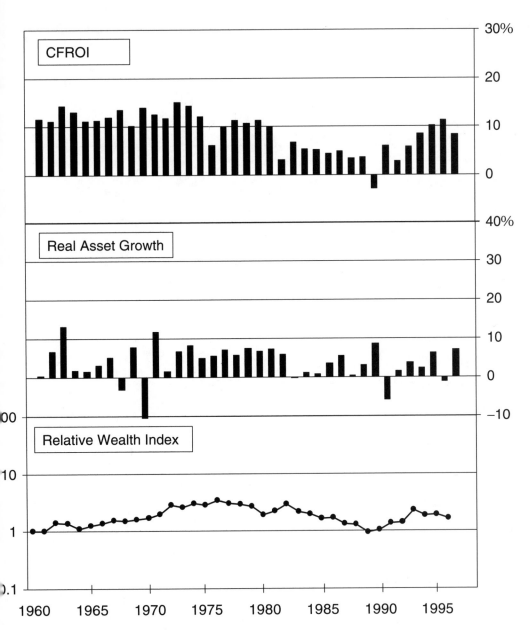

Figure 2.24B Briggs & Stratton.
Source: Compustat and HOLT/*ValueSearch*™

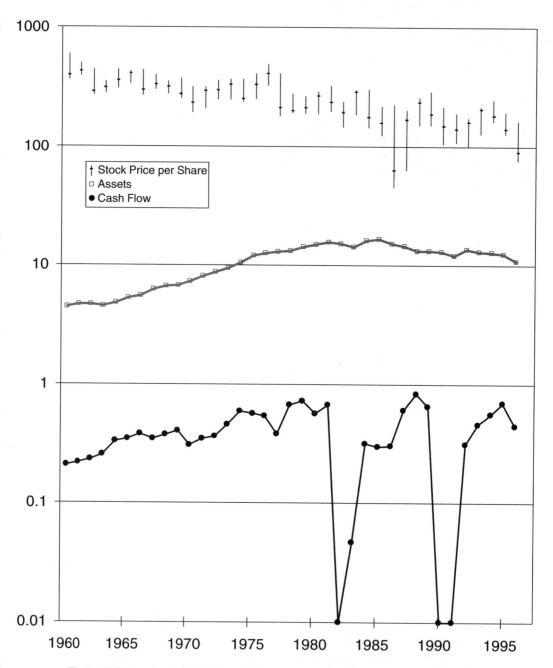

Figure 2.25A   Bethlehem Steel. Bethlehem Steel is a large U.S. steel maker with an abysmal track record. Not only have shareholders suffered in terms of their investment returns, but the economy incurred an opportunity cost by not having resources recycled sooner to far more productive uses. Finally, employees suffered. During the 1980s alone, seventy thousand employees lost their jobs.

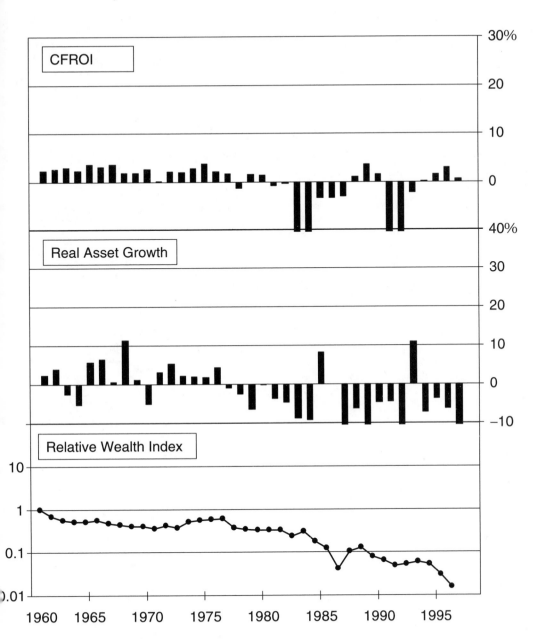

Figure 2.25B   Bethlehem Steel.
Source: Compustat and HOLT/*ValueSearch*™

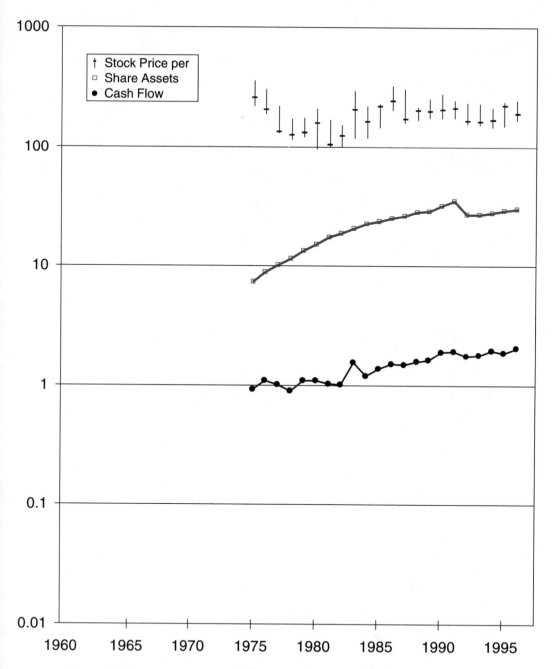

Figure 2.26A Coors. Based on its sales, Coors evidently pleases many beer drinkers. That may be true, but it is also true that management has not been an efficient user of capital, as its CFROI track record demonstrates. The downward Relative Wealth line suggests few long-term shareholders have reason to be pleased with management at Coors.

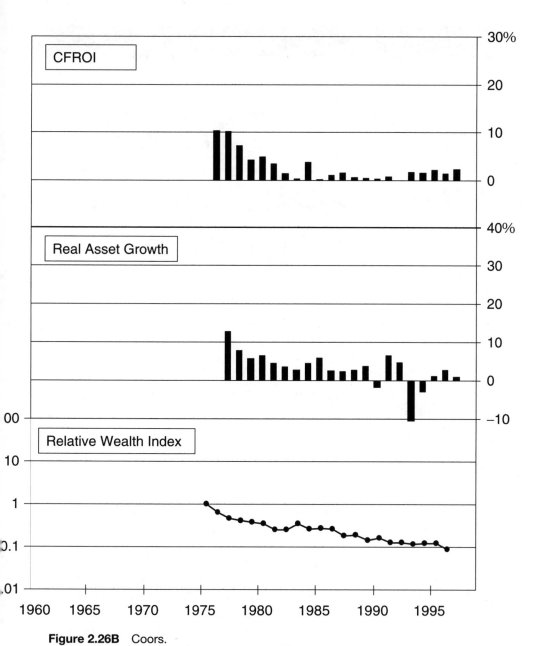

Figure 2.26B Coors.
Source: Compustat and HOLT/*ValueSearch*™

CFROI^{TM} model and DCF/CFROI arithmetic

Summary

- A map of the complete CFROI valuation model reveals the model's major components and serves as a helpful device for identifying and locating the major determinants of the value of firms.
- As a type of discounted cash flow (DCF) model, the CFROI model has three basic variables: forecast net cash receipts (NCRs), a discount rate, and a warranted value.
- Net cash receipts, the heart of valuation analysis, are explained. Because the CFROI model values the total firm, the relevant NCR stream represents receipts to which both debt and equity suppliers have a claim.
- The CFROI model separates the NCR stream into two parts, one from existing assets and one from future investments. A separate net present value (NPV) is calculated for each and the sum of those two values is the total value of the firm. This approach facilitates a plausibility check on the value of future investments by explicit identification of the ROIs and reinvestment rates that drive the NCRs from future investments.
- A simplified model firm is created with necessary financial data for detailed demonstrations of how, for the CFROI model, to (a) value existing assets, (b) value future investments, (c) verify the model has conceptually sound roots, and (d) calculate the CFROI performance metric.

CFROI valuation model map

The major components of the CFROI valuation model are presented in Figure 3.1. Consider the map a thinking apparatus for identifying and locating the major determinants of firms' values. This book's explanation of the components will communicate how (a) financial-statement data link to economic performance and (b) economic performance links to total-firm warranted value, finally expressed as warranted common equity value per share.

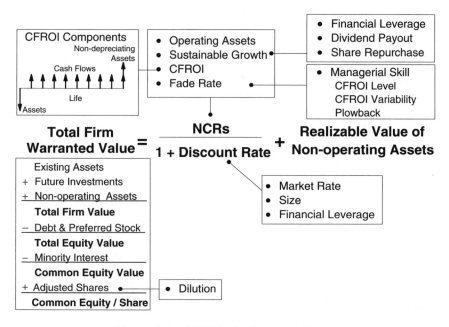

Figure 3.1 CFROI valuation model map.

We now turn to the explanation of the common elements of all DCF valuation models, and then describe via a highly simplified model-firm, the calculation of a CFROI valuation model warranted value, including tying it back to standard DCF treatment. This condensed version is easier to follow than the complete model, yet it enables the reader to grasp how components are calculated and fit together.

Because we stress the importance of logical consistency, this book contains many references to Figure 3.1 and the relationships among the components. As an example of logical consistency, the model includes in operating assets a capitalized value of operating leases. Consistency requires (a) inclusion of the related rental expenses in cash flow and (b) inclusion of the estimated debt value of those leases in the firm's total debt, which impacts on the firm's warranted common equity value.

Pricing equation

Valuation based on discounted cash flow (DCF) is straightforward when it is applied to bonds. Investors forecast a net cash receipt (NCR) stream comprised of the bond's interest and principal payments. Based on returns available from other bonds and on the investor's perception of the relative uncertainty of receiving the interest and principal payments, the investor assigns a discount rate, or opportunity cost of capital, to the forecast NCRs. With these two known values, the warranted value of the bond can be calculated from the following equation, in which the subscript and superscript numbers are the number of years of interest payments. H is the horizon period, i.e., the maturity year of the bond, when principal is repaid and is included in the period's cash receipt.

$$\text{Warranted value} = \frac{NCR_1}{(1+DR)^1} + \frac{NCR_2}{(1+DR)^2} + \cdots \frac{NCR_H}{(1+DR)^H} \quad (3.1)$$

For simplicity, the summation sign and time period specification have been dropped from the discounting expression (NCRs/(1 + Discount Rate)) used in the valuation map of Figure 3.1.

By substituting a known market price for warranted value, a *market-derived* discount rate can be calculated. This discount rate provides a calculated net present value of the NCR stream equal to the market price. In the case of bonds, this is the familiar yield-to-maturity.

The basic DCF valuation model has three elements: (1) forecasted NCRs, (2) discount rate, and (3) a warranted value. It can be applied to valuing business firms as well as bonds. The use in valuing businesses is clearly more challenging because of a much higher degree of difficulty in forecasting NCRs and assigning an appropriate discount rate.

Net cash receipts (NCRs)

A firm's net cash receipts represent what the firm gets less what it gives up along the way. NCRs are the heart of valuation analysis. A logical point is understanding how the firm's inflows and outflows of funds relate to a NCR.

Analyzing a conventional statement of sources and uses of funds, with a focus on net working capital, helps to identify the NCR from both the firm's perspective and from the capital suppliers' perspective. Figure 3.2 displays the change in net working capital (NWC) as the difference between sources of funds and uses of funds. Since the CFROI model utilizes accrual accounting to represent economic transactions, the funds statements based on NWC (not cash) are appropriate.

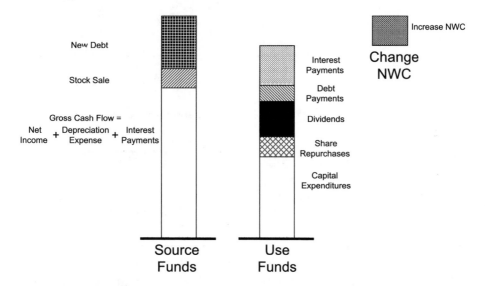

Figure 3.2   Sources and uses: net working capital (NWC).

Capital suppliers, both debt holders and equity owners, have claims on the firm. For a non-financial firm, the standard CFROI perspective is to value the entire firm. The total-firm warranted value less debt provides the warranted equity value. The firm's NCR stream thus represents receipts to which both debt and equity suppliers have a claim.

From the *firm's perspective*, a NCR is gross cash flow less reinvestment, consisting of gross capital expenditures and change in net working capital. Figure 3.3 illustrates that the firm's NCR is identical to the capital suppliers' NCR. From the *capital suppliers' perspective*, cash in their pockets takes the form of interest payments, debt principal repayments, dividends, and share repurchases. The NCR of this group is these cash receipts less new debt and sale of additional equity shares, which is cash out of their collective pockets. This NCR identity of Figure 3.3 is graphically seen as a rearrangement of the sources and uses of funds from Figure 3.2.[1]

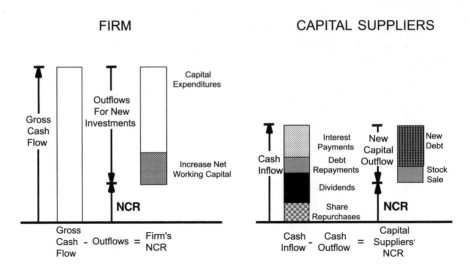

Figure 3.3 Firm's NCR = capital suppliers' NCR.

Packaging the NCR stream

Theoretically, DCF valuation requires forecasting the entire NCR stream for the life of the firm, which becomes an exercise of the imagination in the distant years. One widely used DCF approach keeps the forecast horizon short by truncating the NCR stream at some period and assigning terminal value at that time.

The CFROI model separates the forecast NCR stream into two parts: (1) NCRs from existing assets and (2) NCRs from future investments, as shown in Figure 3.4.[2]

Each of the NCR streams can be separately discounted, giving a separate NPV for existing assets and for future investments. The NCRs from existing assets wind down over the economic life (L years) of these assets, as expressed in Equation 3.2. The NCRs from future investments cover the horizon (H years) representing the life of the firm. In dealing with the wealth created from future investments, the horizon can be shortened to a period of years during which ROIs regress to eventually approximate the discount rate.

$$\text{Warranted value} = \overbrace{\sum_{t=1}^{L} \frac{\text{NCR}_t}{(1+\text{DR})^t}}^{\text{Existing assets}} + \overbrace{\sum_{t=1}^{H} \frac{\text{NCR}_t}{(1+\text{DR})^t}}^{\substack{\text{Future} \\ \text{investments}}} \qquad (3.2)$$

Almost always it is easier to estimate NCRs from existing facilities which wear out over an estimated life than from future investments. Consider a valuation analysis of an oil/gas exploration and production

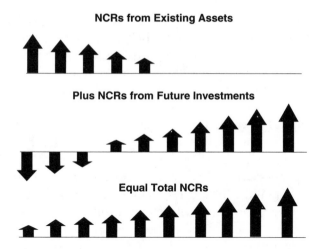

NCRs from Existing Assets

Plus NCRs from Future Investments

Equal Total NCRs

Figure 3.4 CFROI model's approach to forecasting net cash receipts.

firm. Would it not make common sense to calculate a base value from an estimate of the NCR wind-down pattern of existing reserves and then add a value for estimated NCRs from future investments? Notice that this value of existing assets is a forward-looking, cash-flow-driven value. It is totally *independent* of how accountants would record book capital.

This approach to NCRs is particularly useful for making and judging the plausibility of forecast NCRs from future investments, a key part of valuation models. NCRs from future investments are driven by forecasting (a) future *life cycle* of ROIs on capital outlays and (b) the firm's reinvestment rates.

A model firm as a portfolio of projects

The cornerstone for understanding the calculation logic of the CFROI valuation model is a project with a specified ROI. In this section *constant project economics* is assumed, which means the cash receipts at all times are specified in accordance with the project ROI. The model firm is constructed as a portfolio of projects and, at any point in time, has a market value comprised of (1) an existing portfolio of projects and (2) opportunities for future investment in incremental projects.

This simplified environment is used to explain how to: (a) value existing assets; (b) value future investments; (c) verify that the CFROI valuation model is a conceptually sound way to model the firm's NCR stream; and (d) calculate a CFROI as a 'cross-sectional' return measure from a portfolio of ongoing projects.

The constant-project-economics assumption is relaxed when competitive fade is introduced in Chapter 7. Then, project cash receipts are affected by competitive pressures that tend to drive returns on capital towards the average, or cost of capital, rate.

Consider a firm as a portfolio of projects. Each incremental investment, or project, has: (a) an initial outlay that is 80 per cent depreciating assets and 20 per cent non-depreciating assets, or net working capital (NWC); (b) a three year life; (c) equal cash flows over the life of each project; and (d) net working capital released at the end of the project. For simplicity, the firm's life cycle (Figure 3.5) is represented by project ROIs that begin at 20 per cent and trend downward to the assumed 10 per cent cost of capital. Also, for convenience, the reinvestment rate for a year is one half of the ROI for that year. 'T' is the last year when project ROIs exceed the cost of capital; thus, investments made beyond T would create zero wealth.

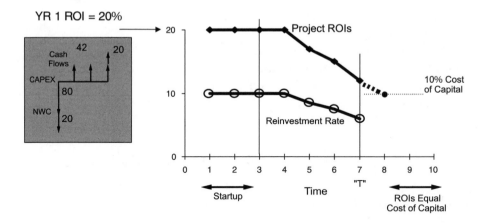

Figure 3.5 Model firm's life cycle.

Investments are made at year-end and are followed by annual cash receipts, which also occur at year-end. As shown in Figure 3.5, the investment outlay in year 1 is 100, the sum of 80 new plant and 20 NWC. A 20 per cent internal rate of return for this project consists of three equal annual cash flows of 42 plus 20 NWC released at the end of the project.

End of Year Data

		...... START UP						"T"	-NO INCREMENTAL INVESTING-		
	1	2	3	4	5	6	7	8	9	10
(A) Growth Rate	20.0%	10.0%	10.0%	10.0%	8.5%	7.5%	6.0%			
(B) Project ROI		20.0%	20.0%	20.0%	17.0%	15.0%	12.0%			
Project Cash Flows										
1		42.0	42.0	42.0	46.2	50.8	55.9	57.2	59.1	58.8
2			46.2	46.2	50.8	55.9	57.2	59.1	58.8	
3				50.8	55.9	57.2	59.1	58.8		
4										
5										
6										
7										
(C) Gross Cash Flow	0.0	42.0	88.2	138.9	152.8	163.9	172.1	175.0	117.8	58.8
(D) Investment NWC	20.0	22.0	24.2	26.6	28.9	31.0	32.9	0.0	0.0	0.0
(E) Released NWC	0.0	0.0	0.0	20.0	22.0	24.2	26.6	28.9	31.0	32.9
(F) Net Change NWC (D-E)	20.0	22.0	24.2	6.6	6.9	6.8	6.3	(28.9)	(31.0)	(32.9)
(G) CAPEX	80.0	88.0	96.8	106.5	115.5	124.2	131.6	0.0	0.0	0.0

$42

$100

Figure 3.6 Model firm's project outflows and inflows.

Figure 3.6 describes in numbers the entire life cycle of the model firm from start up in years 1 to 3 through investment being discontinued in years 8 through 10. Highlighted in Figure 3.6 is the initial project outlay of 100 with cash flows of 42 and released NWC of 20. Lines (A) through (G) present the model firm's performance in terms of outflows and inflows; valuation is not yet addressed. A specified year's capital expenditure (CAPEX), line (G), is calculated by multiplying the prior year's CAPEX by the growth rate, Line (A), for the specified year. (This model firm runs on an Excel spreadsheet and readers can download it from *http://www.holtvalue.com.*)

At the end of year 3, a full portfolio of projects is in place. The performance numbers of those projects (existing assets) are diagrammed in Figure 3.7. Notice that the oldest project, project 1 begun in year 1, has one remaining year of 42 cash flow and 20 of released non-depreciating assets at that time. The newest project, project 3 undertaken in year 3, has a full three years of receipts ahead.

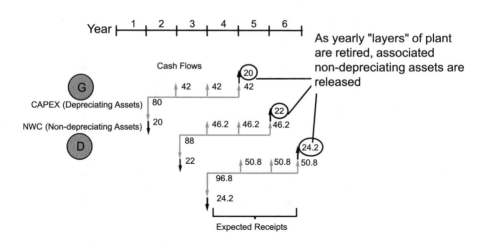

Figure 3.7 Existing assets at year 3. Note: letters in circles correspond to lines in Figure 3.6.

Figure 3.8 adds lines (H) through (T) to Figure 3.6, necessary detail for calculating a CFROI and for demonstrating two methods of calculating a warranted value. Line (H) is the model firm's annual NCR amount that drives the warranted value calculation.

As is shown in Figure 3.9, yearly NCRs (H) equal gross cash flow reduced by investment in new plant and net change in NWC. In year 4, gross cash flow (C) is 138.9, the sum of year 4 cash flows

End of Year Data, 10% Cost of Capital

		START UP		Year				NO INCREMENTAL INVESTING		
	1	2	3	4	5	6	7	8	9	10
(A) Growth Rate	20.0%	10.0%	10.0%	10.0%	8.5%	7.5%	6.0%			
(B) Project ROI		20.0%	20.0%	20.0%	17.0%	15.0%	12.0%			
Project Cash Flows										
1		42.0	42.0	42.0						
2			46.2	46.2	46.2					
3				50.8	50.8	50.8				
4					55.9	55.9	55.9			
5						57.2	57.2	57.2		
6							59.1	59.1	59.1	
7								58.8	58.8	58.8
(C) Gross Cash Flow	0.0	42.0	88.2	138.9	152.8	163.9	172.1	175.0	117.8	58.8
(D) Investment NWC	20.0	22.0	24.2	26.6	28.9	31.0	32.9	0.0	0.0	0.0
(E) Released NWC	0.0	0.0	0.0	20.0	22.0	24.2	26.6	28.9	31.0	32.9
(F) Net Change NWC (D – E)	20.0	22.0	24.2	6.6	6.9	6.8	6.3	(28.9)	(31.0)	(32.9)
(G) CAPEX	80.0	88.0	96.8	106.5	115.5	124.2	131.6	0.0	0.0	0.0
(H) NCR (C – F – G)	(100.0)	(68.0)	(32.8)	25.8	30.4	32.8	34.2	203.9	148.9	91.7
(I) Balance Sheet - NWC	20.0	42.0	66.2	72.8	79.7	86.6	92.8	64.0	32.9	0.0
(J) Balance Sheet - Gross Assets	100.0	210.0	331.0	364.1	398.5	432.8	464.2	319.8	164.6	0.0
(K) % Non-depreciating	20.0%	20.0%	20.0%	20.0%	20.0%	20.0%	20.0%	20.0%	20.0%	
(L) CFROI			20.0%	20.0%	20.0%	18.9%	17.2%	14.6%	13.5%	12.0%
VALUE #1 -PV NCR(t + 1) to YR 10 [H]			354.3	363.9	369.9	374.0	377.3	211.1	83.3	0.0

Figure 3.8 Model firm's CFROI valuation audit. Note: Items might not sum to totals due to rounding. Adapted from Bartley J. Madden. 'The CFROI Valuation Model,' *Journal of Investing*, Spring, 1998, Exhibit B-5.

End of Year Data, 10% Cost of Capital

	START UP —			Year				NO INCREMENTAL INVESTING		
	1	2	3	4	5	6	7	8	9	10
EXISTING ASSETS										
(M) PV This Year of Cash Flow/Wind Down			244.6	269.1	285.4	296.9	300.6	155.7	53.4	0.0
(N) PV Released NWC			54.5	60.0	65.7	71.4	76.6	55.4	29.9	0.0
(O) PV of Total Receipts From Existing Assets (M + N)			299.2	329.1	351.1	368.3	377.3	211.1	83.3	0.0
FUTURE INVESTMENTS										
(P) Investment (D + G)			121.0	133.1	144.4	155.2	164.6	0.0	0.0	0.0
(Q) PV of investment			144.5	158.9	163.9	170.2	170.9	0.0	0.0	0.0
(R) Incremental Wealth Created (Q – P)			23.5	25.8	19.5	14.9	6.3	0.0	0.0	0.0
(S) Future Investments			55.2	34.8	18.8	5.7	0.0	0.0	0.0	0.0
VALUE #2 (O + S)			**354.3**	**363.9**	**369.9**	**374.0**	**377.3**	**211.1**	**83.3**	**0.0**
(T) Shareholders Return ((Value(t) + NCR(t))/ Value(t − 1)) − 1				10.0%	10.0%	10.0%	10.0%	10.0%	10.0%	10.0%

Figure 3.8 *(continued)*.

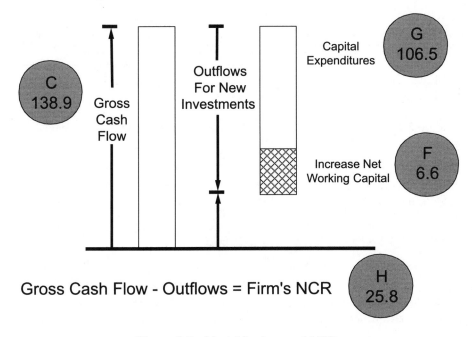

Figure 3.9   Model firm's year 4 NCR.

from projects 1, 2 and 3. Net change in NWC (F) is the amount of new investment NWC (D) less the amount of released NWC (E) from completion of project 1 [see (E) in Figure 3.8]. Note that for the remainder of this chapter, letters in circles correspond to lines in Figure 3.8.

Two valuation methods

Valuing the NCR stream

As described earlier in this chapter, the theoretical DCF calculation incorporates the entire NCR stream. Value #1 of Figure 3.8 is the present value, at the end of the year specified, of the total future NCR stream, with a discount rate of 10 per cent. At year 3, Value #1 is 354.3, calculated as shown in Figure 3.10.

In the CFROI model, a firm's warranted value is the sum of (1) the present value of discounted NCRs from *existing assets* plus a present value of discounted NCRs due to *future investments* [see Equation 3.2, on page 68]. The great benefit of this approach is that the NCR stream from future investments can be viewed as a function of ROIs and reinvestment rates, which make the forecast NCRs subject to useful plausibility checks.

H						Year				
		4	5	6	7	8	9	10	Total
(a)	Net Cash Receipts (NCR)	25.8	30.4	32.8	34.2	203.9	148.9	91.7	
(b)	PV Factor @ 10%	0.909	0.826	0.751	0.683	0.621	0.564	0.513	
(c)	PV NCR (a) x (b)	23.5	25.1	24.6	23.4	126.6	84.0	47.1	354.3

Figure 3.10   Present value of total NCR stream at year 3, end of year, Value #1.

The CFROI model's component parts approach produces Value #2 in Figure 3.8, which for year 3 is 354.3, the same as Value #1 for that year. Let us look at the calculation details.

Present value of existing assets

Back to year 3 in Figure 3.8: line (O) shows the PV of existing assets as 299.2, the sum of 244.6 (M) from the wind-down of cash flows plus 54.5 (N) from released NWC (non-depreciating assets). Figure 3.11 provides the audit trail for this calculation.

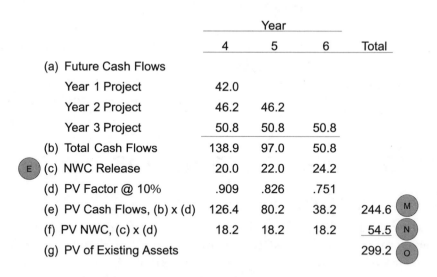

	Year			
	4	5	6	Total
(a) Future Cash Flows				
Year 1 Project	42.0			
Year 2 Project	46.2	46.2		
Year 3 Project	50.8	50.8	50.8	
(b) Total Cash Flows	138.9	97.0	50.8	
E (c) NWC Release	20.0	22.0	24.2	
(d) PV Factor @ 10%	.909	.826	.751	
(e) PV Cash Flows, (b) x (d)	126.4	80.2	38.2	244.6 M
(f) PV NWC, (c) x (d)	18.2	18.2	18.2	54.5 N
(g) PV of Existing Assets				299.2 O

Figure 3.11   Present value of existing assets at year 3.

Present value of future investments

At the end of year 3, investments made in each of the years 4 through 7 constitute all future investments, that is, the model firm stops investing at year 8 and winds down, with operations completely shut down at the end of year 10. The value of the model firm at year 3 would not change if we extended the process for additional years with new projects earning exactly the cost of capital, because we would be including additional years in which zero additional wealth is created.

The value of future investments at any given year is found by calculating the amount of wealth created by the investments made in each future year; discounting the wealth created from yearly investments to a present value at the given year; and then summing those present value amounts. Figure 3.12 takes us through the steps. The total investment made in year 4 is 133.1 (P), consisting of 106.5 in capital expenditures (G) and 26.6 in additional NWC (D). The assumed 20 per cent internal rate of return provides equal cash flows of 55.9 (project 4 cash flows in Figure 3.8). The PV of this project in year 4 with the 10 per cent discount rate is 158.9 (Q). This exceeds the investment cost by 25.8, which represents wealth created in year 4 by the project undertaken in that year.

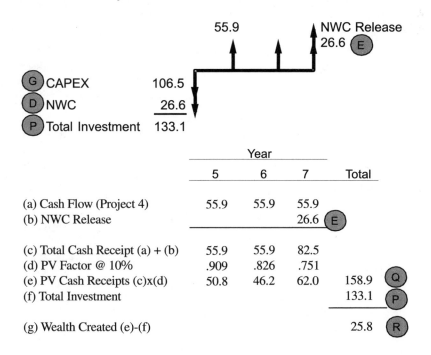

Figure 3.12 Wealth creation from year 4 investment.

Similar calculations for wealth created by investments made in years 5, 6, and 7, are shown on line (a) of Figure 3.13. But those are values at the year the investments were made, and they have to be appropriately discounted to their PV in year 3, which are shown in line (c) of Figure 3.13. The present value at year 3 of the wealth created by all of the firm's future investments is 55.2 (S).

	Investment Year				
(R)	4	5	6	7	Total
(a) Wealth Created	25.8	19.5	14.9	6.3	
(b) PV Factor @ 10%	0.909	0.826	0.751	0.683	
(c) PV of Wealth Created	23.5	16.1	11.2	4.3	55.2
(a) x (b)					(S)

Figure 3.13 Present value of wealth creation from all future investments, at end of year 3.

The 299.2 value of existing assets (Figure 3.11) and the 55.2 value of future investments (Figure 3.13) sum to a total value of 354.3 (Value #2). Value #2 represents the CFROI model's approach and is identical to Value #1. These calculations confirm the DCF mathematical soundness of the CFROI model's approach. Accuracy of the entire process can be checked by calculating the return investors would receive if they bought the firm at the calculated value of one year and sold at the calculated value of the next year: if accurate, the investors' return would be 10 per cent, the model firm's assumed cost of capital. Consider a purchase of the firm in year 3 for 354.3 (S). In year 4, the value has increased to 363.9 (S); in addition, a NCR of 25.8 (H) is received. The owners' return is [(363.9 + 25.8)/354.3] − 1, a 10.0 per cent return (T), the same as the model firm's cost of capital. See Figure 3.14.

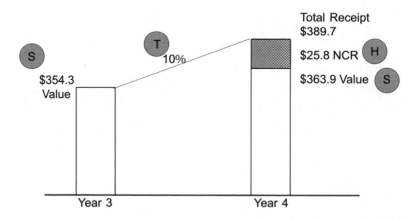

Figure 3.14 Investors' achieved return equals model firm's cost of capital.

We have shown that the investor's achieved return exactly equals the firm's cost of capital under the condition that the firm delivers the exact economic performance expected by investors.

Calculating and interpreting a CFROI

The CFROI metric is a real, cross-sectional internal-rate-of-return calculated at a point in time from aggregate data for a firm. Figure 3.15 reveals graphically the cross-sectional characteristic of the CFROI and the data for calculating it for the model firm at year 4.

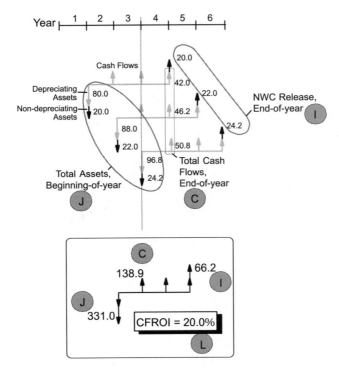

Figure 3.15   CFROI at year 4.

To outside investors, the individual projects (1, 2 and 3 in Figure 3.8) could not be identified from financial statements, so the data for the separate projects would not be available. But financial statements do reveal the amount of total assets, total depreciating assets, total non-depreciating assets, and total cash flow. And it is reasonable to infer that the cash tied up in non-depreciating assets (NWC) is released over the life of the depreciating assets. In practice, asset life is calculated from financial statements. Here we assume it is 3 years.

Thus, we have amounts for each of the four variables determining an internal rate of return — asset cost, periodic gross cash flows, the

	Year			Total
	4	5	6	
(a) Cash Flow	138.9	138.9	138.9	
(b) Released NWC			66.2	
(c) Total Receipts	138.9	138.9	205.1	
(d) PV Factor at 20%	0.833	0.694	0.579	
(e) PV of Receipts (c) × (d)	115.8	96.5	118.7	331.0

Figure 3.16   Check of year 4 CFROI calculation.

life of the project, and the salvage value in terms of released non-depreciating assets. They are shown in cash-flow depiction at the bottom of Figure 3.15, as is the calculated CFROI, 20.0 per cent.

A check of the 20.0 per cent CFROI can be made by using that rate to discount the receipts in calculating a value for the assets. This calculation is shown in Figure 3.16, and the present value equals 331.0, the amount of the asset in the calculation of the CFROI.

The 20 per cent CFROI at year 4 matches the year-4 project ROI only because the project ROIs for the prior years also were 20 per cent [line (B), Figure 3.8]. Notice in Figure 3.8 that as the project ROIs trend downward beginning with year 5 investment, the CFROI (L) also begins to trend downward, but with a lag of one year and less sharply. Pronounced downward or upward trends in CFROIs imply that incremental project ROIs on average have been lower or higher than recent CFROIs. A firm's time series of CFROIs is particularly useful to help forecast ROIs on future projects.

In applying the total system approach to valuation, however, CFROIs should not be calculated in an unquestioned belief that they always are useful. For a business entity having a large portfolio of ongoing projects, CFROIs provide useful indication of average ROIs earned on the portfolio of projects. Due to the varied NCR patterns over time for *specific projects*, all cross-sectional measures based on project data at a point in time will give readouts across time that differ from the real, achieved ROI on the specific projects. However, monitoring trends in CFROI can identify firms which may be investing in distinctly higher or lower project ROIs compared to the firm's average, or CFROI, level.

CFROIs have limited use with start-up operations, where the portfolio of projects as a whole is still being penalized by very substantial expenses and limited revenues. In this instance, operating milestones of a non-financial nature are crucial: e.g., getting a prototype product to meet or exceed target performance standards; engineering the product so that manufacturing costs will not exceed a target level; etcetera. One example is development-stage biotech firms whose current CFROIs are negative due heavy R & D expenditures and very little revenues.

Interestingly, that substantial market values exist for many such firms indicates that investors are using a *long-term* forecast horizon. More telling, a closer analysis of these firms plainly reveals that the market substantially 'marks up' the value of those firms that have achieved key scientific milestones in developing novel drugs with exceptionally large market potential and 'marks down' firms which have the opposite characteristics. In this example, *managerial skill*, so important to forecasting future corporate performance, is being measured with non-accounting variables. Market prices are being driven by longer-term forecasts of CFROIs and sustainable growth which are primarily tied to the firm's research pipeline and the likelihood and timing of FDA approvals.

Market-derived discount rates and company-specific risk differentials

Summary

- Three questions are explored and answered: (1) How are discount rates determined in the CFROI model? (2) What accounts for changes in discount rates over time? (3) What is the empirical support for the CFROI model's company-specific risk differentials?
- Discount rates employed in any DCF-based valuation model should be consistent with the model's net cash receipts forecast method.
- Taxable investors seek to achieve a target real return net of personal taxes; therefore, these investors' demanded returns from the corporate sector at any time are affected by *expected* inflation and *anticipated* personal tax rates, both of which can change dramatically from period to period. The history of real achieved returns on stocks and on bonds since 1960 indicates that investors often do not get what they expect.
- In the manner that a bond's yield-to-maturity can be derived from its market price and its expected stream of interest

payments plus principal repayment, the discount rate employed in the CFROI model is a real *market* discount rate derived from the market's price for an aggregate of firms and a forecasted net cash receipts stream for the aggregate which is consistent with the model itself.

- The discount rate employed in the CFROI model is directly comparable with the CFROI performance metric, which enables users to more readily judge if firms are likely to create or destroy wealth in making future investments. Comparison of market discount rates and CFROIs from 1960 explains a great deal of the market's miserable performance during the 1970s and its highly favorable performance since the early 1980s.
- The market real discount rate is a weighted average of a real debt rate and real equity rate. A real debt rate is calculated as the nominal rate less inflation expectations. With knowledge of the debt rate and the weights of debt and equity, a real equity rate can be calculated. Real equity and real debt rates since 1960 are presented, as are nominal equity and debt rates for comparison.
- A firm-specific discount rate is the market rate plus a risk differential related to the firm's size and financial leverage. The empirical foundation for the magnitude of the differentials is described. The procedure is consistent with the CFROI model and is forward-looking.

Discount rate tied to valuation model

In Chapter 3 a 10 per cent discount rate was assumed in calculating the warranted value of the model firm. The estimate of a discount rate is the subject of this chapter, and we describe the discount rate calculation approach developed and used by HOLT Value Associates in its CFROI model.

An especially important, fundamental point distinguishes our approach from the conventional academic treatment of assigning discount rates, namely, the assignment of a firm's discount rate needs to be integral to the valuation model itself. An estimate of a firm's discount rate is necessarily contingent upon how the NCR stream is forecasted.

Let us explain why. A test of a model's usefulness is the closeness with which calculated warranted equity valuations correlate with firms' actual levels of and changes in stock prices over time. Consider two analysts using different valuation models. Analyst 'O' has an optimistic bias, and tends to forecast that high-return firms will maintain their lofty capital returns for a long time. Analyst 'P' has a pessimistic view, and tends to forecast a fast reduction in the high returns. Should analysts O and P use the same discount rate? No. Analyst O must employ a higher discount rate and P a lower discount rate in order to improve the tracking accuracy of their calculated warranted values with actual stock prices. O's valuation model forecasts too-high net cash receipts, which need to be offset by a higher discount rate. The opposite is true for P.

In practice, users of DCF valuation models often import a CAPM/beta discount rate which is independent of the method used to forecast NCRs. Biases are unrecognized, and the notion of a total valuation system is ignored. In contrast, HOLT's total system approach derives firm-specific discount rates consistent with specified procedures for assigning fade rates for future CFROIs and sustainable growth rates that drive the NCR stream. Three variables determine the CFROI model's company-specific discount rate: market rate, company size, and company leverage.

Investors' demanded returns

Taxable investors seek to achieve a targeted, or demanded, real return net of personal taxes. These are *forward-looking* returns and, therefore, are affected by anticipated decrements resulting from the combined effects of inflation and nominal tax rates on dividends and capital gains (equity owners) and interest (debt holders). These returns compete with expected real, net-of-tax returns from other investments, each adjusted for its perceived risk level.

Historical achieved returns

A useful starting point for analyzing returns demanded by capital suppliers is to observe historical achieved real returns. Figure 4.1 displays *real wealth indices* for equity investors and for debt investors. Beginning wealth is set to $100 for both equity and debt. In 1960, an increase in the S&P Industrials Stock Index plus dividends resulted in a nominal growth of equity wealth. This change was then adjusted for inflation, represented by the change in the GDP Deflator during 1960, and was plotted as the real wealth index value at year-end 1960. This procedure was repeated for each year to 1996. Similarly, a real wealth index for corporate debt owners was calculated and plotted for estimates of investment performance from owning S&P 'A' rated industrial bonds.

Figure 4.1 shows the path over time of $100 invested at the beginning of 1960 becoming $968 in constant dollar pre-tax wealth by the end of 1996 for stock holders (6.3 per cent per year) and $352 for debt holders (3.5 per cent per year). Notice that the vertical scale is logarithmic, so that equal vertical changes represent equal percentage changes regardless of the base value.

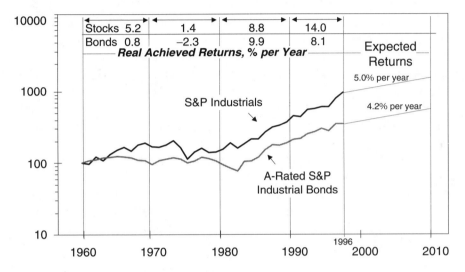

Figure 4.1 US real wealth indices 1960–1996. Year-end 1959 = 100.

Given the uneven pattern of real wealth changes, it is clear that investors often do not get what they expect. For example, during the decade of the 1970s, equity investors achieved a return of just 1.4 per cent per year, and debt holders achieved a negative 2.3 per cent per year. See real achieved returns at the top of Figure 4.1. A sustained bull market for stocks began in the early 1980s, as did one for bonds.

The dashed lines beyond 1996 indicate the pre-personal-tax wealth growth anticipated by equity and debt holders. The figures of 5.0 per cent per year for equity and 4.2 per cent per year for debt are the real discount rates implied by market prices as of September 1997. To firms, these demanded rates represent the average real costs of equity and of debt capital.

The CFROI model does not employ a lower after-tax cost of debt for the benefit of the tax deductibility of interest paid by firms. This benefit is captured by higher CFROIs owing to lower taxes paid. From the capital suppliers' perspective, the cost of debt (or equity) capital is properly viewed as the return that bondholders (or common stock owners) expect to achieve in the future. Bondholders obviously expect to receive full interest and principal payments; therefore, their expected return is understated when the cost of debt capital is reduced for the tax deductibility of interest payments, as is often done in textbook treatments of the cost of capital. Readers should keep in mind that 'cost of capital' in this book refers to the weighted average of equity and debt in real terms without impounding the tax benefit of interest in a lower debt rate.

Effects of taxes and inflation

Equity investors react to changes that affect their expected real, net-of-tax return by lowering or raising share prices to adjust for revisions of firms' NCR forecasts and also to adjust for the expected effects of inflation and taxes on their target return. It is decidedly more difficult to gauge the return demanded by equity owners than by debt owners. Regarding debt, published yields-to-maturity for various debt instruments reflect demanded nominal returns for different levels of risk and maturity.

Figure 4.2 depicts a $100 investment opportunity for investors that after one year is expected to pay back $110 cash. There is a $4 inflation loss and a $3 tax payment, leaving a real after-personal-tax gain of 3 per cent ($3). Investors at the margin having a real 3 per cent target return would be willing to pay $100 for the opportunity.[1]

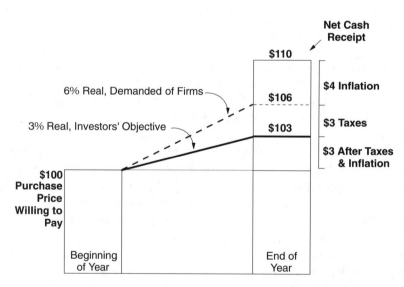

Figure 4.2   Taxable investors seek a net-of-tax real return. Stylized example.

Consider the described investment opportunity as a one-project firm. What is the firm's real cost of capital under the described conditions? The firm's *real* cost of capital is 6 per cent, the investors' demanded *real* before-personal-taxes return required to achieve a target *real* after-personal-taxes return of 3 per cent. This stylized example might help readers to appreciate the consistency between the CFROI real percent-per-year unit of measure of firm performance and investors' demanded return, or firm's cost of capital, also stated in real percent-per-year units.

The stylized example also can be used to illustrate the link between changes in expected personal taxes and valuations of firms. Figure 4.3 depicts the same investment opportunity as shown in Figure 4.2, but personal taxes are expected to be $5. What does this imply for the firm's cost of capital? With expected inflation unchanged at 4 per cent ($4 rounded), investors would be willing to pay only $98.06, not $100, for the return of $110 after one year.

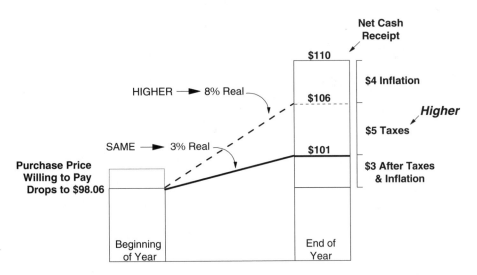

Figure 4.3   Higher personal taxes lead to higher return demanded of firms.

Figure 4.3 indicates that the firm's project investment will be priced at its cost if the firm achieves not a 6 per cent real return but an 8 per cent real return. If the firm invests $98.06 and earns an 8 per cent real return, then its market value will equal the cost of its invested assets. The firm's cost of capital has risen to 8 per cent.

Consideration of investors' thinking in terms of real, after-personal-tax returns suggests that CFROIs demanded from the corporate sector are related to the expected real taxes of firms' capital suppliers. Actual economies will exhibit *divergence* between the corporate sector CFROI and the investors' demanded return. Investors can change stock prices *quickly* in recognition of changing real tax rates. Business firms react more *slowly* by adjusting their capital expenditure programs.

Valuing future investments

Figure 4.4 summarizes the relationship between the investors' discount rate, the CFROI demanded of firms, and the market pricing of new investments above, at, or below their cost. When a firm's future investments are expected to earn CFROIs greater than the investors' discount rate, these investments are priced higher than their cost, and wealth would be created. No wealth would be created from future investments when expected CFROIs equal the discount rate. When future investments are expected to earn CFROIs less than the discount rate, these investments are priced less than their cost, and wealth would be destroyed from the use of resources for such investment projects.

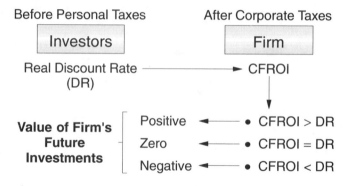

Figure 4.4 Demanded returns.

The firm's warranted value is the sum of net present values owing to (1) NCRs from existing assets and (2) NCRs from future investments:

$$\text{Warranted value} = \overbrace{\sum_{t=1}^{L} \frac{\text{NCR}_t}{(1+\text{DR})^t}}^{\text{Existing assets}} + \overbrace{\sum_{t=1}^{H} \frac{\text{NCR}_t}{(1+\text{DR})^t}}^{\substack{\text{Future} \\ \text{investments}}} \qquad (4.1)$$

This clearly is a forward-looking model keyed to forecasted NCRs. This does not mean the forecast has nothing to do with the past; indeed, the CFROI was initially developed as a performance measure on existing assets to assist in forecasting incremental project ROIs and through them, future NCRs. Yet, we also have emphasized the importance of approaching firm performance and the market's valuation of firm performance as an *adaptive* total system, which implies that the future might well be significantly different from the past.

Rational investors encountering higher personal tax rates would likely adapt to the new expectations by *immediately* raising their demanded before-personal-taxes real return. To use prior history alone—say, captured as a measured average equity premium over a risk-free rate—as the basis for assigning a current equity discount rate is highly dubious.

The market aggregate of firms

As previously noted, HOLT's procedure for assigning discount rates used in the CFROI model has its foundation in the model itself and in market prices, both of which are *forward-looking*. These discount rates are *market derived*, and we call them market discount rates. The procedures described below for calculating a market discount rate are rooted in basic mathematics: if two out of three variables in an equation are known, the third can be derived. Figure 4.5 condenses the basic valuation equation into three variables and applies it not to a single firm, but to an aggregate of firms.

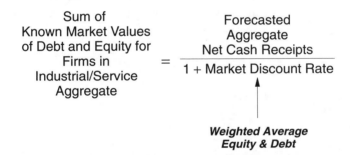

Figure 4.5   Conceptual framework for deriving market discount rates.

The derivation procedure demonstrated

For a specified universe of industrial/service firms, their total market values, including debt and equity, are summed at a point in time. Firms are put into mini-aggregates whose NCR streams are summed. A discount rate is selected and used to calculate a net present value for the NCRs. If too high (low) a discount rate is used, the warranted value will be lower (higher) than the known market value for the aggregate. The *market discount rate* is that rate which results in a warranted value that equals the market value.

Readers might benefit from a demonstration of this procedure. In September 1997, 1,438 firms with monitored forecast data made up HOLT's Industrial/Service Aggregate for the United States. These firms had an aggregate market value of $8.42 trillion, comprised of $2.16 trillion of debt and $6.26 trillion of equity market value. A forecasted year-ahead CFROI for this aggregate was approximately 7.5 per cent, substantially greater than the long-term average of about 6 per cent. The actual calculation routine selects a discount rate and calculates a NPV for NCRs from *existing assets* and a NPV for NCRs from *future investments*. These NPV calculations follow the same procedures as used for valuing an individual firm, as explained in detail in Chapter 7.

Figure 4.6 plots calculated warranted values based on real discount rates ranging from 3 to 10 per cent. With a 10 per cent rate, existing assets have a NPV of $4.46 trillion and future investments have a NPV of negative $1.10 trillion, yielding a total warranted value of $3.36 trillion, much below the known market value of $8.42 trillion. Since 10 per cent is too high a rate, let's try 3 per cent. Existing assets then have a $6.52 trillion NPV and future investments have a positive NPV of $5.61 trillion. Evidently, this rate is too low, since it yields a total warranted value of $12.13 trillion. This trial-and-error process is repeated until a discount rate is found that provides a warranted value equal to the known market value of $8.42 trillion. That rate is 4.8 per cent, as shown in Figure 4.6, and it is the 'market' discount rate.

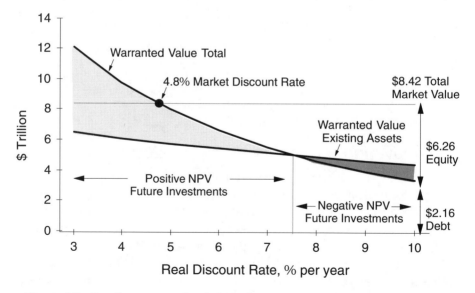

Figure 4.6 Iterative process for deriving September 1997 market discount rate.

Note that the value of future investments is zero based on a discount rate of approximately 7.5 per cent, which corresponds to the forecasted aggregate CFROI. This is an expected result, as no wealth is created from future investments when returns are equal to the discount rate.

Forecasting aggregate net cash receipts

When dealing with the market, it is convenient to use price indices such as the S&P 500 Common Stock Price Index in the United States. Also, when constructing an aggregate of firms, the initial inclination is to pool data and treat the resulting aggregate as one big firm. An aggregate is quite useful for eliminating anomalies inherent in data for individual firms. But, there is a problem with aggregate data: the market prices individual firms, not indices or aggregates.

If a high-CFROI firm is pooled with a low-CFROI firm, the result can be an average CFROI firm. But the high-CFROI firm (e.g. Microsoft) can have a very large market value relative to its assets while the low-CFROI firm (e.g. Bethlehem Steel) can have a decidedly low valuation relative to its assets. The actual combined market values of these two firms can easily diverge from the warranted value calculated for the aggregated firm. The lesson is to avoid combining highly dissimilar firms when dealing with market values.

In order to pool homogeneous firms, the universe is sorted high to low on CFROI level. Mini-aggregates are constructed of pooled firms earning similar CFROIs. That is a start, but the next problem is that the CFROIs of individual firms fade toward the average at different rates. High-CFROI firms with steady CFROIs and modest reinvestment tend to fade slower than high-CFROI firms with volatile track records and high reinvestment. HOLT's current procedure combines enough firms so that an average fade rate for each mini-aggregate's CFROI level is applicable, that is, some member firms in a mini-aggregate fade faster than average while others fade slower than average.

In the US, the long-term averages of CFROIs and discount rates have been approximately 6 per cent. As for the historical experience of CFROI fade towards the longer term average, the typical firm experiences a reduction in the spread of CFROI in relation to the aggregate CFROI of about 40 per cent over a 4 year period.[2] For example, an 11 per cent CFROI firm has a 5 per cent spread over the long-term average 6 per cent CFROI, and approximately 40 per cent of that spread, or 2 per cent, tends to be lost over 4 years, resulting in a 9 per cent CFROI. Firms with CFROIs below 6 per cent would be expected to fade upward.

Market-derived discount rate

Using average fade rates for mini-aggregates, HOLT's current procedure derives market discount rates for 1960 through 1996 as displayed in Figure 4.7.

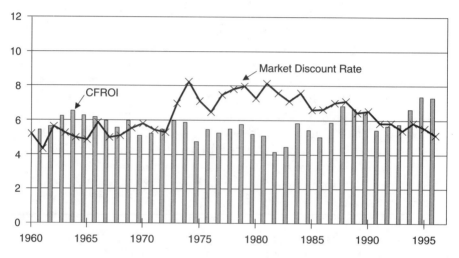

Figure 4.7 CFROIs and market discount rates 1960–1996. Source: HOLT Value Associates historical data file.

HOLT continually tests alternative procedures. A somewhat more complicated procedure is to construct smaller mini-aggregates, so that different fade rates could be used reflecting different characteristics of firms in these more refined mini-aggregates. HOLT's preliminary work along these lines has generated market discount rates close to those derived from its current procedure.

Another approach is to deal with only a subset of the entire universe. Those firms that are earning CFROIs close to the discount rate are not sensitive to varying fade rates for ROIs on future investments. Because very little wealth is created from future investments, a somewhat faster or slower fade rate is inconsequential. Empirical work along these lines has also produced market discount rates similar to those calculated from HOLT's current procedure.

In order to assist in comparing what is demanded with what is being delivered, the market discount rates are plotted in Figure 4.7 along with aggregate CFROIs for industrial/service firms. These CFROIs were calculated by pooling data on the 1000 largest firms (equity capitalization) covered by Compustat in each year. This sample includes firms in a particular year which were not present in later years owing to subsequent mergers, bankruptcies, etc.

Figure 4.7 shows that since 1960, CFROIs in the US have varied around the approximate 6 per cent long-term real level. Remember, the notion of a fade toward the average CFROI is based on the economic proposition of competitive life cycle of individual firms: when one firm underperforms and loses customers, another firm is outperforming it and gaining customers; so for the total of *all* firms the notion of a life cycle would not apply. The competitive process resulting in winners and losers over particular time periods applies to firms with large market values as well as those with small values. For example, in the computer/software industry, Microsoft and Cisco Systems have gained competitively while IBM and Digital have lost.

CFROIs and market discount rates, 1960–1996

Figure 4.7 addresses the question of whether CFROIs in particular years were adequate in meeting the investors' demanded returns. During the 1970s the market discount rate suddenly shot up and remained substantially higher than the CFROIs for the same years. The average firm would find its existing assets and new investments were being priced at less than their cost. In this environment, formerly economically viable projects would become wealth dissipators, and restructuring and contraction would be expected to accelerate. At the beginning of the 1980s, the market discount rate was approximately 8 per cent. This discount rate then began a *downward* trend extending through 1996, while CFROIs were trending upward. For equity investors, this rare combination fueled an extraordinarily long and strong bull market. We will now explain why discount rates change over time.

Market real debt and real equity rates

The market real discount rate is a weighted average of a real debt rate and a real equity rate. After calculating a time series of real debt rates for the industrial/service aggregate, the implied real equity rates can be solved for directly. We then will calculate some rough demanded equity rates from 1960 to 1996, based on tax rates on dividends and capital gains for maximum tax bracket investors.[3] This series is helpful for understanding why demanded real equity rates might differ over time.

A real debt rate is calculated as the nominal rate minus inflation expectations. Inflation expectations are forward-looking, but we do not have available an appropriate forward-looking measure in the US for historical time periods. Comparison of yields-to-maturity of inflation-indexed bonds and of equivalent nominal bonds that differ in no other way seems a sound way to measure inflation expectations. Unfortunately, inflation-indexed bonds have only recently been issued by the US Treasury. Consequently, we have had to settle for a backward-looking measure of inflation expectations for the period 1960 to 1996.

Figure 4.8 displays as vertical bars the annual change in the US GDP Implicit Price Deflator, reflecting the change in the purchasing power of the dollar. The percent-per-year change in the Deflator Index over moving 10 year trailing periods is also plotted. It serves as a proxy for inflation expectations used by investors in pricing bonds. At the present time, bond investors arguably remember the inflationary experience of the 1970s and assign some probability of a significant rise in inflation when pricing bonds. Therefore, it can be argued that longer term expectations probably are not a straight extrapolation of recent low levels of inflation. The 10 year trailing rate of change is used for our analysis.[4]

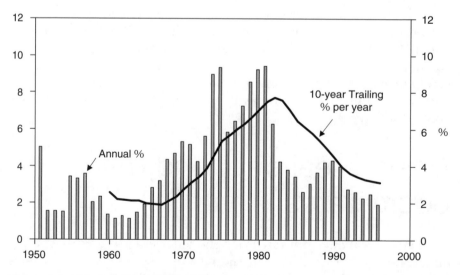

Figure 4.8 US inflation, GDP Deflator 1950–1996. Source: Department of Commerce, Bureau of Economic Analysis.

A time series of nominal yields for Standard & Poors 'A' rated industrial bonds is plotted in Figure 4.9. These are converted to real debt rates by subtracting our estimated inflation expectations for the same years.

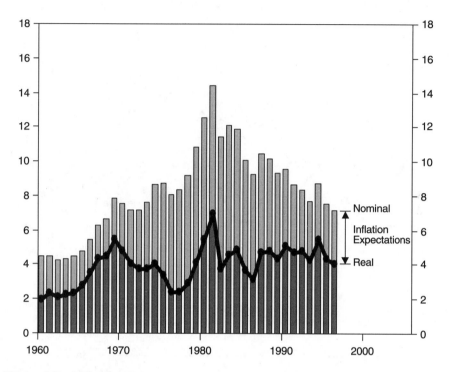

Figure 4.9 S&P industrial bonds 'A'-rated yields, 1960–1996. Source: Standard & Poor's Industrial Bonds 'A' Rated Yields.

The upper left corner of Figure 4.10 displays the equation for the market discount rate being a weighted average of debt and equity rates. With estimates of the real debt rate, and with the calculated annual proportions (weights) of debt and equity, we solve the equation for the implied real equity rate. Those rates are plotted in Figure 4.10, and the time series is called the market-derived real equity rate. The pattern over time of the market discount rate can be better understood by observing changes in its components; i.e. the debt and equity rates.

Real and nominal rates compared

Because HOLT's CFROI valuation model is thoroughly grounded in real units of measurement, it better serves as a lens through which to recognize important patterns. In order to compare the information content of real and nominal discount rates, the real discount rates

shown in Figure 4.10 were converted to nominal rates by adding inflation expectations for the appropriate years. These nominal discount
rates are plotted in Figure 4.11.

Notice in Figure 4.10 that the real debt rate has trended sideways
since the early 1980s, while the Figure 4.11 trend of the nominal debt

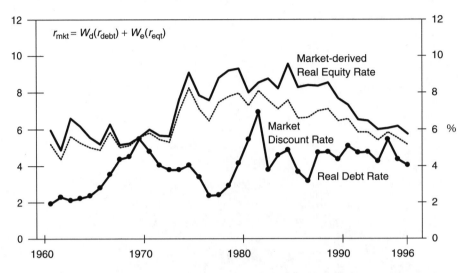

Figure 4.10   Market-derived real discount rates, 1960–1996. Source: HOLT Value
Associates historical data file.

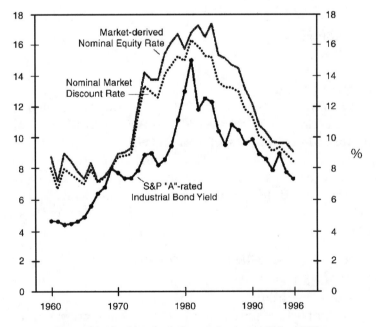

Figure 4.11   Nominal discount rates, 1960–1996.

rate has been clearly downward over the same period. Although it is well known that the rate of inflation has come down since the early 1980s, we dare to say that without the benefit of an inflation-adjusted series, few, if any, analysts could precisely visualize the sideways trend of the real debt rate. With inflation being so varied across time and across countries, important discount rate patterns in time series and relationships are virtually certain to be missed or misinterpreted if models are used that do not include thorough adjustments for inflation. Economists have recently raised the possibility of deflation in certain countries. If deflation were to occur, it would add further confusion to nominal time series.

Effects of taxes and inflation on demanded real equity rates

The conceptual framework discussed at the beginning of this chapter focuses on equity market prices being set by investors to achieve a target real return net of personal taxes. The analysis below uses this framework in conjunction with actual tax rates on dividends and capital gains for *maximum tax bracket* investors, which admittedly over-simplifies a very complex situation. Therefore, assumptions used below for calculating a demanded real equity rate should be viewed as providing a *rough approximation* as to expected levels of and changes over time in the market-derived real equity rate.

Figure 4.12 displays historical maximum dividends and capital gains tax rates and the time series of inflation expectations discussed earlier. Because the capital gains tax rate in the United States is not indexed for inflation, the after-personal-tax proceeds from capital gains are affected by inflation. Using the logic described earlier for computing demanded returns for different tax payments, we calculated a time series of real demanded equity returns for the tax rates and inflation expectations shown in Figure 4.12. This data series is plotted as the dotted line in Figure 4.13, juxtaposed with the market-derived real equity rate series reproduced from Figure 4.10. Computational details are presented in Appendix A.

Let's now focus on the jump in the market-derived real equity rate during the 1970s. One can see from Figure 4.13 that because of higher capital gains tax rates and accelerating inflationary expectations, taxable investors would have been forced to raise their demanded before-personal-taxes rates in order to maintain their after-personal-taxes returns. This alone could account for substantially lower equity valuations and lower equity returns during much

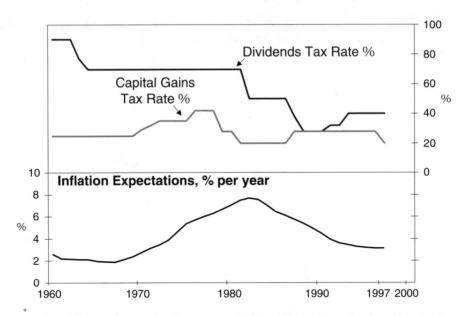

Figure 4.12 Inputs to demanded real equity rate, US maximum tax bracket investor.
Source: HOLT Value Associates historical data file.

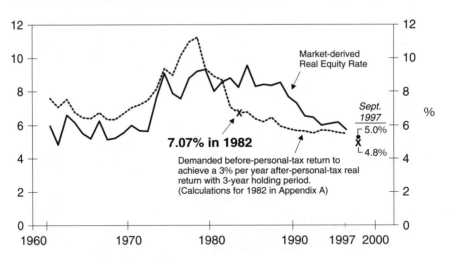

Figure 4.13 Real equity discount rates, 1960–1996.

of the 1970s (see Figure 4.1 on page 85). At the same time that equity investors were demanding a higher real return, firm performance was down somewhat, as revealed in lower aggregate CFROIs (see Figure 4.7 on page 92).

Around 1980, these valuation variables turned favorable. Ronald Reagan was elected President on a platform of reducing inflation, taxes, and the regulatory burden on business, and of generally getting Government 'off the backs of workers.' Tax-law changes put the maximum dividends and capital-gains tax rates on a clear downward course, and inflationary expectations turned downward shortly into the 1980s. From the early 1980s through the latter part of 1997, the demanded before-personal-taxes return declined as the impact of taxes declined. The market-derived real equity rate, an estimate of what equity investors were using to price stocks, also trended downward, as would be expected. With rising CFROIs (Figure 4.7) and declining discount rates, the US stock market generated exceptionally high achieved returns to investors (Figure 4.1).

At September 1997, a 4.8 per cent per year demanded real equity return was calculated, using the recent lowering of the capital gains tax rate to 20 per cent. This approximately equaled the 5.0 per cent market-derived real equity rate at that time.[5] Market-to-book or price-to-earnings ratios contain no information about the effects of expected personal taxes (legal rate in combination with inflation) on either the current levels or historical levels. These popular ratios simply do not reflect the magnitudes of all the important variables and the complex relationships among them to be useful for assessing how expensive the market is at any given time.

Risk differentials

The market discount rate is derived from an aggregate constructed by pooling the data of member firms. In this aggregate, larger firms by market value have more effect than smaller firms. The market discount rate can be viewed as representative of a firm having the characteristics of the aggregate, in which case, 'average' financial leverage of firms will be the aggregate's average leverage. Firms will be judged above or below this average in assigning firm-specific risk differentials. The firm-specific discount rate is the market rate plus a risk differential (positive, negative, or zero).

Concept illustrated for bonds

A useful introduction to the mechanics of HOLT's procedure for estimating risk differentials is to first consider risk differentials in the pricing of bonds. Consider a corporate aggregate comprised of all outstanding bonds of a selected group of industrial/service firms. For illustrative purposes, bonds in this group range from B to AAA rated (see Figure 4.14) and have the same maturity. What is the market-derived discount rate?

To answer that question, the simplified basic valuation equation is used once again. The price is simply the sum of the market values of all the bonds. The forecasted NCR stream is the sum of anticipated

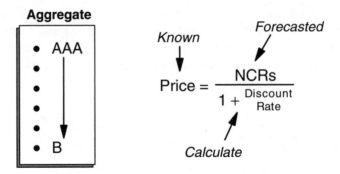

Figure 4.14   Corporate aggregate average bond yield.

interest and principal payments. The discount rate that produces a present value of this NCR stream equal to the known market price is the market rate, or average bond yield.

Figure 4.15 shows the basic idea of empirically deriving risk differentials applicable to the bonds of a particular firm. The notion is to observe different yields, calculated as the firms' bond yields less the market rate. Then these implied risk differentials are related to characteristics of firms that are likely to cause investors to demand more or less than the average yield. This analysis would provide, as shown in Figure 4.15, an estimated firm-specific bond yield equal to the market rate (average) at a point in time plus an empirically based risk differential.

Figure 4.15   Firm-specific bond risk differential.

Risk-differential determinants: leverage and size

A company-specific discount rate is the market discount rate plus a risk differential (positive, negative, or zero). The effects of financial leverage and size (equity market values) cannot be eliminated through portfolio diversification, and arguably they are key determinants of firms' risk differentials.[6]

First, consider financial leverage. CFROIs are calculated from gross cash flow to all the firm's capital suppliers (debt holders and equity owners), and because cash flows are higher due to the tax deductibility of interest payments, CFROIs and forecast NCRs are also higher. The offset to this favorable effect on a firm's NCR stream should be a higher discount rate. As for size, transactions costs are higher for investing in smaller firms; hence, investors should demand a higher expected return before transactions costs as compensation.[7] In addition, at some level of 'small' size, firms are less able to cope with major setbacks from management mistakes or economic downturns, and investors should want to be compensated for that risk also.

Empirical test design

To test this hypothesis, we used a variation of the procedure described above for ascertaining firm-specific bond-rate risk differentials. Consider a firm at a point in time with a known market value and a forecasted NCR stream. The implied discount rate can be calculated; it is the rate that equates the present value of the firm's NCR stream to the firm's total market value. The *difference* between the firm's implied discount rate and the market's discount rate can be inferred to be the discount rate risk differential assigned to the firm by investors. Errors in these derived risk differentials arise when the forecasted NCR stream used in the calculation is different from that used by investors. This potential source of error *increases* the difficulty of empirically verifying the hypothesis that leverage and size are significant to risk differentials.

An empirical study, published in the *Journal of Investing*, was performed using HOLT's Historical Backtest File.[8] This is a monthly file beginning in 1986 containing firms' financial statement data that would have been available at that time and forecasted CFROIs consistent with security analysts' EPS forecasts available at that time. At 12 month intervals, a large sample of industrial firms were partitioned into deciles by leverage and size. As depicted in Figure 4.16, each

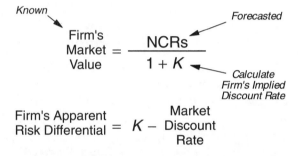

Figure 4.16 Calculating a firm's apparent risk differential.

firm's apparent risk differential was calculated as the difference between the firm's implied discount rate (K) and the market discount rate at that time.

Empirical test results

The study contained 10,350 observations, and median risk differentials were calculated for both leverage and size deciles. Figure 4.17 displays these median real risk differentials. They confirm the hypothesized effects of (1) higher leverage and higher risk differentials and (2) smaller size and higher risk differentials. For example, firms whose leverage is at the highest leverage decile had a positive median real risk differential of 1.3 percentage points and firms whose size is at the smallest size decile had a positive real risk differential of about 0.9 percentage points. Company-specific real discount rates for such firms would be higher than the market real discount rate. A negative risk differential for low leverage, and/or large size would reduce the company-specific real discount rate to below the market real discount rate.

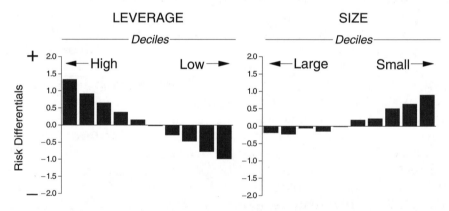

Figure 4.17 Real discount rate differentials for firm financial leverage and size, US industrial/service firms, 1986–1996. Source: Bartley J. Madden, 'The CFROI valuation model,' *Journal of Investing*, Spring, 1998, exhibit 10.

Example firm-specific risk differentials

The computation of risk differentials and the assignment of a company-specific discount rate should not be rote exercises. HOLT uses regression analysis to continually refine weightings for combining the effects of leverage and size on risk differentials. Figure 4.18 displays risk differentials for a variety of firms from the HOLT/*ValueSearch*™ Database of September 1997 when the market discount rate was 4.8 per cent per year.

Firm	Equity Market $billion	(A) Size Differential % per year	% Leverage, Debt/(Debt+Equity)	(B) Leverage Differential % per year	(C) = (A) + (B) Risk Differential % per year	(D) = 4.8 + (C) Firm's Discount Rate % per year
Baseline for the Market	2.6	0.0	27	0.0	0.0	4.8
Wal-Mart	66.3	-0.6	18	-0.3	-0.9	3.9
Emerson Electric	22.7	-0.4	13	-0.5	-0.9	3.9
Maytag	2.3	0.0	24	-0.1	-0.1	4.7
Polaroid	2.1	0.0	23	-0.1	-0.1	4.7
Dana	3.7	-0.1	37	0.3	0.2	5.0
Dryer's Grand Ice Cream	0.5	0.3	42	0.5	0.8	5.6
Bombay	0.2	0.5	51	0.9	1.4	6.2

Figure 4.18 Example firm-specific risk differentials, September 1997. Source: HOLT/*ValueSearch*™ Database, September 1997.

The top line of Figure 4.18 shows baseline values for the market, that is, an average firm is represented by $2.6 billion of equity market value. Think of sorting the member firms in the industry high to low on market equity values and, for September 1997, half of the total aggregate equity value is contained by firms at or above $2.6 billion in equity size. Similarly, average leverage represents 27 per cent of total market value being debt. Deviations from these baseline values result in positive and negative risk differentials as displayed in Figure 4.18.

CFROI™ calculation details

Summary

- The CFROI performance metric is typically calculated from publicly available financial statements. By way of an actual company example, this chapter provides details of the many adjustments made to such data in the calculation of a CFROI. The adjustments are logically consistent with each other and with the complete CFROI valuation model.
- The cash in/cash out perspective of the CFROI metric is that of all capital suppliers, both debt holders and equity owners, because the metric measures returns on total resources committed to the firm's operations. This perspective requires that all cash in/cash out amounts be measured in monetary units of equivalent purchasing power.
- Calculation of a CFROI requires four major inputs: (1) life of the firm's assets, (2) amount of the firm's assets, (3) periodic gross cash flow and (4) nondepreciating asset release in the final year of asset life.
- An adjusted gross plant amount is divided by depreciation expense to estimate life of the firm's assets.
- Included in the gross plant amount are, among other things, a capitalized value of leased operating assets and an appropriate amount of goodwill. HOLT's procedure for marking up reported historical-dollar plant amount to current dollars is described.
- The handling of goodwill is shown to be related to the type of performance/valuation issue explored. Because historical

asset amounts are lost when purchase accounting is used for acquisitions, it can hinder some performance/valuation analyses. A proposed solution is to use pooling accounting in financial statements and record the components of goodwill in a footnote.

- In calculating the amount of non-depreciating assets for industrial/service companies, significant financial subsidiaries must be treated as special cases to avoid erroneous CFROI measurement. Spread-derived earnings on an equity base should be the foundation of performance measurement and valuation of financial businesses.
- Because some of the items used in calculating a CFROI metric have a connection to the way debt and minority equity interests are treated in the CFROI model, capital structure also is explained by use of this example company.

Improved accuracy requires comprehensive calculations

Chapters 2 and 3 briefly introduced the CFROI performance metric. The work required to calculate a CFROI from financial statements is extensive, as this chapter reveals. In fact one criticism sometimes made of the CFROI metric is that the calculations require too much additional work. But to conclude the calculation work is too much simply because it is more, even a lot more, than that of other performance metrics is to ignore the greater benefit of the CFROI valuation model over the models in which the more simple performance metrics are used.

We are not suggesting that every reader should understand every detail presented in this chapter. A high level of accounting and valuation expertise is necessary for that. Yet, we encourage all readers to at least page through this chapter to gain an appreciation of the extensive adjustments required to calculate economic performance as accurately as practicable.

This chapter details the calculation of a CFROI from fiscal-year 1993 financial statements for Hershey Foods Corporation. Hershey's 1993 financials (see Figure 5.1) were used in a widely distributed Association for Investment Management and Research (AIMR) monograph that compared a number of performance metrics. That monograph's treatment of the CFROI was necessarily abbreviated and ignored many important details.[1] By using the same financials,

Balance Sheet

Assets	
Cash and cash equivalents	15.959
Net receivables	294.974
Inventories	453.442
Other current assets	124.621
Total current assets	888.996
Gross plant, property, and equipment	2,041.764
Accumulated depreciation	580.860
Net plant, property, and equipment	1,460.904
Intangibles	473.408
Other assets	31.783
Total assets	2,855.091
Liabilities	
Long-term debt due in one year	13.309
Notes payable	354.486
Accounts payable	108.458
Taxes payable	35.603
Accrued expenses	301.989
Total current liabilities	813.845
Long-term debt	165.757
Deferred taxes	172.744
Other liabilities	290.401
Equity	
Common stock	89.922
Capital surplus	9.681
Retained earnings	1,431.704
Less Treasury stock	118.963
Common equity	1,412.344
Total liabilities and equity	2,855.091

Income Statement

Sales	3,488.249
Cost of goods sold	1,895.378
Gross profit	1,592.871
Selling and general administrative expense	1,035.519
Operating income before depreciation and amortization	557.352
Depreciation	100.124
Operating profit	457.228
Interest expense	34.870
Nonoperating income and (expense)	7.875
Special items	80.642
Pre-tax income	510.875
Total income taxes	213.642
Income before extraordinary items	297.233
Extraordinary items	(103.908)
Net income	193.325

Figure 5.1 Summarized 1993 Hershey Foods Corporation financial statements ($ millions).

our presentation might clarify some things for readers familiar with the AIMR monograph.

A note on calculation methods

HOLT Value Associates maintains a monitored database of historical and forecast data for nearly all firms worldwide of interest to professional money managers. HOLT's CFROI calculations are based on information contained in originally published financial reports and do not use restated data. In order to maintain year-to-year comparability of CFROIs, balance sheet and income statements are used for the same fiscal year. An argument can be made that cash flow taken from the income statement for a year should be matched with an end-of-year asset base for the prior fiscal year (the beginning of 'this' year). But this often would result in substantial errors when processing data for thousands of firms on a worldwide basis, because acquisitions and divestitures during a year render such beginning-of-year figures incompatible with end-of-year financial statements.

The important point is that readers understand how the CFROI calculations are logically consistent and fit within the complete valuation model. For example, the handling of pensions and other postretirement liabilities affects the CFROI, and it also affects the amount of debt used in calculating a firm's warranted equity value. Some of the estimating procedures described below could be improved upon if one had more in-depth information concerning a particular firm. Trade-offs in choosing one calculation procedure over another are unavoidable, and they will be discussed as applicable. Valuation work should be an exercise in *critical thinking*, not an exercise in mechanistically plugging accounting numbers into a net present value formula. This becomes particularly clear from the analysis of goodwill appearing in a later section of this chapter.

It is important to note that cash flows from operating activities, as US firms report in conformance with FAS No. 95, is not the cash flow concept used in either the calculation of net cash receipts or CFROIs. *We accept the principles of accrual accounting for measuring economic performance.*

Provisions for miscellaneous reserves can easily be manipulated. For Hershey and other US companies, HOLT's database does not include adjustments for these provisions. If more detailed analysis suggests that reserves are both substantial and being manipulated, then adjustments should be made. HOLT makes adjustments for German firms where 'other risk provisions' is a well-known source of substantial earnings manipulation.

Units of measurement and inflation adjustments

Real numbers used in CFROIs, asset growth rates, and discount rates help to make a performance/valuation model useful on a world-wide basis. A short overview on units of measurement and related terminology follows.

From the accountants' perspective, performance centers on *earnings* available to the firm's *equity* owners. Cash available from depreciation charges is implicitly deemed to be reinvested, under the 'going concern' assumption. From an *economic* perspective, performance focuses on total cash generated from all the firm's assets, whether the capital for such has been supplied by debt holders or equity owners. If a business cannot generate cash returns from total committed resources at least equal to combined debt and equity capital costs, wealth will be dissipated if cash is reinvested. From an economic viewpoint, such a firm should not remain on a business-as-usual path. It is not an economically going concern.

The cash-in/cash-out framework of a real ROI handles inflation differently than does the replacement-cost accounting approach. This can be shown with a simple illustration. Consider: a $100 investment in a machine with a one-year life; the machine generates $200 of cash during the year; the general level of prices remains unchanged (zero inflation); and the replacement cost of an identical machine is $200 at year-end. By the replacement-cost accounting procedure, net income would be zero, because the depreciation charge would be the machine's replacement cost, $200.[2] But if the machine were not replaced and instead the $200 cash were distributed to the capital suppliers, they would achieve a 100 per cent gain in purchasing power: $100 was committed, and one year later $200 was received.

The point here is that inflation adjustments need to be made from the perspective of the firm's capital suppliers, not from the going-concern accounting perspective. The capital-suppliers' perspective requires that all monetary values — all cash-in/cash-out amounts — be measured in monetary units of equivalent purchasing power. Because purchasing power terminology is loose, related definitions used at HOLT and in this book follow.[3] They are in terms of US dollars, but apply to other monetary units also.

(1) *Constant dollars.* Dollar amounts for different years are expressed in dollars having the same purchasing power.

(2) *Current dollars*. Dollar amounts for different years have the purchasing power of the dollar for the year for which the amount is recorded. ('C\$' will be used as an abbreviation for current dollars.)

(3) *Historical dollars*. Dollar amounts for a given year that are summations of different-year current-dollar amounts, and thus are amounts of mixed-purchasing-power dollars.

CFROI calculation example

Four major inputs to CFROI

In order to assist readers in maintaining perspective about the CFROI as the detailed example is presented, the 'CFROI Valuation Model Map' is reproduced here as Figure 5.2 with items shaded that are discussed in this chapter. The CFROI is the key variable involved in forecasting the stream of expected net cash receipts that are discounted in calculating a firm's warranted value. The map also shows in the upper left box the four inputs to a CFROI calculation: (1) the life of the assets; (2) the amount of total assets (both depreciating and non-depreciating); (3) the periodic cash flows assumed over the life of those assets; and (4) the release of non-depreciating assets in the final period of the life of the assets.

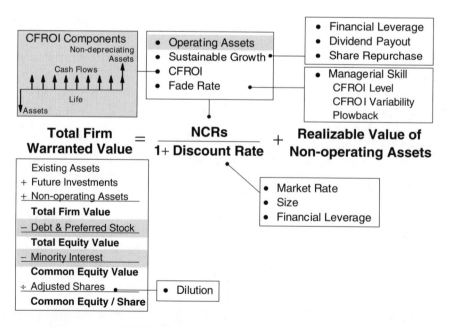

Figure 5.2   CFROI valuation model map. CFROI calculation issues.

A firm's warranted value is the present value of a NCR stream generated from *operating* assets plus the estimated realizable value of *non-operating* assets. In the US, non-operating investments typically are not significant and can be included in operating assets with related income included in cash flow. If firms' non-operating investments are substantial, as they often are in France, the preferred treatment is to classify them as non-operating and to estimate their after-tax realizable value. Of course, their contribution to cash flow must then be removed.

Land is part of the plant account and is recorded at historical cost in the financial statements of US firms. In terms of the Valuation Map, the first question is whether land is an operating or non-operating asset. If a portion of the firm's land should be separated from operating assets, then the estimated after-tax proceeds from sale of this land is put into non-operating assets. This avoids placing a very 'high' value for land into the operating asset base which would produce inappropriately low CFROIs and understate the firm's operating economic performance. Interestingly, this part of the CFROI model immediately raises fundamental questions for top management concerning the firm's basic business and the reasons for holding any non-operating assets.

Recall that the CFROI is a *cross-sectional* measure of project ROIs at a point in time, which projects (in an amalgamated sense) constitute the firm's operating assets at that point in time. The cross-sectional make-up of a CFROI is clearly shown in Figure 3.15 on page 79. In calculating a CFROI, both depreciating and nondepreciating assets

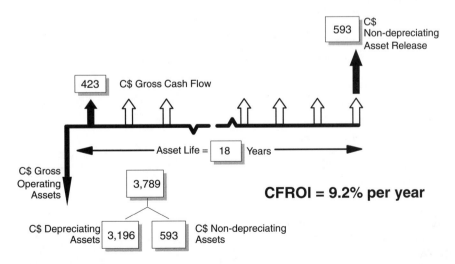

Figure 5.3 CFROI calculation. 1993 Hershey Foods Corporation, requires four major inputs.

are expressed in current dollars (C$) corresponding to cash flow measured in current dollars. Although the CFROI calculation from financial statements for a given year uses the cash inflow for that year alone, that amount is assumed to be the periodic inflow for *each* of the asset-life years. Thus, the CFROI is an average internal rate of return of the firm's existing projects (Figure 5.3).

Figure 5.4 summarizes the major components to the four inputs required to calculate a CFROI based on the financial information for Hershey Foods. Many of the component calculations are related

———————— Asset Life ————————	
(a) Adjusted Gross Plant	1,822
(b) Depreciation of Gross Plant	100
(c) Project Life (a)/(b)	18
———————— C$ Gross Operating Assets ————————	
C$ Depreciating Assets:	
Gross Plant Less Land & CIP	1,822
+Gross Plant Inflation Adjustment to C$	428
+Construction in Progress (CIP)	171
+Gross Leased Property	313
+Adjusted Intangibles	473
−Pension Intangibles	(11)
TOTAL	3,196
C$ Non-depreciating Assets:	
Current Assets Other than Inventories	436
−Current Non-debt Liabilities	(446)
Net Monetary Assets	(10)
+Inventories	453
+Last In, First Out (LIFO) Inventory Reserve	59
+Land	48
+Land Inflation Adjustment to C$	11
+Other Long Term Assets	32
TOTAL	593
———————— C$ Gross Cash Flow ————————	
Net Income	297
+Depreciation & Amortization	113
+Adjusted Interest Expense	30
+Rental Expense	25
+Monetary Holding Gain (Loss)	0
−First In, First Out (FIFO) Profits	(3)
+Pension Costs (Gains)	44
−Pension Service Cost	(32)
−Gain on Special Items After Tax	(51)
+Minority Interest Expense	0
TOTAL	423

Figure 5.4   Major components to Hershey CFROI calculation.

to (1) the CFROI being a measure from the viewpoint of all capital suppliers, (2) the CFROI being in real units, and (3) the need to maintain logical consistency in the treatment of all components and sub-components. The remainder of this chapter describes the conversion of Hershey's 1993 balance sheet and income statement (Figure 5.1) and related footnote information to key inputs in HOLT's calculated CFROI of 9.2 per cent per year (Figure 5.3).

Asset life

Asset Life is the estimated average economic life (in years) of the tangible fixed assets of a company. It is calculated as adjusted gross plant divided by depreciation expense.

$$\text{Asset Life} = \frac{\text{Adjusted Gross Plant}}{\text{Depreciation of Gross Plant}}$$

The Gross Plant amount is the cost of all tangible fixed property. Although land & improvements and construction in progress are considered tangible fixed property, they are excluded from the Adjusted Gross Plant because there is no associated depreciation expense. Note though, there are occurrences when construction in progress can be depreciated. Land is classified as a non-depreciating asset and construction in progress as depreciating.

Gross Plant	$2, 041.76
Less: Land & Improvements	(48.24)
Construction in Progress	(171.10)
Adjusted Gross Plant	$1, 822.42

Depreciation accounting allocates, in a systematic manner, the cost of the tangible fixed assets over their estimated service lives. The systematic methods allowable by GAAP include the straight-line method and accelerated methods, including sum-of-the-years-digits and declining-balance methods. The predominant method used by US firms for book purposes is the straight-line method. Under the straight-line method, the periodic depreciation charge is the cost of an asset (less salvage value) divided by the estimated service life. The Depreciation of Gross Plant should represent only the actual current-period depreciation expense against the Adjusted Gross Plant; therefore, this item does not include amortization of goodwill.

Depreciation & Amortization	$113.06
Less: Amortization of Goodwill	(12.94)
Depreciation of Gross Plant	$100.12

With aggregate data from the firm's financial statements, the calculation of average life is as follows:

$$\text{Asset Life} = \frac{1,822.42}{100.12} = 18 \text{ (rounded to whole years)}$$

Figure 5.5 is a map of the asset life calculation. Similar maps are used for more complex calculations later in this chapter. The calculated life should receive a plausibility check. Possible problems include non-straight-line depreciation methods, fully-depreciated-but-not-yet-retired assets, restructuring charges included in depreciation expense (as done by IBM in 1992), acquisitions involving purchase accounting, etcetera. Comparison with industry peers is helpful. Asset life is typically rounded to the nearest integer. If asset life is short, or if more fine-tuned CFROI answers are desired, a life to one decimal place might be used.

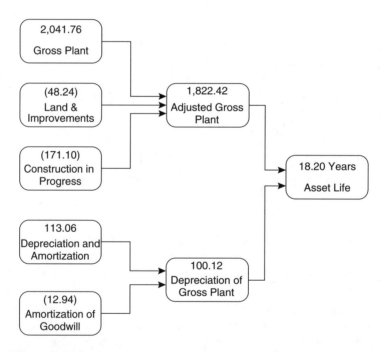

Figure 5.5   Asset life calculation. 1993 Hershey Foods Corporation.

Current-dollar depreciating assets

Together with C$ Non-depreciating Assets, C$ Gross Depreciating Assets comprise the amount of C$ Gross Operating Assets (the cash outflow, or investment) employed in the generation of the periodic cash inflow. Because the CFROI is a measure of the return to all capital suppliers, not equity owners only, the assets figure needed here should also include (1) a capitalized value of operating assets whose usage has been obtained via operating lease (excluded from the balance sheet) and (2) appropriate amount of any goodwill paid for operating assets. Goodwill is discussed in a separate section below.

Gross plant inflation adjustment

The cash inflow for a specified year is recorded in dollars having the purchasing power of the specified year, that is, in current dollars. Gross Plant assets, however, as reported in financial statements, are in historical dollars—that is, in dollars having mixed purchasing power. This mismatch of purchasing-power dollars would result in an erroneous calculation of CFROI except for the situation of a repetitive zero per cent per year inflation environment over the entire Gross Plant Project Life. Adjustments are needed so that both cash inflow and cash outflow amounts are in dollars having the same purchasing power. It is convenient to use the current dollars in which cash inflow is measured.

Mark-up of plant illustration

An understanding of the mark-up procedure for plant might be gained most readily through the use of simple illustration. Figure 5.6 displays important components of the illustration. A 1993 balance sheet would report the amount of gross plant in historical dollars.

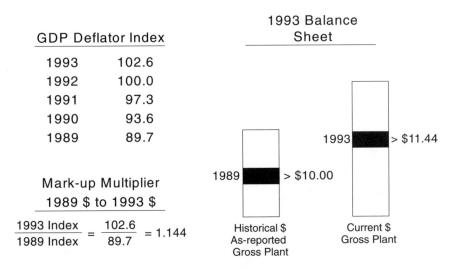

Figure 5.6 Gross plant mark-up illustration. Historical $ to current $, 1993.

The amount is apportioned to earlier years; say $10.00 is apportioned to 1989. The amount for each historical outlay year is marked-up to 1993 dollars based on the change in the GDP Deflator price index. With the GDP Deflator having a value of 89.7 in 1989 and 102.6 in 1993, the $10.00 plant outlay in 1989 dollars would be valued at $11.44 in 1993 dollars.

If this mark-up procedure is followed for each outlay year and amount, the sum is the Gross Plant amount in 1993 dollars. A 'Gross Plant Inflation Adjustment Factor' would be calculated by dividing the current-dollar gross plant amount by the historical-dollar gross plant amount.

HOLT's mark-up procedure for plant

Since complete data on original outlays comprising a particular year's plant is not available in published financial statements, an estimating procedure is required. Appendix B presents a method for mathematically approximating the ratio of current $ plant/historical $ plant. It uses the asset life, real growth rate in plant over the asset life, and the GDP Deflators over the asset life.

The mark-up of gross plant to current dollars is typically the largest inflation adjustment. (Inflation adjustments for inventory profits and for monetary holdings are described later in this chapter.) With inflation, the longer the asset life and the lower the real historical growth rate of assets, the larger the Gross Plant Inflation Adjustment Factor. An idea of the magnitude of the effects of asset life and asset growth rate associated with the history of inflation in the United States can

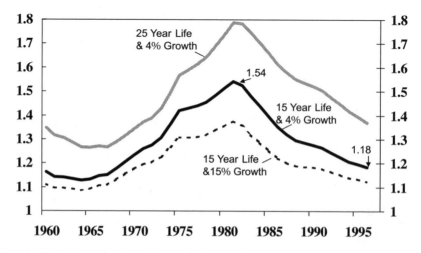

Figure 5.7 US gross plant inflation adjustment factors, based on GDP Deflator.

be gleaned from Figure 5.7. The chart should be interpreted in this way: For a firm having a 15 year asset life in 1981 and a 4 per cent real asset growth rate (the middle line plotted) over the 15 years ending 1981, the 1981 financial-statement historical-dollar gross plant amount would have to be multiplied by about 1.54 in order to restate the gross plant to 1981 current dollars. With no change in asset life or real asset growth rate, the multiple to be applied to 1996 financial-statement gross plant would be only 1.18 due to the lower inflation over the 15 years preceding 1996 versus the 15 years preceding 1981.

Gross plant inflation adjustment to 1993 dollars

The amount of Gross Plant (less Land and CIP) for 1993 in *historical dollars* was presented in the section on Gross Plant Life: $1,822.42. HOLT's Gross Plant Inflation Adjustment Factor for 1993 for firms having Hershey's Asset Life (18 years) and its real historical asset growth rate of 8 per cent is 1.23. Gross Plant adjusted to 1993 dollars then is $2,250.29, the product of $1,822.42 multiplied by 1.23. The difference between Gross Plant in 1993 dollars, $2,250.29, and Gross Plant in historical dollars, $1,822.42, is $428 (rounded) and is the amount of the Gross Plant Adjustment to 1993 Dollars.

In the absence of complete details on original cost of all existing layers in the plant account, the historical real asset growth is used as a proxy for the age of the plant. High (low) asset growth corresponds to newer (older) plant.

For fiscal 1993, HOLT used an approximate 8 per cent real historical growth rate. If a firm had no acquisitions or divestitures, its gross plant in current dollars for a number of years could be translated into constant dollars. A real growth rate (using constant-dollar amounts) could then be calculated. Hershey divested plant in 1988. The 8 per cent real growth rate is for 'normalized' growth, which excludes 1988. A Net Plant/Gross Plant ratio with land excluded can also be used to estimate plant age and to link it to an historical real asset growth rate. Non-straight-line depreciation and fully-depreciated-but-not-yet-retired plant can severely distort this ratio.

Revaluations

In reply to the criticism that the CFROI calculation is highly complex, we note that the overall completeness of the CFROI model makes it *easier* to analyze firms, especially firms with complex accounting issues. As an example, the United Kingdom allows plant revaluations.

Whitbread PLC has extensively used this opportunity to change its as-reported amount of plant. Clearly, an analyst using as-reported data for Whitbread has a serious problem in working with an accounting return-on-capital-employed (ROCE).

In contrast, the CFROI procedures easily accommodate this accounting issue. In Figure 5.8 one line plots as-reported gross plant for Whitbread, which includes revaluations. Using footnote information, HOLT strips out each year's revaluation amount and replaces it with the historical-cost amount. The historical plant amount is then marked up to current pounds and plotted as HOLT's Inflation Adjusted Gross Plant. These adjustments contribute to the end result of a CFROI time series that is more reflective of economic performance than accounting returns based on as-reported assets.

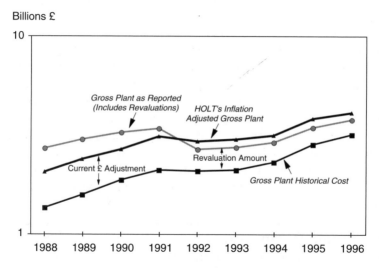

Figure 5.8   Revaluations and inflation adjustments. Whitbread PLC.

Construction in progress

Construction in Progress (CIP) is not included in the Gross Plant amount that is layered back for marking up to current dollars, because CIP is known to belong in the current-year plant layer and is already stated in current-year dollars. When CIP projects are completed and put in service, they become depreciable; thus, the CIP amount belongs in the Depreciating Assets category.

Current-dollar gross leased property

Whether the use of operating assets is obtained by purchasing or leasing is a financing decision. In either case, the assets are employed in the generation of the firm's cash inflow. Inasmuch as *operating* lease payments are charged to rental expense over the term of the lease, no asset or liability is recorded on the balance sheet of a company. (In contrast, *capitalized* leases which meet the criteria of FAS 13 'Accounting for Leases' are presented on the balance sheet as assets and liabilities.) For the purpose of calculating a cash rate of return on all assets employed by the firm, the value of operating assets whose use has been obtained by lease must be included in the firm's total gross assets. Rental expense is added to net income in calculating cash inflow, and the future obligation of operating leases is included as debt in the capital structure.

In order to determine the gross value of the operating leases, i.e., the amount to include as a Depreciating Asset, the assumptions are made that the lease life is approximately equal to asset life and that rental payments will be adjusted upward with inflation. Therefore, a stream of current year rental expense is in constant dollars and is discounted at the real debt rate to give an amount for gross leased property. The real debt rate is the estimated nominal rate of interest on the company's debt reduced by inflation expectations. It is 3.9 per cent for the Hershey example.[4] This estimating procedure improves upon merely using the minimum rental commitments disclosed in footnotes. Nevertheless, other procedures should be considered when the analyst has more information, especially when operating leases are substantial, as with airlines for example.

Eighteen years of equal payments of $24.52 (rental expense from the footnotes) discounted at a rate of 3.9 per cent generates a present value of $313.00, the current-dollar capitalized value of leased property.

Key issues concerning intangibles/goodwill

The importance of critical thinking to performance measurement and valuation work is especially apparent with respect to the handling of intangibles. Intangibles include patents, trademarks, goodwill, and the like. For practical purposes, the main concern is goodwill, measured as the excess of cost over the 'fair value' of the acquired net assets.

Treatment depends on question explored

Consider Firm A, which acquires Firm B for $P. Firm B is maintained as a stand-alone business, and some years later it is taken public. Based on its prospects at that time, the stock market values the spinoff at a market value of $S. From the perspective of the capital owners of Firm A, how should economic performance of the acquisition investment be measured? The answer is that performance is reflected in the real internal rate of return that equates the present value (at time of purchase) of subsequent NCRs and spinoff market value $S to the purchase price $P. This rate is the real achieved return (Figure 5.9), and it is not affected by the method of accounting for the transaction (purchase or pooling accounting) as long as taxes paid and NCRs are not affected.

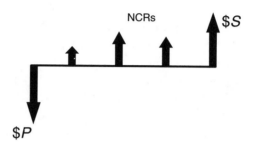

Figure 5.9   Achieved ROI for acquisition investment.

In the above example, which takes the perspective of Firm A's capital suppliers, the full amount of any goodwill must be included as investment in Firm B. Now consider goodwill from a different perspective, namely, when we want to estimate the spinoff market value, $S.

Figure 5.10 displays the major components of *purchase accounting*. It reveals that an acquired firm's gross asset amount is lost, because it is replaced with a 'fair value' amount and goodwill amount, which is the excess of the purchase price over fair value.

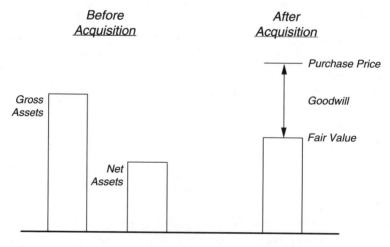

Figure 5.10   Major components of purchase accounting.

In contrast to purchase accounting, consider pooling accounting whereby the acquired firm's assets are pooled (aggregated) with the acquiror's. The amount of aggregated gross assets (and related depreciation) is not affected by any fair value appraisal, and goodwill is not recorded.

Now, the value to Firm A of Firm B as a spinoff is highly related to the likely returns on Firm B's *future* investments. This argues for excluding goodwill. More precisely, the figure needed is the original cost basis of B's assets, because the CFROIs on B's *operating assets* would be most useful for gauging likely returns on new investments.

We have dealt with two distinct situations involving acquisition goodwill, and we have shown that full inclusion or full exclusion of the effects of goodwill is appropriate depending on the question being asked.

In HOLT's Database, the amount of intangibles (goodwill) is included in assets for measuring CFROIs. Consequently, a firm's track record of CFROIs is 'tilted' towards the perspective of the firm's capital suppliers who, in fact, paid for the goodwill. By necessity, HOLT has to treat all firms in a consistent manner using publicly available financial data.

In recognizing the need to assess the likely returns on future investments, an argument can be made to examine CFROIs with and without intangibles. The lower CFROIs, calculated with intangibles in the asset base, may be 'closer to the mark' for firms that are likely to make substantial goodwill-creating acquisitions on an ongoing basis in future years, without fundamentally improving the performance of the acquired businesses. A more optimistic CFROI, closer to ongoing returns from operations excluding intangibles in the asset base, may be more appropriate for gauging ROIs going forward when: (a) substantial acquisitions are unlikely to occur in future years or (b) large scale performance improvements in acquired firms have been demonstrated and will likely be repeated with future acquisitions.

An example of a highly skilled management that continually makes a large number of acquisitions is Danaher Corporation whose stock price has risen over seven-fold in the last seven years. Danaher's primary businesses are tools and process/environmental controls. Danaher has reached a high level of proficiency in the continuous improvement practices of lean manufacturing pioneered by Toyota. Danaher earns above-average returns on the purchase price of its acquisitions because it quickly transfers its operating skills to acquired firms and thereby achieves extraordinary efficiency gains.[5] Danaher's acquisition strategy *extends* its demonstrated skill to new, growth opportunities to the benefit of its long-term shareholders.

HOLT's treatment of goodwill

In HOLT's Database used by professional money managers, the near-term forecasted CFROI is shown with and without intangibles. For most firms there is little difference. When there is a substantial difference, the analyst is alerted to examine more deeply management's track record on the performance of acquired businesses and management's likely future acquisition strategy.

With US firms, goodwill can be amortized over 40 years. Inclusion of the gross amount of goodwill in operating assets would depress CFROIs to a lower figure for a very long time, and CFROIs often would reflect acquisitions made by managements long gone. Such lower CFROIs might easily misrepresent the skill of current management and the returns to be expected from incremental investments. Consequently, goodwill is treated on a net basis.

Given the limitations of existing data in the US on goodwill, another approach might be considered. This rough method focuses on gross plant life. Notice that prior to the acquisition, an analyst could calculate a clean number for asset life. But with purchase accounting, a new gross plant figure emerges, namely, the accountant's estimate of fair value. In most instances, asset life computed as fair value divided by revised depreciation charges would contribute to a shorter consolidated life, thereby biasing CFROIs downward. As new plant is added and older layers are retired, this bias is eliminated over the next cycle of plant replacement. So, amortizing goodwill over the asset life seems to be a reasonable way to circumvent the 40 year retiring problem while helping to compensate for the above-mentioned bias occurring during a cycle of plant replacement. HOLT has recently implemented this method in the United Kingdom where acquisition goodwill is immediately written off to equity and is easily identified.

Proposal: use pooling, footnote goodwill

In the light of the above analysis of goodwill, is there a way to resolve the problems of purchase accounting yet still address the fact that goodwill is a genuine cost in the eyes of the acquiring firms' shareholders? Our proposed solution is:

(1) Use pooling, and thereby avoid both fair-value-induced problems and the need to assign a specific amortization schedule for goodwill.
(2) Record in a footnote the amount of goodwill, computed as purchase price less net book assets of the acquired firm.

Analysts would then have the flexibility to include goodwill in whatever way is appropriate for the *particular measurement problem* faced.

Adjusted intangibles

Pension Intangibles are also included in Intangibles. Pension Intangibles are created when a company increases pension benefits and retroactively gives credit to employees for the portion of these benefits that have been earned.

For example, an employee who has worked 20 years of a pension-plan-projected 30 year tenure, has earned 67 per cent of the plan's benefits. When the plan benefit level is retroactively raised, instantaneously the employee would be entitled to 67 per cent of the newly

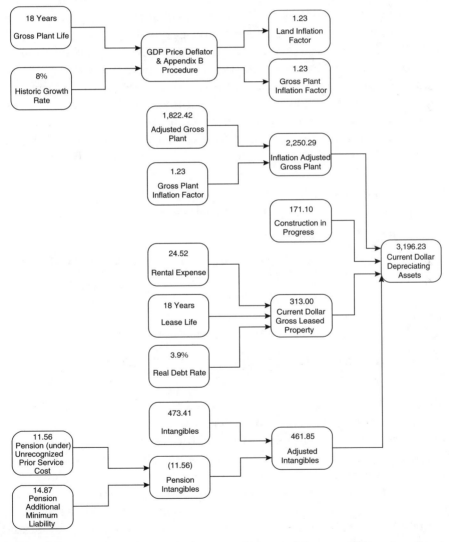

Figure 5.11 Current-dollar depreciating assets calculation. 1993 Hershey Foods Corporation.

granted benefits. Based on the opinion that increased pension benefits result in improved employee morale, lower turnover, and other
unquantifiable benefits to the company, the Financial Accounting
Standards Board (FASB) in the US has determined that such assets
should be amortized over the future economic-benefit period. Because
such assets are a FASB accounting creation and are quite different
from the typical operating assets of a business, their amounts are
removed from the amount of depreciating assets used in the CFROI
calculation.

Although Hershey's balance sheet labels Intangibles as resulting
from business acquisitions, a note in the annual report indicates that
other intangibles are included. The portion of the intangibles related
to pensions needs to be excluded from Depreciating Assets. According
to FAS 87, 'Employers' Accounting for Pensions,' Pension Intangibles
are equal to the *lesser of* the Pension Unrecognized Prior Service
Cost, $11.56, or the Pension Minimum Liability, $14.87. Note that
the Pension Intangibles relate only to under-funded plans, because
over-funded plans would have a zero minimum liability amount. Once
the Pension Intangible amount has been determined, that amount is
subtracted from total Intangibles to obtain Adjusted Intangibles, as
follows:

Intangibles (Total)	$473.41
Less: Pension Intangibles	(11.56)
Adjusted Intangibles	$461.85

A map of Hershey's Depreciating Assets Calculation is shown in
Figure 5.11.

Current-dollar non-depreciating assets

Along with C$ Depreciating Assets, C$ Non-depreciating Assets
constitute C$ Gross Operating Assets (the cash outflow, or invest-
ment) employed in the generation of the periodic cash inflow. The
amount of C$ Non-depreciating Assets also is a cash inflow (addi-
tional to the periodic cash inflow) received upon completion of the
project life. Conceptually, the components are: the net working
capital investment required in connection with the firm's projects
(which includes inventory stated in current dollars), land stated
in current dollars, and any other tangible non-depreciating asset
used in the generation of the periodic cash flow. HOLT's CFROI

procedure organizes Non-depreciating Assets into Monetary Assets, and All Other Non-depreciating Assets, which include Investments & Advances, Inventory, Land, and when appropriate, a reduction of a portion of the firm's Deferred Tax Assets.

Financial subsidiaries: a special case

Before we get into the calculation of monetary assets, financial subsidiaries require attention as a special case. Hershey does not have a significant finance subsidiary, but many industrial/service firms do. It is essential that financial subsidiaries be treated appropriately in order to avoid errors in calculating CFROIs and warranted valuations.

The nature of a business determines how economic performance is appropriately measured. For example, if a firm invests in land for the primary purpose of capital gains, then the realized market value of those properties is at the heart of performance. If a firm is like a Home Depot or Wal-Mart, the issue of the market value of land under their stores is almost always immaterial, compared with the importance of factors related to generating operating cash flows.

Consider an industrial firm that has a finance arm (business) with all assets reported on a consolidated basis. A loan by the finance arm is recorded as an asset on the consolidated balance sheet. That asset is used to generate interest income. The difference, or spread, between interest income and interest expense on the supporting debt should be compared to the equity used by the finance business. Spread-derived earnings on an equity base, with consideration for the risks involved should be the foundation for the valuation of financial businesses.

In the US, FAS 94, 'Consolidation of All Majority-owned Subsidiaries,' has resulted in the consolidation of financial subsidiaries for a large number of industrial firms. If the CFROI valuation model is applied to industrial firms that have consolidated substantial financial subsidiaries, and if no adjustments are made, the following occur:

(1) CFROIs are too low, because assets are substantially boosted by loans on the books and cash flow is only modestly increased due to including interest expense on associated debt.
(2) The forecasted NCR stream is based on a starting asset base that is too high, coupled to CFROIs that are too low.
(3) Too high a risk differential for financial leverage is assigned due to ignoring that a significant portion of consolidated debt is associated with the financial business.

(4) Because industrial firms' CFROIs are forecasted to fade to a competitive average level of approximately 6 per cent real in 40 years, the model implies a dramatic increase in the spread earned by financial assets over time.

The above effects illustrate the importance of a complete logical blueprint for valuation analysis, such as that of the CFROI model. Note that effects may be offsetting, but it is risky to assume that. Given that stock prices are inherently noisy, users of more simple valuation models may be unaware of errors such as described above.

Effect (4) above requires additional explanation. In Figure 5.12 the top panel shows the longer-term fade-to (downward or upward) level of 6 per cent for CFROIs on $100 of industrial assets. Consider a financial operation (middle panel) that has $10 of equity and $90 of debt for each $100 of loans. Also, assume that the real debt cost is 3.0 per cent and the real return on loans is 3.6 per cent. For $100 of loans, interest earned is $3.60, and for $90 debt, interest expense is $3.00, giving a spread of $0.90 on an equity base of $10.00; all in inflation-adjusted terms. This gives a 9.0 per cent real pretax Earnings/Book.

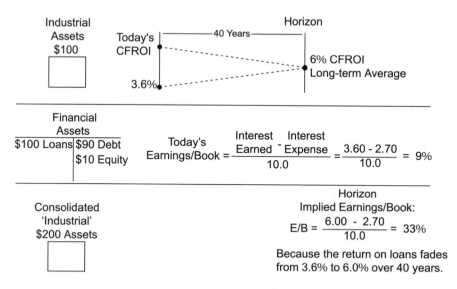

Figure 5.12 Financial subsidiaries are a valuation special case.

The valuation distortion is apparent in the bottom panel. After consolidation, a total of $200 of assets is forecasted within the model to fade to a 6 per cent CFROI level. But $100 of the $200 in consolidated assets are loans that currently earn 3.6 per cent resulting in a 9 per cent Earnings/Book. All else equal, if these loans earn the implied 6.0 per cent, pretax Earnings/Book for the financial business would jump to 33 per cent.

Testing proposed fixes

A thorough valuation of industrial/service firms with very large finance businesses (e.g., General Electric, John Deere) requires separate analyses for the industrial and finance business units. Nevertheless, for many firms with financial subsidiaries a shortcut procedure can resolve the problems described above. This procedure has three steps and involves estimates when the financial subsidiary is not separately broken out in the annual report:

(1) Reduce receivables by the amount that is estimated to be carried by financial subsidiary debt.
(2) Reduce gross interest expense by the amount of interest estimated to be related to financial subsidiary debt.
(3) Reduce debt used to calculate warranted equity value by the estimated amount of financial subsidiary debt.

The above steps have the effect of putting the equity portion of the finance subsidiary, and related spread income, into the CFROI calculation. In effect, the financial subsidiary is de-consolidated and treated as an equity investment.

Many industrial/service firms have a finance-type business in the consolidated financial statements. For example, the 1996 annual report for Sears, Roebuck and Co. shows a *retailing* business in which 60 per cent of the net assets are credit card receivables. Hillenbrand Industries has five operating groups primarily dealing with funeral services and health care. Hillenbrand sells both pre-paid funeral services and life insurance, and invests in bonds with maturities that match expected cash outflows from these operations. These are clearly financial spread businesses.

Although the adjustments discussed above seem logical, an added degree of confidence accrues when empirical tests support the logical fixes. The top panels of Figure 5.13 display CFROI data for Hillenbrand. The 'No Adjustment' panel of Figure 5.13 presents the firm's track record of CFROIs with no adjustment for Hillenbrand's spread businesses. The 'With Adjustment' panel presents the CFROI track record after stripping out the financial assets and after treating these assets as an equity investment to avoid the errors discussed earlier.

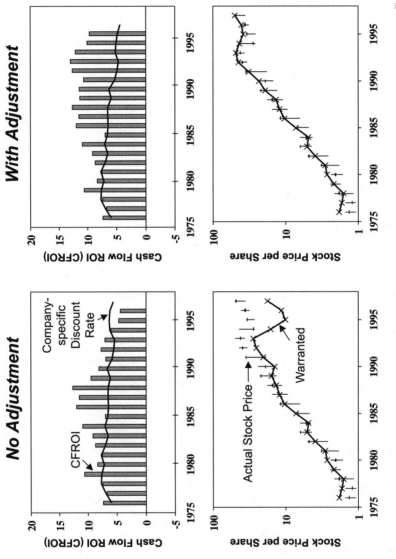

Figure 5.13 Hillenbrand Industries (financial subsidiaries). Source: Compustat and HOLT/*ValueSearch*™.

After the adjustments are made, CFROIs since 1988 have remained well above the market discount rate.

The bottom panels of Figure 5.13 display historical tracking of warranted versus actual stock prices for Hillenbrand. In recent years, as Hillenbrand's financial assets grew larger, the before-adjustment deviation between warranted and actual stock prices became substantial. After the adjustments, the four sources of errors previously noted were corrected, and the result was substantially improved tracking of warranted versus actual stock prices.

Monetary assets

Monetary Assets (excluding inventories) are cash and short-term items and are susceptible to loss of purchasing power of the monetary unit. Monetary Assets are calculated as the accumulation of Cash & Short-term Investments; Receivables, Adjusted for Financial Subsidiary Debt; and Other Current Assets. Hershey does not have a finance subsidiary, so the Receivables Total is used without adjustment.

Cash & Short-term Investments	$ 15.96
Receivables Total	294.97
Other Current Assets	124.62
Monetary Assets	$435.55

Net monetary assets

Net Monetary Assets is Monetary Assets reduced by adjusted current liabilities, which includes accounts payable, income taxes payable, accrued expenses, and all other liabilities not considered as debt holders in the CFROI model. Although GAAP provides that the current portion of long-term debt and any short-term debt are current liabilities, those items are excluded from HOLT's Net Monetary Assets. Such debt is included in a company's Capital Structure, consistent with the CFROI model's treatment of debt holders as capital suppliers along with equity owners.

Net Monetary Assets is calculated as Monetary Assets less Current Liabilities (excluding debt & deferred tax liability). An adjustment is made to the accounts payable amount, due to Hershey maintaining an overdraft position at certain banks. Bank overdrafts represent checks honored by a bank without the account having sufficient funds to cover the checks. For logical consistency, the overdraft amount is taken out of the accounts payable amount and reclassified as short-term debt.

Account Payable	$108.46
Income Taxes Payable	35.60
Other Current Liabilities	301.99
Current Liabilities	$446.05

(Excluding debt & deferred tax liability)

Current-dollar inventory

Valuing inventory in current dollars is important to the CFROI calculation for the same reason that valuing Gross Plant in current dollars is important, namely, to eliminate distortions in values due to varied purchasing power of the monetary unit and, thereby, to have a more accurate series with which to observe patterns across time. Inventory is stated in current dollars when valued under the FIFO (first-in, first-out) method. Under the FIFO method, it is assumed that goods are used or sold in the order in which they are purchased, i.e., the first goods purchased (first ones in) are the first taken out of inventory. The remaining goods (those in inventory) therefore must represent the most recent purchases, and they typically would be stated in current dollars.

Some companies value inventory by the LIFO (last-in, first-out) method. Under LIFO, the remaining goods in inventory might have been purchased some time ago. Since inventory typically is valued at cost (purchase prices), purchases made before the current period would be stated in dollars having purchasing power different from current dollars, unless inventory prices remained constant.

The LIFO reserve represents the difference between the inventory valued at LIFO and the inventory valued at FIFO. As a practical matter, the LIFO reserve is easily obtained, since it is a required footnote disclosure under GAAP. LIFO inventories are converted to current dollars by adding the LIFO reserve.

Current-dollar land

As with Plant, land (including improvements to land) is stated in an amount of historical dollars, the component parcels and improvements having been purchased at various times and valued at their then-current dollar costs. Financial statements for outsiders do not give detail needed to 'age' total land into component amounts purchased in various years, which amounts then could be marked-up to current dollars by a procedure similar to that for Gross Plant. Lacking a better alternative, HOLT marks up land and improvements to current dollars with the same adjustment factor as the Gross Plant Inflation Adjustment.

Other long-term assets

This is a catch-all category for non-depreciating *long-term* assets that do not belong in the other identified categories.

Investments & advances

In this category belong long-term receivables and advances, and other investments, including investments in unconsolidated companies in which there is no significant control. When investments are an insignificant element in the firm's assets, it is convenient to treat them as a non-depreciating asset, otherwise a more detailed analysis is required to estimate their realizable value to the firm. In such situations, they would not be included in the operating asset base used to calculate CFROI, and their effect on the cash flow input to CFROI would be removed.

Deferred tax assets (excluded)

If a portion of deferred tax assets is the result of FAS 106, 'Employers' Accounting for Postretirement Benefits Other Than Pensions', that portion needs to be excluded from Non-depreciating Assets. FAS 106 changed the prevailing accounting practice for such benefits from a pay-as-you-go (cash) basis to an accrual basis. This caused firms to record as a liability the expected cost of providing future non-pension postretirement benefits for an employee during the year in which the employee renders service to earn the promised benefit. More than 95 per cent of companies required to adopt FAS 106 opted to book, in the year they adopted the statement, a liability for all previously earned promised benefits. Because the IRS does not allow a tax deduction for postretirement expenses until actually paid, in many instances the implementation of FAS 106 substantially boosted deferred tax assets.

The FAS 106 liability is a component of debt in the firm's capital structure. By increasing debt, all else equal, the firm's warranted *equity* value is reduced. The key point is that FAS 106 effects are properly viewed as a debt-like reduction from total warranted value and not part of the operating assets used to calculate CFROIs. In the CFROI model, the amount of long-term, deferred tax assets owing to FAS 106 is excluded from Non-depreciating Assets (and thus from the amount of Gross Operating Assets), while the associated unfunded liability needs to be translated to an estimated market value of debt in the company's capital structure.

The excluded portion of deferred tax assets is limited by FAS 109, 'Accounting for Income Taxes.' It specifies that all current deferred tax assets and liabilities shall be offset and presented as a single amount with a similar treatment for non-current assets and liabilities. Thus, although a company may have a large FAS 106 long-term deferred tax asset, it might also have a long-term deferred tax liability. In such a situation, the long-term deferred tax asset is netted against the long-term deferred tax liability. If the net is a long-term liability, the amount of the liability appears on the balance sheet. Inasmuch as the deferred tax asset would not be included as an asset on the balance sheet, no

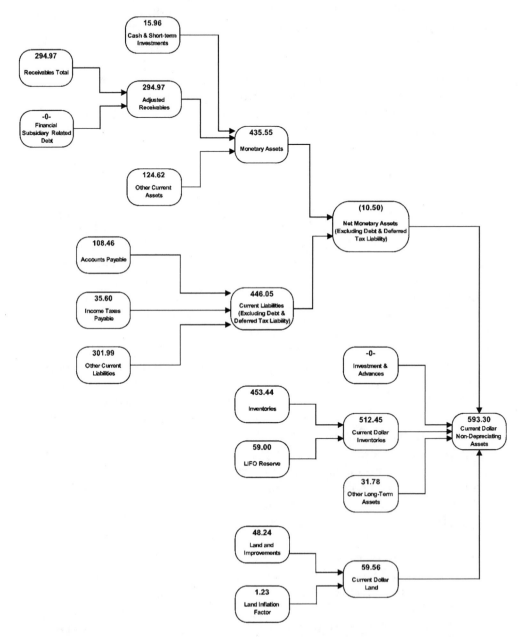

Figure 5.14 Current-dollar non-depreciating assets calculation. 1993 Hershey Foods Corporation.

adjustment to the amount of non-depreciating assets would then be needed, as is the case for Hershey's 1993 financial statements.

The calculation map for Current-dollar Non-depreciating Assets is shown as Figure 5.14.

Current-dollar gross cash flow

The Current-dollar, or Inflation Adjusted, Gross Cash Flow is the final amount needed for the example CFROI calculation. Conceptually, we seek to capture the amount of cash flow resulting from the company's business *operations*, regardless of how financed. The items added to accounting Net Income are Depreciation & Amortization, Adjusted Interest Expense, Rental Expense, Monetary Holding Gain (Loss), LIFO Charge to FIFO Inventories (subtractive item), Net Pension Expense, Special Item After Tax, and Minority Interest.[6]

Depreciation & amortization

Depreciation and Amortization are added to Net Income because they are non-cash operating expenses.

Adjusted interest expense

Interest Expense is added to Net Income because, in the CFROI model, it is viewed as a financing cost, not an operating cost. This cash flow adjustment is consistent with the handling of the associated debt in the capital structure, where it is deducted from the total value of the company in deriving the economic equity value of the company.

As we discussed in the Non-depreciating Assets calculation, Hershey does not have a financial subsidiary of significant size, but many industrial firms do, and such subsidiaries require special treatment. In order to adjust the cash flow for a finance subsidiary, the gross reported Interest Expense for the industrial company is reduced by the estimated portion attributable to the finance subsidiary's debt, leaving an Interest Expense (Adjusted) comprising only the company's core-business Interest Expense. Thus, when there is a finance subsidiary, it is this Adjusted Interest Expense that is added to Net Income in deriving cash flow for the CFROI calculation. For a financial subsidiary that finances the firm's receivables, the *spread* of interest earned on the receivables, less the interest on the associated debt, flows through to net income.

The Adjusted Interest Expense is calculated as Gross Interest Expense less Capitalized Interest Expense less Financial Subsidiary Interest Expense. Gross Interest Expense is $34.87 and Capitalized

Interest Expense is $4.65 and both are obtained from a note in the financial statements. If Hershey had a financial subsidiary, the Financial Subsidiary Interest Expense could be estimated by taking the Gross Interest Expense multiplied by the proportion of debt represented by Financial Subsidiary Debt. Calculation of Adjusted Interest Expense is as follows:

Gross Interest Expense	$34.87
Less:	
Capitalized Interest Expense	(4.65)
Financial Subsidiary Interest Expense	(0.00)
Adjusted Interest Expense	$30.22

Rental expense

Recall that in the Depreciating Assets calculation, leases were capitalized, with the capitalized amount considered part of the operating-asset investment (cash-out) used to generate the periodic cash inflow. The future obligation of operating leases is included in debt in the Capital Structure calculation. Rental expense (lease payments) thus is added to net income in deriving cash flow generated from *all* operating assets, which is the cash flow needed for the CFROI.

Monetary holding gain (loss)

If a country's monetary unit exactly retained its purchasing power year-to-year, this item would be unnecessary. Moreover, when the rate of inflation is low, the amount of this item is typically insignificant. Yet, all monetary units, including the US dollar, have had significant rates of loss of purchasing power in some years over the past few decades, and the timing of such has varied among countries. The monetary holding gain or loss is another adjustment needed to make CFROIs comparable across time and across countries.

Here is the rationale for it: If inflation were 10 per cent during a year, it would take $110 at the end of a year for $100 in monetary assets at the beginning to have maintained its purchasing power. If the $100 monetary asset earned, say, 10 per cent tax-free, $10 interest would have been received and, all else equal, would have boosted net income by $10. But it would not be a real return, since the $10 was required just to maintain the purchasing power of the initial $100 principal. Cash flow would have to be reduced by the monetary-holding loss of $10 to put the cash flow into real units.

The above illustration applies if Net Monetary Holdings are positive. If a company has a negative Net Monetary Holdings, inflation results in a real gain, because the company would settle the net obligation with dollars of reduced purchasing power. Such gains should be added to Net Income in deriving Current Dollar Gross Cash Flow. (So that monetary-holding gains or losses do not dominate cash flow, it is advisable to put a size limit for such gains or losses; e.g., no more than 10 per cent of the total of Earnings Cash Flow plus Depreciation & Amortization plus Adjusted Interest Expense.) The calculation is as follows:

Net Monetary Assets (excluding debt & deferred tax liability)	($10.50)
Percent Change in GDP Deflator, 2.61 per cent	X0.0261
Monetary Holding Gain (Loss)	= $0.27

LIFO charge to FIFO inventories

Previously we described why in an inflationary environment the *FIFO* method more accurately values the balance-sheet amount of inventory stated in current dollars, and thus why inventories recorded under LIFO method should be restated to their FIFO value.

When income-statement effects are considered, however, the *LIFO* method results in a more accurate current-dollar cost-of-goods-sold figure, and thus a more accurate net income figure. Recall that the implicit assumption under LIFO is that the last goods purchased (the last in to inventory) are the first ones taken out of inventory for use or sale. These goods would be the most recently purchased, and thus their cost more likely would be recorded in current dollars. In an inflationary environment, cost-of-goods-sold is more likely to be understated when inventory is kept under the FIFO method, in which case net income would be overstated, and so would cash flow. Therefore, a subtraction from Net Income needs to be made in the amount of the estimated FIFO profits, that is, the overstatement of Net Income due to the use of FIFO.

This inventory charge is a soft number. Using the published financial statements, an estimate is made of the proportion of the firm's inventories on FIFO and this amount is multiplied by the percentage change in the Producer Price Index (PPI) for the same year. The result is an approximate amount by which Net Income would be reduced if the firm had been on LIFO instead of FIFO.

The above assumption can easily be improved by more detailed knowledge of a particular firm's inventory. A firm's actual inventory prices can change at dramatically different rates than the PPI. For this reason, HOLT limits the size of this adjustment.

For Hershey, the 1993 inventory charge is calculated as follows:

Total Inventory	$453.44
Percent Inventory on FIFO, 40 per cent	X0.40
Amount Inventory on FIFO	= $181.38
Percent Change in Producer Price Index, 1.45 per cent	X0.0145
LIFO Charge to FIFO Inventories	= $2.63

Net pension (and other post-retirement benefit) expense

CFROIs measure how well management is using resources, independent of how those resources are financed. HOLT therefore reverses the net financing effects of pensions (and other post-retirement benefits) on earnings in the calculation of cash flow. Consistency is maintained by including in the firm's debt the difference between the company's retirement-plan obligation (liabilities) and assets held to meet the obligations.

For convenience of expression, 'pension' will often be used for 'pension and post-retirement benefits.' In the language of pension accounting, 'service cost' is the cost of the promised pension benefit incurred due to the service of employees during the accounting period; it thus is the operational cost of the benefit. 'Pension expense' is the 'service costs' plus financing effects, and financing effects include interest cost, expected return on plan investments, and other financing items:

$$\text{Pension Expense} = \text{Service Cost} + (\text{Interest Cost} - \text{Expected Return} + \text{Other})$$

For cash flow calculation, reversal of the income effects of financing can be achieved by adding Pension Expense and subtracting Service Cost.

Hershey's Total Pension Expenses are:

Pension	$27.83
Post-retirement	16.61
Total pension expense	$44.44

The Total Service Costs are:

Pension	$27.83
Post-retirement	3.99
Total service cost	$31.83

Gross Cash Flow is calculated by deducting only service costs, but including the financing costs, similar to how interest is included as a return to the debt holders.

Minority interest

Net Income is reported after reduction for the amount of any Minority Interest. The minority owner is treated as a supplier of capital in the CFROI valuation model. Therefore, Minority Interest is added back to Net Income in calculating gross cash flow. After the firm's total warranted value has been reduced by the claims of debt and preferred stock holders, the residual is split between minority interest and common equity in proportion to their book values.

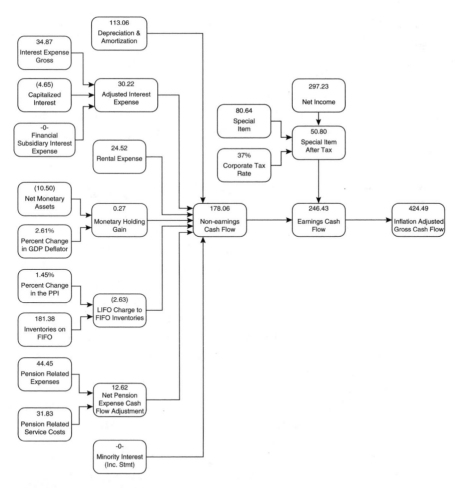

Figure 5.15 Current-dollar gross cash flow calculation. 1993 Hershey Foods Corporation.

Special item after tax

The income statement can include a pretax special item due to, for example: (a) adjustments applicable to prior years; (b) nonrecurring profit or loss on the sale of assets, investments, and securities; and (c) write-downs or write-offs of receivables and intangibles.

It is impossible to have a single rule for the treatment of special items. In HOLT's CFROI calculations, Net Income is adjusted to exclude the effects of such items. Because reported Net Income would include the after-tax effect of the Special Item, the adjustment is the after-tax amount. Alternatively, an analyst might conclude, in a particular situation, that the special item (gain/loss) should be prorated to adjust up/down CFROIs over past years because the special item properly reflects the level of managerial skill.

The calculation for Hershey is:

Special Item	$80.64
Taxes at 37 per cent rate	(29.84)
Special Item After Tax	$50.80

In the map for the calculation of current-dollar gross cash flow (Figure 5.15), Net Income plus Special Item After Tax are labelled Earnings Cash Flow. Non-earnings Cash Flow consists of all the other items.

Concluding remarks on CFROI

This completes the description of the four major inputs to the CFROI calculation for the Hershey example. The calculation itself can be done on a financial calculator by using the key strokes for calculating an internal rate of return. The Hershey example CFROI is 9.2 per cent per year.

Other performance metrics do not include the comprehensive adjustments incorporated in the CFROI metric. The broad comparability of calculated CFROIs gives that metric a high usefulness as a benchmark for making and judging the plausibility of forecast CFROIs, and thus of forecast NCRs.

In contrast, Earnings/Book ratios are easy to calculate, but changes in the rate of inflation, together with GAAP treatment of many activities, undermine their comparability across time, companies, and surely national borders. Problems with Earnings/Book comparability are most severe when accounting rules are changed. For example, when FAS 106, dealing with non-pension post-retirement benefits, was issued in the United States, companies took large write-offs to equity that boosted Earnings/Book, yet total assets and economic performance were unaffected.

What about ROCE (return-on-capital-employed) as a performance-metric competitor to CFROI? The conventional ROCE is computed as [(net income + interest expense)/net assets]. That's easy, especially in relation to the computation complexity of a CFROI. Moreover, ROCE incorporates asset life implicitly via the effects of assigned depreciation schedules on net income and net assets. If one ignores inflation biases due to historical cost, and denominator biases due to fully-depreciated-but-not-yet-retired plant, ROCE might seem to be a strong performance-metric competitor to CFROI.

While ROCE incorporates asset life, it does so *implicitly* and with *tacit acceptance* of accounting depreciation schedules, which are reflected in the amounts of net income and net assets. In contrast, CFROI requires an *explicit* estimate of asset life. Inappropriate asset life, for example that arising from the use of accelerated depreciation schedules in Japan, distorts calculated CFROIs, which in turn distorts the estimated value of existing assets and of future investments. This would result in observed systematic deviations between the warranted stock price and actual stock price, which would indicate a problem with the valuation. Asset life is one of the tracks HOLT can travel down in search of the source of a problem and a resolution of it. HOLT's asset-life benchmarks by industries and by countries are helpful for these purposes. In general, the explicit details of the CFROI calculations greatly help in identifying and resolving performance measurement problems.

Today's CFROI calculation procedures incorporate the resolutions of many earlier problems uncovered in our work with clients. Analysts using HOLT's services no longer encounter these particular problems; performance measurement and valuation accuracy has been improved.

Capital structure

As mentioned earlier, the CFROI was originally developed to assist in forecasting ROIs on incremental investments. The ROIs apply to all operating assets, regardless of how they are financed, by debt or equity. Thus, the cash flow relevant to the CFROI metric is that available to both the firm's equity owners and debt holders, and the warranted value calculated from the CFROI model is the total value of the firm. In the CFROI model the sources of capital (capital structure) are taken into account after the total value of the firm is calculated. As is shown in Figure 5.2 on page 110, debt-holder claims and non-common-equity-owner claims are subtracted from the total value of the firm to arrive at the value of the common stock.

For each component of debt, we would prefer to use a market value. But book value is often used for lack of better information. If figures more reflective of market value are available, they should be used. Total Debt is the sum of Conventional Debt, Operating Lease Debt, Pension Debt, Other Liabilities, and Preferred Stock.

Conventional debt

This figure will be used for calculating a firm's financial leverage used in assigning company-specific risk differentials. It is reduced by the estimated amount of related finance subsidiary debt when applicable, but Hershey does not have a finance subsidiary of significant size.

Short-term debt	$337.29
+ Current portion of long-term debt	13.30
+ Book overdraft (short-term loan)	17.20
+ Long-term debt	165.76
− Adjusted Finance Subsidiary Related Debt	0.00
Conventional Debt	$533.55

Operating lease debt

In the section on Depreciating Assets, the current-dollar Gross Leased Property amount was calculated from rental payments, asset life, and a real debt rate. Gross Leased Property less accumulated depreciation reserves gives net leased property, which is the amount of Operating Lease Debt.

To derive the amount of accumulated depreciation reserves, HOLT first calculates an historical real asset growth rate for a company by averaging real asset growth rates over a seven year period, after eliminating those years having significant acquisitions, and/or divestures. This gave an 8 per cent rate for Hershey in 1993.

With that growth rate, the assumption is made that over the leased property life each year's addition was 8 per cent larger in constant dollars than the prior year's addition. One can then mathematically derive the relationship between accumulated depreciation reserves and gross leased property. Under this procedure, high historical growth implies relatively new facilities having relatively low accumulated depreciation reserves, which in turn implies a relatively high net leased property amount (debt).

Pension debt

This consists of two items, FAS 87 (Pension) and FAS 106 (Non-pension Post Retirement) Net Liabilities. The FAS 87 Net Liabilities is the difference between the Projected Benefit Obligation for both over-funded and under-funded plans, less the assets of those plans (if any). These amounts can be found in notes to the financial statements. The FAS 106 Postretirement Benefit Liability is the Projected Benefit Obligation balance, which also can be found in a note.

FAS 87	
Pension Projected Benefit Obligation	$417.90
Pension Plan Assets	(348.54)
FAS 87 Net Liabilities	$69.36
FAS 106	
Post-retirement Benefit Liability	$198.41

Pension Debt will show a value only if the plans in the aggregate are in an under-funded position relative to the projected benefit obligations of the plans. If the plans are in an over-funded position, Pension Debt would be zero, as the pension assets exceed the pension liabilities. The calculation follows:

FAS 87 Net Liabilities	$69.36
FAS 106 Post-retirement Benefit Liability	198.41
Pension Debt	$267.77

Other liabilities excluding pension obligation

Other Liabilities Excluding Pension Obligation is calculated by subtracting both the Postretirement Benefit Liability (FAS 106) and the Accrued Pension Cost (FAS 87) for both over-funded and under-funded pension plans from Liabilities Other. This is done because the Liabilities Other contains both of these items within the total. Note, however, that if a plan is in a Prepaid Pension Cost (asset) position, the amount would not be included here, because the Prepaid Pension Cost is reported as an asset on the balance sheet. The Other Liabilities Excluding Pension Obligation amount is calculated as follows:

Liabilities Other	$290.40
FAS 106 Postretirement Benefit Liability	(198.41)
Accrued Pension Cost (Over-Funded)	(6.68)
Accrued Pension Cost (Under-Funded)	(43.90)
Other Liabilities Excluding Pension Obligation	$41.41

Preferred stock

For most firms, when market value of preferred stock is unavailable, the dividend yield on the preferred stock can be used to estimate market price. Convertible preferred stock requires more detailed analysis of the conversion terms.

Minority interest (balance sheet)

The Minority Interest balance is zero, as review of the balance sheet and the footnotes makes no mention of Minority Interests.

A summary map of Capital Structure is shown as Figure 5.16.

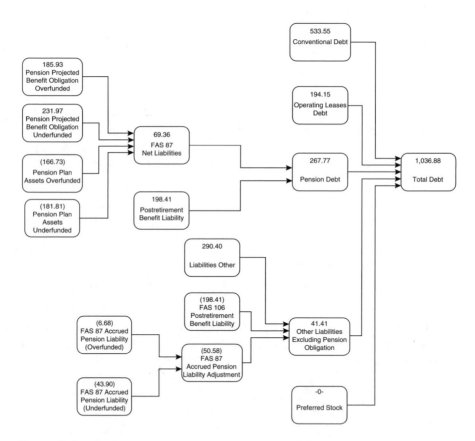

Figure 5.16   Capital-structure debt calculation. 1993 Hershey Foods Corporation.

HOLT's DualGrade® corporate performance scorecard

DualGrade® is a registered trademark of HOLT Value Associates.

Summary

- To give readers a break from technical details, this chapter demonstrates the model's usefulness in the form of an easy-to-appreciate summary grading system: HOLT's DualGrade® Corporate Performance Scorecard for 2000 US companies, which is presented in Appendix C.
- This performance scorecard can be used to: (a) quickly learn the relative rankings of firms for expected near-term and long-term performance, (b) initially assess a firm's managerial skill, (c) benchmark peers, (d) screen for buy/sell candidates, (e) test one's thoughts about an industry or firm, and (f) search for possible 'best practices'.
- DualGrade® is a two-grade structure with one grade for expected *near-term economic performance* and one grade for expected *long-term wealth creation* as a percentage of total firm value. Possible grades for each characteristic are A through E, determined by the firm's quintile rank within its size category. The highest grade is AA; the lowest, EE.

- Commentaries for example companies and general observations are presented to help readers interpret the dual grades. Insights can be gained from studying the grades for firms within industry groups.
- A preview of the 5-year forecast window used in calculating warranted values and described in Chapter 7 is illustrated. With a +1-year forecasted CFROI level, the model can be used to translate a firm's stock price into the market's implied +5-year CFROI level for the firm. In a graphical presentation, a line connecting the +1-year and +5-year CFROIs visually displays the market's forecasted performance fade trajectory for the firm. This is called 'setting the line' on market expectations.
- Reasons are given as to why HOLT's DualGrade® Scorecard is more helpful than other popular scorecards, including earnings/book, total shareholder return, and Market Value Added.

Introduction

We have emphasized the importance of feedback information as a check on our knowledge-base. Feedback is critical both for correcting erroneous knowledge and for raising confidence in reliable knowledge. HOLT's DualGrade® Performance Scorecard is a valuable source of feedback information. It is inexpensive in terms of both cash-outlay (it's free) and search cost (it's readily available on the Internet at *http://www.holtvalue.com*, and takes relatively little time to peruse). Yet, it conveys much useful information.

Grounded in HOLT's CFROI valuation model, the DualGrade® Performance Scorecard carries many of the advantages of the CFROI model over alternative valuation models and of grading (ranking) structures based on them. Some of the model's advantages carried over to DualGrade® are: a sound economic performance metric expressed in real units, minimization of accounting distortions, and suitability for direct comparisons across industries, borders, and time. Yet, DualGrade® suffers from the limitations of any grading system—primarily, significant factors might well be excluded from the grading system and, therefore, might go unobserved from reliance on the grade(s) alone.

Nevertheless, DualGrade® is an important tool. It can be used to:

- learn the relative ranking of firms according to expected near-term performance and according to expected wealth creation from future investments;

- get an initial assessment of a firm's managerial skill;
- benchmark peers;
- identify buy/sell candidates;
- get a 'reality check' of one's viewpoints about an industry or firm;
- identify firms that are superior at creating economic wealth, in order to learn 'best practices'; and
- identify issues deserving further consideration and research.

In this chapter the construction of the DualGrade® Performance Scorecard is described, and its applications, interpretations, and limitations are explained. The machinery industry is used as an example.

Two components to performance = DualGrade®

One major benefit of the CFROI metric is its comparability across time, across firms with different asset compositions, and across borders. A time series of a particular firm's CFROIs is a helpful indicator of the overall skill of that firm's management.

Expected near-term CFROI

Expected near-term levels of CFROIs are an excellent gauge of how efficiently management is running a firm's existing operations. The comprehensive comparability of CFROIs enables them to serve well as a measure of each firm's expected near-term operating efficiency relative to that of other firms. Expected near-term CFROIs thus is one performance component of the DualGrade® rankings.

% Future

While current operating efficiency is obviously important, positioning the firm now to create wealth in the future is an even greater challenge. The CFROI model provides a way to make a reasonable inference about the proportion of a firm's total market value that is due to *expected* wealth creation or dissipation from future investments. This proportion is labeled '% Future' and serves as the second component of DualGrade® rankings.

The total value of a firm is the sum of a value from existing assets and a value from future investments. The forecasted +1-year CFROI is used to make a reasonable estimate of the firm's value due to its existing assets. We describe in the next section how the CFROI model's estimate of a firm's value due to existing assets is used in the calculation of the firm's % Future.

DualGrade® data

HOLT maintains a proprietary database covering companies in all the major countries. This database includes nearly all the publicly traded companies of interest to professional money managers. Data include: each firm's track record of CFROIs and sustainable growth, forecasted CFROIs, HOLT-derived real discount rates, estimated value of firm's existing assets, and extensive supporting data. From the monitored database, HOLT produces a scorecard for industrial/service firms in each country.

The first performance measure of DualGrade® is the firm's forecasted CFROI, at a point 12 months ahead, consistent with security analysts' current forecasted EPS for the next two fiscal years. The method of assigning a grade to the +1-year CFROI is presented below.

The second measure, % Future, captures how much of today's market value is due to future investments. It is the excess of today's market value over the value of the firm's existing assets, expressed as a % of total market value. HOLT's procedure for calculating the value of a firm's existing assets is described in Chapter 3 and is further explained in Chapter 7. The firm's total market value is the sum of its equity value plus its debt value. The total market value less the estimated value of existing assets is the implied market valuation of the firm's future investments. These values are expressed on a per share basis, as shown in Figure 6.1 for contrasting firms in the Machinery Industry with data as of December 1997. Dover had a robust 48 per cent of its total market value due to future investments versus the industrial average of 35 per cent. With a −19 % Future,

	Per share dollar amounts, rounded	
	Dover Corp.	Mine Safety Appliances Co.
(a) Equity	36	66
(b) Debt	5	11
(c) Total Market Value = (a) + (b)	41	76
(d) Existing Assets Value	21	90
(e) Future Investments Value = (c) − (d)	20	−14
(f) % Future = (e)/(c)	48%	−19%

Figure 6.1   Sample % Future calculations.

Mine Safety Appliances was priced with expectations that future investments would dissipate wealth.

DualGrade® in Appendix C

Appendix C presents the 2000 industrial/service firms comprising HOLT's USA 2000 DualGrade® Performance Scorecard as of month-end December 1997. Page 258 shows that the 68 industries in the USA 2000 have an aggregate estimated value of existing assets of $6.16 trillion and a total market value of $9.43 trillion, implying $3.27 for future investments. This gives a % Future for the aggregate of 35 per cent (3.27/9.43). Industries are listed from high to low by % Future, with the Healthcare Information System Industry highest at #1 (page 256) and Metals & Mining (Diversified) lowest at #68. On the subsequent Appendix pages 259 through 342 company data are displayed by industry, arranged in alphabetical order.

Typically, as firms grow larger, it becomes increasingly difficult to maintain high CFROIs. Therefore, since company dynamics change with size it is helpful for peer comparisons to not mix firms of substantially different size. For this reason, HOLT divides the industrial/service universe into Very Large, Large, Medium, and Small groups based on equity market capitalization. Rankings and related grades for +1-year CFROI and for % Future are done within these size groups. In this manner, Very Large firms are graded against Very Large firms, and likewise for other size firms. Figure 6.2 provides information on how the 2000 firms were grouped. The size break points change during the year as market values change.

Consider the Very Large group of industrial/service firms, which consists of the top 300 of the 2000 firms ranked by equity market capitalization. Within this group, rankings are done by quintiles, with the top quintile graded A (best), and the others graded B, C, D, and E (worst). The first letter grade is for the +1-year CFROI rank, and the

	Number Firms	Equity Market Capitalization ($)
Very Large	300	3.93 billion +
Large	500	1.03 to 3.93 billion
Medium	600	0.42 to 1.03 billion
Small	600	154 million to 425 million
	2000	

Figure 6.2 HOLT USA 2000 DualGrade® size groupings, 31 December 1997.

second letter grade is for the % Future rank. The highest double rating is AA, and the lowest, EE.

The Appendix presents company data and related grades arranged by industry, which is generally the more useful way to study the data. Yet, for some purposes it is more informative to look at relative corporate performance without regard to the industry. Therefore, HOLT presents rankings by size group, where all Very Large firms are ranked relative to one another, and similarly for other size categories. Due to space limitations, this ordering of corporate performance is not included in Appendix C, but it is available at *http://www.holtvalue.com.*

Example dual grades

Based on this size ordering, five paired companies were selected from the Very Large category. The paired firms had the same grades for near-term performance but different grades for long-term performance (Figure 6.3). The pairing structure is helpful for illustrating how the market can see much different long-term futures for firms whose near-term CFROIs are similar. It is worth repeating that the inference as to what the market sees results from subtracting the estimated value of existing assets from the firm's total market value, including debt and equity. This *implied* value for future investments is expressed via the % Future.

The market expects Coca-Cola's (AA) extraordinarily strong, global franchise to preserve Coke's high returns long into the future. In contrast, Philip Morris (AC) has a less bright future, as the company faces increased regulation and large litigation costs.

Harley-Davidson's expected near-term CFROIs are not as high as Coke's, but it has a very strong franchise, as does Coke. There is a lengthy list of customers waiting to buy Harley-Davidson motorcycles. Its brand name enables Harley to charge premium prices. In contrast, the market apparently believes that competition will be more successful in lowering Deere's (BD) CFROIs from near-term high levels.

Monsanto (CB) divested its chemical division and has focused its long-term R & D programs on innovative products in agriculture, food ingredients, and especially pharmaceuticals. With a solid 'B' grade for % Future, the market expects that Monsanto's future investments will be rewarding. In contrast, Eastman Kodak (CD) embarked on an ill-conceived diversification strategy. A new CEO is reorganizing the firm while facing increasingly stiff competition from Fuji. The % Future 'D' grade implies the market doubts that Kodak will significantly improve its CFROIs.

LONG TERM, % FUTURE

Grades	A	B	C	D	E
A	Coca-Cola (265)		Philip Morris (340)		
B		Harley-Davidson (324)		Deere (300)	
C		Monsanto (271)		Eastman Kodak (320)	
D		Hasbro (324)		Air Products & Chemicals (268)	
E	Genentech (282)				Kmart (330)

NEAR TERM, +1-year CFROI

Figure 6.3 DualGrade® matrix, example companies, 31 December 1997. Companies can be located in Appendix C using the page numbers in parentheses.

Hasbro (DB) is one of the world's largest toy makers. Management has emphasized global brand management and product development. The market believes that management has positioned the firm to earn high CFROIs in future years. Air Products & Chemicals (DD) has been earning CFROIs close to or below the cost of capital for a long time, and the market expects more of the same.

Genentech (EA) is a leading biotechnology company whose CFROIs have been depressed by heavy R & D expenditures. Continued success in obtaining FDA drug approvals would result in sharply higher CFROIs. The % Future 'A' grade implies the market is expecting such. Kmart (EE) has not done well in competing against Wal-Mart in the mass merchandise market. Kmart is also in the home improvement market, where it has fared poorly in competition with Home Depot. As far as the market is concerned, Kmart's future is bleak.

Some general observations about DualGrade®

Readers are encouraged to get a feel for the DualGrade® data by reviewing industries with which they have considerable knowledge about specific firms. *The DualGrade® Scorecard reflects relative economic performance, not relative attractiveness as investments.* 'AA' graded firms might be priced with overly optimistic expectations and 'EE' firms might contain overly pessimistic expectations. Here are a few observations to keep in mind:

1. Double grades of A's and B's indicate high economic wealth-creating efficiency currently and expected in the future. High levels of capital expenditures by these firms will create economic wealth, but also will tend to drive the high CFROIs downward towards the average CFROIs.
2. Managements of middle-of-the-pack graded firms should strive for CFROI improvement. For example, firms with solid technical skill levels in areas that are becoming less valued in the marketplace might add new core competencies either through acquisition or internal development.
3. Double grades of D's and E's indicate a need for change. Be wary of managements' forecasts that large expenditures for new plant and equipment will solve the low productivity problem. A clear break from business-as-usual is needed. Such a break might require substantial contraction of assets and major restructuring.

4. Firms graded 'A' for % Future deserve thorough study and under-standing. The market believes these firms will be unusually successful, and that generally entails innovation. You should want to analyze in detail those 'A' % Future firms which are your competitors (directly or indirectly). You should also want to know about many non-competitor firms with an 'A' % Future grade. Some of these firms might excel at a process or prac-tices that could be implemented at your firm, thereby securing a competitive advantage.

5. Use DualGrade® as a quick 'reality check' of your thinking about an industry. If you disagree with the vast majority of grades for firms within an industry, be sure to identify why you see the industry so differently.

6. Select firms as *potential* buy/sell candidates *deserving further research* if their double grades seem overly pessimistic/optimistic. This opportunity often arises when firms report particularly weak/strong quarterly EPS and you are confident that the market is incorrectly extrapolating short-term results.

Industry data

Page 258 shows that the Machinery Industry has 68 firms with $142 billion of total market value. The estimated value of these firms' existing assets was $118 billion and, by implication, the value of their future investments was $24 billion. This provided the Machinery Industry with a 17 % Future, 50th highest out of 68 industries.

Pages 300–2 display the 68 machinery firms grouped by the four size categories. Firms are initially ranked on +1-year CFROI within their size group, and then sorted high to low on % Future.

As we explain in Chapter 7, the value of a firm's future investments depends on more than its near-term CFROI. Other key determinants are: (1) the rate at which CFROIs fade over the long term towards the cost of capital; (2) the forecasted sustainable growth rate; (3) its related fade rate; and (4) the firm-specific discount rate. Neverthe-less, the DualGrade® data illustrate that firms' 5-year Median and +1-year CFROIs have a major impact on determining % Future. A comparison of the +1-year forecasted CFROI to the 5-year past Median CFROI gives some indication of whether the firm is forecasted to significantly deviate from its past performance. Finally, firms that are in a startup/development stage can have high % Future that seems inconsistent with the +1-year CFROI because the market is anticipating a rising CFROI as the firm becomes more established.

The plausibility of DualGrade® has been tested by an interesting experiment sometimes done when HOLT consultants are meeting with corporate executives. Quite often, corporate managers express deep doubt about the market's ability to rationally value firms' economic performance in general, and their own firm in particular. Yet, when asked to sort their competitors by level of managerial skill, their ordering of firms closely correspond to rankings of % Future and CFROI level, that is, to DualGrade®.

Changing competitive landscape

DualGrade® data displayed in Appendix C provide an efficient way to assess firms' track records of economic performance (past 5-year median CFROI), likely near-term performance (forecast +1-year CFROI), and the market's assessment of their long-term potential (% Future). Firms cannot escape the forces of the competitive life cycle. It becomes increasingly difficult to sustain above-average CFROIs as firms grow larger, especially if their industry's pace of innovation slows. Nevertheless, even in so-called mature industries, firms with truly innovative managements can earn stellar CFROIs and be accorded high % Future for an extended period.

Appendix C takes a snapshot at 31 December 1997 and grades 2000 industrial/service firms. In paging through the alphabetical order of the industries, readers can benefit from putting aside detailed knowledge about certain firms and focus on a bigger picture 'reality check' embodied in the double grades. The following eight observations are presented simply to give the reader a sense of what might be gleaned from the DualGrade® Performance Scorecard.

(1) A vivid illustration of the so-called transition from the Machine Age economy to the Information Age is the preponderance of 'E' % Future grades for larger firms in these industries: Air Transport, Cement and Aggregates, Metals & Mining, Natural Gas (Diversified), Paper & Forest Products, Petroleum (Integrated), Railroad, and Steel (Integrated). In sharp contrast are Information Age industries such as Computer Software & Service, Telecommunication Equipment, and Drugs.

(2) The sheer number of dual grades of A and B in the Computer Software & Services Industry (pages 274–9) attests to the wide opportunity for and scope of innovation in this industry.

(3)   There is not even one 'A' % Future firm of any size in the entire Chemical (Basic) Industry (page 271). Perhaps Monsanto's management saw the limitations of that industry when it decided to restructure by moving into biotechnology and drug development. There are many A and B % Future grades in the Drug Industry (page 281).

(4)   Dell Computer, Computer & Peripherals Industry (pages 271–4), is known to have achieved great efficiencies from implementation of lean operating processes. How much might Dell's CFROIs decline as its competitors accelerate their implementation of lean processes? The +1-year CFROIs (pages 271–2) show Dell at 32.0 per cent, Gateway 2000 at 24.2 per cent, Compaq Computer at 18.4 per cent, and Hewlett Packard at 13.2 per cent. Is Dell's management skillful enough to implement the next innovation before its competitors and thereby maintain its extraordinarily high CFROI?

(5)   Give the managements of Campbell Soup and Wrigley high praise for delivering AA grades in the 'dull' food processing industry (page 289). In contrast, a succession of managements at Eastman Kodak (CD) and Polaroid (ED) have been unable, thus far, to buck the competitive life cycle (pages 320–1).

(6)   Performance that is strikingly above industry peers warrants investigation, not only for insights applicable to that particular industry but also for 'ways of doing business' that might be employed in other industries. Fastenal (AA) stands out above its industry peers on page 329 with a 5-year median CFROI of 18.5 per cent and a 19.2 per cent forecast CFROI in the retail building supply industry. Heartland Express (AA) on page 342 has a 5-year median CFROI of 18.4 per cent and a 14.5 per cent +1-year CFROI, while most other firms of its size in the Trucking and Transport Leasing Industry are graded much lower.

(7)   The onset of radical change in an industry offers increased opportunities for innovation and for earning above-average CFROIs. At the same time, old-line firms accustomed to the former slow pace of change in the industry, can fare poorly in the new, rapidly changing environment. Very Large firms in the Telecommunications Services Industry have below-average grades for +1-year CFROI and % Future (page 337). Many more A and B grades are observed for smaller firms in this industry, perhaps indicating there are highly profitable niches to exploit.

(8)   Have there been across-the-board big winners in telecommunication? The *equipment suppliers* (pages 335–7) generally have achieved outstanding performance grades.

'Setting the line'

Consider the Machinery Industry on page 300 and note Stanley Works, a global manufacturer of hardware and tools with $2 billion of sales. It is a CB dual grade, very large firm that apparently is improving, as indicated by its 5-year 6.0 per cent median CFROI increasing to 9.9 per cent forecast +1-year CFROI. The market apparently has confidence in the firm's management, as reflected by a 47 % Future. If one has an interest in the machinery industry, one would want to understand what is happening at Stanley Works.

Its CFROI life-cycle chart (Figure 6.4) indicates something favorable has recently happened. See section 'Life-cycle examples' (page 21) for a description of the Relative Wealth Index. The firm's CFROIs had been stuck near the 5 to 6 per cent level for most years from 1977 to 1996, but forecasted CFROIs for 1997 and 1998 are substantially higher. The firm has hired a new CEO who has a demonstrated level of high skill and has undertaken a large-scale reorganization of the firm. Whatever is happening at Stanley Works will have effects on its competitors. Firms with sharply rising CFROIs, and especially firms with A and B grades for % Future, could be planting the seeds of destruction for competitors. DualGrade® data can be used for identifying possible losers as well as winners.

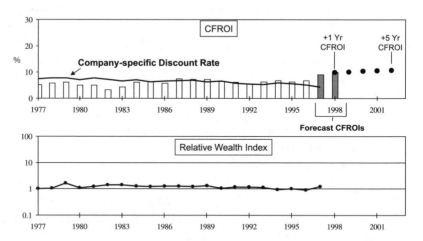

Figure 6.4 Stanley Works. CFROIs, actual and forecasted. Source: Compustat and HOLT/*ValueSearch*™.

Stock price reveals the market's 'line' for expected CFROI fade

In Figure 6.4, forecasted CFROIs for fiscal years 1997 and 1998 are weighted to yield a forecasted +1-year CFROI of 9.9 per cent for

12 months hence. At a month-end December 1997 stock price of $47, the *market's revealed expectation for +5-year CFROI*, according to the CFROI model, is shown as a line from the +1-year 9.9 per cent CFROI to 10.7 per cent. At HOLT, this process is called 'setting the line'. The 'line' indicates the market is bullish on the *economic* performance of Stanley Works, inasmuch as the 'line' for most firms with above-average CFROIs is a downward pattern from +1-year to +5-year. This calculation is explained in Chapter 7. As for *investment* performance, if Stanley Works delivers CFROIs greater (less) than expected, shareholders that pay $47 per share will likely achieve returns greater (less) than the return of the general market over the same period.

CFROI market expectations are incorporated in the remaining charts in this chapter as a preview of the more extensive explanation of the CFROI valuation variables in Chapter 7 and as a demonstration of some quick applications of the model. The model's usefulness for (1) improving understanding of firms' past performance, (2) identifying near-term forecasted performance, and (3) 'setting the line' on market expectations is evident in working with actual company data. Some additional examples from the Machinery Industry follow.

Simple example applications

Under-performance expected to continue

Innovation and continuous improvement to eliminate waste and provide more value to customers is necessary for the long-term success of any business firm—whether in a glamorous industry like high tech or a mundane industry like machinery manufacturing. Mine Safety Appliances Co., EE on page 302, and JLG Industries, AB on page 301, illustrate the potential for change, negative and positive, lurking in many of the 68 firms in the machinery industry.

The Figure 6.5 display of CFROIs for Mine Safety reveals a dismal economic performance, with CFROIs well below the market discount rate. The firm makes products to protect the safety and health of workers. At recent prices, the market is expecting no significant change in CFROIs. Radical change is needed.

Effects of implementing lean manufacturing

JLG Industries manufactures self-propelled aerial work platforms. The CFROI track record of JLG (Figure 6.6) through 1993 documents an under-performing firm. Since 1993, JLG has achieved a dramatic

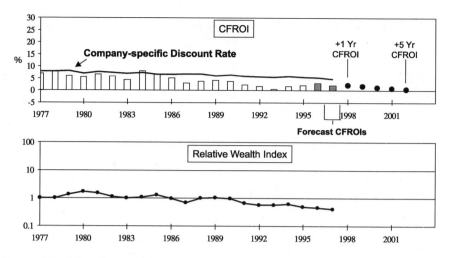

Figure 6.5 Mine Safety Appliances Co. CFROIs, actual and forecasted. Source: Compustat and HOLT/*ValueSearch*™.

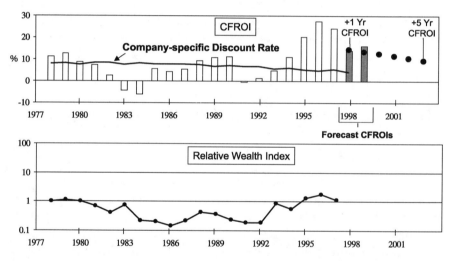

Figure 6.6 JLG Industries. CFROIs, actual and forecasted. Source: Compustat and HOLT/*ValueSearch*™.

improvement in its overall business results, as reflected in sharply higher CFROIs of more than 20 per cent in recent years. Near-term forecast +1-year CFROI is about 13 per cent. A noteworthy part of JLG's turnaround is its excellence in implementing lean manufacturing and related continuous improvement practices which have greatly raised customer satisfaction. Improved economic performance is the result of these fundamental improvements in work processes. *Lean manufacturing* is one term for the *Toyota-style* production system; another is *demand-pull* manufacturing.

JLG's improved leanness was illustrated in its *1996 Annual Report*, with management noting that inventories had increased less than $2 million over the latest five years while sales had increased $319 million. At year-end 1997, JLG's stock price implied that the +1-year CFROI of 13 per cent would fade to about 10 per cent by +5-year.

CFROIs, 'the line', and growth

We complete our review of examples from the Machinery Industry by examining two AA firms, Chart Industries and Helix Technology, both on page 301. CFROIs for Chart Industries (Figure 6.7) plummeted in 1993 and 1994, and during this time its stock price fell from $8 to a low of $2 per share. Subsequently, new management restructured the firm and dramatically improved CFROIs. Its stock rose to $23 by year-end 1997.

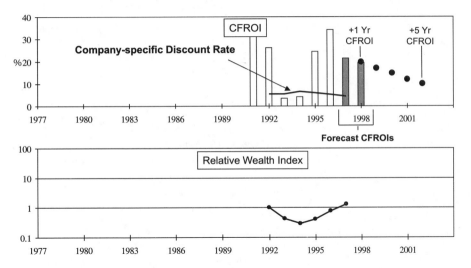

Figure 6.7 Chart Industries, Inc. CFROIs, actual and forecasted. Source: Compustat and HOLT/*ValueSearch*™.

The firm is a leading supplier of engineered equipment to four major markets: air separation, hydrocarbon processing, cryogenic and high-vacuum applications, and speciality products. Corporate managements of engineered products that compete with Chart Industries should pay attention to this firm. The firm has an aggressive growth strategy that, when coupled to extraordinarily high CFROIs, boosts the value of near-term future investments. But higher growth tends to drive CFROI downward. To calculate with HOLT's CFROI model a $23 warranted equity value per share equal to the $23 share price, as explained in Chapter 7, requires the 20 per cent +1-year CFROI to fade towards 10 per cent in +5-year. Investors who view this *line* as pessimistic should research Chart Industries as a possible buy candidate.

Our second company, Helix Technology Corporation (Figure 6.8) specializes in the development and application of cryogenic and vacuum technology. Management notes that its products are considered links in the 'global electronics food chain'. Production equipment dependent on Helix vacuum products is used for manufacturing semiconductors, flat panel displays, magnetic recording heads, and magnetic and optical storage media. Helix cryogenic systems are also facilitating the commercialization of emerging applications for superconducting electronics in the growing wireless telecommunications market.

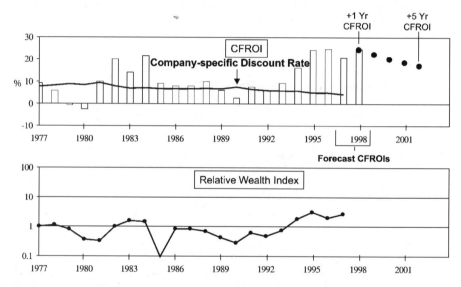

Figure 6.8 Helix Technology Corp. CFROIs, actual and forecasted. Source: Compustat and HOLT/*ValueSearch*™.

The surge in Helix's CFROIs during the last five years has resulted in a substantial cash balance, and dividends have been greatly increased. This recycling of cash to shareholders via dividends is consistent with maximizing shareholder value when the firm's wealth-creating opportunities are fully funded and 'excess' cash remains. The month-end December 1997 share price implied that a 24 per cent CFROI +1-year would fade to a 17 per cent by +5-year.

Providing highly specialized machinery to Information Age firms offered Helix a way to avoid commodity-type competition. This example should be kept in mind when researching other firms that have the potential to make their products or services a critical link in the food chain of a high-growth industry.

Comparison with other performance scorecards

Any relative grading structure based on summary indicators has limitations, and DualGrade® is no exception. However, compared to other summary rankings of corporate performance, DualGrade® is far superior.

A variety of corporate performance scorecard measures are available, and many are published in the financial press. For example, the earnings/book ratio is frequently used, as is shareholder return. In addition, *Fortune* magazine has printed an annual ranking based on Stern Stewart's MVA® (Market Value Added). Readers should experiment with DualGrade® data and these other measures, and then decide for themselves which is most useful. We offer a few comments about these other measures.

Earnings/book is an easily manipulated accounting ratio and should not be considered a satisfactory gauge for comparisons across companies, even within a single country. For comparisons across national borders, earnings/book ratios are essentially worthless. Cross-border differences in accounting practices are too significant.

Shareholder rate of total return, that is, dividends plus price appreciation, might seem to be an appropriate gauge of the firm's *economic performance*. Not so. Although over the long-term, economic performance and the level of firm value are related, during any particular time period, excess shareholder return (positive or negative) is driven by *actual* economic performance that is higher/lower than *expected* at the beginning of the period. It often happens that a firm for which the market has low economic performance expectations at the *end* of a given period, up from dismal expectations at the *beginning* of the period, will generate positive excess shareholder return. Over the same period, preeminently-valued firms might generate only average shareholder return, because their actual economic performance was in line with the market's very high expectations. In the CFROI framework, we would expect to observe for the example low-performing firm above, improvement from dismally low levels of CFROIs (perhaps an E first grade) to merely low levels (a D perhaps).

The challenge for investors always is to gauge the soundness of market expectations embodied in current stock prices. The argument made in this book and reflected in the CFROI model is (1) that the market gives a great deal of weight to the skill of management in formulating its expectations of a firm's future economic performance and (2) that a firm's track record of CFROIs is a key determinant of those expectations.

Stern Stewart promotes MVA® as the best scorecard measure. MVA®, or market value added, is calculated as the difference between a firm's total market value and adjusted book capital. HOLT's DualGrade® is, we believe, superior to MVA® in three important respects. We agree with Stern Stewart's emphasis on the need to measure firms' expected performance on *future* investments. HOLT's % Future is superior to MVA® for this purpose. HOLT's % Future reflects a better estimate of the value of existing assets, and since the value of future investments is the difference between total value and the value of existing assets, it follows that a better estimate of existing assets translates to an improved estimate for future investments. The MVA® approach is rooted in book capital, which reflects how accountants recorded *past* events. Stern Stewart's MVA® is total market value less book capital with assorted adjustments.[1] It does not use forward-looking estimates of cash flows from existing assets.

Second, the MVA® calculation is heavily influenced by firm size. Only big companies make it to the top of MVA® rankings, thereby implying that all these firms are also top *economic* performers. Firms of substantially different size cannot be meaningfully compared on MVA®. For example, a superbly performing medium-size firm with a dual grade of AA can be far behind a larger competitor on MVA® ranking, even though the larger firm is perhaps a CC. The DualGrade® solves this problem by ranking firms within four separate size categories and using not an absolute number for the market's assessment of future investments but a percentage of market value (% Future). Stern Stewart might elect to show their MVA® as a proportion of book capital, but this still would not address the need for a forward-looking estimate of the value of existing assets.

Finally, annual MVA® rankings do not capture changes in firms' expected performance during the year. HOLT updates its database weekly for both market prices and year-ahead CFROIs consistent with changing security analysts' EPS forecasts. The intra-year effects of changing debt levels and shares outstanding are also incorporated into the database. With this up-to-date information users can more effectively monitor *changes* in expected corporate performance as they occur.

7

Valuing expected performance, an application

Summary

- Over the long term, firms' NCR streams reflect managerial skill and competition. The skill level of management is revealed in the track records of firms. While the level of CFROIs is a key indicator of management skill, variability of CFROIs and the rate of asset growth are others.
- Consistent with the competitive life cycle, empirical results indicate that competition tends to compress CFROIs toward the average. The *direction and magnitude of change* over four-year spans for firms grouped by CFROI was: (1) top-quintile-CFROI firms faded downward the most; (2) second-quintile firms faded downward; (3) middle-quintile firms, those with CFROIs near the average, faded little; (4) fourth-quintile firms faded upward; and (5) bottom-quintile firms faded upward the most. The fade effects of CFROI variability and asset growth also were consistent with life-cycle reasoning.
- *Sustainable growth* for any year is the asset growth that would result from a continuation of the existing capital structure, the existing dividend-payout policy, and the CFROI for the same year. HOLT's growth-rate calculation procedures resolve end-of-year and beginning-of-year data problems.
- Warranted-value calculations are traced step-by-step for an actual company. In treating all companies similarly and objectively, and in being consistent with the complete CFROI model, HOLT's life-cycle procedures serve as useful baselines

for organizing data and thought, but they should not be considered sacrosanct. If users have better information about ROIs on future projects and asset growth for near-term than is implied by the baseline procedures, it should be used.

- The advantages of a total system way of thinking become clear in enumerating the different effects of variables involved with quantifying the impact of share repurchase.
- Finally, hypotheses are suggested for empirical tests to investigate why firms' quarterly earnings *surprises* affect stock prices so differently. They invoke the key CFROI model components of (a) CFROI level, (b) importance of future investments to warranted value, and (c) the market's assessment of management's skill.

Growth and fade

A review

The preceding chapters present either summarily or in detail the major components of HOLT's CFROI valuation model. Figure 7.1 below, is the Valuation Model Map with shading for growth and

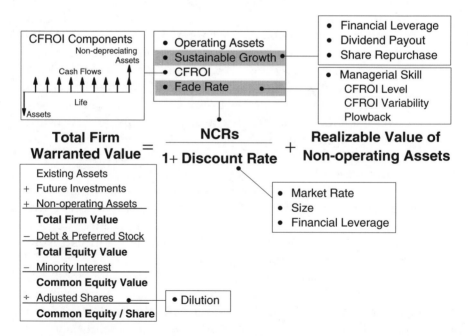

Figure 7.1 CFROI valuation model map. Growth and fade issues.

fade — the two major inputs to forecast NCRs that are covered in detail in this chapter. Both growth and fade are introduced in Chapter 2 in the context of the stylized competitive life cycle, which portrays the proposition that competition tends to force CFROIs toward the average. Both also appear in the series of charts demonstrating the usefulness of track records of CFROIs and real asset growth rates. Some of these charts reveal that above-average firms have been able to maintain superior CFROIs and substantial asset growth for extended periods — they have been able to 'beat the fade'. This is indicative of highly skilled management.

In Chapter 3, growth and fade are referred to in the context of the simplified model firm used to illustrate the CFROI model's fundamental components and to demonstrate the calculation of a warranted value. There it is mentioned that the CFROI model benefits from a procedure for forecasting NCRs from the firm's *future* investments based on the notion of a life-cycle of ROIs on incremental projects and of asset growth. But for numerical simplicity, the gross cash flows for a particular project are assumed to remain constant for each year covering the project life, and the reinvestment rate for any year is assumed to be one-half the ROI for that year.

Fade is also mentioned in Chapter 4 in the context of HOLT's procedure for deriving market discount rates consistent with, and applicable to, the CFROI model. In this procedure, a forecast of NCRs is required, which involves the concept of fade. The section 'Setting the Line' in the immediately preceding chapter explains the CFROI-model's usefulness for translating a firm's current stock price into +5-year CFROI and then judging the plausibility of that being achieved based on the firm's track record, the track records of its competitors, and *typical fade patterns*. Throughout, we have argued for the usefulness of the CFROI model because it is an adaptive system that integrates a firm's actual performance with the stock market's valuation of the firm's expected *future* performance.

The need: forecasting NCRs

For our discussion of growth and fade, consider two long-established firms earning CFROIs well above the cost of capital, and reinvesting at about the same rate. To value firms, NCRs must be forecasted: both NCRs from *existing assets* and NCRs from *future investments*. What information is available for making forecasts of future ROIs on new investments? Because of their comparability across time, companies, and countries, firms' CFROI track records contain useful information: the longer the period of superior CFROIs and the smaller the variation in CFROIs, the higher the perceived level of *managerial skill* and, in most instances, the greater the confidence one can have that the past will carry over to the future.[1]

Compare the track records of Emerson Electric (Figure 2.11 on page 33) and Advanced Micro Devices (Figure 2.20 on page 51). Emerson management has demonstrated a high level of skill by maintaining CFROIs very near 10 per cent, well above the US industrial/service universe long-term average of 6 per cent, for over three decades. The consistency of Emerson's level of CFROI is missing from Advanced Micro's track record.

Advanced Micro has had some CFROI years well above 10 per cent, but also some well below. Its growth rate has been very high, but also quite variable. Firms' CFROI fade rates are affected by asset growth. High growth opportunities together with above-average CFROIs are high inducements for the entry of competitors, who bring the powerful forces that tend to drive superior performance toward the average. In addition, the overall degree of difficulty in managing a business increases as growth accelerates. Compared to Emerson, the management of Advanced Micro has been less in control of its firm's performance. Focusing on the level of managerial skill implied in CFROI track records suggests that, for the same near-term CFROI forecast, it is more plausible to expect a slower CFROI fade rate for Emerson than for Advanced Micro. We would expect empirical analysis of actual CFROI fade rates to support this view, and it does.

Baseline fade patterns

Empirical guidelines for assigning baseline, or typical, CFROI fade rates should not be mechanistically employed.[2] For example, IPOs of startup biotechnology firms involve intellectual capital and, almost always, large accounting losses due to substantial startup R&D outlays. Our emphasis on managerial skill suggests that the track records of top management, and especially key scientific personnel, should play a major role in the valuation of these IPOs. In this instance, financial data are of little use in gauging managerial skill. On the other hand, for established businesses, historical financial data can be quite useful in assessing likely fade rates.

The calculating procedures described use as-reported financial statements combined with security analyst EPS forecasts for the next two years, typically. HOLT Value Associates has software tools suitable for use 'inside' firms, where more specific data are available, and for use by security analysts who work with detailed line-item forecasts of balance sheets and income statements.

Empirical evidence for CFROI fade rates

Empirical test design

Empirical support for the patterns of CFROI fade by CFROI level, CFROI variability, and firm growth has been published.[3] The data sample for this study consisted of 'plain vanilla' industrial/service firms in the United States. Regulated and financial firms, oil and gas firms, and other specialized asset firms were excluded. CFROI fade was measured by the change in four-year median CFROI. The median was calculated as the average of two CFROIs after excluding the highest and lowest CFROIs. For example, in 1969 a firm's *past* four-year median was based on CFROIs for fiscal years 1966, 1967, 1968, and 1969. The firm's *future* four-year median used 1970, 1971, 1972, and 1973. CFROI fade involves a comparison of the future CFROI with the past CFROI.

At each of six points in time—1969, 1973, 1977, 1981, 1985, and 1989—the largest 1000 firms by equity market value were selected. Median CFROIs were calculated for past and future CFROIs at the specified times. For the six points in time, the 1000 firms were ranked high to low on past CFROI. Each firm received a normalized rank score ranging from 1 (lowest) to 100 (highest). An advantage to normalized ranks, for homogenous firms, is that observations across time can be pooled. Fade classes were constructed based on firms' past CFROI level (quintiles) and, for a given CFROI level, further classification was based on past CFROI variability and on growth opportunities, measured by dividend payout ratio.

Figure 7.2 is a diagram of the fade class construction, and it shows that variability and growth were divided into high and low classes by comparing firms within a given CFROI level. If in a given year a firm's past median CFROI is assigned a rank between 81 and 100, it is assigned to CFROI quintile 1 (top). For each of the selected six sampling years, a total of 1000 firms are divided into CFROI quintiles of 200 firms each. Each quintile has its member firms ranked on variability measured by a standard deviation for CFROIs over a four-year span. Variability was labeled 'high' for ranks above 50 and 'low' for ranks 50 and below. Similarly, firms fall into 'high' or 'low' categories depending on their growth rankings. Figure 7.2 diagrams the construction of four fade classes from the middle quintile. This procedure is done for all five quintiles, yielding a total of 20 fade classes.

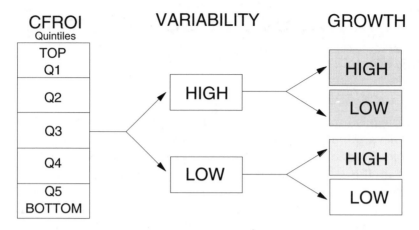

Figure 7.2　Fade class construction.

Empirical results

The basic empirical results shown in Figure 7.3 used pooled observations of ranked variables ranging from 1 (lowest) to 100 (highest), like rungs on a ladder. With six time periods, the total number of observations is 6000, with 300 observations for each of the twenty fade classes shown in Figure 7.3. Consider the fade class for Q1 (quintile 1) with high variability and high growth. The average change in CFROI rank (i.e., the fade) is −27, based on 300 observations. This is equivalent to dropping 27 rungs on the CFROI 'ladder' over a four year time frame.

The empirical results are in conformance with the life cycle premise that, over time, competition tends to fade CFROIs toward the average. The highest CFROI firms ('All' by variability and growth in Q1) show a 15 decline, followed by Q2 with 9 decline. Firms in Q3 on average stay at that level, with a zero fade. Q4 firms on average improve 9 rungs on the CFROI ladder, and the lowest quintile (Q5) firms on average gain 15. Let's take a further look at variability and growth classes.

One would expect that high CFROIs coupled to high growth opportunities would attract substantial competition. Moreover, high growth by itself increases the degree of difficulty in successfully managing a business. Indeed, the data show that *high-growth* Q1 firms do fade faster than *low-growth* Q1 firms (−19 versus −12). Similarly, if variability for above-average CFROIs is useful in discerning the level of managerial skill, then low-variability Q1 firms should fade more slowly. The data show that they do: i.e., −9 for all firms with low variability in Q1 versus −22 for high variability. The observed relationship of managerial skill and growth opportunities also is observed

		Growth		
CFROI	Variability	High	Low	All
Q1	High	−27	−17	−22
Q1	Low	−11	−7	−9
Q1	All	−19	−12	−15
Q2	High	−17	−9	−13
Q2	Low	−8	−1	−5
Q2	All	−13	−5	−9
Q3	High	−4	−2	−3
Q3	Low	2	5	3
Q3	All	−1	1	0
Q4	High	9	10	9
Q4	Low	10	10	10
Q4	All	9	10	9
Q5	High	16	18	17
Q5	Low	12	13	13
Q5	All	14	15	15
All	High	−5	0	−2
All	Low	1	4	2
All	All	−2	2	0

Figure 7.3 Change in CFROI rank over four years. Averages for each fade class. Source: Bartley J. Madden, 'The CFROI life cycle,' *Journal of Investing*, Vol. 5, No. 2, Summer 1996, exhibit 7.

in Q2 and Q3, but the magnitude of change is smaller as CFROIs approach the average level.

CFROIs that are below average (Q4 and especially Q5) may indicate a need to substantially restructure the firm. Restructuring typically adds volatility to CFROIs and reduces asset growth. Low variability for below-average CFROI firms can be associated with a 'business as usual' complacency by top managements, which may not be favorable for these firms. Consequently, variability and growth for Q4 and Q5 firms have understandably different implications than for firms in higher CFROI quintiles. This is reflected in the data, which show that CFROI fade as not strongly related to variability or growth for Q4 and Q5 firms.

Donaldson Company's CFROI-model track record

Donaldson Company is a member of the Machinery Industry, which is reviewed in Chapter 6. It is a world leader in separation technology with a strategic focus on air and liquid filtration systems.

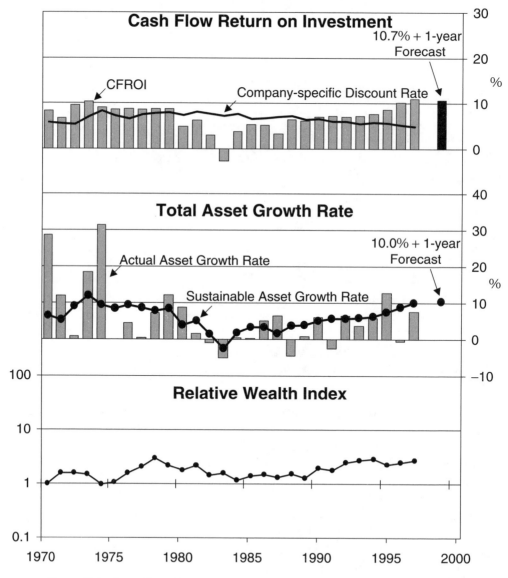

Figure 7.4   Donaldson Company, historical life cycle, 1970–1997. Source: Compustat and HOLT/*ValueSearch*™.

From below-average in the early 1980s, Donaldson's CFROIs show a solid upward trend to a recent 10 to 11 per cent level. Its stock has substantially outperformed the general market over this time period, as shown by the upward trend of the Relative Wealth line in the bottom panel. CFROIs cover fiscal years (ending in July) 1970 through 1997, with a forecasted +1-year CFROI of 10.7 per cent also plotted in the upper panel. This 10.7 per cent forecast CFROI is based on median security analysts' EPS forecasts for fiscal years 1998 and 1999 from Zacks Investment Research as of month-end December 1997. HOLT/*ValueSearch*™ database translated these forecasted EPS into a CFROI. Market real discount rates are also plotted in the upper panel, for easy recognition of Donaldson's economic performance (CFROIs) in relation to real returns demanded by capital suppliers.

The middle panel shows both actual and sustainable total asset growth rates. Actual asset growth rate is the yearly per cent change in the firm's CFROI-model gross assets. In order to calculate a real growth rate, each year's assets are expressed in monetary units having the same purchasing power. The *sustainable asset growth rate* is also a real number and is tied to the CFROI for a particular year. If a firm has no debt in its capital structure and has a zero dividend payout, then its reinvestment, or plowback, will produce a sustainable growth rate approximately equal to the CFROI. The sustainable growth rate is the asset growth that would result from a continuation of the existing capital structure, the existing dividend payout policy, and the CFROI for that year.

Analysts should understand the reasons for large differences between actual and sustainable growth. Acquisitions and the sale of new debt or equity are common reasons for actual asset growth to exceed sustainable growth for a given year. Divestitures, pay-down of debt, and share repurchase are typical causes for asset growth to be less than sustainable growth. Sustainable growth rates are more useful for forecasting NCRs from future investments because they are closely related to the level of CFROIs and, in HOLT's procedures, are 'normalized', i.e., not too high or low due to non-sustainable effects.

Sustainable growth calculation challenges

If we ignored problems arising from mixing financial statement data from different fiscal years, then the calculation of sustainable growth

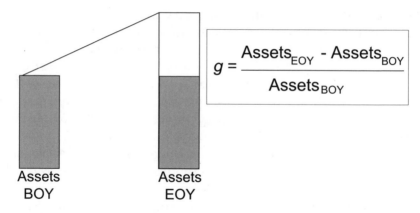

Figure 7.5 Basic asset growth rate calculation.

could use the basic relationship between beginning-of-year (BOY) assets and end-of-year (EOY) assets as shown in Figure 7.5.

But acquisitions, divestitures, and write-offs are frequent occurrences that make BOY assets not comparable to EOY assets. The sustainable growth rate calculation procedures described below are used by HOLT in processing worldwide data in a manner that circumvents the problems of using as-reported data from one fiscal year that is not comparable to as-reported data from another fiscal year. The equation expressing HOLT's procedure is shown in Figure 7.6.

$$g = \frac{P - R + \Delta D}{A - (P - R + \Delta D)}$$

where

g is sustainable growth rate
P is simple plowback
R is asset retirements
ΔD is change in debt
A is EOY gross assets

Figure 7.6 Sustainable asset growth rate calculation.

During the year, plant is retired and, on average, new debt financing is secured to maintain the firm's target proportion of debt to equity. Change in assets is calculated as Plowback less Retirements plus Change in Debt. BOY assets (the denominator) is calculated as EOY assets less change in assets during the year, which avoids the use of the prior fiscal year's amount of assets. Simple Plowback is gross cash flow less payments to capital suppliers. The normalized amount of retirements represents the expected portion of the plant account 'worn out' and retired during the year.[4]

Change in debt (Δ*D*) is the 'normal' amount of debt-financed new investment, assuming the company maintains the same debt to equity ratio (*D*/*E*). For a specified ratio of debt to equity to be maintained, Δ*D*/Δ*E* must equal *D*/*E*.

Rearranging: $\Delta D = (D/E)\ (\Delta E)$, and where $\Delta E = P - R$, $\Delta D = (D/E)(P - R)$. See Figure 7.7.

P − *R* is the difference between the Simple Plowback (*P*) and Retirements (*R*), or the net increase in equity before any debt-financed new investment. Simple Plowback is reduced by the Retirements, because it is assumed that current year Retirements are replaced with new assets. Equity (*E*) is net assets less debt. Net assets is gross depreciating assets less accumulated depreciation, plus non-depreciating assets plus investments (see Chapter 5).

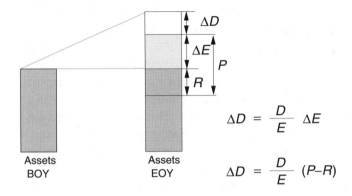

$$\Delta D = \frac{D}{E}\ \Delta E$$

$$\Delta D = \frac{D}{E}\ (P{-}R)$$

Figure 7.7 Change in debt calculation.

Consider a capital structure of Net Assets 1.00 − Liabilities 0.20 = Equity 0.80. This represents a firm that is 25 per cent leveraged; i.e., a *D*/*E* ratio of [0.20/(1.00 − 0.20)]. If the current-year increase in Equity were 0.30, representing *P* − *R*, the new capital structure would be Net Assets 1.30 − Liabilities 0.20 = Equity 1.10, and leverage would be 18.2 per cent. To maintain the capital structure existing at the beginning of the year, debt would have to increase by an additional .075, $\Delta D = (D/E)(\Delta E) = (0.25)(0.30) = .075$. Leverage then would be 25 per cent, with Assets 1.375 − Liabilities 0.275 = Equity 1.10.

Caveats

Our procedure might raise questions about the use of sustainable growth for forecasting future NCRs. Suppose that the analyst has confidence in *detailed* forecasts covering a firm's financial statements over the next two to five years and that these forecasts indicate unusually high or low *actual* reinvestment amounts in relation to the anticipated CFROIs. Are not these forecasts superior to those generated from sustainable growth method? When detailed financial statements forecasts are available, these should be used to directly calculate NCRs. As the forecast horizon lengthens, however, forecast ROIs on new investments and sustainable growth rates should take over as NCR drivers. When forecasts are made for distant years in absolute value terms, they can easily incorporate *unrecognized* economic-performance assumptions that simply are not plausible.

CFROIs and sustainable growth become more useful as the forecast horizon lengthens and, absent detailed line-item forecasts of near-term financial statements, they provide useful drivers of NCRs for these early years. A *major advantage* of displaying the next one to five forecast years as CFROIs and sustainable growth rates is that these data can be directly compared with track records, thereby facilitating plausibility judgements about the forecast. With data for industry peers also displayed as CFROIs and sustainable growth, users gain additional perspectives on the likelihood of forecast performance being achieved.

Use of the CFROI model also can improve communication of forecasts and plans. Non-financial experts can relate their perceived level of managerial skill of a business to forecast patterns of CFROIs and sustainable growth and, in so doing, gain an intuitive understanding of what a forecast implies. This is extraordinarily difficult to achieve when forecast data are expressed in absolute terms. And as we have pointed out earlier, less rigorous performance measures are unreliable for connecting the past to the future and for cross-company comparisons in most cases.

Example valuation calculation: Donaldson Company

HOLT's database and software

HOLT/*ValueSearch*™ database and software employ warranted value calculations summarized in this section. The source data are as-reported financial statements from Compustat for the US and security analysts' annual EPS forecasts from Zacks Investment Research for the US. All firms are treated similarly, thus providing objectivity and useful baseline comparisons. The valuation software is often used for setting the line on market expectations for CFROIs and asset growth over the coming five years. Various scenarios of future CFROIs and sustainable growth can be tested for their effects on warranted values.

With HOLT's more extensive LIVM™ (Line Item Valuation Model) software, users can override key variables and analyze how historical tracking changes. Also, with LIVM™, detailed financial forecasts for near-term forecast years can be inserted.

Forecast life cycle

ValueSearch will contain for a typical company, median security analysts' EPS forecasts for the coming two fiscal years. These data are adjusted for fiscal year-ends, and translated into a +1-year CFROI. A +1-year sustainable growth rate also is calculated, consistent with the +1-year CFROI. Figure 7.8 contains data from *ValueSearch* as of month-end December 1997. The +1-year CFROI for Donaldson was 10.7 per cent. The +5-year CFROI was forecasted to be 8.8 per cent, based on HOLT's procedures which give weight to Donaldson's level of CFROI, past variability of CFROI, and sustainable growth—the key variables in the empirical fade results reported at the beginning of the chapter.

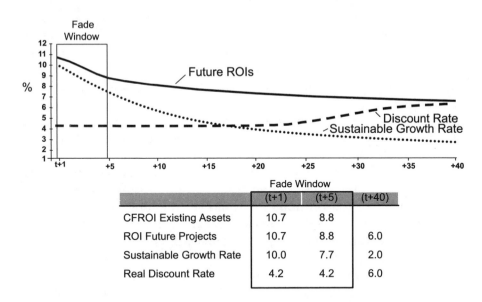

	Fade Window		
	(t+1)	(t+5)	(t+40)
CFROI Existing Assets	10.7	8.8	
ROI Future Projects	10.7	8.8	6.0
Sustainable Growth Rate	10.0	7.7	2.0
Real Discount Rate	4.2	4.2	6.0

Figure 7.8 Donaldson Company. Forecast life cycle as of year-end 1997.

Donaldson's ROIs on new investments were set equal to the forecasted CFROIs for future years.[5] There are times when *incremental* investments justify ROIs significantly different from CFROIs calculated from *aggregate* financial statements. These situations are far more frequent in smaller firms, and especially in startups. *Users need to explicitly decide on whether ROIs on new investments can be satisfactorily approximated by forecasted near-term CFROIs.*

At year-end 1997, the market discount rate was 4.8 per cent, and Donaldson's company-specific discount rate was 4.2 per cent. HOLT's procedures gave Donaldson a small increase in risk differential for size, which was more than offset due to a large decrease for financial leverage because Donaldson had very little debt. Figure 7.8 shows the forecasted life-cycle of Donaldson regressing over a 40-year period to a 6.0 per cent ROI and a 2.0 per cent sustainable growth rate. The 6.0 per cent level is an approximate long-term average CFROI for the United States. Since 1960, market discount rates have fluctuated above and below the 6.0 per cent level.

Readers should note that the standard HOLT fade pattern for high CFROI firms is downward towards 6.0 per cent and for low CFROI firms, upward. With HOLT/*ValueSearch*™ software, *any fade pattern* can be utilized and the resulting warranted value calculated. For example, an analyst might believe that Coca-Cola can sustain a particular level of ROI on new investments and a particular level of reinvestment rate for a very long time before regressing towards average. A relevant question: How long is this zero fade period implied in today's price? Longer time periods of zero fade would be input until a warranted value was calculated which matched today's value for Coca-Cola. The analyst thereby obtains an idea of how long the superior performance would have to hold to justify a current stock price.

Beyond year +5 in Figure 7.8, ROIs on new investments, using the standard HOLT fade forecast, are regressed towards 6.0 per cent at year +40. The 6.0 per cent level is a sensible long-term target based on historical levels of CFROIs and discount rates in the United States. Yet it is not a crucial assumption for valuing future investments. The crucial assumption is that over the long term the spread between ROIs and discount rates approaches zero. This implies essentially zero wealth for today's shareholders due to far-distant future investments.

Each year, 10 per cent of the spread between that year's ROI and the long-term 6.0 per cent level is dissipated. This fade rate of 10 per cent is representative of typical fade patterns observed in the empirical research described at the beginning of this chapter. It results in a negligible spread by year +40.

The *company-specific discount rate* of Figure 7.8 is held constant for 20 years, which covers the wind-down years for cash flows from existing assets for most industrial/service firms. Beginning in year +21, the discount rate also regresses towards 6.0 per cent by systematically reducing the spread between the discount rate and the long-term 6.0 per cent level. Each year, 10 per cent of the remaining spread is dissipated in the same way that ROIs are regressed.

Simply forecasting that all firms' ROIs in the distant future regress to company-specific *current* discount rates results in puzzling situations. For example, a Coca-Cola (low company-specific discount rate currently) would be forecast to achieve $t + 40$ ROIs substantially lower than a Bethlehem Steel (high company-specific discount rate currently).

Plausibility benchmarks from historical data

Net cash receipts can be calculated from the firm's perspective or from the capital suppliers' perspective. Dividend discount valuation models take the latter approach, while the CFROI valuation model takes the former. Why? The answer lies in analyzing how a NCR forecast is made and how it can be judged for plausibility.

In the CFROI model, the NCR drivers are CFROIs and sustainable asset growth rates. By using real magnitudes in time series, the *forecast* patterns for these variables can be directly *connected* to the firm's *historical* performance of these same variables. This performance continuum communicates the degree of optimism or pessimism reflected in the forecast. This continuum does not work so well with dividends. Firms can be achieving high CFROIs with high reinvestment and not pay any dividends. With this type of firm, sizable dividends would be in the distant future, and forecasting far-distant dividends can easily become an exercise of the imagination. With the CFROI model, ROIs on future investments are assumed to regress towards the discount rate; therefore, as the forecast horizon lengthens, the present value of these diminishing-wealth-creating investments tends to have a small effect on today's warranted value. In contrast, dividends are typically forecasted to continue rising in distant years and, as previously noted, pose precarious problems in judging plausibility, particularly for firms currently paying zero dividends. Also, in our opinion, CFROIs and sustainable growth rates are more suitable for empirical fade research which can guide analysts in making the +1-year to +5-year forecast of financial performance.

In summary, the CFROI valuation model helps users visualize what a forecast represents. The starting point is the firm's track record. An analyst's forecast of CFROIs is basically a continuation of the historical life-cycle chart.

Value of existing assets

The forecasted CFROI +1-year represents year-end 1998. The firm's warranted value will be calculated for year '0' which is year-end 1997.

The forecasted 10.7 per cent CFROI +1-year is based on $651 million of current dollar gross assets, which includes $202 million non-depreciating assets; $85 million gross cash flow; and an asset life of 14 years. Over years +1 to +14, as shown in Figure 7.9, the *existing assets* are forecasted to wear out and their cash flows to wind down. Portions of the plant account will be retired and non-depreciating assets released, *based on the same logic as described in the calculation procedures for the model firm in Chapter 3*.

The upper table of Figure 7.9 focuses on the total firm from years +1 to +14, and includes new investments beginning in year +1. The lower table focuses on the receipts derived from assets existing at year 0; i.e., gross cash flow [line (7)] and released non-depreciating assets [line (8)]. Line (14) shows a cumulative present value of these receipts equal to $642 million, which is the warranted value of Donaldson's *existing assets* at year-end 1997.

Besides asset life, the key determinants of the receipts in years +1 to +14 are the age of existing plant and the forecasted fade rate for CFROIs. The older the plant, the more rapid the wind down of cash flows because of larger plant retirements in earlier years.[6]

Compare future total gross cash flow to the firm [line (4)] with gross cash flow received from existing assets [line (7)]. As new investments are made beginning at +1-year, they account for an increasingly larger share of total cash flow which begins at +2-year. Meanwhile, existing year 0 assets wear out and account for a decreasing share of total cash flow. As plant is retired, year 0 gross assets [line (5)] decline and non-depreciating assets are released [line (8)]. Note that the sum of released non-depreciating assets [line (8)] equals 184 (rounded), which is the amount of non-depreciating assets included in existing assets at year 0.

Value of future investments

There are two basic steps in calculating the present value of the NCR stream generated by *future investments* that follow the forecasted life cycle shown in Figure 7.8. The two steps are described in Chapter 3, beginning on page 76. First, the *incremental wealth* created from each future investment is computed as the present value of that investment in the year undertaken less the amount invested. Second, that incremental wealth is then discounted to a present value for 'today'. The cumulative amount of these present values represents the estimated value of the firm's future investments.

Figure 7.10 presents data related to the calculation of wealth created in year +3 from new investments in that year. Earlier in this chapter we discussed that, in displaying historical time series,

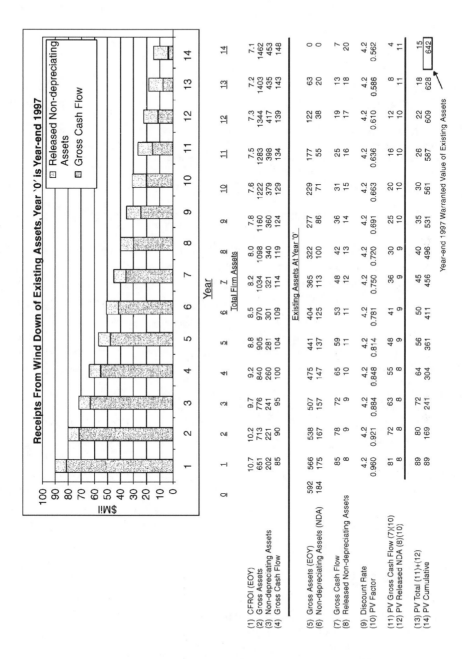

Receipts From Wind Down of Existing Assets, Year '0' is Year-end 1997

Legend: Released Non-depreciating Assets; Gross Cash Flow

(Y-axis: $Mil; X-axis: Year)

Total Firm Assets

	1	2	3	4	5	6	7	8	9	10	11	12	13	14
(1) CFROI (EOY)	10.7	10.2	9.7	9.2	8.8	8.5	8.2	8.0	7.8	7.6	7.5	7.3	7.2	7.1
(2) Gross Assets	651	713	776	840	905	970	1034	1098	1160	1222	1283	1344	1403	1462
(3) Non-depreciating Assets	202	221	241	260	281	301	321	340	360	379	398	417	435	453
(4) Gross Cash Flow	85	90	95	100	104	109	114	119	124	129	134	139	143	148

Existing Assets At Year '0'

	0	1	2	3	4	5	6	7	8	9	10	11	12	13	14
(5) Gross Assets (EOY)	592	566	538	507	475	441	404	365	322	277	229	177	122	63	0
(6) Non-depreciating Assets (NDA)	184	175	167	157	147	137	125	113	100	86	71	55	38	20	0
(7) Gross Cash Flow		85	78	72	65	59	53	48	42	36	31	25	19	13	7
(8) Released Non-depreciating Assets		8	9	9	10	11	11	12	13	14	15	16	17	18	20
(9) Discount Rate		4.2	4.2	4.2	4.2	4.2	4.2	4.2	4.2	4.2	4.2	4.2	4.2	4.2	4.2
(10) PV Factor		0.960	0.921	0.884	0.848	0.814	0.781	0.750	0.720	0.691	0.663	0.636	0.610	0.586	0.562
(11) PV Gross Cash Flow (7)(10)		81	72	63	55	48	41	36	30	25	20	16	12	8	4
(12) PV Released NDA (8)(10)		8	8	8	8	9	9	9	9	10	10	10	10	11	11
(13) PV Total (11)+(12)		89	80	72	64	56	50	45	40	35	30	26	22	18	15
(14) PV Cumulative		89	169	241	304	361	411	456	496	531	561	587	609	628	642

Year-end 1997 Warranted Value of Existing Assets

Figure 7.9 Donaldson Company. Value of existing assets.

Forecast	+1-year	+2-year	+3-year
(1) CFROI (EOY)	10.7%	10.2%	9.7%
(2) Sustainable Growth Rate (BOY)	10.0%	9.4%	8.9%
(3) Asset Life	14	14	14
(4) Gross Cash Flow	85	90	95
(5) C$ Gross Assets (EOY), $Mil	651	713	776
(6) C$ Non-depreciating Assets (EOY), $Mil	202	221	241
(7) CFROI (BOY)	12.2%	11.6%	11.0%
(8) Project ROI (BOY), No Fade			11.0%
(9) Project ROI (BOY), With Fade			8.8%
(10) New Investment, $Mil			93
(11) NPV at +3-year @ 4.2% Discount Rate Using Project ROI, No Fade, $Mil			52
(12) NPV at +3-year @ 4.2% Discount Rate Using Project ROI, With Fade, $Mil			33
(13) PV Factor @ 4.2%, Year 3 to Year 0			0.884
(14) Wealth Created with Fade, (12) × (13)			29

Figure 7.10   Donaldson Company. Value of +3-year future investment.

a BOY orientation for CFROI would have been preferred except for the severe problems associated with acquisitions, divestitures, and write-offs when mixed-fiscal-year data are used. Therefore, an EOY orientation is used for CFROI time-series display, and this requires an adjustment in the valuation calculations. That adjustment is to make an EOY CFROI into a BOY CFROI, which in turn becomes a BOY project ROI. The wealth creation from future projects is tied to BOY project ROIs and to sustainable growth rates which are calculated on a BOY basis.

The forecasted +3-year CFROI is 9.7 per cent [line (1), Figure 7.10] based on EOY data. This can be verified using the four basic inputs shown in Figure 7.10 lines (3), (4), (5), and (6). The 9.7 per cent EOY CFROI is converted to 11.0 per cent BOY CFROI as shown on line (7). This internal rate of return is based on +3-year gross cash flow of 95, +2-year gross assets of 713, +2-year non-depreciating assets of 221, and a 14-year asset life. With a CFROI fade rate of zero, the +3-year project ROI is identical to the BOY CFROI, as displayed in line (8).

Effect of fade

The fade-toward-average effect of competitive forces applies to both the wind down of cash flows from existing assets and the ROIs on future investments. For the future investment in year +3, Figure 7.11 depicts the decline in cash flows implied by the basic fade pattern of CFROIs for years +4 to +17. The project ROI of 11.0 per cent with no fade (equal cash flows each year) decreases to 8.8 per cent after the effects of fade are included.

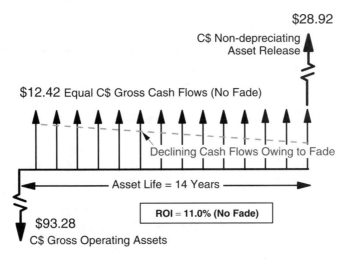

$28.92

C$ Non-depreciating
Asset Release

$12.42 Equal C$ Gross Cash Flows (No Fade)

Declining Cash Flows Owing to Fade

◄─── Asset Life = 14 Years ───►

ROI = 11.0% (No Fade)

$93.28
C$ Gross Operating Assets

Figure 7.11   Donaldson Company. Fade and +3-year project ROI.

The cost of the project (new investment) in year +3 is 93.28 [line (10), Figure 7.10]. Applying a 4.2 per cent discount rate to *equal cash flows* of 12.42 over 14 years coupled with released non-depreciating assets in the final year of 28.92 gives a present value of 146.19. When *faded cash flows* are used, the present value is 126.81. The difference between the 126.81 present value and the 93.28 cost of the investment is 33.51 which is the *net* present value, or wealth created, at year +3. The present value of that sum today (year 0) is $33.51/(1.042)^3$, or 29.62. When this procedure is repeated for all the investment years +1 to +40 using faded ROIs, the cumulative wealth created from *future investments* has a present value today of $450 million. See Figure 7.12.

We want to reiterate a point made earlier about the completeness of the CFROI model. The procedures for incorporating CFROI fade into the present value calculations for existing assets and future investments are part of a total valuation system approach. The calculation of a market-derived discount rate and the assignment of risk differentials are integrally connected with the approach to fade rates. Conceptually, one could construct a model that would give all firms the identical discount rate and then make company-specific adjustments in fade rates; i.e., 'risky' firms would be assigned less favorable fade rates.

Total-firm warranted value and warranted share price

Figure 7.13 shows how Donaldson's warranted value at year-end 1997 is comprised of contributions from existing assets and future

Year	CFROI %	Discount Rate %	(a) Future Investments $Mil	Wealth Created $Mil	(b) PV Factor	(c)=(a)(b) PV at Year 0 of Wealth Created $Mil
1	10.7	4.2	86	35	0.960	34
2	10.2	4.2	90	34	0.921	31
3	9.7	4.2	93	33	0.884	29
4	9.2	4.2	97	32	0.848	27
5	8.8	4.2	100	31	0.814	26
6	8.5	4.2	102	30	0.781	24
7	8.2	4.2	104	30	0.750	22
8	8.0	4.2	106	29	0.720	21
9	7.8	4.2	108	28	0.691	19
10	7.6	4.2	110	27	0.663	18
11	7.5	4.2	113	26	0.636	17
12	7.3	4.2	115	26	0.610	16
13	7.2	4.2	118	25	0.586	15
14	7.1	4.2	122	25	0.562	14
15	7.0	4.2	143	27	0.539	15
16	6.9	4.2	147	26	0.518	14
17	6.8	4.2	150	25	0.497	12
18	6.7	4.2	153	24	0.477	11
19	6.6	4.2	155	22	0.458	10
20	6.6	4.2	157	20	0.439	9
21	6.5	4.4	159	19	0.421	8
22	6.5	4.5	160	17	0.402	7
23	6.4	4.7	162	16	0.384	6
24	6.4	4.8	165	15	0.367	5
25	6.3	4.9	167	14	0.350	5
26	6.3	5.0	170	13	0.333	4
27	6.3	5.1	173	12	0.316	4
28	6.2	5.2	177	11	0.301	3
29	6.2	5.3	199	12	0.286	3
30	6.2	5.4	203	11	0.271	3
31	6.2	5.4	206	11	0.257	3
32	6.2	5.5	209	10	0.244	2
33	6.1	5.5	212	10	0.231	2
34	6.1	5.6	215	9	0.219	2
35	6.1	5.6	217	9	0.207	2
36	6.1	5.7	220	8	0.196	2
37	6.1	5.7	222	8	0.185	1
38	6.1	5.7	226	8	0.175	1
39	6.1	5.8	229	7	0.166	1
40	6.1	5.8	233	7	0.157	1

Year-end 1997 Warranted Value of Future Investments   450

Figure 7.12 Donaldson Company. Value of future investments.

**Total Firm
Warranted Value**

Existing Assets	642
+ Future Investments	+ 450
+ Non-operating Assets	+ 0
Total Firm Value	**1092**
− Debt & Preferred Stock	− 55
Total Equity Value	**1037**
− Minority Interest	− 0
Common Equity Value	**1037**
÷ Adjusted Shares	÷ 49.45
Common Equity/Share	**$ 20.97**

Figure 7.13   Donaldson Company. Warranted equity value per share.

investments. Donaldson's estimated total-firm warranted value, less the value of debt and minority interests, translates into a warranted equity value of $20.97 per share. The Donaldson example completes the warranted value section of our basic valuation map.[7]

The $20.97 warranted share price is quite close to Donaldson's actual stock price of $22.53 at year-end 1997. The HOLT forecast +1-year CFROI of 10.7 per cent fading to 8.8 per cent by +5-year entails the sustainable growth rate following a similar path downward, because its calculation is tied to the CFROI. Inasmuch as the warranted equity value per share was very close to the actual price, it is reasonable to assume that market expectations are quite close to the forecast. If the actual price were substantially higher (lower) than our warranted price, the +5-year CFROI could be raised (lowered) until it yielded a warranted equity value equal to the actual share price. This is the procedure for *setting the line* on market expectations, discussed in Chapter 6. This visual display of market expectations is exceptionally useful to investors making buy/hold/sell decisions and to corporate managements needing to gauge what the market expects of their firm.

Comparing actual prices with warranted prices

The comprehensiveness of the CFROI model is well suited to comparison of actual prices to warranted prices in order to gain insights and uncover measurement problems involving variables in the basic CFROI Valuation Model Map. Comparisons also can verify that the inputs to the model for a particular firm seem to capture economic performance adequately over time.

By country, HOLT maintains Backtest Files that are monthly time series of data which would have been available at those times. These data include, among others, forecast EPS, and corresponding calculations of warranted equity value per share. With the US Backtest File, warranted equity values per share for Donaldson were calculated at year-end for 1986 through 1997. These are displayed in Figure 7.14.

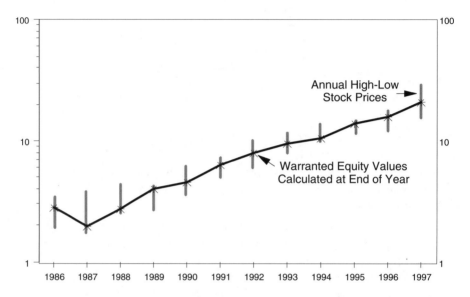

Figure 7.14   Donaldson Company. Stock prices and warranted equity values.

The above series shows a close fit, as expected for a firm like Donaldson. The firm has 'clean' accounting, and typically its forecast ranges for CFROIs based on security analysts' EPS forecasts are not large.

Stock price volatility and plausible range of forecast economic performance

Investors often want to compare a stock's *upside potential* to its *downside risk*. HOLT's CFROI valuation model and software accommodates this need by providing users the ability to input different forecast scenarios of CFROI and growth, and then to calculate the related warranted equity values. Investors can study firms' track records and, at various points in time, assess plausible forecast ranges for both CFROIs and sustainable growth. These can be translated into high-low ranges of warranted equity values. By comparing these ranges with actual stock price ranges, investors gain insights to the cause of stock price volatility.

High CFROI firms with substantial variability in CFROIs, and/or reinvestment rates, invariably have above-average betas. Beta is a measure of a firm's stock price volatility relative to the general market. Such firms have a wide range of potential *wealth creation* from future investments although the exact magnitude to this potential may be quite difficult to forecast. In contrast, below-average CFROI firms can have a steady pattern of CFROIs with a narrow range of reinvestment rates which result in low betas. Importantly, these business-as-usual, below-average users of capital can easily be priced with negative values for future investments, reflecting anticipated *wealth dissipation.*

Portfolio approach versus firm-specific value approach

How does the capital asset pricing model (CAPM), a centerpiece of modern finance, view the 'riskiness' of the above firms? With its *portfolio focus* and a host of mathematically convenient assumptions, the CAPM breaks risk into two components: (1) unique, or *diversifiable* risk and (2) *undiversifiable risk*, associated with general market moves, which cannot be eliminated through portfolio diversification. Undiversifiable risk, in the CAPM world, is captured in beta. The CAPM/beta encourages investors to view the aforementioned wealth-creating firm as 'more risky' (higher beta) than the wealth-dissipating firm (lower beta). Although this may be logical in the portfolio-analysis context of CAPM, it is not useful in the context of the CFROI valuation model. We argue for an *individual firm focus*, one that links firm economic performance with warranted value and quantifies the plausible range of *future* economic performance and related shareholder returns.

The firm-specific orientation of the CFROI valuation model does not ignore the issue of *market efficiency*. Indeed, the more investors work with the CFROI model and company data, the more aware they become of the evidence that the market is exceptionally astute, on average, in forecasting future economic performance. For particular investors with their selected universe of stocks, it helps clarify their degree of difficulty in consistently earning returns well in excess of the general market. Consistently superior shareholder returns require forecasting CFROIs better than the market does.

Evaluating share repurchase programs

The importance of critical thinking and a *total system perspective for valuation variables* is illustrated here in connection with an analysis of share repurchase. Articles in the popular press and security analysts' reports often exhibit considerable muddled thinking on this topic, primarily due to a lack of a total system perspective.

The magnitude of wealth-creating investment opportunities

In analyzing Coca-Cola and Abbott Laboratories in 1998, one extraordinarily important valuation issue to both firms is their repetitive and very large share repurchases. Both firms have very high CFROIs and very high sustainable growth rates. Although share repurchase tends to be erratic for most firms, these two firms have systematically made large repurchases over the past decade. Therefore, analysts must form an opinion on whether or not this activity will continue at such large levels. Do these top managements believe their stock prices are undervalued, or do they face a shortage of investment opportunities at well-above-average CFROI levels?

The key variables requiring analysis are highlighted in Figure 7.15. Remember that a forecast of continued large share repurchase entails a much lower actual plowback, which affects the CFROI fade rate. For high-CFROI firms, *all else equal*, lower reinvestment rates reduce the present value of future investments. An offsetting effect is that, *all else equal*, lower reinvestment provides a slower CFROI fade, which increases the value of future investments. At times, share repurchase might substantially impact financial leverage. This affects the firm's risk differential and CFROIs via gross cash flow. The completeness of the CFROI valuation model helps the analyst to work through these relationships.

Estimating the per share impact

The use of warranted value in analyzing share repurchase is explained as follows. Take a simplified share repurchase where the firm has a non-operating asset that is converted to cash in order to finance a share repurchase. By this assumption, the forecasted NCR stream from operating assets is not impacted by share repurchase. Assuming that the firm will deliver NCRs implied by the warranted value (WV), the per share gain or loss to *non-selling* shareholders is calculated as

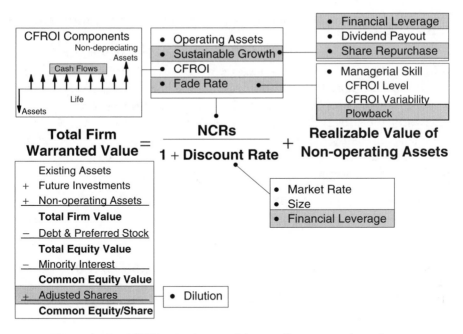

Figure 7.15 CFROI valuation model map. Share repurchase issues.

follows:

$$\text{PER SHARE GAIN} = \frac{\text{WV} - P(\text{SBUY})}{\text{SORIG} - \text{SBUY}} - P$$

Where:

P = Price per share received by selling shareholders
WV = Warranted equity value
SORIG = Original Shares outstanding
SBUY = Shares Bought
WV − P(SBUY) = Warranted equity value reduced by the amount of non-operating assets used to finance share repurchase
SORIG − SBUY = New shares outstanding

The above expression is readily understandable given the simplified conditions. The greater the gap between warranted value per share and actual price, the greater the per share gain. Realizing this gain requires the share price to reach the warranted value over some 'reasonable' length of time.

The firm's NCR stream was not affected by assumption. So, a gain to non-selling shareholders is a loss to the selling shareholders. That is, the sellers suffer an opportunity loss of not participating in the market's repricing of the firm's stock price. If there is no repricing (i.e., actual price equals warranted value), then share repurchase has a zero impact.

The numerical example below illustrates the importance of the difference between warranted value and current price and this gap closing in the near future. Repurchasing shares, in a sense, 'levers' this gap-closing to the benefit of non-selling shareholders. But in many share repurchases this leverage tends to be small in relation to the effect of closing the value gap. In this hypothetical example, $400 of non-operating assets is used to repurchase 10 shares from a total of 100 shares outstanding.

$$WV = OPERATING\ ASSETS + NON\text{-}OPERATING\ ASSETS$$
$$WV = 4600 + 400 = 5000$$
$$P = 40$$

Note that there is a value gap of $10 per share, $(5000/100) - 40$.

$$PER\ SHARE\ GAIN = \frac{5000 - 40(10)}{100 - 10} - 40 = 11.11$$

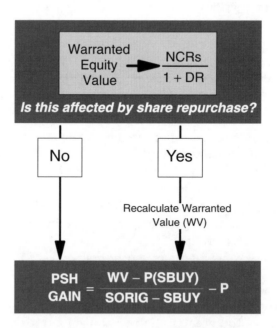

Figure 7.16 Share repurchase analysis.

In summary, the non-selling shareholders enjoyed a per share gain of $11.11. Even though shares outstanding were reduced by 10 per cent, only $1.11 of the $11.11 total resulted from share repurchase. The bulk of the gain, $10.00, was due to *closing the value gap*. This type of example can be illuminating to those who believe that share repurchase, by itself, is automatically beneficial to share prices.

Figure 7.16 shows the steps for analyzing the more complex situations that require recalculation of the warranted value.

Life-cycle perspective on stock price reactions to quarterly reports

This chapter has dealt with forecasts of firms' *long-term* NCR streams driven by a life cycle of CFROIs and sustainable growth. In concluding this chapter, we would like to comment on how this long-term perspective might help to take the mystery out of perceived *irrational* stock price reactions to quarterly reports.

Have you ever heard the comment: firm X reported a bad quarter but the stock went up, while firm Y posted a good quarter but its stock dropped; therefore, the market must be rooted in crowd psychology and emotion rather than rational economics? One explanation is that the market's reaction does, in fact, make sense when *actual* quarterly EPS are compared to *expected* EPS. The CFROI life-cycle perspective suggests ways to improve upon this explanation by: (1) measuring surprise as deviation of actual CFROI from expected CFROI, thereby removing the effects of financial leverage, and (2) incorporating current market expectations for firms' life cycle of future CFROIs and sustainable growth. The notion is to make quantitative estimates of the expected magnitude of short-term price reactions to quarterly report surprises. Three empirically testable hypotheses are:

(1) The higher the proportion of a firm's value owing to future investments, the larger the change in warranted value for a given revision in forecasted CFROIs and growth. For established firms, all else equal, (e.g., holding financial leverage constant), firms with a higher proportion of value attributable to future investments should exhibit larger short-term changes in stock price for the same quarterly CFROI surprise.

(2) Firms that have been earning CFROIs close to the average rate for many years are likely to continue to remain near that level of profitability, consistent with the empirical results presented in Figure 7.3. All else equal, these cost-of-capital-type firms should

exhibit smaller short-term changes in stock price for the same quarterly CFROI surprise.

(3) Established firms that steadfastly have been earning CFROIs well below average have inferior managerial skill, and/or a flawed business strategy. The initiation of a potential resolution of this problem (replacement of top management or exiting one or more uneconomic businesses) should dominate the market's forecasting of long-term NCRs regardless of short-term quarterly financial results. All else equal, low CFROI firms that are in the process of fundamentally fixing the root cause of their sub-standard CFROI performance should be most likely to show positive stock price changes even while reporting negative quarterly operating results.

This way of thinking about the market's reaction to quarterly report announcements also applies to other corporate announcements. The basic idea is to first use the long-term perspective of the CFROI model to identify the key valuation issues. Then, quantify the likely stock price reaction to a corporate announcement, paying particular attention to how it might impact a key valuation issue.

8

Evaluating valuation models

Summary

- For more than 30 years, mainstream finance has devoted surprisingly little attention to detailed individual-firm valuation models. This is the result of a research methodology that (a) reveres elegant mathematical theorizing, (b) accepts a theory's assumptions as not needing to correspond to reality, and (c) treats the stock market as such an *efficient* mechanism for forecasting firms' economic performance that valuation analysis becomes unproductive.
- With its foundation in elegant mathematical specification of *efficient portfolios*, the capital asset pricing model (CAPM), first elucidated in the early 1960s, was quickly embraced by finance academics even though it requires a host of assumptions that have no counterpart in the way *investors actually value individual firms*.
- The primary competitor *individual-firm* model to the CFROI model is the *residual income* (RI) model. *Residual income* is what a firm earns in excess of that required to compensate owners for the cost of their capital. RI valuation models have appeal for their simplicity.
- For the firm's equity discount rate, RI models use the CAPM/beta approach, in which the firm's discount rate is calculated as a base risk-free rate for the time of the valuation plus a risk premium. This risk premium begins with the excess return of the general equity market over the risk-free rate for some selected historical period. It is then adjusted depending upon a firm's stock price volatility as measured by beta. The *historical* nature of the CAPM/beta risk premium is a severe

flaw. In addition, the use of betas often results in cost of capital, or discount rate, estimates that *are counter to common sense.*

- Stern Stewart's EVA® is a variation of the standard RI model. Although EVA® has significant differences, it uses the same compact algebra and perpetuity assumptions for valuation, nominal rather than real magnitudes, and the CAPM/beta discount rate procedure—all of which are major drawbacks.

- We present six criteria for evaluating competitor valuation models: (1) insights gained from analyzing firms' track records, (2) identification of key valuation issues, (3) valuation accuracy, (4) usefulness for making plausibility judgements about forecasts used in the models, (5) ease of implementation, and (6) process for model improvement. We argue that the CFROI model is superior to RI/EVA® by all criteria other than ease of implementation, which favors RI/EVA®.

- *Free cash flow* is a vague concept. It can divert attention away from the much more important issue of a firm's level of *managerial skill.*

We began this book by saying its purpose is to explain HOLT's CFROI valuation model with enough detail and clarity for readers to understand it and have a basis for judging its usefulness. The special characteristic of the CFROI model is its focus on relationships among variables in a total system, as differentiated from isolating pieces of the total system. These relationships entail a level of detail and a way of thinking that fosters a process of problem recognition → generation of hypotheses → empirical feedback → adequate solutions. The model has a process within itself for continual improvement, which is one of the six criteria we propose as reasonable for evaluating valuation models.

Some readers might wonder why we feel a need even to articulate evaluation criteria. Why not simply look to mainstream academic finance to see what is 'the best' valuation model? This relates to another question, why does the CFROI model ignore mainstream finance theory on CAPM/beta cost of capital? In taking up these questions directly, we return to some fundamental issues discussed in Chapter 1 about what constitutes knowledge.

Our organization for this chapter is to first briefly discuss important historical issues that explain the practices of mainstream finance. It describes a mainstream orthodoxy that reveres elegant mathematical theorizing in the extreme and promotes a heavy-handed influence on empirical researchers to fit their studies into the reigning theories accepted by the editorial boards of top finance journals. This illuminates why the CFROI model can differ from the mainstream so radically in its discount rate mechanism.

CAPM/beta is an integral part of a finance student's education in corporate finance and valuation. It is employed in the currently leading academic contender for 'best' valuation model, namely the residual income (RI) model. Stern Stewart & Co. promotes a version of RI that it labels as EVA® (economic value added). After describing RI and EVA®, we apply six criteria to evaluate the advantages and disadvantages of the RI, EVA®, and CFROI valuation models.

The mainstream finance method

Learning need: feedback, testing of assumptions

We have emphasized that learning, or knowledge improvement, is the product of the basic knowledge and action process discussed in Chapter 1, and this applies to valuation model improvement, too. Figure 8.1 reproduces the knowledge and action flowchart with shaded emphasis on feedback and testing of assumptions. Both are essential to understanding the focus and method of modern finance and its implications for guiding advances in valuation understanding in the future.

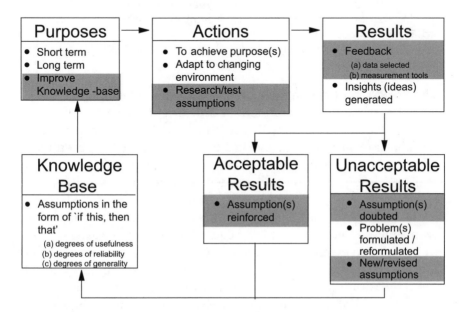

Figure 8.1 Knowledge and action system. Testing assumptions.

Readers who do not follow academic finance might be surprised at the lack of attention over the last three decades given to building and improving detailed models for calculating warranted values. We offer an explanation for this.

Origin of the CAPM: mathematics and efficient portfolios

In the early 1950s Harry Markowitz cleverly devised mathematical relationships to operationalize efficiency in the context of a portfolio of stocks.[1] In the early 1960s William Sharpe extended this mathematical portfolio orientation to a capital asset pricing model (CAPM) based on a host of assumptions that clearly have no counterpart in actual practices of investors.[2] The CAPM specifies the expected return on a stock as the expected return on a risk-free asset plus a risk premium. This risk premium is the product of (a) the excess of the expected return for the general equity market over the risk-free return multiplied by (b) the individual stock's beta.

By the 1960s, the economics profession was rapidly transitioning towards highly abstract mathematical model building, a trend that continues unabated today. Concerning this reverence for formal abstract models, Ronald Coase remarked in early 1996:[3]

> Economics has been becoming more and more abstract, less and less related to what goes on in the real world. In fact, economists have devoted themselves to studying imaginary systems, and they don't distinguish between the imaginary system and the real world. That's what modern economics has been and continues to be. All the prestige goes to people who produce the most abstract results about an economic system that doesn't exist.

The CAPM was a congenial foundation for academic finance to follow the economics profession. It led to a massive outpouring of academic journal articles with roots in mathematical specifications of equilibrium pricing and market efficiency. Note that a valuation model deals with differences between warranted and actual stock prices. As such, a valuation model does not necessarily require elegant, high-level mathematics. It is basically a net cash receipt forecasting mechanism combined with a discount rate mechanism. Advancements in understanding require not so much abstract theory development as extensive, detailed empirical analysis and refinement. Moreover, academics could point out that market efficiency implies that all relevant information as to firms' future economic performance is already contained in market prices. That being the case, why expend effort to calculate warranted values?

Assumptions become unchallengeable, deductive logic rules

To understand the habits of mainstream finance academics, one needs to examine their methodological underpinnings, evident in a 1953 paper by Milton Friedman 'The Methodology of Positive Economics'.[4] In this paper, Friedman argues, among other things, that the realism of assumptions is immaterial as long as the world behaves 'as if' the assumptions were true:

> ... [T]he important question to ask about the 'assumptions' of a theory is not whether they are descriptively 'realistic', for they never are, but whether they are sufficiently good approximations for the purpose at hand. And the question can be answered only by seeing whether the theory works, which means whether it yields sufficiently accurate predictions.

> page 15

In his 1964 formulation of the CAPM, Sharpe builds upon Friedman's position:

> [Italics added]

> ... [S]ince the proper test of theory is not the realism of its assumptions but the *acceptability of its implications*, and since these assumptions imply equilibrium conditions which form a major part of classical financial doctrine, it is far from clear that this formulation should be rejected.

> page 434

At this point, the reader might be getting a sense of 'how research is done' in mainstream finance. In their book *Toward Finance With Meaning — The Methodology of Finance: What It Is and What It Can Be*, George Frankfurter and Elton McGoun provide an insightful critique of mainstream methodology and the CAPM. Sharpe's position quoted above receives this criticism:[5]

> [Italics added]

> Although Sharpe builds on Friedman (the test of a theory is not the realism of the assumptions), the distinction between the two is critical. Sharpe moves from Friedman's acceptance of a theory if it provides a 'sufficiently good approximation' of reality 'for the purpose at hand' to adopting a doctrine based on the 'acceptability of its implications.' In essence, *Sharpe eschews dependence on predictive ability (as Friedman's litmus test of the quality of a theory) and instead, condones logical consistency with accepted doctrine*. It is sufficient for such logical consistency to exist when a model's mathematical structure is internally consistent, and/or when the theory's extra-mathematical implications are not in conflict with rudimentary economic precepts that

dominate, indeed rule, the literature. In other words, any theory that tells us not to put all of our eggs in one basket is a good theory.

pages 30–31

Our critique of mainstream finance's lack of concern for skepticism of a model's assumptions is shared by Frankfurter and McGoun:

[Italics added]

... [W]e discussed in general terms the problems associated with building theories on simplifying assumptions. Such assumptions are not only unproven, but also never even tested. In fact, it is not considered necessary to test them. If the theories built on the assumptions fail to predict adequately, then they are abandoned and replaced by new theories built on new (and equally simplifying) assumptions. Had the assumptions of the failed theory been thoughtfully considered in advance and their inherent limitations and contradictions recognized, the failure might have been anticipated.

page 99

... [O]ne of the premier theories of finance, the CAPM, has been a notoriously dismal failure at prediction. The model was obviously built with a cavalier disregard for the realities of risk and uncertainty, which disregard led to their wholly inappropriate translation into the language of mathematical probability. *The failure of the CAPM makes an excellent case study of the belief that greater attention to assumptions — especially assumptions concerning the different 'languages' in which problems are suggested, theories constructed, and theories tested — might have prevented decades of futile effort.*

page 99

... As we have tried to show, the finance of the last four decades has had no success, especially with acute problems such as asset valuation, capital structure, and dividend policy; therefore, finance's so-called paradigm has nothing to do with any scientific achievement, but with a supposedly 'scientific' method. Finance's paradigmatic method is justified by its rhetorical elegance, not by its results.

page 240

This discussion on mainstream finance methodology is not of historical interest only; it is important for understanding how research tends to be conducted in mainstream finance today. It is also important that the finance profession pay serious attention to the criticisms raised by researchers such as Frankfurter and McGoun, who have a deep knowledge of both finance and methodology.

From observations to new/revised theory

The procedure of inquiry diagramed in Figure 8.1 is rooted in common sense attention to what works. This is crucially important, very *basic* stuff that has enormous implications for how we will observe valuation problems, learn about them, develop workable solutions, and take more successful actions — or not. The issue is well articulated by Robert Haugen:[6]

[Italics in original]

> Finance scholars have long embraced the notion that we advance faster and better by *first* creating theories that make predictions about the way the world works. *Next* we turn to the data to see if the numbers conform to the predictions. If we find that they do not, we either (a) 'refine' the theories, by altering the assumptions upon which they are based, or (b) 'refine' the empirical tests until the data speaks in a voice we can *appreciate and understand.*

page 136

> ... But most of the major advances in the frontier of human knowledge did not follow an arrow running through the theories into the empirical tests. Rather, *most of our greatest triumphs proceeded in the opposite direction from data to theory.* The arrow goes from straightforward empirical observation to the development of theories which give us the insights *to understand what we have seen.*

page 136

> ... We have two choices. We can *advance* by developing radically new theories to help us understand what we now see in the data. Or we can *go back*, denying what is now readily apparent to most, bending the data through ever more convoluted econometric processes, *until it screams its compliance with our preconceptions.*

page 138

Readers might keep in mind the above background on mainstream finance in considering our discussion of the development of residual income and EVA®.

Residual income

A little history

Residual income is what a firm earns in excess of that required to compensate owners for the cost of using their capital. There is a long history in the accounting literature of linking accounting numbers to equity values via a residual income model. As discussed below, in specifying a warranted value for a firm, the RI valuation relies on 'offsetting' biases in the accounting numbers that drive the valuation. As far back as 1937, Gabriel Preinreich noted:[7]

[Italics added]

A fundamental truth about accounting is that, *given perfect and unlimited foresight*, no matter at what value an asset is placed on the books and no matter in what haphazard way it is amortized over its unexpired life, the discounted excess profits plus the recorded value will always give the true fair market value, even though both the investment and the excess profits are measured incorrectly. This statement is a simple theorem of arithmetic.

page 220

This line of thinking was pursued by Edwards and Bell in their influential 1961 book, *The Theory and Management of Business Income.*[8] Mainstream finance subsequently moved away from this 'fundamental analysis' approach to valuing business enterprises and began a journey of elaborate mathematical theorizing about risk and return under conditions of equilibrium.[9] In recent years, Ohlson, Feltham, Penman, Lee and others have resurrected the residual income model.[10] The accelerating RI academic research is one reason for spending time on this topic. To the extent that EVA® is a hot topic in the popular press, RI is equally a hot topic in the accounting literature and may eventually play a significant role in mainstream finance. Also, since EVA® is a version of RI, it is helpful to understand the similarities and differences.

Foundation in accounting

The standard RI academic treatment has an equity orientation keyed to earnings (E), common equity, or book value (B), and an equity discount rate (c).[11] B, book value, is the result of myriad accounting rules that may be judged as having more or less conservative biases. Residual income to the equity holder for period 't' is earnings less a charge for the use of capital:

$$RI_t = E_t - (c)B_{t-1} \text{ which can be rearranged as} \tag{8.1}$$

$$RI_t = \left[\frac{E_t}{B_{t-1}} - c \right] B_{t-1} \tag{8.2}$$

E_t/B_{t-1} is return on equity (ROE_t), and Equation 8.2 then can be expressed as

$$RI_t = (ROE_t - c)B_{t-1} \tag{8.3}$$

This expresses the familiar spread notion of a rate of return compared to the cost of capital.

Staying with *accounting-based* data, the RI academic treatment is to configure, at time t, the firm's value (V_t) as book capital (B_t) plus the present value of future annual RI amounts beginning in year $t + 1$. This valuation can be shown mathematically to provide the identical answer as that from valuing the firm's future dividend stream. If RI in future periods is zero, the firm's value is book capital $(V_t = B_t)$. The point here is that accounting biases are assumed to offset in the present value mathematics under the assumption of 'clean surplus' accounting in the future, wherein change in common equity book value is due to earnings less dividends. If book value is under (over) its 'true' value, then E/B compensates by being overly high (low).

Now to the matter of forecast horizon. Equation 8.4 implies that the value-added terms are to be estimated over an infinite horizon.

$$V_t = B_t + \frac{(ROE_{t+1} - c)B_t}{1 + c} + \frac{(ROE_{t+2} - c)B_{t+1}}{(1 + c)^2} + \cdots \tag{8.4}$$

To make this manageable, the model's proponents develop a finite-horizon model by adding a final term to the above equation. Typically they assume that after T periods, excess earnings on the capital base at time T persist indefinitely and new investments beyond T will match the cost of capital and, therefore, will have a zero impact on today's value.

Remember that the present value of $1 (beginning one year hence) received in perpetuity is $1 divided by the discount rate. Consequently, the final term of Equation 8.4 expresses value added for that year as a perpetuity, dividing it by c:

$$V_t = B_t + \frac{(ROE_{t+1} - c)B_t}{1 + c} + \frac{(ROE_{t+2} - c)B_{t+1}}{(1 + c)^2} + \cdots$$
$$+ \frac{(ROE_T - c)B_{T-1}}{(1 + c)^T c} \tag{8.5}$$

In fact, the user can select any horizon, say three years, and then use a perpetuity assumption (or some other manipulation) to assign a terminal value in year 3. There are a variety of ways to rearrange the basic RI model of Equation 8.5. The hallmark of these models is simple and compact algebra.

CAPM equity cost of capital

The cost of capital, or discount rate, in RI valuation models encountered in the academic literature employ the conventional CAPM/beta approach. In this approach, a firm's nominal equity cost of capital is a base risk-free rate plus a general equity risk premium adjusted for a firm-specific risk measure, beta (see Figure 8.2). The equity rate is the return investors are seeking to achieve when buying a particular firm's common shares. It is a *forward-looking* rate. The yield on long-term government bonds at any particular time, which is a forward-looking rate, is typically used as the risk-free rate at that time.

Figure 8.2　CAPM equity cost of capital.

Wide range of historical measures of equity premium

A severe flaw with CAPM/beta as a tool for estimating investors' demanded equity return resides in the method of calculating the premium. The premium for investing in the general equity market is measured by the excess return of equities over the risk-free rate for *some selected historical period*. An adjustment is made for an individual stock's volatility using beta. Firms that are more (less) volatile than the market have betas greater (less) than 1.0. Here again, firms' betas vary depending on the particular time period used for measurement. A firm-specific risk premium is the product of beta multiplied by the general equity risk premium.

The particular historical period used in calculating the general equity risk premium is a notorious source of wide variation in the resulting answer. Moreover, this procedure ignores today's 'uniqueness'. For example, today's equity investors may expect personal tax rates and inflation to be quite different from those expected during the historical period used. That period could include a lengthy period when bonds substantially underperformed stocks due to a lag in appropriately adjusting inflationary expectations. Arguably, after such a bad experience investors would demand higher real returns from bonds than in earlier periods, so today's demanded premium for stocks over bonds could be substantially less than revealed in the selected historical relationship. The market-derived discount rate analysis of Chapter 4 suggests that was the case in late 1997. Finally, the historical market risk premium used in the CAPM approach is unable to incorporate new information that has a substantial impact on discount rates. HOLT's market-derived approach described in Chapter 4 is designed to track the changing demands of investors as reflected in up-to-date market prices.

Examples of unreasonable CAPM/beta risk premiums

Suppose a CAPM user selected a 6 per cent general equity risk premium. This means that a firm with a beta of 1.5 would have a 9 per cent total risk premium (6 × 1.5). This implies that the firm's equity cost of capital is 300 basis points higher than average, based on a beta of 1.0 being the average. Obviously, betas have a significant effect.

If a valuation model is not subjected to feedback that points out weaknesses, then one or more of its components can be grossly inaccurate and go unnoticed. In our opinion, the lack of attention by mainstream finance to *detailed* valuation models and related feedback has led to the continued use of grossly inaccurate CAPM/beta equity discount rates. Even, in the *absence* of detailed feedback of warranted versus actual stock prices, a common-sense *reality check* should give CAPM users reason to question their procedure.

The example companies in Figure 8.3 were presented in a short note on cost of capital that used Value Line betas published in September 1995.[12] The company charts display monthly high-low stock prices. Firms on the left are industry leaders and those on the right are laggards from the same Value Line industry groups.

In 1995, Edison Brothers Stores had over 2,700 speciality retail stores concentrated in shopping malls. Better value to the customer offered by Wal-Mart and other retailers had reduced the appeal of mall shopping and devastated the core business approach of Edison Brothers. The stock plummeted from $40 per share in 1993 to $1 to $2 by 1995. The firm was on the verge of bankruptcy by September 1995.

With the market risk premium taken to be 6 per cent (an often-used figure), Wal-Mart's beta of 1.25 implies its equity risk premium is 7.50 per cent (6 × 1.25 = 7.50) and Edison Brothers' beta of 0.95 implies its equity risk premium is 5.70 per cent (6 × 0.95 = 5.70). This would make Wal-Mart's cost of equity capital 180 basis points (7.50 − 5.70) *higher* than Edison Brothers' cost of equity capital.

Hechinger had been taking a severe competitive beating from the larger superstores, pioneered by Home Depot, in the retail building supply industry. Hechinger lost money in 1994 and 1995. Not unrelated, its stock lost two-thirds of its value in 1995. With a beta of 1.60, Home Depot's cost of equity capital by the same process as above would be 420 basis points *higher* than Hechinger's, with its beta of 0.90.

Is it at all reasonable to believe that investors would have demanded substantially *lower* equity returns from such troubled companies than from their large, preeminent competitors? Plainly not. But that is what CAPM/beta indicates.

In our approach, a firm's discount rate is the sum of the market rate plus a risk differential for size and leverage, both of which are

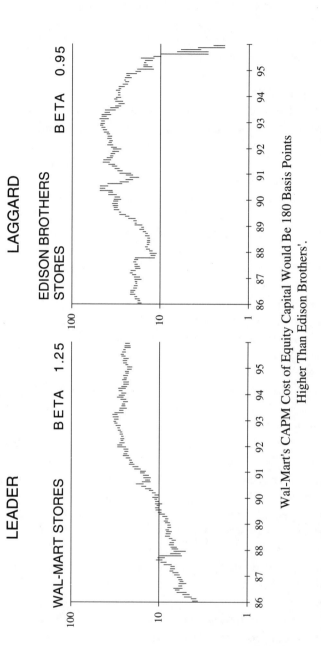

Figure 8.3 Examples of unreasonable CAPM/beta costs of equity capital. Source: Bartley J. Madden and Sam Eddins, 'Different approaches to measuring the spread of return on capital in relation to the cost of capital,' *Valuation Issues*, July/August 1996, pp. 4–7.

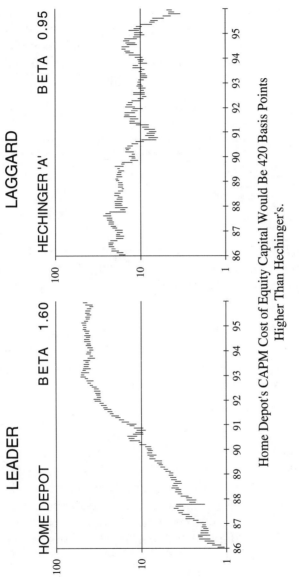

Home Depot's CAPM Cost of Equity Capital Would Be 420 Basis Points Higher Than Hechinger's.

Figure 8.3 *(continued)*

also used for firms' credit ratings. Large firms with low leverage, such as Wal-Mart and Home Depot, have negative risk differentials and therefore *below-average* discount rates, or costs of capital, by our approach.

In a widely cited 1992 article, Eugene Fama and Kenneth French provided substantial empirical evidence that beta had very little power in explaining shareholder returns.[13] In other words, high-beta firms achieved returns approximately the same as low beta firms. That it should have taken over three decades for the academics to discover this problem speaks volumes about the little importance of feedback to mainstream finance academics.

Criteria for evaluating valuation models

EVA® as a type of RI model

In his book, *The Quest for Value*, Bennett Stewart describes Stern Stewart's version of a residual income valuation model. Compared to the previously discussed academic RI model, the primary differences are:

(1)   A total asset orientation replaces a common equity orientation.
(2)   Return-on-total-capital-employed (ROCE) replaces ROE.
(3)   Adjustments for some accounting distortions are made.
(4)   Weighted average cost of capital (WACC) replaces equity cost of capital.

The resulting RI is labeled EVA®, a trademarked term for Stern Stewart's version of RI. The EVA® valuation model uses the same RI compact algebra and perpetuity calculations. Neither RI nor EVA® deals with real (inflation-adjusted) numbers. Neither addresses our fundamental point that a discount rate should be an integral part of the valuation model. Rather, both models import a CAPM/beta equity discount rate derived independently of the valuation model and having all the problems mentioned earlier.

How do we judge if the EVA® valuation model is better than the standard RI valuation model? Do the adjustments that Stern Stewart touts as translating accounting to true economic performance really improve its valuation calculation over RI? How do both models compare to the CFROI valuation model? In addressing these questions, our approach is to begin by focusing on criteria of key importance to *users* of valuation models. Figure 8.4 lists six criteria.

1. Insights from Analyzing Firms' Track Records
2. Identification of Key Valuation Issues
3. Accuracy
4. Plausibility Judgements
5. Ease of Implementation
6. Process for Model Improvement

Figure 8.4 Six criteria for evaluating valuation models.

Our conclusions summarized

Before discussing these criteria in detail, we offer a brief summary of our viewpoints.

(1) From our vantage point, there should be no doubt whatsoever that the CFROI valuation model is superior to RI/EVA® regarding criteria 1, 2, 4, and 6.

(2) Regarding accuracy, criterion 3, the CFROI valuation model is, in our opinion, *substantially more accurate* than RI/EVA®. HOLT's extensive client base of money management firms that use the CFROI valuation model is an especially strong endorsement of the model's accuracy. These are sophisticated, knowledgeable portfolio managers and analysts whose *job performance is dependent on valuation accuracy.* Nevertheless, accuracy entails subtle technical issues and deserves rigorous, extensive empirical tests by independent researchers. The technical material in this book might facilitate academic research on the CFROI model's accuracy.

(3) Ease of implementation, criterion 5, favors at some level RI/EVA® over CFROI. There is no free lunch. Among other things, the CFROI model's rigor in inflation and accounting adjustments, its discount rate improvements over the easy-to-calculate CAPM/beta discount rates, its detailed fade rates in place of simple perpetuity calculations, and its total system emphasis on relationships among variables involve a greater level of complexity. In sharp contrast, the RI model is extraordinarily compact and uses just a few standard accounting variables.

Criterion 1: insights from analyzing firms' track records

In the CFROI model, the baseline NCR forecast is driven by a forecast life-cycle of CFROIs and sustainable growth. An inherent part of the model is the display of firms' track records of CFROI juxtaposed with the market discount rate and of actual asset growth juxtaposed with sustainable growth. With accounting biases minimized and with inflation adjustments made, a long-term time series of CFROIs can indicate likely ROIs on new investments. With a Relative Wealth index also displayed, periods of outperforming/underperforming the equity market can be seen in the context of contemporaneous performance of CFROIs and asset growth. Shareholder returns greater/less than the market are highly associated with changes in firms' CFROI level. With this historical display and users' detailed knowledge of firms' businesses, insights are often gained that are helpful in forecasting firms' future economic performance.

The RI model does not incorporate the benefit of historical data displays. With its claim of measuring *economic* performance, the EVA® model might appear to be useful for analyzing firms' past *economic* performance. This is not the case. EVA® computes the difference between an adjusted ROCE and a dubious cost of capital estimate, and multiplies this difference by an adjusted capital base. The result is a single *deceptively simple* amount that, in fact, contains a myriad of assumptions built into the calculation. It is in absolute value terms and not adjusted for inflation, resulting in severe limitations for time series analysis. Because it is directly tied to the firm's capital base, EVA® for a growing firm earning more than the cost of capital will nearly always increase over time, even if CFROIs are decreasing.

EVA® limitations revealed

Figure 8.5 displays EVA® for Wal-Mart calculated by following the guidelines in Bennett Stewart's book *The Quest for Value*. These data will not match the published Stern Stewart EVA® numbers for many reasons. The assignment of a CAPM equity cost of capital is fraught with wide variation based on minor differences in estimating either beta or market risk premium. In addition, Stern Stewart refers to a large number of possible adjustments used in its EVA® calculations. We do not claim to be reproducing all of those adjustments. Using published Stern Stewart material, we are able to plot its EVA® calculations for selected years in Figure 8.5.

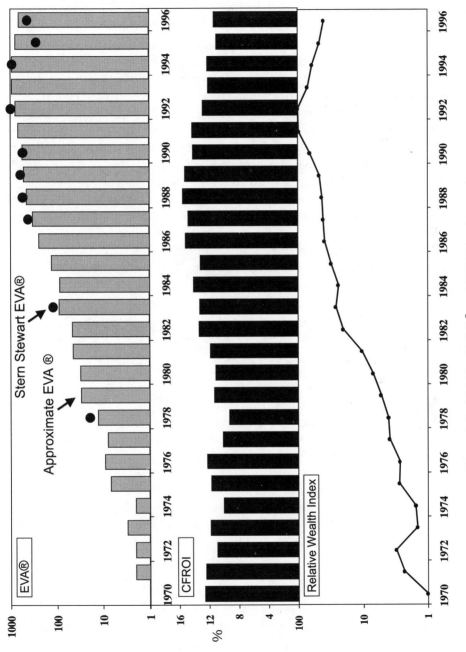

Figure 8.5 Wal-Mart's EVA® and CFROI track record.

The Relative Wealth Index of Figure 8.5 shows that Wal-Mart's stock outperformed the market substantially until the early 1990s. EVA® also rose sharply over that time, as did Wal-Mart's earnings and cash flow (see Figure 2.8A on page 26). The key to Wal-Mart's outperformance was its rising trend of high CFROIs (counter to the market's expectation for a normal fade) coupled with exceptionally large reinvestment rates (Figure 2.8B). These revealing *components* to a firm's track record cannot be observed in an EVA® time series.

We challenge motivated readers to take a large sample of companies and display time series of CFROIs and EVA®s alongside firms' Relative Wealth lines. *Declining* CFROIs and *declining* Relative Wealth lines will often be observed accompanied by *rising* EVA®s. The conclusion will be that the relative performance of firms is much more closely related to CFROI changes than to EVA® changes.

EVA® proponents might argue that EVA® is not designed for time series analysis, that EVA®s ROCE could be adjusted for inflation, and that a real ROCE is a more appropriate comparison to CFROI. We agree. The basic point remains, though: EVA® by itself is a poor metric for gaining insights from analyzing firms' track records. CFROI is superior by criterion 1.

Criterion 2: identification of key valuation issues

One purpose of analyzing firms' track records is to spot a firm's key valuation issue(s). For below-average CFROI firms, the key issues are CFROI improvement and avoidance of business-as-usual reinvestment plans. For firms in a growth mode, a key issue is the extent of investment opportunities at returns clearly in excess of the cost of capital. Comparison of actual asset growth rates to sustainable growth rates is helpful. For example, the Chapter 7 discussion of share repurchase noted the much slower reinvestment rates for Coca-Cola and Abbott Labs due to large share repurchases. This was apparent from actual asset growth rates that have been much lower than sustainable growth rates. For firms with downward trends in CFROIs, the key issue is that ROIs on future investments might well be much lower than current CFROI levels.

In the HOLT/*ValueSearch*™ database, the +1-year forecast CFROI is displayed two ways: one includes goodwill and the other excludes goodwill. A substantial difference almost always raises an important analytical issue about management's plans for future acquisitions. If a large portion of future growth is expected to come via acquisitions (including the cost of goodwill associated with future acquisition premiums), ROIs on new investments would likely be forecasted at a lower level than if future growth is mostly internally generated.

The primary reason why the CFROI model rates higher than RI/EVA® regarding criterion 2 is the CFROI model's completeness and its visual display of firms' track records which greatly facilitates the identification of key valuation issues.

Criterion 3: accuracy

Criteria 1 and 2 suggest that helping valuation model users assemble essential 'intelligence' about specific firms is an integral part of improving the accuracy of forecasts. In actual valuation work, *accuracy involves not only the firm's NCR forecast but also the market's NCR expectation.*

A truly insightful analysis that more accurately forecasts corporate performance of a firm than the market may not lead to the right decision. The success of buy/hold/sell investment decisions depends on the accuracy of the analyst's forecast of *both* corporate performance and the market's expectations of the firm's performance. To illustrate, let's say an analyst *correctly* forecasts a major improvement in a firm's wealth creation but *wrongly* interprets that today's stock price reflects expectations for such improvement. In such a case, the analyst might well miss an attractive buying opportunity—a bad decision.

The forecast 'five year window' illustrated for Donaldson Company in Chapter 7 is particularly effective for relating a user's forecast to market expectations. With accounting distortions minimized and inflation effects removed, forecast economic performance can be directly viewed as an extension of past performance. With *ValueSearch* software, users can employ different fade rates and calculate corresponding warranted values in a visual, easy-to-follow manner. In our opinion, the RI or EVA® valuation mechanics are not nearly as effective. We are confident that those who experiment with company data using RI, EVA®, and CFROI forecasting procedures will agree that CFROI is superior.

Consider a valuation, perhaps for a company of interest to an investor or for a possible acquisition target to a corporate management. Would users not want to have an idea of how well their valuation model worked in the past for this particular firm? *ValueSearch* database displays time series of actual stock prices and of warranted values for essentially all the firms of investment interest in the major countries. Professional money managers using the HOLT system place considerable importance on this *valuation audit*. It enables one to assess if there are systematic problems of continued overtracking or undertracking of actual prices versus warranted share values. As the CFROI Valuation Model Map suggests, the model provides a blueprint for identifying the source of the problems, and likely fixes. Consider a situation in which warranted values are consistently less than actual. First, note that it is important to *identify* this problem before using a calculated warranted value to make an investment decision—likely a bad decision. Second, one wants to *fix* the problem if possible. Perhaps, the firm uses accelerated depreciation and this has not been properly adjusted for, with the consequence that the asset life input is substantially understated. Computing a more realistic asset life and recalculating warranted values with historical data might well bring warranted values close to actual historical prices and that would suggest the proposed fix is indeed a fix. Accuracy is not the consequence of an isolated act. It involves a *process* for identifying sources of inaccuracy and resolving such problems.

Missing from the applications of RI and EVA® that we have seen is any detailed audit of differences between warranted and actual prices. In our experience, improvements in accuracy accelerate as all components of the valuation model are treated as a total system. As procedures for estimating CFROI fade rates, risk differentials, and the like are improved, the model will be more useful for *identifying* and fixing measurement problems that might otherwise go unnoticed. If mainstream finance followers had studied the results of CAPM/beta cost-of-capital estimates within the context of detailed, company-specific valuation audits, we believe this cost-of-capital procedure would have been discarded long ago for valuation purposes.

Criterion 4: plausibility judgements

The CFROI model presented in this book adjusts accounting data to better reflect economic performance. Also, all component parts of the model are expressed as real, or inflation-adjusted, magnitudes. These features are essential for long-term time series analysis of data and cross-company comparisons within a specific country. They are even more important for extending analyses to different countries. The CFROI model's completeness is well suited to handling the wide array of international accounting treatments, and adjusting for distinctly different country inflation histories. Although the technical sections of this book might indicate that the CFROI model is complex, the complexity is due to a completeness which makes it easier to convert worldwide accounting data to comparable measures of economic performance. Comparability across companies of varying asset composition, across time, and across national borders is essential for making improved plausibility judgements about specific levels of forecasted corporate performance — criterion 4.

Life-cycle performance is, at bedrock, determined by managerial skill and competition. In studying firms' track records, users can associate levels of CFROI and sustainable growth with levels of managerial skill. Financial data thereby gain a measure of intuitive meaning. Consequently, forecasts of CFROIs and sustainable growth are more easily interpreted for the degree of optimism or pessimism they reflect than are forecasts made in absolute dollar terms such as EVA®. Plausibility judgements involve comparisons with other firms, especially competitors. Here again, a forecast of better (worse) performance than a competitor is typically more acceptable if this is consistent with demonstrated levels of managerial skill for the firm and its competitors, i.e. their CFROI track records.

Plausibility judgements are further enhanced by the CFROI model's five year forecast window, which forces explicit attention to the CFROI fade rate. A firm's current stock price can be translated to expectations of a CFROI level at the end of the five year period. The market's expected fade can be compared to a standard HOLT forecasted fade rate based on the firm's level of CFROI, CFROI variability, and reinvestment rate. In addition, the +5-year CFROI communicates the level of managerial skill being forecasted by the market.

Wal-Mart offers an example of the practical use of the five year window in judging a stock's upside potential and downside risk. During 1992, Wal-Mart was trading around $30 per share. At that price, HOLT clients could calculate that the market expected over the five year forecast window zero fade in CFROIs while Wal-Mart maintained its historically high reinvestment rate. Application of HOLT's CFROI model helped users judge the upside potential as small and the downside risk as large, and the conclusion was to sell Wal-Mart at that time. Some years later, a September 1996 *Forbes* article described how money managers used HOLT's CFROI model. In that story, attention was given to HOLT's earlier analysis of Wal-Mart and its then current analysis with the stock around $25. The conclusion was that Wal-Mart had become a buy, because the current market price implied a +5-year CFROI forecast close to the long-term 6 per cent corporate average. Such a rapid fade to an average company, while certainly possible, was deemed unlikely. Subsequent to the buy recommendation, Wal-Mart outperformed the market and ended 1997 at around $40 per share.

Criterion 5: ease of implementation

We granted earlier that RI/EVA® is easier for corporations to implement than the CFROI model. The *benefit* of the CFROI model's greater accuracy comes at the *cost* of added technical details. This additional complexity should not be a deterrent for implementing the CFROI model within money management firms. Success or failure in money management hinges on a sound research process and valuation accuracy, both of which are enhanced by the CFROI model.

A legitimate debate exists as to the benefits of managing solely by the *accounting value drivers* at deeper levels within business firms. In Chapter 9 we specifically address the central point that accounting data measure *results* of business processes and that a high level of controlling by accounting data, whether expressed as EVA® or CFROI, could easily misdirect attention from underlying business processes. On the other hand, *simple* internal measures that force business unit managers to be accountable for resources are certainly useful. The original concept of residual income is rooted in charging managers for the cost of capital they are using. The clear benefits of RI/EVA® are in those situations where gross inefficiencies exist due to an internal performance measurement system based on sales or operating income, without any accountability for the assets employed to produce the results.

We think the CFROI model is better suited than RI/EVA® at higher levels of the firm, where valuation accuracy is particularly important as, for example, in measuring market expectations, acquisition pricing, valuing business unit plans, and the like. At lower operating levels, the challenge is to transition to more simple accounting-based tools that help to improve the business processes that drive the accounting results.

The importance of *first* striving for the most accurate valuation model and *second* learning how to simplify for internal corporate use was well articulated by David Walker, VP-Finance at Procter & Gamble, in a letter to the editor in the December 1996 issue of *CFO* magazine:

> Here is my advice to anyone considering or using shareholder value approaches:
>
> 1. Spend the internal time and resources necessary to really understand the weak spots in these approaches.

2. Use the most theoretically valid approach you can find at the corporate level—regardless of complexity.
3. Develop an in-house business unit translation that is simpler to use.
4. Get some experience with the tools before linking to compensation.

Criterion 6: process for model improvement

Regarding criterion 6, the point has been made that the CFROI model contains within itself a process for improvement. The heart of this process is ongoing empirical feedback, especially time series of warranted versus actual stock prices in combination with the CFROI Valuation Model Map referred to throughout this book. Example of this improvement process includes the problem of dealing with financial subsidiaries (pages 125–9) and the evaluation of share repurchases (pages 184–7).

Many of the HOLT CFROI valuation model's calculating processes will be improved over time as deeper problems are uncovered and solutions developed. Nevertheless, the model incorporates foundational ideas that we expect will not change. They are:

1   Within a total system approach to valuation, the key parameters are endogenous. For example, the specification of a discount rate is dependent on the model's NCR forecasting procedures.

2   The market discount rate for an aggregate of firms also depends on how firms' NCRs are forecasted. It is, as it should be, a forward-looking rate derived from current stock prices.

3   More reliable company-specific discount rates will follow from better estimates of firms' CFROI fade rates, which then leads to improved estimates of company-specific risk differentials.

4   All components of the model need to be expressed in sound, logically consistent units of measurement. Time series data must be real numbers, adjusted for changes in the purchasing power of the monetary unit.

5   For established firms, a time series of CFROIs is especially helpful for gauging likely real ROIs on new investments.

6   It is useful to split the firm's anticipated NCR stream into an existing assets component and a future investments component.

7   For established firms, plausibility judgements of forecast CFROIs and asset growth require benchmarks. Fundamental benchmarks include the firm's CFROI life-cycle track record, competitors' track records, and the market discount rate.

Postscript: 'free cash flow' ambiguity

A discussion of cash flow and valuation of business would be incomplete for many readers without addressing the notion of free cash flow. It is a prime example of muddled thinking.

The investment community has at least three notions of free cash flow (FCF):

1. FCF is the same as NCR. In this case, why not use unambiguous words like *net cash receipt* and avoid the confusing *free* notion?
2. FCF is gross cash flow reduced by interest and dividend payments and some portion of capital expenditures that the analyst feels is an appropriate deduction.
3. FCF is 'cash flow in excess of that required to fund all projects that have positive net present values when discounted at the relevant cost of capital,' according to Michael Jensen.[14]

Focus on managerial skill, not free cash flow

Jensen's FCF takes complex issues and converts them into simplistic blackboard exercises in net present value calculation. It easily leads to the notion that if an industry has overcapacity, it should shrink. Overcapacity exists, according to Jensen, when internally generated cash flows by industry member firms could be fully reinvested only by accepting negative NPVs for future capital expenditures.

There is always a genuine risk that net present value calculations made by corporate staffs are biased toward answers top managements and boards want to hear. Moreover, inept managements almost always argue that productivity-improving capital outlays, once made, will restore wealth-creating returns. Would Jensen propose blindly accepting project assessments made by inept managements who documented their internal forecasts with spreadsheets demonstrating positive net present values? Jensen ignores the critical issues of plausibility judgement and managerial skill.

Although industry capacity can be important to long-term planning, it has the potential for reinforcing a business-as-usual attitude, that is, of considering adequate 'capacity' for producing the 'usual' products in the 'usual' way. Wal-Mart, Nucor, and Enron—led by skillful top managements—created highly innovative and successful businesses in mature industries with arguable overcapacity at times.

Rather than relying solely on internal NPV forecasts, we suggest useful information can be found in the market expectations embodied in the value of firms' future investments. A large part of Chapter 6 is devoted to HOLT's % Future computation and to 'setting the line' expressing the market's expectations for CFROI fade. Using this information, investors and board members might rightly conclude that low values attributed to firms' future investments reveal a substantial shortfall of *managerial skill*. If so, the solution is to replace top management, not necessarily to automatically distribute cash to shareholders. A new management team might decide to downsize the firm or might choose to redirect cash to economically viable projects.

More FCF is not necessarily favorable

In addition to confusion arising from the different notions of FCF described above, FCF suffers from misperception that it is a favorable sign, that is, the more FCF a firm has, the better. Indeed, security analysts' reports often contain price multiples of FCF, typically implying that high multiples are expensive stocks and low multiples are cheap stocks.

If FCF is identical to NCR, it is apparent that higher FCF is not necessarily better. High capital outlays for high ROI projects can depress NCRs in the early years but result in substantial positive values for future investments. If this same firm were to lose these wealth-creating opportunities, its capital expenditures might well decline, and higher FCF could result in the near term. But that would not be favorable.

Valuation analysis should involve a total system approach and a focus on critical thinking. Muddled thinking and wrong answers often result when valuation is viewed simply as NPV arithmetic.

Thinking about critical issues

Summary

- Because wealth creation stems from the efficient use of scarce resources in satisfying customer needs, the corporate goal of maximizing *shareholder* value requires that management skillfully weigh the economic trade-offs among the competing interests of *stakeholders*.
- Irrespective of the industries in which firms operate, it is increasingly recognized that knowledge is essential for superior performance. Key top-management skills now include (a) providing a vision, (b) focusing on total-system efficiency, (c) promoting an innovative environment, (d) guiding and fostering adaptability and (e) creating a continuous-learning organization.
- A corporate vision is a core purpose that inspires and guides persons within the firm to want to do those things that ultimately make the firm financially successful. When shareholder value is viewed and communicated in terms of CFROIs and sustainable growth, the connection between *non-financial* drivers and corporate performance is more apparent.
- Managing by 'accounting value drivers' carries a high risk of misdirection. Accounting data should be used to improve the efficiency of a total system centered on business processes tied to customer satisfaction and employee satisfaction. The causal direction is *from* sound processes *to* successful results.
- Firms have failed largely because management did not recognize that the foundation assumptions of the business no longer fit reality. Firms' structures and processes need to actively promote feedback so that innovation in response to an

ever-emerging future occurs continuously. The stock market is a valuable source of feedback concerning managements' assumptions about the future, and the model by which the stock market is observed, interpreted, and communicated is critical to the 'messages' received.

- Internal accounting systems should serve as a tool to assist creative thinking—thinking that addresses important elementary issues as to *how* work is done.
- Firms successfully configured as learning organizations continuously create and leverage knowledge that results in more efficient business processes for designing, making, selling, and servicing products.
- A valuation perspective such as that provided by the CFROI model is essential to developing more useful accounting treatments for soft assets, such as intellectual capital.
- Firms' internal performance measurement involves complex issues and needs to be addressed as a learning process.

The total system diagram introduced in Chapter 1 is reproduced as Figure 9.1. The shaded area of this figure highlights critical elements inside the firm, which serves to organize the major topics of this

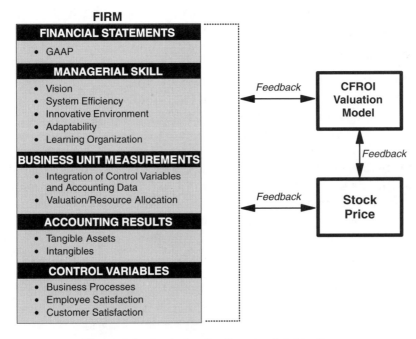

Figure 9.1 Analyzing the firm as a total system.

chapter and provides a context for pertinent excerpts from the writings of some leading researchers. The chapter reveals how key CFROI valuation concepts are compatible with work being done by others on unfolding critical issues.

Shareholders, stakeholders, and government policy

Valuation models and public policy

Public misperceptions about firm performance and the market's valuation of it has enormous trouble-making potential in the national attitude about the role of government as overseer of business. While public enthusiasm for government direction of business activity is much diminished from its heights, it is probably safe to say there remains, worldwide, a large segment of the people that highly doubts the business goal of maximizing shareholder value is aligned with the interests of society at large. One expression of this doubt is the notion that businesses should be managed not in the interest of *shareholders* alone, but of *stakeholders*, including employees, customers, suppliers, and the community at large. Some writers support government policies intended to encourage business to be more socially responsible, which includes taking better care of their employees generally and especially by providing greater job security.

This notion of stakeholder interests has its roots in a myopic analysis that runs along these lines: In pursuing the interests of shareholders, top management is continually, quarter-to-quarter, under pressure to improve the *bottom line and to make the numbers* expected by Wall Street analysts. Reducing costs becomes the top priority, and downsizing becomes the way of life in Corporate America and is making its way to other countries. Operations are consolidated; major plants are shut down; large numbers of long-service employees are forced to take early retirement or are fired; suppliers local to the shuttered plants lose major customers and they too are forced to reduce their workforces; economic multipliers magnify the economic contraction and its related losses of wealth across the community. At the consolidated operations, remaining employees become overburdened and overstressed by the additional work; product quality and customer service worsens. Yet, company's profits increase substantially, as does the price of its stock. Shareholders and top executives are handsomely enriched at the expense of everyone else.

Efficient resource allocation, trade-offs, and skilled managements

This line of argument is riddled with flawed thinking related to an erroneous implicit valuation model and to a truncated view of the wealth creation system. A basic proposition of market economics is that society as a whole benefits as resources continually shift away from lower-valued uses and towards higher-valued uses as revealed in the ever-changing price structure of the market for goods and services. Self-employed workers and workers organized within firms have different performance levels in efficiently developing, producing, and delivering products and services that consumers want. Wealth grows as scarce resources continually shift away from below-average-performing firms/workers towards above-average performers. In the financial markets, capital has a cost. Firms/workers that steadfastly underperform are dissipating society's wealth, because their use of capital means that opportunities are missed for society to earn at least the average return on investments.

Those who support the stakeholder case must argue not only that markets are inefficient, but also that there is a more efficient mechanism for harnessing society's scarce resources for the betterment of society at large. How *performance, efficiency* and *economic viability* are measured is crucially important to this issue. If a total system approach like that of Figure 9.1 is applied to the stakeholder issue, it will be recognized that the role of stakeholders must be incorporated in management's calculus of firm performance. Managements necessarily weigh *trade-offs* among the interests of various stakeholders. How many great companies have consistently mistreated employees or polluted the environment? The misperception about maximizing shareholder value *at the expense* of employees and local communities has its roots in *under-performing managements* who eventually cause layoffs and restructuring. Maximizing shareholder value is a means of transferring resources away from these under-performers and towards firms that can better use these resources. The more efficient an economy is in maximizing shareholder value, the sooner resources are recycled to better uses, thereby reducing the need for large scale layoffs and restructurings.

Successful managements often anticipate change or, at a minimum, recognize and adapt to it early. Managements that ignore change and conduct business-as-usual on the assumption that the future will mirror the past are on a path of under-performance and wealth dissipation. Except for the very individuals who would have retained their jobs for a time longer, society as a whole would have been worse off if, for example, resources were continually invested in plants for manufacturing stagecoaches and gas-lamps in spite of their imminent obsolescence.

New management that inherits a sinking ship is faced with tough decisions to make the firm into a viable enterprise. The popular press and fired employees tend to give too little attention to the root cause — deficient management from years past and, most probably, an under-performing board of directors.

Managerial skill: vision

In their insightful book *Built To Last: Successful Habits of Visionary Companies*, James Collins and Jerry Porras analyze the characteristics of exceptional companies, among them Hewlett-Packard, Merck, Minnesota Mining and Manufacturing (3M), and Wal-Mart.[1] Their comments about maximizing shareholder value are important:

[Italics in original]

> Contrary to business school doctrine, 'maximizing shareholder wealth' or 'profit maximization' has not been the dominant driving force or primary objective through the history of the visionary companies. Visionary companies pursue a cluster of objectives, of which making money is only one — and not necessarily the primary one. Yes, they seek profits, but they're equally guided by a core ideology — core values and sense of purpose beyond just making money. Yet, paradoxically, the visionary companies make more money than the more purely profit-driven comparison companies.
>
> ... A key role of core purpose is to guide and inspire. 'Maximize shareholder wealth' does not inspire people at all levels of an organization, and it provides precious little guidance. *'Maximize shareholder wealth' is the standard 'off-the-shelf' purpose for those organizations that have not yet identified their true core purpose.* It is a substitute ideology, and a weak substitute at that. Listen to people in great organizations talk about their achievements and you'll hear very little about earnings per share. Motorola people talk about impressive quality improvements and the effects of the products they create on the world. HP people talk with pride about the technical contributions their products have made to the marketplace. Nordstrom people talk about heroic customer service and remarkable individual performance by star sales people.

For those employees who do not have a meaningful ownership stake in the firm, the goal of maximizing shareholder value is not likely to be an effective motivator. But motivating employees is not the functional purpose of that goal. Although price changes for apples or gasoline may not be inspirational to consumers, these prices are part of a valuation mechanism essential for the allocation of society's scarce resources. This, in turn, improves society's standard of living.

Similarly, the goal of maximizing shareholder value is critical to better *economic* trade-off decisions by managements.

Example of success

Consider Hewlett-Packard's long-term track record, Figure 2.9B on page 29. CFROIs in 1996 equaled the well-above-average 12 per cent level achieved in the early 1960s. HP not only beat the CFROI fade, but did so with high reinvestment rates maintained over many years.

Society in general also benefits when skillfully managed firms invest in large-scale, innovative projects. In 1960, HP had 3,000 employees and an equity market value of $1.3 billion (1996 $); by 1996 HP had 112,000 employees and $51 billion market value. HP created a great deal of shareholder value and a great many jobs—probably well-paying jobs. HOLT's DualGrade® for HP is a solid BB, with a forecast +1-year CFROI of 13.2 per cent and with 52 per cent of the firm's total market value attributable to future investments.

HP has excelled in undertaking what Collins and Porras describe as BHAGs, Big Hairy Audacious Goals. For HP these have involved leveraging core technologies to deliver innovative products that satisfy customers. Another essential ingredient to HP's long-term success is the firm's core values—what employees refer to as the 'HP way'. The *end result* of the way HP operates is a preeminent long-term track record of CFROIs and asset growth rates that clearly created shareholder value. From the perspective of shareholder value, long-term life-cycle charts such as HP's and Wal-Mart's (Figure 2.8B on page 27) are the financial results of *skilled* managements with the ability to organize and inspire their employees to achieve BHAGs. When shareholder value is viewed and communicated in the context of past and forecast levels of CFROIs and asset growth rates, the meaning of shareholder value is readily understandable.

Managerial skill: total system efficiency

Local accounting efficiencies

The Information Age of the 1990s can be differentiated from the earlier Machine Age. The Machine Age is identified by mass production of standardized products, orchestrated by top managements using command-and-control systems tied to accounting numbers, with firms gaining competitive advantage through economies of scale in using tangible assets. In contrast, the Information Age is characterized by the widespread dissemination of information and the creation and exploitation of knowledge. Intangible assets are much more important in the Information Age, and a heated debate has arisen about how these assets should be reflected on firms' financial statements. A consensus is developing that to deliver exceptional corporate performance and create substantial shareholder value, firms need to be configured as learning organizations, whether the industry is low-tech or high-tech.

Firms that regularly improve their *core business processes* usually also achieve improved financial performance as recorded in their accounting statements. Unfortunately, this causal direction is often turned around: the causal variables are taken to be the *accounting value drivers* rather than the improvements to the underlying business processes. A firm's economic performance and valuation are likely to suffer when management disregards total system efficiency in devotion to some single business issue or narrow set of them, such as corporate mission, product quality, inventory levels, employee loyalty, customer service, costs, and the like. Managing a business to accounting targets is especially likely to emphasize local efficiencies and obscure the need to manage the efficiency of the total system.

Company example

Take Lincoln Electric Company as an example of a firm that seems to be breaking some of today's popular management rules when they are viewed in isolation. Lincoln Electric manufactures arc welding equipment, and has an unusual organizational structure that motivates teamwork and high quality while simultaneously paying employee bonuses tied to piece rates. The following quote describes important components of the firm's operating system.[2]

> As is widely understood, paying piece rates encourages output-directed effort. The high employee earnings suggest both that the piece rates encourage them to work at more than the standard rate and that there is probably a selection effect as well, with highly motivated, able workers being differentially attracted to the firm. However, piece rates also give incentives to skimp on quality if quality is not easily monitored and if maintaining quality competes with generating volume. The bonus system helps counter this. In fact, each unit is stencilled with the initials of the people who worked on it, and if it fails after delivery because of a flaw in production, the responsible worker loses as much as 10 per cent of his annual bonus. The bonus for cooperation also helps overcome the tendency for workers to resist helping one another or taking on temporary special tasks that need doing but cannot be paid on a piece rate (both of which would take away from the time when they could be producing and earning money). Thus the bonus and the

piece-rate pay scheme are complementary: Using either one makes it more attractive to use the other.

Obviously, if piece rates are effective, different workers will work at different rates, making it necessary to shift workers around to balance the production line. This makes flexible work rules especially valuable and creates a need for work-in-progress (WIP) inventories to allow individual workers to continue their production even when there is a temporary slowdown in the preceding or following production step. Thus, Lincoln's exceptionally high WIP inventory levels and flexible work rules are complementary with its piece-rate pay system.

An operating structure based on typical accounting ratios would attack the WIP inventory as excessively high and direct effort toward reducing it, if WIP were considered in isolation. To properly understand Lincoln Electric, one must analyze the firm as a total system, in which case high WIP inventory is recognized as a necessary part of a structure of no layoffs, flexible tasking, piece-rate compensation with a bonus-component to incent teamwork and high quality, and trust that management will be fair.

The message of the Lincoln Electric example is not that it is a model of the right organizational system but rather that managing by accounting numbers in isolation is dangerous. Accounting numbers and other rules that make a complex system more manageable should always be viewed with constructive skepticism within a meaningful context. The successful bonus system in the US proved to be a failure when Lincoln implemented it in Germany.[3] The radically different German culture was a new aspect that severely disrupted Lincoln's 'proven' bonus system.

Performance results from business processes

An excellent example of the benefit of a focus on business processes is the dramatically improved performance of American Standard in recent years. The firm has 44,000 employees engaged in air conditioning, plumbing, and automotive businesses. From 1988 to 1995, inventory turns increased from 3.3 to 10.7; its goal is 15. Working capital as a per cent of sales decreased from 16.3 per cent to 4.9 per cent; its goal is zero. What was the root cause of these improved accounting results?

In the *1995 Annual Report* Emmanuel Kampouris, American Standard's CEO, attributed it to the firm's implementation of a 'demand flow' management system similar to Toyota's production system:

[Italics in original]

... The Company is a worldwide leader in Demand Flow® Technology ('Demand Flow' or 'DFT'), having implemented Demand Flow processes in its manufacturing facilities and administrative activities.[4] DFT enhances customer service by reducing manufacturing cycle time, increasing flexibility and improving product quality. It also improves productivity by reducing non-value-added work, increasing inventory turnover, reducing working capital requirements and liberating both manufacturing and warehouse space.

... The success we have attained in improving manufacturing productivity and efficiency has inspired us to expand the DFT model to all areas of our operations. Our vision in undertaking this massive change is to become a truly *responsive* and *learning* organization. In January of 1995, we took the first steps toward becoming a process-structured Company, one which is organized around processes as opposed to traditional functions.

... We continue to eliminate both visible and unseen cultural barriers that impede the exchange of information. Removing these barriers will encourage shared learning, thus enhancing our associates' professional growth and our Company's competitiveness. The end result of all our efforts must be the creation of stockholder value.

... DFT, a customer-responsive business system, focuses on building quality products by integrating and synchronizing work processes in a continuous flow. DFT optimizes all resources—people, machines and materials—within a process providing a mathematically defined solution for maximizing their potential. It is a powerful tool to both evaluate and change work processes. Experimentation and change are constants in DFT, leading to continuous improvement. The flow process is designed to be fast and efficient, enabling our companies to gain competitive advantages by better serving customers through speed in product design and order fulfillment while improving quality and productivity.

... We are attacking the 'functional silos' rooted in the traditional organizational hierarchy. In their place, you will find a wholly reorganized company structured around processes.

American Standard's *1995 Annual Report* describes much more about the firm's vision, strategies, organization, operating efficiencies and learning capabilities. At December 1997, American Standard had a forecasted +1-year CFROI of 13.7 per cent, a striking improvement from the ho-hum 6 per cent CFROIs achieved prior to implementing the new system. Clearly, the firm has gained a competitive advantage.

With a focus on controlling processes, American Standard strives to optimize the total system. This way of organizing work is better suited to continued improvement and efficient use of resources in order to achieve high customer satisfaction. It is the reverse of a top-down hierarchical system which controls behavior based on accounting data alone. Here the operating results *cascade up the organization*, at some point taking the form of accounting statements that can be translated to economic performance via CFROIs, sustainable growth, and fade, with related effects on the firm's warranted value.

Managerial skill: innovative environment

Drucker on assumptions and failure

One of the critical tasks of management is organizing feedback mechanisms so that change is not threatening and innovation is the rule rather than the exception. To innovate is to avoid obsolescence. Figure 9.2 highlights the paramount importance of testing assumptions so that the firm avoids operating under 'comfortable' but obsolete and dysfunctional assumptions.

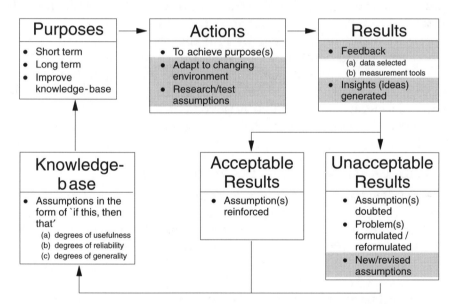

Figure 9.2 Knowledge and action system. Testing assumptions.

Examples abound of firms that at one time achieved preeminent levels of performance and dominant industry positions before eventually falling into down-sizing and searching for ways to revitalize their organizations. In his analysis of such deterioration, Peter Drucker described the key role of assumptions:[5]

[Italics in original]

The root cause of nearly every one of these crises is not that things are being done poorly. It is not that the wrong things are being done. Indeed, in most cases, the *right* things are being done—but fruitlessly. What accounts for this apparent paradox? The assumptions on which the organization has been built and is being run no longer fit reality. These are the assumptions that shape any organization's behavior, dictate its decisions about what to do and what not to do, and define what the organization considers meaningful results. These assumptions are about markets. They are about identifying customers and competitors, their values and behavior. They are about technology and its dynamics, about a company's strengths and weaknesses. These assumptions are about what a company gets paid for. They are what I call a company's *theory of the business.*

... When a theory shows the first signs of becoming obsolete, it is time to start thinking again, to ask again which assumptions about the environment, mission, and core competencies reflect reality most accurately—with the clear premise that our historically transmitted assumptions, those with which all of us grew up, no longer suffice.

Drucker's views make a strong case for the need for feedback that indicates if top management's strategies are viable and innovation is flourishing or if strategies are outdated and products and services meet a demand of the past. In principle, a firm's structures and processes should continually provide feedback, or listening, so that the entire organization becomes smarter and incrementally adapts to an ever-emerging future. As this ideal is approached in practice, innovation accelerates. Consequently, layoffs and restructurings become obsolete as products and services continually improve to better serve the firm's customers.

Feedback from bottom up, from outside in

Although feedback is often viewed as most essential to top management's strategy, it is indispensable at all levels of a viable business enterprise. Consider these remarks by John Seely Brown concerning feedback/listening as part of the innovation process:[6]

[Italics in original]

Strategy has to be informed by insights that percolate from the bottom up, from the outside in. Traditional strategic planning tends to be little more than a calendar-driven ritual in which deeply held assumptions and industry conventions are reinforced rather than challenged.

... A company that has control-oriented hierarchical organizational structures limits its ability to listen to a changing world by not honoring its periphery, from which new ideas often emerge. I'm not proposing anarchy or chaos; the organizations that will prove most effective are those that have discipline with *enabling*—rather than coercive—business processes and that have the ability to hear and act on unusual signals before others do.

... Organizations ground themselves through listening. If an organization's researchers are grounded—that is, if they have a deep and intuitive understanding of why the problems they are working on are important—and the organization has enabling business processes with systems to support emergent communities of practice, it is in a position to create meaningful strategies that are informed by what has come up from the bottom, in from the outside, from where the rubber hits the road. That's when the sparks start to fly and innovation takes hold.

From outside in, the stock market

The stock market is an especially viable outside-in source of feedback for assessing top management's crucial assumptions about the future, and the valuation model by which the stock market is observed, interpreted, and communicated is critical to the feedback messages 'received'. Boards of directors, top managements, and business unit managers all need to clearly communicate on performance/valuation issues. This book presents the case for the CFROI valuation model as both a critical lens by which to observe the stock market and a common language by which to communicate about performance and valuation.

Feedback facilitates *early* adaptation to a fundamentally changing environment, and/or obsolete assumptions. Strongly held beliefs tend to filter out observations at odds with those beliefs, the very observations that could expedite needed changes.[7] The comparability of the CFROI metric and the completeness of the CFROI valuation model reduce the *subjectivity* of what is perceived. When this is recognized, individuals are more inclined to trust the messages of the metric and model.

The CFROI model's valuation details make visible and explicit the key inputs to a specific warranted value calculation. When portfolio managers and security analysts disagree on a buy/hold/sell conclusion, they can communicate the sources of disagreement by explicitly arguing for different inputs (e.g., fade rate) and quantifying the valuation impacts of those differences.

Corporate management could also benefit from the completeness and detail of the CFROI model. When management thinks the market is undervaluing its stock, the disagreement with portfolio managers and stock analysts can be identified and explored in terms of the model's explicit components. By using the CFROI model in communications with investors, management will be more successful in 'correcting' erroneous views of investors and thereby raise the valuation of the firm, or will learn something from investors and 'correct' its thinking and policies inside the company and thereby raise the valuation of the firm, or both. The market is not the enemy of a management team truly committed to maximizing shareholder value. To the contrary, the market is an ally of such management, able and willing to supply information that could be highly useful.

Managerial skill: adaptability

Accounting data and creative thinking

We use adaptability to refer to the managerial task of dynamically integrating strategies, opportunities, and core competencies.[8] There is a large body of literature covering these topics, including ways to think about them, case studies, and a variety of ideas on implementing proposed improvements. Nevertheless, a critical issue in managing the firm as a highly productive, adaptive system is neglected. This issue is the subtle manner in which accounting data can either help or hinder improvement in *how work is done*. Tom Johnson makes this point as follows:[9]

> Accounting must go beyond providing measurements of results. By providing a means for exploring the assumptions and worldview that drive behavior in an organization, accounting can serve the larger organizational purpose of promoting inquiry into the relationships and patterns that give rise to the results we see.

Our concern about the potential of internal accounting systems to stifle creativity and learning in business firms can be illustrated by an anology with a scientific laboratory. In a very real sense, successful work in laboratories requires the same type of integration of strategies, opportunities, and core competencies as needed by business firms. Although there are generally accepted principles for reporting experimental results and these are important to the scientific process, it is stating the obvious to say that the reporting procedures do not produce the results. Insights and creative thinking clearly are key to scientific advances.

Likewise, internal accounting systems by themselves are insufficient for fundamentally improving the firm's efficiency. Accounting systems can be exceptionally valuable tools when developed in concert with creative thinking. This point is missed by those who ignore total-system complexities and advocate managing solely by *accounting value drivers*.

This analogy between business work and scientific work is articulated in an excellent study, 'The Factory as laboratory,' by Peter Miller and Ted O'Leary. In studying the redesign of a factory floor in a particular plant of Caterpillar Inc, these researchers note that:[10]

[Italics in original]

> ... For the factory is as much a site of invention and intervention as the laboratory populated by physicists, chemists, and the like. This is self-evident for the products made in the factory. But the factory is a

site for invention and intervention in a further important sense. It is here, on the shop floor, that new realities are created out of the dreams and schemes of diverse agents and experts based in a multiplicity of locales. The rearranging of persons and things on the factory floor proposed recently by advocates of cellular manufacturing, just-in-time systems, customer-driven manufacturing, and designs for the 'Factory of the Future' have made the factory into a laboratory *par excellence.* Out of such interventions have emerged new physical spaces on the shop floor, new ways of calculating, new forms of work organization, and new modes of economic citizenship.

... Henceforth, authority would flow directly from the customer to the work process, along the Assembly Highway, in accordance with the ideal of empowered workers responding immediately to the wants and wishes of the customer. Authority would no longer be embodied in the character of the supervisor, or in the routine calculations of a technique such as standard costing, but would inhere in the process itself.

The spirit in the walls

In manufacturing and marketing heavy trucks and buses, the Swedish firm Scania has a long-term record of successfully matching strategy to market opportunities while utilizing a particularly strong competency in modular product design. In analyzing the key reasons underlying the firm's success, Tom Johnson and Anders Bröms return to the basic notion of how work is done:[11]

[Italics in original]

Scania, the Swedish maker of heavy-duty trucks, buses and diesel engines, has parlayed a modular product design strategy into a robust formula for low costs and sustained profitability. But modularization has contributed to Scania's high performance for more reasons than just effective design, component standardization and parts commonality. It also has created a customer-focused mode of thinking among the company's managers that is referred to as 'the spirit in the walls.' This spirit supports a unique web of relationships with patterns that transmit profit-enhancing behavior among Scania people.

... Their approach to modularization enables them to build increasingly complex varieties of consumer-pleasing products and services upon a foundation of exceedingly parsimonious means. More than anything else, their ability to execute results that are 'rich in ends, but simple in means' accounts for Scania's remarkable success.

... However, it is not well understood that cost-driver information may capture only a small fraction of the financial improvement that part-number austerity makes possible. This is because such information assumes a linear and essentially static relationship between costs and part-number count. It focuses attention on what work to do — reduce the number of different part numbers — but it implicitly assumes that continuing to pursue business as usual is *how* work is to be done. In other words, activity-based cost-driver information tells managers to reduce costs by eliminating a cost driver (such as part numbers); it does not necessarily provoke inquiry into how a company's *modus operandi* causes part-number count to affect profitability. Managers who are driven by these cost-based targets to economize on part numbers, but who still conduct business as usual, never will know if a different approach to doing business might reduce part numbers and yield even deeper and longer-lasting financial improvement.

... It is inconceivable that top-down cost-focused pressure to reduce part proliferation could have generated the disciplined and persistent campaign of experimentation and testing that Scania's design engineers carried out in the name of component standardization over the past few decades. That campaign is an indication that the difference in Scania's overall financial performance comes from people attending to patterns in *how* things are done. They do much more than focus, in the name of results-oriented targets, on *what* is done.

... The spirit of disciplined service engendered in Scania's management by modular thinking is quite different from the spirit that finance-oriented manage-by-results thinking has engendered in most business in America and Europe during the past three to four decades. Most European and American companies, in contrast to Scania, manage by results, not by pattern (or process). They leave the determination of *how* things are done to the whim of each individual worker or manager. Employees are told to pursue cost or profit targets by manipulating people and processes, not by mastering the discipline of a standardized pattern of work. In other words, the *means* is subordinated to the *end*. To manage by pattern, however, implies giving priority to the means. This makes every act valuable in its own right, not just something to finish while racing mindlessly to reach an end result down the road.

The example of Scania illustrates the importance of committing to a lasting process for improving how work is done. It also suggests that internal performance measurement poses formidable challenges and exciting opportunities for total-system-type accounting data. Rather than rely on 'sophisticated' valuation/measurement systems that blindly use conventional accounting value drivers, managements should seek to develop measurement systems that initially might provide only rough answers concerning tough issues, but answers that are in the right direction and are useful because the systems deal meaningfully with valuation effects. Over time, precision of the measurement procedures, like other processes, can be improved.

Managerial skill: learning organization

Ray Stata, CEO of Analog Devices, is in the forefront of implementing systems thinking and positioning the firm as a learning organization — one of the five key responsibilities comprising managerial skill. We share Stata's concern for *business processes* (see control variables in Figure 9.1) as a cornerstone of learning organizations.[12]

> I would place greater emphasis on process standardization, improvement, and redesign as a cornerstone in building learning organizations. Business processes define the ways people interact as well as the information content of these interactions in order to achieve intended results. Often these processes are ill-defined or even random in nature, especially between functions and organizations. If that is the case, it is difficult to discover or create new ways to improve the interactions. Standardized processes, improved continuously and occasionally redesigned, can be powerful vehicles through which to discover new insights about how organizations behave, and, as a result, to modify behavior and improve performance. Standardized processes also provide effective means for transferring best practice experiences from one organization to another.

In 1989, Stata authored an insightful article, 'Organizational Learning — The Key to Management Innovation,' which described the central elements in significantly improving efficiency and accelerating Analog Device's progress as a learning organization. (Figure 2.19B, page 49, displays the surge in Analog's CFROIs during the late 1980s and into the 1990s.) The following excerpt reinforces the role of feedback and adaptation and the importance of awareness regarding strongly held assumptions, which may be the root causes of today's problems or of missed opportunities.[13]

[Italics added]

> My approach to strategic planning for our most recent five-year plan, 1988 to 1992, was strongly influenced by discussions with Arie deGues in the New Management Style Project. In a recent article, deGeus suggested that the benefits accruing from planning are not just the objectives and strategies that emerge, but the learning that occurs during the planning process. He contends that one form of organizational learning results from *understanding the changes occurring in the external environment and then adapting beliefs and behavior to be compatible with those changes.* If learning is a goal, then the way you structure the planning process and who you involve in it can make an important difference.
>
> Analog Devices is a highly decentralized company; in the past top management set the broad corporate objectives and assumptions, but most of the detailed strategic planning was carried out in the divisions. But this time, in order to encourage organizational learning, we formed fifteen corporate wide product, market, and technology task forces that drew together 150 professionals from throughout the company. We wanted to better understand the opportunities we faced as a corporation and how we needed to change to fully exploit those opportunities. The result of twelve months of deliberations was a delineation of nine

imperatives for change, as well as specific recommendations for how to bring about those changes. An even more important result was that a broad cross-section of our top professionals understood why some *basic beliefs and assumptions* that had served us well in the past needed modification.

For example, one of our *strongest beliefs* was that the best way to organize our resources was to use relatively small, autonomous divisions. However, as we worked our way through the planning process, it became clear to all of us that our most fanatical commitment to decentralization was impeding progress.

... Another *strong belief* that melted under scrutiny was that we had to choose between a proprietary, differentiated product strategy and a low-cost producer strategy. This either/or choice has proven to be a false and misleading alternative not only for Analog Devices, but for many other US companies, as well.

Intangible assets and valuation

Implications for accounting systems

In the Information Age, more and more firms are making greater expenditures for intangible assets that are not part of GAAP data. In the case of American Standard, as employees gain expertise in demand flow processes and leverage their knowledge throughout the firm, the increasing stock of intellectual capital will not appear on the balance sheet. Note that as the know-how in process technology increases, less tangible assets are needed for any given level of output.

What are the implications for the accounting system of the increasing importance of intangible assets as the Information Age continues to evolve? We now offer some thoughts about these accounting challenges — again from a total-system perspective.

Consider these thorny intangibles issues: (1) Management must decide how much to budget for a new employee training program, if anything. (2) Often times, firms are acquired at substantial premiums for their acknowledged brand names. Is it misleading to expense advertising outlays that create brand names? (3) Consider 3M's policy of encouraging its technical staffers to devote 15 per cent of their time to any research they believe to be important. How should the 15 per cent of employee costs be treated for accounting purposes?

Three basic approaches

We can think of three basic approaches to handling these kinds of intangible outlays. One, stick with GAAP accounting to measure effects. In practice, this typically means minimizing accounting costs.[14] Two, implement accounting rules that are presumed to resolve GAAP shortcomings, e.g., capitalize and amortize R&D expense, employee training, advertising, and the like. And three, use qualitative, intuitive judgement.

With approach two (capitalize and amortize), outside security analysts or inside managers adjust the balance sheet and income statement so that an adjusted return-on-capital-employed can be calculated, which then can be run through a valuation model. The result is often touted as an economic analysis adjusted for GAAP distortions. The serious problem here is the tendency for the accounting rules to become mindlessly applied, even when they are arbitrary, much as how goodwill is treated under GAAP. The resulting valuation analysis has a veneer of sophistication, but it can easily be significantly misleading.

Let us consider 'brand names' to illustrate our point. Brand-name value suggests that advertising expenses can have a future benefit, but how advertising expenses should be capitalized and amortized is not straightforward. Depending on the intensity of competing-brands' advertising and the strength of the particular brand name, it seems probable that some portion of advertising expenses is necessary to realize the forecasted NCR stream from *existing* assets. In other words, some portion of the future benefit may already be captured in a favorable wind-down pattern used in the forecasted NCRs from existing assets. Moreover, if the firm's track record of superior CFROIs is forecasted to continue via forecasted superior ROIs on future investments, that, too, may be due to the firm's reputation, and/or product brand name. In such instance, the *future* benefit of the brand name is handled explicitly by a slower fade rate for ROIs on future investments. With this approach, the brand name could be valued as the difference between warranted values from forecasted NCR streams with and without the brand name.

Approach more important than precision

Let us discuss how these three approaches would address 3M's 15 per cent policy. Over the last 20 years, CFROIs for 3M have been well above average at approximately 10 per cent and have held there—an impressive achievement for a very large firm. It is generally acknowledged by 3M's top management, its employees, and those who research the firm that 3M's superior economic performance is driven by a steady stream of innovative products from a platform of core technological capabilities. These capabilities are attributable in large measure to the 15 per cent rule, coupled with an ongoing corporate goal of delivering a high per cent of sales from products recently developed. Question: How should the 15 per cent of employees' time be treated?

Approach one above would lower net income by the full amount of employee salary costs and would ignore the future benefit. Approach two would recognize the future benefit, but would require the use of a set rule for capitalizing and amortizing the time employees devote to their personal 'skunk works'. Approach three, 'gut feel', is not so lacking of rationality as it might first appear. Management of 3M initiated this 15 per cent rule as part of a process for promoting innovation to keep 3M at an above-average level of performance. They succeeded. What is more important to 3M's success, the innovation process or the precision of the accounting treatment? *The central criterion for internal accounting treatments should be how well the proposed treatment helps improve the business processes that drive the accounting results.*

Learning from the market

In dealing with non-GAAP/soft assets we should keep firmly in mind that stock prices over time do, in fact, represent astute forecasts of future NCR streams, which incorporate the effects of outlays for non-GAAP assets. Much research is needed to better understand how the market values complex, hard-to-analyze, intellectual-capital-intensive firms. Such an effort requires explicit valuation models, not merely excess-shareholder-return studies that can be conveniently produced via regression equations. The empirical feedback we have in mind would reveal the kinds of information investors need to improve their decision making, their valuations of firms. This approach stands in sharp contrast to deciding *the* best way to handle an accounting treatment solely on the basis of logical arguments.

Management of Thermo Electron found a highly effective solution for the interrelated problems of employee motivation/compensation and the valuation of its early-stage business units that were contributing to dismal accounting earnings. Management was convinced that these businesses were creating value which was obviously unrecognized in their earnings. Thermo Electron spun out these businesses as publicly traded firms, while retaining a controlling interest. As publicly traded businesses, the ongoing development programs of these intellectual-capital-intensive firms receive intensive scrutiny and are directly appraised via stock prices.

Asking the right question

For significant issues involving soft numbers, we suggest that the softer the number, the more one should be inclined to avoid capital-izing and amortizing and, instead, to explicitly assess the benefits in terms of the CFROI fade rate. The issue should not be framed: What is the best way to capitalize and amortize intangible assets? The right question is: What is the best way to develop a learning process for estimating the contribution of soft assets to firms' warranted market value, and then to accelerate the realization of these values?

We believe it would be useful if there were greater acknowledgement that (a) our current knowledge about how market valuations are impacted by investments in intangible assets is quite limited; (b) the problem is extraordinarily difficult and thus open-minded inquiry is warranted; and (c) progress would be accelerated by empirical analysis in connection with specified valuation models that address the *level* of firms' market values, as well as *changes* in their values.

Managements may have enough relevant *internal* information to develop workable capitalization and amortization schedules for some intangible outlays that involve future benefits. Nevertheless, we believe it is a mistake for the accounting rule-making organizations to hard-wire rules for treating intangible assets in *external* financial statements. The accounting profession should avoid rules for capitalization and amortization which result in aggregated information that reduces potentially useful data for specific valuation models being developed by investors.

The above argues for the accounting governing bodies to encourage or to require firms to disclose detailed supplementary information about intellectual capital and related intangible assets. For example, this information would show which business units account for what portions of the total R&D expense, and would break out R&D by useful classifications. Investors would then be able to incorporate R&D information into their valuation models in ways that they *learn* are most insightful and useful. We would expect sophisticated investors to continually modify and improve how soft numbers are used in their valuation analyses, and their practices could be feedback for use in further changes to the information disclosed.

Our view is compatible with a 1996 proposal by former SEC commissioner Steven Wallman:[15]

[Italics in original]

... We need to move towards a model where financial statements and related disclosures are viewed more as different layers of information—just as a finely textured color picture can provide more information than a black and white representation.

... In this model, the primary focus is on providing *relevant* information, with specification of both the items to be reported and the form and level of assurance of these items. The most relevant and reliably measured items would represent the core of the financial reports—the clear black and white, with no shades of gray or color—similar to the recognized content of the financial statement items in today's model.

Successive outer layers of the financial reporting picture would consist of information that meet some—but not all—of the requirements of recognition, or that are not as susceptible to verification procedures.

Under this approach, instead of starting with the question of whether an item must be recognized in the financial statements, the first question would be whether an item should be part of the firm's financial disclosure, with a progression then to a discussion of the appropriate layer in which the item should be reported. Such a framework—where the different layers of information could reflect, in essence, different levels of satisfaction of the traditional recognition criteria concepts (e.g., relevance, reliability, measurability), or could reflect entirely different concepts—will be useful in progressing beyond the current recognition versus non-recognition debates.

Internal performance measurement challenge

A learning process

Internal performance measurement is not merely a task of arranging some accounting variables and some non-accounting variables into a scorecard. It involves inquiry into how work is done and how the firm as a total system can improve. It involves a bridge from the CFROI valuation model (long-term NCR forecasts) through conventional accounting data to non-accounting data, including process-oriented measurements. It involves a learning process in which valuation and economic trade-offs play a central role in the evolution of improvements in both company-specific internal measurements and in GAAP-based financial statements.

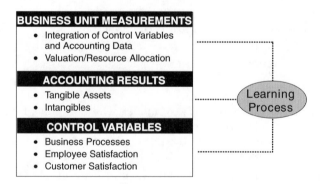

Figure 9.3   Internal performance measurement challenge.

In Figure 9.3, accounting results are explicitly separated from the control variables related to business processes, employee satisfaction, and customer satisfaction. The *ideal* internal performance measurement system uses accounting data creatively to bring a needed *economic rationality* to decision-making. This is the only way to progressively improve decisions about the right amount of employee training, advertising, product quality, and the like.

Kim Clark and Takahiro Fujimoto described how Japanese car manufacturers sometimes have expanded consumer choice (product quality) with too little regard for cost.[16] This is a recipe for increasing market share while accepting less-than-satisfactory CFROIs. Efficiency in allocating the firm's resources (and by extension, the economy's resources) requires the discipline of expected ROI in relation to cost of capital. Even quality, the most sacred cow of today's devotion to customer satisfaction, needs an economic cost-benefit test.

The bullet-point item of Valuation/Resource Allocation is included in Figure 9.3 to stress the importance of not burying economic/valuation issues within some arbitrary rules for capitalization. Ever-changing and difficult-to-handle issues, such as the examples involving intangible assets discussed earlier, require a commitment to a learning process for measurement itself.

The CFROI valuation model facilitates the measurement of warranted value and change in it. But the benefits that come from *completeness* of the CFROI valuation model entail a cost of not offering *simple* valuation guidelines within business units.

The internal performance measurement challenge is threefold:

(1) to continually learn how control variables relate to accounting information,
(2) to use accounting information to improve the business processes that produce the accounting results, and
(3) to connect detailed valuation analysis being made at higher levels of the firm with more simple resource allocation guidelines at lower levels.

Looking ahead

CFROI model's improvement process

Anyone who has had upper-level corporate management responsibility, and anyone who has had experience in analyzing the fundamental performance of companies and valuing their stocks, will have a deep appreciation for the difficulty of managing a company and achieving a long-term record of success. Complexity and uncertainty abounds in the trade-offs, both short-run and long-run, that have to be made among stakeholder interests in the pursuit of the goal of maximizing shareholder value. Then there is the dynamic dimension — everything is in a state of change, requiring continual identification of the changes, weighing their significance, and then appropriately adapting to them. Plainly, companies have to learn and adapt — or fail. And so do those of us seeking to better understand how to assess and value company performance.

The CFROI valuation model in its current stage of development at HOLT Value Associates has been described in this book. Users of this model gain insights and increased accuracy while developing a deeper understanding of the complexities of corporate performance/valuation. The completeness of the model facilitates both identifying measurement problems and developing useful solutions.

As this book is being written, HOLT Value Associates has approximately 250 worldwide money management firms as clients. A companion book being written by William Mahoney, *CFROI Portfolio Management: Buy, Sell, Hold .... How Money Managers Use CFROI to Help Decide*, presents case studies of money managers' application of HOLT's CFROI valuation model and database in their buy/hold/sell decision making. For many of these clients, HOLT is the single biggest research outlay in their budgets. These are no-nonsense, demanding clients whose job performance depends on the reliability of their valuation analyses of companies on a worldwide basis. They do not engage HOLT merely to process the calculations discussed in earlier chapters.

Rather, HOLT is a source of insights and new perspectives arising from our continued efforts to improve the model's calculation procedures for both corporate performance measurement and valuation. This effort involves: an endless stream of company-specific conceptual issues; over-riding subtle input data errors; myriad international accounting issues, which are beyond coverage in this book; and ongoing basic research. Basic research entails, among other things, grappling with challenging issues such as risk differentials, fade rates, market-derived discount rates for countries, intangible assets such as goodwill, R&D expenditures, analyzing write-offs to better judge ROIs on future investments, and improving forecast procedures for natural resource and financial firms. Work is progressing on refining the CFROI metric to better address: leasing businesses, substantial depreciating assets having unusually short or long asset lives, and highly specialized accounting, such as encountered in the entertainment industry. Finally, we strive to make the HOLT CFROI valuation model more valuable as a thinking apparatus by improving our proprietary *ValueSearch* and LIVM™ products and database that cover most publicly traded firms of investment interest in all major countries.

Our purpose in describing HOLT's business is not to insert a commercial plug. We are suggesting that advances in linking corporate performance to valuation and progress in handling tough issues requires intensive, company-specific empirical feedback, the kind that generally is missing from the statistical manipulations that constitute empirical support in academic studies. With *ValueSearch*, clients can investigate the differences between model-generated warranted values and actual stock prices and can incorporate their own forecast data and over-rides. Consequently, security analysts and portfolio managers with in-depth knowledge of companies in particular countries actively *participate* in problem recognition→ hypotheses testing→ empirical feedback→ that is, the knowledge improvement loop.

HOLT Alliance Services, a separate business unit of HOLT Value Associates, serves corporate management needs through a broad array of strategic alliances. As the HOLT framework is more widely employed in corporate applications, we fully expect it will become the global standard for benchmarking and valuation. The same knowledge-building loop involving stock-market feedback will be used with a new group of hard-nosed, demanding corporate clients with in-depth knowledge of the measurement problems within their firms. We anticipate bringing valuation insights, rooted in the ideas presented in this book, to the task of connecting non-accounting control variables with accounting data in ways that lead to improved value-creating corporate decisions. Better understanding of treatments for non-GAAP assets will also carry over into valuation insights for our portfolio managers. Corporate managers will benefit from increased valuation accuracy through an interface that makes operational, at the business unit level, the full benefit of the CFROI valuation model. That interface will also facilitate simplifications of the CFROI valuation model, as needed, to fully integrate shareholder-value-based management throughout the firm.

Readers interested in ongoing updates on HOLT's activities and access to DualGrade® Scorecard data can tap into *http://www.holt value.com*. I would appreciate and benefit from receiving your comments and criticisms on material covered in this book. My e-mail address is *bmadden@holtvalue.com*.

Chapter notes

Chapter 1

1. The comments here about knowledge do not address full-range philosophical issues of what knowledge is. For an extensive description of, and argument for, the type of inquiry and knowledge with which we substantially agree, see Paul Kurtz, *The New Skepticism: Inquiry and Reliable Knowledge*, Prometheus Books, Buffalo, New York, 1992.

2. For some situations, 'desired' could be a misleading modifier of 'results'. Take hurricanes, for example. Humans cannot take action to control or eliminate them (the ultimate desired result), but with improved hurricane-forecasting techniques, humans can take action to avoid the loss of lives and reduce property damage. Both highly desired results.

3. Thomas Lys and Linda Vincent, 'An analysis of Value Destruction in AT&T's Acquisition of NCR,' *Journal of Financial Economics*, Vol. 39, 1995, 353–378.

4. See Hadley Cantril, Adelbert Ames, Jr., Albert H. Hastorf, and William H. Ittelson, 'Psychology and Scientific Research, Part I, The Nature of Scientific Inquiry,' *Science*, November 4, 1949, Vol. 110, for an illuminating discussion on improving the knowledge base. The following excerpt (p. 462) is consistent with the Knowledge and Action System diagram of Figure 1.1.

> What man brings to any concrete event is, then, an accumulation of assumptions, of awarenesses, and of knowledge concerning the relatively determined aspects of his environment as derived from his past experiences. But since the environment through which man carries out his life transactions is constantly changing, any person is constantly running into hitches and trying to do away with them. The assumptive world a person brings to the 'now' of a concrete situation cannot disclose to him the undetermined significances continually emerging. And so we run into hitches in everyday life because of our inadequate understanding of the

conditions giving rise to a phenomenon, and our ability to act effectively for a purpose becomes inadequate.

When we try to grasp this inadequacy intellectually and get at the why of the ineffectiveness of our purposeful action, we are adopting the attitude of scientific inquiry... [S]cience is an activity designed by man to increase the reliability and verifiability of his assumptive world ... [R]eal progress in any science involves an awareness of our assumptive worlds, a consciousness of their inadequacy, and a constant, self-conscious attempt to change them, so that the intellectual abstractions they contain will achieve increasing breadth and usefulness.

5. 'Warranted value' means the value calculated from use of the model; it should not be uncritically read as 'the right' value.
6. See Gordon Donaldson, 'A New Tool for Boards: The Strategic Audit,' *Harvard Business Review*, July–August, 1995, 99–107.
7. Insightful discussions of the pitfalls of internal accounting control systems and the need for a total system approach are presented in H. Thomas Johnson, *Relevance Regained: From Top-down Control to Bottom-up Empowerment*, New York: The Free Press, 1992.
8. The following two articles contain useful empirical research on the valuation effects of 'soft' assets:
   Eli Amir and Baruch Lev, 'Value-relevance of non-financial information: The wireless communications industry,' *Journal of Accounting and Economics*, Vol. 22, 1996, 3–30.
   Baruch Lev and Theodore Sougiannis, 'The capitalization, amortization, and value-relevance of R&D,' *Journal of Accounting and Economics*, Vol. 21, 1996, 107–138.
   The implications of soft assets, or knowledge, on the wealth creation ability of an economy are covered in Paul Romer, 'Idea gaps and object gaps in economic development,' *Journal of Monetary Economics*, Vol. 32, 1993, 543–573.

Chapter 2

1. Strictly speaking, the achieved real ROIs (return on investments) for a collection of projects should be compared to each project's risk-adjusted, real discount rate. The intent here is to present a workable definition of economic performance at a broad level. We are not proposing ROI replace net present value for detailed capital budgeting analysis.
2. The model firm in Exhibit 2.4 uses a 6.5 per cent real project ROI and a life of 15 years, 20 per cent of current-dollar gross assets is non-depreciating and released in the fifteenth year, and gross cash flows are equal over the project life. Straight-line

depreciation is used. Debt has a maturity equal to the project life and pays nominal interest at the rate corresponding to the long-term bond yield for the year of issuance.

The annual real asset growth rate is three per cent, which determines the constant-dollar investment outlays for each year's new plant and related net working capital. Nominal outlays are computed consistent with the time series of inflation rates. Common dividends represent 25 per cent of the sum of net income plus depreciation. Debt approximates 35 per cent of as-reported net assets.

The model firm takes 15 years (project life) to build up to a full portfolio of projects; this covers the years 1889 to 1903. Beginning in 1904, year-by-year additions to plant and new debt also involve plant retirements and debt repayments. Equity financing and share repurchase are the year-by-year balancing variables; for the assumptions employed, these amounts are quite small.

3. George Stigler, *Capital and Rates of Return in Manufacturing Industries*, Princeton: Princeton University Press, 1963, 54.

4. The growth rate (g) in the Relative Wealth Index involves a multiplicative relationship. If 10 per cent per year was the total shareholder return when the S&P 500 provided a 5 per cent per year return, then $1.10 = (1 + g)(1.05)$. Hence, $g = 4.76$ per cent per year. The Relative Wealth Index increases from 1.00 to 1.0476, which is 1.05 rounded.

Chapter 3

1. Although capital suppliers' NCRs do in fact equal the firm's NCRs, it does not necessarily follow that investors will achieve 'above-average' returns from buying shares in 'well managed' firms; i.e., those earning high returns on capital. There is the matter of the firm's cost for its assets differing from the price investors pay to have a claim on the firm's assets. When the firm's total value (debt and equity) coincides with the firm's net assets (book cost) at time of purchase and time of sale, then the return earned by the firm on its capital equals the return achieved by the capital suppliers. Such a situation almost never occurs. The market values of well-managed high-return firms are much higher than the cost of assets, and the reverse holds for low-return firms.

2. This framework was originally developed in Merton H. Miller and Franco Modigliani, 'Dividend Policy, Growth, and the Valuation of Shares,' *Journal of Business*, October, 1961, 411–433.

Chapter 4

1. In calculating a real rate of change for an annual period, the inflation index, or price deflator, is used to express an end-of-year number in units of purchasing power that match the beginning-of-year number. For simplicity, this precise calculation was not used in Figures 4.2 and 4.3 in order to focus on the key concepts using rounded dollar figures to approximate the effects of inflation and taxes.

2. On a year-to-year basis, aggregate CFROIs for a universe of firms will vary from their long-term level. Detailed measurement of firms' fade rates towards a long-term average (approximating the cost of capital) needs to compensate for year-to-year movements in aggregate CFROIs.

3. Constructing a demanded real equity discount rate is a complex problem. The calculation logic based on maximum tax bracket investors is a useful *starting point*. Complicating issues include investors with lower tax rates (e.g., non-taxable); the appropriate holding period assumptions; and the potential for personal tax rates to be correlated with corporate sector profitability (e.g., low capital gains tax rates being associated with less government regulations).

   Charles G. Callard has done significant research on the effects of personal tax rate changes on market-demanded discount rates. For a brief overview, see his 'Tax premiums available for tax-exempt investors may help offset inflation,' *Pensions & Investments*, October 13, 1980.

4. A more sophisticated model of inflation expectations has not yet been pursued. One reason is the calculation of a warranted value for a firm uses a company-specific discount rate which is the market discount rate plus a risk differential. The derivation of a market discount rate does not require an estimate of inflation expectations because it is based on a forecasted NCR stream that is in constant dollars.

5. The nominal A-rated corporate bond yield was 7.3 per cent (N). Inflation expectations were 3.0 per cent (I). The real debt rate was $(1 + N)/(1 + I)$ or 4.2 per cent. Using the weighted average equation of Figure 4.10 with a market rate of 4.8 per cent and 25 per cent weight for debt and 75 per cent weight for equity, a real equity rate of 5.0 per cent was computed.

6. Financial leverage is measured as the percentage of debt to total market value (debt and equity). Debt is calculated as Total Debt less Pension Debt as explained in Chapter 5 (see Figure 5.16).

7. The potential to lower firms' cost of capital by reducing trans-actions costs in trading stocks seems not to be widely appre-ciated. Recent regulatory changes in the US that force Nasdaq market-makers to display orders which are between their bid-ask spreads should reduce trading costs for retail investors in particular. The potential benefits from periodic, single-price call auctions for Nasdaq stocks is discussed in Bartley J. Madden and Ernest P. Welker, 'Give Small Investors an Alternative to Nasdaq,' *Wall Street Journal*, 16 January 1995.

    Money managers trading large blocks of stock on the NYSE and elsewhere incur excess trading costs as they attempt to move a block without revealing the sizes of their orders. The NYSE could choose to address this 'problem' from the customers' perspective and upset the status quo of their specialist system. This is not a likely choice, unless competition forces the exchange to adapt. A simple mechanism, 'Yellow Light Trading,' to solve the confiden-tiality problem of large orders was detailed in Bartley J. Madden, 'Structural Changes in Trading Stocks,' *Journal of Portfolio Mana-gement*, Volume 20, No. 1, Fall, 1993, pp. 19–27. A vastly more complicated version of this idea is represented by OptiMark's supercomputer trade matching system scheduled to be launched soon on the Pacific Stock Exchange.

8. Bartley J. Madden, 'The CFROI Valuation Model,' *Journal of In-vesting*, Spring, 1998, Vol. 7, No. 1, 31–44.

Chapter 5

1. Pamela P. Peterson and David R. Peterson, 'Company Performance and Measures of Value Added,' The Research Foundation of the Institute of Chartered Financial Analysts, AIMR, 1996.
2. The example is hypothetical. Technically, a one-year-life machine is expensed. Let's assume the machine has a life of one year plus one day and therefore is depreciated.
3. Would non-comparable measurement be used in engineering and the sciences in general? No engineer would divide 12 feet by 4 inches and claim that the answer 3 has useful content. Yet, many valuation models hinge on the relationship between the conventional CAPM/beta estimate of the firm's *nominal* cost of capital and the firm's accounting return, which is *not* a pure nominal number. The accounting return, which is typi-cally calculated as the sum of net income and of interest divided by net assets, has net plant in the denominator. The net plant amount is an aggregation of expenditures made with dollars of

varied purchasing power. So, the economic-value-added spread, measured as accounting return less cost of capital, lacks consistency of measurement units. This problem is acute with long-term time series; it is less severe if inflation has been close to zero over the life of the plant account.

4. Hershey carried a 'AA-' corporate debt rating in 1993. This gave a 7.4 per cent nominal debt rate. Inflation expectations (Figure 4.8) were 3.4 per cent. The calculated real debt rate was 1.074/1.034, or 3.9 per cent.

5. Clifford F. Ranson III and James C. Lucas, 'Special Situations Report: Danaher Corporation,' NatWest Securities, 31 January 1997.

6. HOLT's calculation of gross cash flow does not add back deferred taxes reflected in the income statement, which make cash taxes paid less than book taxes. For consistency, the associated deferred tax liability recorded on the balance sheet is not considered a debt claim—which, all else equal, would reduce the firm's warranted *equity* value. The primary reason HOLT has adopted this treatment is to improve forecasts of CFROI fade. In Chapter 7, we review empirical results that link actual CFROI fade rates to management's demonstrated skill at controlling operations as reflected by CFROI variability over time. We found that the add-backs for deferred taxes increased CFROI variability and constituted 'noise' from the perspective of assessing management's control over operational results. Analysts implementing CFROI might reasonably employ other ways of handling this and other variables. The essential point is to maintain a total system perspective and logical consistency among variables.

Chapter 6

1. G. Bennett Stewart, III, *The Quest for Value*, New York: Harper Collins, 1991.

Chapter 7

1. Longer track records of performance recorded by performance metrics that are not rigorously adjusted for inflation are unreliable as indicators of future performance, because users cannot gauge for different sub-periods of the past the degree to which the record reflected the firm's economic performance or the

currency's performance. Short-period track records have limited usefulness as indicators of management skill simply because they are too short to reveal much about long-term performance. The unreliability of such other metrics as measures of *economic* performance is unavoidably carried over into inaccuracy of valuation models that incorporate those metrics.

2. Valuation of business firms is an extraordinarily complex task. As the Information Age accelerates, firms are utilizing proportionately more intangible assets and less hard assets which are recorded in GAAP financial statements.

    Internet firms such as America Online and Yahoo!, and biotechnology firms with massive R&D outlays such as Agouron Pharmaceuticals and Human Genome Sciences represent businesses that involve little in the way of hard assets. Although the basic underpinnings of the CFROI valuation model are applicable to these Information Age firms, much needs to be learned. For example, R&D is expensed in the current HOLT model and users adjust for more or less successful R&D programs by forecasting a more or less favorable CFROI fade rate. R&D outlays pose deep valuation problems. What kind of R&D is the firm involved in — a one-shot chance at a home run drug, or an extensive R&D program which builds up an enabling technology platform that addresses a portfolio of drug candidates? For a specified treatment of R&D, what are the implications for CFROI fade rates and the related forecast wind-down pattern of cash flows from existing assets? What are the implications for discount rate risk differentials? One wants to develop improved procedures for handling R&D that are logically sound and improve the historical tracking of actual stock prices versus warranted values.

    Ongoing progress at HOLT on basic research issues, including R&D, fade rates, risk differentials, and a host of issues related to more difficult-to-analyze firms will change the model's current numerical processes. What does not change is the underlying framework for how the NCR stream and the discount rate interrelate. Consequently, our treatment of some of HOLT's specific estimating procedures in Chapter 7 is somewhat abbreviated. The emphasis is on important calculations requiring critical thinking, not on mindless computations.

3. Bartley J. Madden, 'The CFROI Life Cycle,' *Journal of Investing*, Summer 1996, Vol. 5, No. 2, 10–20.

4. Appendix D describes a procedure for estimating retirements that has logic similar to that used for adjusting the plant account to current dollars (see Appendix B).

5. Donaldson does not have any significant amount of goodwill. If it did a judgement would be required about ROIs on new investments versus CFROIs calculated with and without goodwill (see 'Key issues concerning intangibles/goodwill,' beginning on page 119).

   If R&D expense (or other soft-asset outlays) has been capitalized as part of Intangibles, the assigned amortization schedule provides an estimate of retirements. This is a complex issue and should not be treated casually. Chapter 5 describes the issues of purchase accounting and goodwill. Retirements of acquisition goodwill included in Intangibles is not straightforward. It requires in-depth analysis of the details of each situation.

6. For example, if the real historical growth was zero, asset life was four years, and zero CFROI fade was forecasted, then one-fourth of the cash flow in year 0 would be a receipt [line (7), Figure 7.9] in years $+1, +2, +3$, and $+4$. Also, one-fourth of the non-depreciating assets in year 0 would be a receipt, line (8), in years $+1, +2, +3$, and $+4$.

   In *ValueSearch* software, a real historical asset growth rate is computed and used as a proxy for plant age. This procedure has proven to be quite useful for publicly available data. If detailed information is available concerning the productive capacity and economic life of individual portions of the plant account, this information can improve the forecast and should be used.

7. On a per share basis the total firm market value is 23.64 comprised of 22.53 equity market value and 1.11 debt. The per share estimate for existing assets is 642/49.45, or 12.98. Consequently the implied value of future investments is $23.64-12.98$, or 10.66. On a percentage basis, 10.66 compared to the total firm value of 23.64 is 45 per cent which can be reconciled with the 45 % Future for Donaldson shown in the DualGrade®, Appendix C, page 300. Donaldson had a two-for-one split in January 1998. This split was incorporated into the per share data presented in Chapter 7.

Chapter 8

1. H. M. Markowitz, 'Portfolio Selection,' *Journal of Finance*, Vol. 7, 1952, 77–91.
2. William F. Sharpe, 'Capital Asset Prices: A Theory of Market Equilibrium under Conditions of Risk,' *Journal of Finance*, Vol. 19, No. 3, September 1964, 425–442.

3. Ronald Coase interviewed by Thomas W. Hazlett, 'Looking for Results,' *Reason,* January 1997, 40–46.
4. Milton Friedman, 'The Methodology of Positive Economics,' pp. 3–43 in *Essays in Positive Economics*, Chicago: University of Chicago Press, 1953, page 15.

Friedman's 1953 essay, 'The Methodology of Positive Economics,' probably has led to more controversy than any other published article in economics. In his own research, Friedman has certainly concerned himself with empirical feedback. But others seem to have used the 'as if' methodology to justify any and all types of elaborate mathematical model building. The following quote from Friedman's paper seems to me to be at the heart of how researchers, especially finance academics, use the 'as if' argument to avoid methodological criticism:

> Viewed as a body of substantive hypotheses, theory is to be judged by its predictive power for the class of phenomena which it is intended to 'explain'... The only relevant test of the validity of a hypothesis is comparison of its predictions with experience. (pp. 8–9)

In 'A Transactional Approach to Economic Research,' (*Journal of Socio-Economics*, 1991, Vol. 20, No. 1, 57–71) I commented in the final section:

[Italics in original]

> It can be argued that in many instances of complex economic phenomena, much can be learned by organizing and studying data as if certain assumptions applied. This learning opportunity need not be abandoned even though particular assumptions are inaccurate on close scrutiny. The difficulty lies in generalizing Friedman's approach as a preferred methodology for economic theory improvement. Practitioners of Friedman's positive economics all too easily construct theory by transforming strongly held beliefs from their assumptive worlds into unrealistic assumptions. They contend that their theories should be viewed as descriptions as if the assumptions were true. The argument is then made that prediction is the ultimate proving ground and, consequently, criticism of assumptions is not relevant. A skeptical attitude toward particular assumptions is labeled as a misguided attempt to test the realism of assumptions. In addition, any criticism that the selection of assumptions may erroneously fix, at an early stage, the formulation of the problem is presumably deflected by Friedman's qualifying phrase 'for the class of phenomena which it is intended to "explain".' The practical result, however, may often be to severely restrict both potential reformulations of the problem and the process of feedback-theory improvement.

Consider the following theory's superb record for prediction about when water will freeze or boil. The theory postulates that water behaves *as if* there is a water devil who gets angry at 32 degrees and 212 degrees Fahrenheit and alters the chemical state accordingly to ice or steam. In a superficial sense, the water-devil theory is successful for the immediate problem at hand. But the molecular insight that water is comprised of two molecules of hydrogen and one molecule of oxygen not only led to predictive success, but also led to 'better problems' (i.e. the growth of modern chemistry).

The transactional approach strives for theory improvement that not only improves predictive accuracy, but also nurtures further insights as to if and how variables are apparently related to the phenomena under inquiry. Strict adherence to Friedman's myopic goal of prediction can be counterproductive, because predictive accuracy may well be restricted to only a highly limited range of relevant experiential needs while hindering what should be the scientist's healthy skepticism.

pages 67–69

In personal correspondence to me, (3 April 1990), Friedman wrote, '... I have read your final section, I have no quarrel with it and it has no quarrel with me, so let us leave it at that.'

5. George M. Frankfurter and Elton G. McGoun, *Toward Finance with Meaning — The Methodology of Finance: What It Is and What It Can Be*, Greenwich, CT: JAI Press, Inc. 1996.

6. Robert A. Haugen, *The New Finance: The Case Against Efficient Markets*, Prentice Hall, 1995, 136 and 138.

7. Gabriel A. D. Preinreich, 'Valuation and Amortization,' *Accounting Review*, September 1937, 209–226.

8. E. O. Edwards and P. W. Bell, *The Theory and Measurement of Business Income*, University of California Press, 1961.

9. Stephen H. Penman, 'Return to Fundamentals,' *Journal of Accounting, Auditing, and Finance*, Fall, 1992, 465–484.

10. Some important articles concerning residual income include:
Victor L. Bernard, 'The Feltham–Ohlson Framework: Implications for Empiricists,' *Contemporary Accounting Research*, Spring, 1995, 733–747.
Gerald A. Feltham and James A. Ohlson, 'Valuation and Clean Surplus Accounting for Operating and Financial Activities,' *Contemporary Accounting Research*, Spring, 1995, 689–731.
Richard Frankel and Charles M. C. Lee, 1998, 'Accounting valuation, market expectation, and cross-sectional stock returns,' working paper, University of Michigan and Cornell University.
Richard Frankel and Charles M. C. Lee, 1997, 'Accounting diversity and international valuation,' working paper, University of Michigan and Cornell University.

Stephen Penman, 1997, 'A synthesis of equity valuation techniques and the terminal value calculation for the dividend discount model,' working paper, University of California at Berkeley.

James A. Ohlson, 'Earnings, Book Value, and Dividends in Security Valuation, *Contemporary Accounting Research*, Spring 1995, 661–687.

11.   Charles M. C. Lee, 'Measuring Wealth,' *CA Magazine*, April 1996, 32–37.

12.   Bartley J. Madden and Sam Eddins, 'Different Approaches to Measuring the Spread of Return on Capital in Relation to the Cost of Capital,' *Valuation Issues*, July/August 1996, 4–7.

13.   Eugene Fama and Kenneth French, 'The Cross-Section of Expected Stock Returns,' *Journal of Finance*, June, 1992, 427–466.

14.   Michael C. Jensen, 'Agency Costs of Free Cash Flow, Corporate Finance, and Takeovers,' *American Economic Review*, May, 1986, 323–329. This paper expounds upon a particular aspect of CFROI life cycle; namely, the restructuring (desired or forced) of firms likely to invest in below-cost-of-capital projects. This issue was also articulated by Dennis Mueller in 'A life cycle theory of the firm,' *Journal of Industrial Economics*, 20, July 1972, 199–219.

Chapter 9

1.   James C. Collins and Jerry I. Porras, *Built To Last: Successful Habits of Visionary Companies*, paperback edition, Harper Business, NY, 1997.

2.   Paul Milgrom and John Roberts, 'Complementarities and fit, strategy, structure, and organizational change in manufacturing,' *Journal of Accounting & Economics*, Vol. 19, 1995, 179–208.

3.   Richard M. Hodgetts, 'A Conversation with Donald F. Hastings of The Lincoln Electric Company,' *Organizational Dynamics*, Winter, 1997, 68–74.

4.   Demand Flow® is a registered trademark of J-I-T Institute of Technology, Inc.

5.   Peter F. Drucker, 'The Theory of the Business,' *Harvard Business Review*, September/October, 1994, 95–104.

6.   John Seely Brown, editor, *Seeing Differently: Insights on Innovation*, Harvard Business Review Book, 1997, xvi–xvii.

7. Useful guidelines for circumventing the 'emotional blinders' that interfere with strategic planning are contained in Clayton M. Christensen, 'Making Strategy: Learning By Doing,' *Harvard Business Review*, November/December, 1997, 141–156.

8. Adaptability, as we use it, is close to 'dynamic capabilities' described in an excellent article by David J. Teece, Gary Pisano and Amy Shuen, 'Dynamic Capabilities and Strategic Management,' *Strategic Management Journal*, 1997, Vol. 18:7, 509–533.

9. H. Thomas Johnson, 'Management Accounting: Catalyst for Inquiry or Weapon for Control?', *Systems Thinker*, November 1995, 1–5.

10. Peter Miller and Ted O'Leary, 'The factory as laboratory,' in *Accounting and Science: Natural Inquiry and Commercial Reason*, edited by Michael Power, Cambridge University Press, 1994, 120–150.

11. H. Thomas Johnson and Anders Bröms, 'The Spirit in the Walls: A Pattern for High Performance at Scania,' *Target*, May/June 1995, 9–17.

12. From a letter to the editor of the *Harvard Business Review*, September/October 1993, p. 190.

13. Ray Stata. 'Organizational Learning—The Key to Management Innovation,' *Sloan Management Review*, Spring 1989, 63–74.

14. For an insightful empirical study that measures the productivity effects of 'soft' human resource variables, see Casey Ichniowski, Kathryn Shaw, and Giovanna Prennushi, 'The Effects of Human Resource Management Practices on Productivity: A Study of Steel Finishing Lines,' *American Economic Review*, June, 1997, Vol. 87, No. 3, 291–313.

15. Steven M. H. Wallman, 'The Future of Accounting and Financial Reporting, Part II: The Colorized Approach,' *Accounting Horizons*, June, 1996, 138–148.

16. Kim Clark and Takahiro Fujimoto, 'The Product Department Imperative: Competing in the New Industrial Marathon,' in *The Relevance of a Decade*, edited by Paula Barker Duffy, Harvard Business School Press, Boston, 1994.

Personal tax rates and cost of capital

Figure 4.13 of Chapter 4 highlights a 7.07 per cent per year demanded real equity return in 1982. This figure was calculated for maximum tax bracket investors seeking a 3 per cent per year real, after-personal-tax return over a three year holding period. The procedure for this calculation develops anticipated tax payments as one step in determining the required real, before-personal-tax return, i.e. the 7.07 per cent return. After taxes are paid, the 7.07 per cent reduces to a 3.0 per cent return. Figure A-1 displays required before-tax real returns for different assumed holding periods and after-tax-return targets.

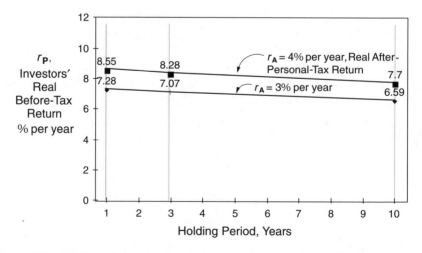

Figure A-1   1982 maximum-tax-bracket investors demanded real before-tax equity returns by holding period.

The process to calculate the 7.07 per cent before-tax return can be described in the following steps. Remember, the before-personal-tax return is the rate demanded of firms. If a firm's new investment is expected to earn an ROI equal to this demanded return, that marginal investment has a market value equal to its cost, and the investment would neither create nor destroy real wealth.

Step 1 (Figure A-2) lists the inputs. The calculation is keyed to solving for a nominal price at the end of the 3-year holding period, i.e., $P_{t=3}$.

$$r_A = \text{Demanded Real Return After Personal Taxes}$$
$$r_P = \text{Demanded Real Return Before Personal Taxes}$$
$$Y_{CAP} = \text{Capital Gains Tax Rate} = 20\%$$
$$Y_{DIV} = \text{Dividends Tax Rate} = 50\%$$
$$\Pi = \text{Inflation Expectations} = 7.7\% \text{ per year}$$
$$t = \text{Period, in years}$$
$$P_{t=0} = \text{Price of Stock at Beginning Period} = \$100$$
$$DIV_{t=0} = \text{Beginning Dividend} = \$100 \times \text{Dividend Yield S\&P}$$
$$\text{Industrials} = 100(0.0452) = \$4.52$$

Assumptions:
(1) 3-year Holding Period
(2) Constant-dollar Dividends Grow at Rate r_A
(3) $r_A = 3.0\%$ per year Real

$P_{t=3} = $ Nominal price of stock after three years, consistent with $r_A = 3.0\%$ per year

Figure A-2 Variables for calculating demanded real equity return before personal taxes.

Step 2 (Figure A-3) shows that the 3 per cent real return after taxes (r_A) requires a nominal price at year end 3 of \$134.07 ($P_{t=3} = 134.07$), based on a beginning price of 100.

		After Tax Constant Dollars		
$\$100 =$	$\dfrac{DIV_{t=0}(1+r_A)(1-Y_{DIV})}{(1+r_A)}$	$PV_{t=0}$ of $DIV_{t=1}$	$4.52(0.5)$	$= 2.26$
$+$	$\dfrac{DIV_{t=0}(1+r_A)^2(1-Y_{DIV})}{(1+r_A)^2}$	$PV_{t=0}$ of $DIV_{t=2}$	$4.52(0.5)$	$= 2.26$
$+$	$\dfrac{DIV_{t=0}(1+r_A)^3(1-Y_{DIV})}{(1+r_A)^3}$	$PV_{t=0}$ of $DIV_{t=3}$	$4.52(0.5)$	$= 2.26$
$+$	$\dfrac{P_{t=3}-(P_{t=3}-100)Y_{CAP}}{(1+\Pi)^3(1+r_A)^3}$	$PV_{t=0}$ of $Sale_{t=3}$	$\dfrac{134.07-(34.07)(0.2)}{(1.077)^3(1.03)^3} = 93.22$	
			$\overline{100}$	

Figure A-3 Calculating $P_{t=3} = \$134.07$. PV = Present Value.

Step 3 (Figure A-4) shows receipts of dividends and ending price in constant dollars without any deduction for taxes. This before-tax stream provides a present value of 100 (equaling the beginning price) when discounted at a real rate of 7.07 per cent per year.

No Taxes
Constant Dollars

$$\$100 = \frac{DIV_{t=0}(1+r_A)}{(1+r_P)} \qquad PV_{t=0} \text{ of } DIV_{t=1} \qquad \frac{4.52(1.03)}{1.0707} = 4.35$$

$$+ \frac{DIV_{t=0}(1+r_A)^2}{(1+r_P)^2} \qquad PV_{t=0} \text{ of } DIV_{t=2} \qquad \frac{4.52(1.03)^2}{(1.0707)^2} = 4.18$$

$$+ \frac{DIV_{t=0}(1+r_A)^3}{(1+r_P)^3} \qquad PV_{t=0} \text{ of } DIV_{t=3} \qquad \frac{4.52(1.03)^3}{(1.0707)^3} = 4.02$$

$$+ \frac{P_{t=3}}{(1+\Pi)^3(1+r_P)^3} \qquad PV_{t=0} \text{ of } Sale_{t=3} \qquad \frac{134.07}{(1.077)^3(1.0707)^3} = 87.44$$

100

Figure A-4   Verifying $r_P = 7.07$ per cent per year.

Inflation adjustment factors

In principle, the mark-up of historical dollars in the plant account to current dollars is a process of following the procedure shown in Figure 5.6 for each layer, or vintage, of plant. This requires knowledge of the age of each layer, which is typically unavailable to investors. A useful mathematical approximation can be derived by partitioning the plant account into layers based on: (a) gross plant life (L) and (b) a constant real asset growth rate (g) over the historical years covering the plant life. With these layers specified, the GDP Deflators are applied consistent with the procedure of Figure 5.6. CAPX is the capital expenditure outlay, or layer. Other symbols are self-evident. The derivation below constructs the plant in current-dollar layers and then derives the original-cost (historical-dollar) layers. A mark-up factor is the ratio of the total current-dollar gross plant to the total historical-dollar gross plant.

Consider a gross plant amount in current dollars where current reflects a particular year, such as 1993. The variables shown below would be stated in 1993 dollars.

Start with the identity,

$$\text{BEG PLANT} + \text{CAPX} - \text{RETIREMENT} = \text{END PLANT}$$

Assuming a constant, real historic growth rate (g) in building up the plant account, then:

$$\text{BEG PLANT} = \text{END PLANT}/(1 + g)$$

Since RETIREMENT is CAPX made L years ago:

$$\text{RETIREMENT} = \text{CAPX}/(1 + g)^{L}$$

After substitution, the beginning identity becomes the equation:

$$[\text{END PLANT}/(1+g)] + \text{CAPX} - [\text{CAPX}/(1+g)^L] = \text{END PLANT}$$

In this equation, CAPX can be solved for:

$$\text{CAPX}\left[1 - \frac{1}{(1+g)^L}\right] = \text{END PLANT}\left[1 - \frac{1}{1+g}\right]$$

$$\text{CAPX} = \text{END PLANT}\frac{\left[1 - \dfrac{1}{1+g}\right]}{\left[1 - \dfrac{1}{(1+g)^L}\right]}$$

END PLANT can be decomposed into a summation of past capital expenditures as follows:

$$\text{END PLANT}_t = \text{CAPX}_t + \text{CAPX}_{t-1} + \text{CAPX}_{t-2} + \cdots$$
$$+ \text{CAPX}_{t-L+1}$$

With the assumption of a constant, real historical asset growth rate (g) and a steady asset project life (L), and knowing CAPX, then:

$$\text{END PLANT} = \text{CAPX} + \text{CAPX}/(1+g) + \text{CAPX}/(1+g)^2 + \cdots$$
$$+ \text{CAPX}/(1+g)^{L-1}$$

In the above, END PLANT is the gross plant amount stated *in current dollars* and is the sum of the individual prior *current-dollar layers*. These layers are converted to historical cost when multiplied by the appropriate adjustment factors.

(A) Current Dollar Layers	(B) Adjustment Factor to Original Cost
CAPX_t	1.0
CAPX_{t-1}	GDP Deflator$_{t-1}$/GDP Deflator$_t$
CAPX_{t-2}	GDP Deflator$_{t-2}$/GDP Deflator$_t$
...	
CAPX_{t-L+1}	GDP Deflator$_{t-L+1}$/GDP Deflator$_t$
Current $ Gross Plant	

The summation of CAPX in (A) provides the current-dollar gross plant. The summation of each CAPX times its adjustment factor (A × B) provides the historical-dollar gross plant. Dividing current-dollar gross plant by historical-dollar gross plant yields the inflation adjustment ratio:

$$\text{Inflation Adjustment Factor} = \frac{\text{Current \$ Gross Plant}}{\text{Historical \$ Gross Plant}}$$

HOLT's DualGrade® performance scorecard, United States, December 1997

HOLT % Future Industry Summary

Data As Of 31 December, 1997
Source: Compustat and HOLT/ValueSearch™

Industry Name	Number of Firms	(a) Equity	(b) Debt	(c = a + b) Total Market Value	(d) Value Existing Assets	(e = c − d) Value Future Investments	(f = e/c) % Future
Healthcare Information Systems	8	21 187	682	21 869	5 752	16 117	74
Computer Software & Services	160	429 585	27 222	456 807	137 783	319 024	70
Beverage (Soft Drink)	6	235 429	26 872	262 301	82 375	179 925	69
Drug	47	608 928	39 927	648 855	219 991	428 865	66
Toiletries/Cosmetics	13	78 141	10 721	88 862	32 874	55 988	63
Telecommunication Equipment	37	94 780	14 019	108 799	42 995	65 804	60
Medical Supplies	76	274 364	28 213	302 577	127 308	175 269	58
Household Products	21	200 213	29 365	229 578	101 085	128 493	56
Electrical Equipment	32	332 712	39 993	372 706	171 803	200 903	54
Retail Building Supply	6	54 369	6 553	60 921	28 256	32 666	54
Entertainment	23	130 885	45 248	176 133	87 540	88 593	50
Industrial Services	80	75 277	18 402	93 680	47 675	46 004	49
Advertising	10	20 954	8 644	29 598	15 111	14 487	49
Computer & Peripherals	66	421 829	56 289	478 117	245 681	232 436	49
Newspaper	14	62 929	14 490	77 418	40 366	37 052	48
Food Processing	40	228 632	56 933	285 566	155 821	129 745	45
Semiconductor (Capital Equipment)	8	22 278	1 750	24 027	13 303	10 724	45
Drugstore	6	36 327	11 786	48 113	26 684	21 429	45
Semiconductor	41	213 155	18 250	231 406	129 918	101 488	44
Recreation	30	55 591	8 869	64 460	37 793	26 668	41
Oilfield Services	49	148 045	21 633	169 678	102 223	67 455	40
Office Equipment & Supplies	22	68 148	23 309	91 457	56 315	35 143	38

% of Total Market Value Attributed to Future Investments (% Future) — $ Billions

Tobacco	7	132 427	42 648	175 075	110 218	64 857	37
Electronics	61	62 929	10 926	73 855	47 709	26 146	35
Shoe	10	17 065	4 948	22 013	14 513	7 500	34
Manufactured Housing/Recreational Vehicles	8	7 829	572	8 401	5 570	2 831	34
Publishing	31	46 328	19 385	65 713	44 412	21 301	32
Furniture/Home Furnishings	19	17 287	4 454	21 741	14 734	7 007	32
Diversified Company	53	143 342	49 235	192 577	130 590	61 986	32
Precision Instrument	44	48 584	12 136	60 720	41 350	19 370	32
Metal Fabricating	21	29 179	5 803	34 982	24 153	10 829	31
Grocery Store	18	64 645	32 666	97 311	67 239	30 071	31
Telecommunications Services	51	538 980	151 657	690 638	483 815	206 823	30
Auto Parts (Replacement)	14	21 327	10 519	31 847	22 637	9 210	29
Retail (Special Lines)	84	107 174	53 446	160 620	115 947	44 674	28
Aerospace/Defence	26	113 590	39 332	152 922	113 162	39 760	26
Food Wholesalers	8	14 230	7 737	21 966	16 351	5 615	26
Apparel	22	22 545	7 436	29 981	22 374	7 607	25
Retail Store	38	219 439	98 694	318 134	237 612	80 522	25
Environmental	20	54 469	30 108	84 578	63 521	21 057	25
Packaging & Container	18	29 229	16 273	45 502	34 193	11 309	25
Medical Services	62	107 955	51 234	159 189	120 036	39 153	25
Hotel/Gaming	33	57 162	29 656	86 818	66 452	20 365	23
Chemical (Speciality)	55	86 359	28 968	115 327	89 777	25 550	22
Home Appliance	6	12 334	8 279	20 612	16 107	4 505	22
Chemical (Diversified)	23	89 651	30 767	120 418	96 110	24 308	20
Restaurant	35	64 063	30 597	94 660	76 739	17 921	19
Homebuilding	10	9 452	7 231	16 683	13 687	2 996	18
Beverage (Alcoholic)	7	40 586	10 306	50 892	41 976	8 916	18

(continued overleaf)

HOLT % Future Industry Summary *(continued from overleaf)*

Industry Name	Number of Firms	(a) Equity	(b) Debt	(c = a + b) Total Market Value	(d) Value Existing Assets	(e = c − d) Value Future Investments	(f = e/c) % Future
Machinery	68	104 468	37 813	142 281	118 256	24 024	17
Building Materials	28	29 331	15 791	45 122	37 728	7 395	16
Chemicals (Basic)	13	135 836	46 236	182 072	153 734	28 338	16
Auto Parts (Original Equipment)	19	32 842	17 298	50 140	42 899	7 241	14
Textile	14	9 136	5 261	14 397	12 406	1 991	14
Auto & Truck	7	135 375	128 365	263 739	241 419	22 321	8
Petroleum (Integrated)	29	432 791	156 564	589 355	564 049	25 306	4
Trucking & Transport Leasing	23	17 469	18 494	35 962	34 502	1 461	4
Cement & Aggregates	11	11 317	2 382	13 700	13 225	474	3
Air Transport	24	62 010	113 586	175 596	173 832	1 764	1
Tire & Rubber	5	14 601	6 181	20 782	20 659	124	1
Petroleum (Producing)	38	46 852	18 453	65 304	68 598	−3 293	−5
Maritime	11	6 967	9 737	16 704	17 550	−847	−5
Paper & Forest Products	41	92 499	68 629	161 128	171 720	−10 591	−7
Steel (General)	18	13 536	6 664	20 199	21 687	−1 487	−7
Natural Gas (Diversified)	30	74 479	45 041	119 520	129 415	−9 895	−8
Railroad	9	69 477	65 898	135 375	159 562	−24 186	−18
Steel (Integrated)	10	7 917	17 604	25 521	31 883	−6 363	−25
Metals & Mining (Diversified)	23	44 812	32 169	76 981	105 072	−28 092	−36
Industrial/Service Aggregate:	2000	7 313 635	2 116 346	9 429 982	6 157 830	3 272 152	35

% of Total Market Value Attributed to Future Investments (% Future)

------- $ Billions -------

HOLT DualGrade® Performance Scorecard
HOLT USA2000 - Industrial/Service, 31 December 1997

Source: Compustat and HOLT/ValueSearch™

HOLT USA2000 Universe
Size / #cos / mkt cap
Very large / 300 / $3.93B+
Large / 500 / $1.03–3.93B
Medium / 600 / $.42–1.03B
Small / 600 / $154–425M
Grouped by Forecast +1 year CFROI Grade (Near Term)
which is then sorted high-to-low on numerical % Future

			HOLT DualGrade® Performance		CFROI Cash Flow Return on Investment			% of Total Market Value Attributed to Future Investments	
			#1 Near Term Fcst +1-year CFROI Grade	#2 Long Term % Future Grade	Past 5-year Median CFROI	Forecast +1-year CFROI	Forecast +1-year CFROI Rank	% Future	% Future Rank
					Advertising Industry				
VERY LARGE (V) - 300 Cos.			*Group*				**x300 (V)**	*Sort*	**x300 (V)**
V	OMC	OMNICOM GROUP	B	B	9.5	10.3	118	57	65
V	IPG	INTERPUBLIC GROUP OF Cos.	C	B	8.8	10.0	131	55	77
LARGE (L) - 500 Cos.			*Group*				**x500 (L)**	*Sort*	**x500 (L)**
L	HHS	HARTE HANKS COMMUN INC	C	B	6.8	9.0	261	53	111
L	UOUT	UNIVERSAL OUTDOOR HLDGS INC	D	A	3.0	6.0	378	59	79
L	OSI	OUTDOOR SYSTEMS INC	E	B	6.5	4.1	452	41	180
MEDIUM (M) - 600 Cos.			*Group*				**x600 (M)**	*Sort*	**x600 (M)**
M	HMK	HA-LO INDS INC	A	A	8.6	16.7	66	60	97
M	AD	ADVO INC	A	B	10.6	17.5	56	49	163
M	AK	ACKERLEY GROUP INC	B	B	9.4	12.0	177	36	231
M	BGF	BIG FLOWER HOLDINGS INC	B	E	9.0	13.7	128	–7	537
M	TNO	TRUE NORTH COMMUNICATIONS	D	D	6.6	6.3	465	17	378
SMALL (S) - 600 Cos.			*Group*				**x600 (S)**	*Sort*	**x600 (S)**
					Aerospace/Defence Industry				
VERY LARGE (V) - 300 Cos.			*Group*				**x300 (V)**	*Sort*	**x300 (V)**
V	GD	GENERAL DYNAMICS CORP	C	C	7.0	8.7	164	31	170
V	LMT	LOCKHEED MARTIN CORP	C	D	6.7	9.2	150	20	210

(continued overleaf)

HOLT USA2000 Universe
Size / #cos / mkt cap

Very large / 300 / $3.93B+
Large / 500 / $1.03–3.93B
Medium / 600 / $.42–1.03B
Small / 600 / $.154–425M

Grouped by Forecast +1 year CFROI Grade (Near Term) which is then sorted high-to-low on numerical % Future

			HOLT DualGrade® Performance		CFROI — Cash Flow Return on Investment			% of Total Market Value Attributed to Future Investments	
			#1 Near Term Fcst +1-year CFROI Grade	#2 Long Term % Future Grade	Past 5-year Median CFROI	Forecast +1-year CFROI	Forecast +1-year CFROI Rank	% Future	% Future Rank
V	BA	BOEING CO	D	C	6.0	8.0	186	31	172
V	NOC	NORTHROP GRUMMAN CORP	D	D	1.0	7.3	201	20	212
V	GMH	GENERAL MOTORS CL H	E	D	6.4	3.8	286	18	220
LARGE (L) - 500 Cos.			**Group**				**x500 (L)**	**Sort**	**x500 (L)**
L	GAC	GULFSTREAM AEROSPACE	A	B	10.0	18.0	36	52	114
L	COT	COLTEC INDUSTRIES	A	B	15.3	13.7	98	45	155
L	SNS	SUNDSTRAND CORP	B	C	8.2	11.5	149	37	205
L	PCP	PRECISION CASTPARTS CORP	C	C	7.9	9.1	254	27	278
L	TKC	THIOKOL CP	C	C	6.5	8.9	266	27	280
L	LIT	LITTON INDUSTRIES INC	D	D	4.3	5.6	395	24	306
MEDIUM (M) - 600 Cos.			**Group**				**x600 (M)**	**Sort**	**x600 (M)**
M	BEAV	BE AEROSPACE INC	A	D	8.9	15.5	80	16	389
M	WYMN	WYMAN-GORDON CO	B	D	3.9	10.5	228	16	388
M	ATK	ALLIANT TECHSYSTEMS INC	B	D	15.0	12.2	168	15	397
M	AIR	AAR CORP	C	C	4.8	8.4	336	33	254
M	RHR	ROHR INC	C	D	5.3	9.7	270	9	451
M	ORBI	ORBITAL SCIENCES CORP	E	B	0.6	4.5	550	46	176
SMALL (S) - 600 Cos.			**Group**				**x600 (S)**	**Sort**	**x600 (S)**
S	KELL	KELLSTROM INDUSTRIES INC	B	B	7.4	13.6	123	46	125
S	DCO	DUCOMMUN INC	B	B	7.4	10.6	218	43	146
S	SDII	SPECIAL DEVICES INC	B	B	8.0	13.4	127	33	220
S	AVL	AVIALL INC	B	C	1.1	12.4	160	26	276
S	HEI	HEICO CORP	C	A	3.1	9.5	272	61	59
S	NRES	NICHOLS RESEARCH CORP	E	A	6.9	5.2	522	48	117

	Ticker	Company	Group				x###	Sort	x###
S	BAR	BANNER AEROSPACE INC	E	D	5.0	5.7	491	14	373
S	MOG.A	MOOG INC -CL A	E	D	2.8	5.5	506	2	461
S	ESE	ESCO ELECTRONICS CORP	E	E	4.8	5.5	504	-3	486

Air Transport Industry

VERY LARGE (V) - 300 Cos. — Group | | | | x300 (V) | Sort | x300 (V)

	Ticker	Company	Group				x300 (V)	Sort	x300 (V)
V	U	US AIRWAYS GROUP INC	C	D	1.9	8.8	158	12	237
V	LUV	SOUTHWEST AIRLINES	D	E	5.0	6.2	234	9	244
V	NWAC	NORTHWEST AIRLINES CORP	D	E	6.8	7.9	187	2	259
V	DAL	DELTA AIR LINES INC	D	E	4.0	6.0	236	-5	271
V	UAL	UAL CORP	D	E	4.6	6.0	238	-18	286
V	FDX	FEDERAL EXPRESS CORP	E	E	3.8	3.9	284	6	249
V	AMR	AMR CORP/DE	E	E	5.0	5.3	251	2	260

LARGE (L) - 500 Cos. — Group | | | | x500 (L) | Sort | x500 (L)

	Ticker	Company	Group				x500 (L)	Sort	x500 (L)
L	AEIC	AIR EXPRESS INTERNATIONAL	B	B	9.5	10.6	176	42	173
L	COMR	COMAIR HOLDINGS INC	C	C	7.9	9.8	217	34	234
L	CAI.B	CONTINENTAL AIRLS INC -CL B	D	E	2.3	7.6	327	2	427
L	ABF	AIRBORNE FREIGHT CORP	D	E	4.6	7.2	346	1	429

MEDIUM (M) - 600 Cos. — Group | | | | x600 (M) | Sort | x600 (M)

	Ticker	Company	Group				x600 (M)	Sort	x600 (M)
M	EUSA	EAGLE USA AIRFREIGHT INC	A	A	17.2	15.4	82	62	92
M	EXPD	EXPEDITORS INTL WASH INC	A	B	10.6	15.0	88	54	131
M	CGO	ATLAS AIR INC	C	E	6.9	8.5	331	-6	535
M	ASAI	ASA HOLDINGS INC	D	D	8.4	8.0	366	12	422
M	AWA	AMERICA WEST HLDG CP -CL B	D	E	5.8	6.5	456	-4	528
M	ALK	ALASKA AIRGROUP INC	E	E	4.3	5.4	520	-2	518

SMALL (S) - 600 Cos. — Group | | | | x600 (S) | Sort | x600 (S)

	Ticker	Company	Group				x600 (S)	Sort	x600 (S)
S	ANS	AIRNET SYSTEMS INC	A	B	9.1	15.8	76	40	161
S	MEH	MIDWEST EXPRESS HOLDINGS	A	B	17.5	15.9	74	37	189
S	KITTY	KITTY HAWK INC	A	D	15.4	15.8	77	1	466
S	XPRSA	US XPRESS ENTP INC -CL A	D	B	9.3	7.5	383	37	187
S	MAIR	MESABA HOLDINGS INC	D	C	6.4	7.5	390	28	258

(continued overleaf)

	HOLT USA2000 Universe Size / #cos / mkt cap Very large / 300 / $3.93B+ Large / 500 / $1.03–3.93B Medium / 600 / $.42–1.03B Small / 600 / $154–425M _Grouped by Forecast +1 year CFROI Grade (Near Term) which is then sorted high-to-low on numerical % Future_	HOLT DualGrade® Performance		CFROI Cash Flow Return on Investment			% of Total Market Value Attributed to Future Investments	
		#1 Near Term Fcst +1-year CFROI Grade	#2 Long Term % Future Grade	Past 5-year Median CFROI	Forecast +1-year CFROI	Forecast +1-year CFROI Rank	% Future	% Future Rank
S SKYW	SKYWEST INC	E	D	5.0	5.5	507	11	391
S ACAI	ATLANTIC COAST AIRLINES INC	E	D	3.7	5.8	487	7	417

Apparel Industry

VERY LARGE (V) - 300 Cos.		*Group*				**x300 (V)**	*Sort*	**x300 (V)**
V VFC	VF CORP	C	C	10.1	10.2	121	34	160
LARGE (L) - 500 Cos.		*Group*				**x500 (L)**	*Sort*	**x500 (L)**
L JNY	JONES APPAREL GROUP INC	A	B	15.8	16.9	45	49	126
L TOM	TOMMY HILFIGER CORP	A	D	17.7	18.2	33	22	315
L LIZ	LIZ CLAIBORNE INC	B	C	9.0	10.9	162	29	266
L WAC	WARNACO GROUP INC -CL A	B	C	13.3	12.0	140	28	271
L FTL	FRUIT OF THE LOOM INC -CL A	D	D	8.1	6.4	369	16	354
MEDIUM (M) - 600 Cos.		*Group*				**x600 (M)**	*Sort*	**x600 (M)**
M NAUT	NAUTICA ENTERPRISES INC	A	B	14.1	18.0	50	49	159
M SJK	ST JOHN KNITS INC	A	B	17.9	17.0	62	45	184
M KWD	KELLWOOD CO	E	E	5.9	5.3	525	1	501
M RML	RUSSELL CORP	E	E	6.0	4.7	541	-13	561
SMALL (S) - 600 Cos.		*Group*				**x600 (S)**	*Sort*	**x600 (S)**
S DLIA	DELIAS INC	A	A	10.5	14.7	91	68	34
S GES	GUESS INC	A	E	25.0	14.7	93	-4	497
S ASM	AUTHENTIC FITNESS	B	C	11.0	12.1	165	29	251

	Ticker	Company	Group				Sort	
S	QFAB	QUAKER FABRIC CORP	B	8.8	10.8	212	-6	502
S	DK	DONNA KARAN INTL INC	B	18.3	11.6	188	-10	516
S	URBN	URBAN OUTFITTERS INC	C	12.4	10.1	245	42	153
S	TNFI	NORTH FACE INC	C	10.3	8.6	334	38	180
S	GOSHA	OSHKOSH B'GOSH INC-CL A	C	5.9	8.8	324	28	263
S	OXM	OXFORD INDUSTRIES INC	D	5.7	8.1	358	-1	476
S	DSH	DESIGNER HLDGS LTD	B	10.6	4.4	543	34	213
S	PVH	PHILLIPS-VAN HEUSEN	D	6.4	4.5	542	7	420
S	HMX	HARTMARX CORP	D	5.9	4.6	537	0	472

Auto & Truck Industry

VERY LARGE (V) - 300 Cos.

	Ticker	Company	Group			x300 (V)	Sort	x300 (V)
V	C	CHRYSLER CORP	E	13.6	14.9	57	10	242
V	PCAR	PACCAR INC	C	6.7	11.5	88	34	161
V	F	FORD MOTOR CO	E	9.4	11.3	94	-3	268
V	GM	GENERAL MOTORS CORP	D	9.0	9.5	143	16	225

LARGE (L) - 500 Cos.

	Ticker	Company	Group			x500 (L)	Sort	x500 (L)
L	NAV	NAVISTAR INTERNATIONAL	B	6.3	11.6	147	17	345

MEDIUM (M) - 600 Cos.

	Ticker	Company	Group			x600 (M)	Sort	x600 (M)
M	WNC	WABASH NATIONAL CORP	C	10.9	9.1	300	24	322
M	TWI	TITAN INTERNATIONAL INC	E	11.2	9.6	276	-5	531

SMALL (S) - 600 Cos.

	Ticker	Company	Group			x600 (S)	Sort	x600 (S)

Auto Parts (Original Equipment) Industry

VERY LARGE (V) - 300 Cos.

	Ticker	Company	Group			x300 (V)	Sort	x300 (V)
V	MGA	MAGNA INTERNATIONAL -CL A	E	10.6	11.0	108	0	264
V	ETN	EATON CORP	D	7.2	8.3	178	21	209
V	DCN	DANA CORP	E	7.8	8.1	181	10	241

LARGE (L) - 500 Cos.

	Ticker	Company	Group			x500 (L)	Sort	x500 (L)
L	LEA	LEAR CORP	C	7.3	9.9	210	25	296
L	BWA	BORG WARNER AUTO	D	7.5	9.8	213	13	374
L	IIN	ITT INDUSTRIES INC	E	5.4	7.8	313	5	417

(continued overleaf)

HOLT USA2000 Universe
Size / #cos / mkt cap

Very large / 300 / $3.93B+
Large / 500 / $1.03–3.93B
Medium / 600 / $.42–1.03B
Small / 600 / $154–425M

Grouped by Forecast +1 year CFROI Grade (Near Term) which is then sorted high-to-low on numerical % Future

			HOLT DualGrade® Performance		CFROI — Cash Flow Return on Investment			% of Total Market Value Attributed to Future Investments	
			#1 Near Term Fcst +1-year CFROI Grade	#2 Long Term % Future Grade	Past 5-year Median CFROI	Forecast +1-year CFROI	Forecast +1-year CFROI Rank	% Future Sort	% Future Rank
MEDIUM (M) - 600 Cos.			**Group**				**x600 (M)**	**Sort**	**x600 (M)**
M	GNTX	GENTEX CORP	A	A	17.9	18.7	44	65	72
M	OEA	OEA INC	B	C	12.3	12.2	167	27	302
M	SUP	SUPERIOR INDUSTRIES INTL	B	C	14.3	11.3	199	26	305
M	MSX	MASCOTECH INC	B	C	7.2	10.7	217	19	356
M	MODI	MODINE MFG CO	C	C	7.8	8.7	322	26	309
M	BDT	BREED TECHNOLOGIES INC	C	D	15.0	9.5	277	16	383
M	TWR	TOWER AUTOMOTIVE INC	C	D	7.2	8.1	356	11	430
M	INMT	INTERMET CORP	D	D	2.4	8.0	362	11	437
M	ARV	ARVIN INDUSTRIES INC	D	E	4.7	6.4	461	2	499
M	SPD	STANDARD PRODUCTS CO	D	E	6.4	7.4	402	-6	536
M	CKC	COLLINS & AIKMAN CORP	E	B	12.5	6.0	483	36	234
SMALL (S) - 600 Cos.			**Group**				**x600 (S)**	**Sort**	**x600 (S)**
S	EXC	EXCEL INDUSTRIES INC	C	E	7.8	10.1	246	-22	561
S	SMPS	SIMPSON INDUSTRIES	D	E	7.8	7.3	403	-15	534

Auto Parts (Replacement) Industry

VERY LARGE (V) - 300 Cos.			**Group**				**x300 (V)**	**Sort**	**x300 (V)**
V	GPC	GENUINE PARTS CO	B	C	12.8	12.3	77	40	139
V	TEN	TENNECO INC	E	D	4.2	5.2	253	25	195
LARGE (L) - 500 Cos.			**Group**				**x500 (L)**	**Sort**	**x500 (L)**
L	FMO	FEDERAL-MOGUL CORP	B	B	3.8	12.6	126	41	178
L	ECH	ECHLIN INC	D	D	8.2	7.8	314	18	341

MEDIUM (M) - 600 Cos.

		Group			x600 (M)	Sort	x600 (M)
M	WAB	A	26.6	18.3	46	53	138
M	SPW	A	5.0	14.6	103	46	178
M	ITP	B	6.4	11.2	202	39	213
M	ORLY	D	10.0	7.6	389	25	318
M	EX	E	5.2	5.4	521	10	439

WESTINGHOUSE AIR BRAKE CO, SPX CORP, INTERTAPE POLYMER GROUP, O REILLY AUTOMOTIVE INC, EXIDE CORP

SMALL (S) - 600 Cos.

		Group			x600 (S)	Sort	x600 (S)
S	WN	B	6.9	12.8	146	41	156
S	DRRA	C	10.3	8.2	349	22	302
S	DON	E	7.0	8.2	352	-16	538
S	SMP	D	6.3	6.3	461	2	454
S	OSL	E	6.5	7.4	395	-11	517

WYNN'S INTERNATIONAL INC, DURA AUTOMOTIVE SYS -CL B, DONNELLY CORP, STANDARD MOTOR PRODS, O'SULLIVAN CORP

Beverage (Alcoholic) Industry

VERY LARGE (V) - 300 Cos.

		Group			x300 (V)	Sort	x300 (V)
V	BUD	C	8.9	9.0	153	31	173
V	VO	E	8.3	4.3	269	-6	276

ANHEUSER-BUSCH COS INC, SEAGRAM CO LTD

LARGE (L) - 500 Cos.

		Group			x500 (L)	Sort	x500 (L)
L	BF.B	B	11.4	10.5	182	40	189
L	ACCOB	E	1.6	3.5	465	-19	473

BROWN-FORMAN -CL B, COORS (ADOLPH) -CL B

MEDIUM (M) - 600 Cos.

		Group			x600 (M)	Sort	x600 (M)
M	CBRNA	D	6.4	9.7	271	16	386
M	MOND	C	6.9	7.8	380	34	248

CANANDAIGUA BRANDS -CL A, MONDAVI ROBERT CORP -CL A

SMALL (S) - 600 Cos.

		Group			x600 (S)	Sort	x600 (S)
S	SAM	B	19.5	12.4	159	26	277

BOSTON BEER INC -CL A

Beverage (Soft Drink) Industry

VERY LARGE (V) - 300 Cos.

		Group			x300 (V)	Sort	x300 (V)
V	KO	A	23.5	21.5	13	80	9
V	PEP	A	9.0	11.9	81	59	59
V	CCE	D	6.4	7.6	192	20	213

COCA-COLA CO, PEPSICO INC, COCA-COLA ENTERPRISES

(continued overleaf)

HOLT USA2000 Universe
Size / #cos / mkt cap

Very large / 300 / $3.93B+
Large / 500 / $1.03–3.93B
Medium / 600 / $.42–1.03B
Small / 600 / $.154–425M

Grouped by Forecast +1 year CFROI Grade (Near Term) which is then sorted high-to-low on numerical % Future

			HOLT DualGrade® Performance		CFROI — Cash Flow Return on Investment			% of Total Market Value Attributed to Future Investments	
			#1 Near Term Fcst +1-year CFROI Grade	#2 Long Term % Future Grade	Past 5-year Median CFROI	Forecast +1-year CFROI	Forecast +1-year CFROI Rank	% Future Sort	% Future Rank
		LARGE (L) - 500 Cos.	*Group*				**x500 (L)**	**x500 (L)** *Sort*	**x500 (L)**
		MEDIUM (M) - 600 Cos.	*Group*				**x600 (M)**	**x600 (M)** *Sort*	**x600 (M)**
M	TRY	TRIARC COS INC -CL A	C	C	4.7	8.3	341	24	325
M	COTTF	COTT CORP QUE	C	D	9.3	9.5	280	11	435
M	COKE	COCA-COLA BTLNG CONS	E	B	5.4	5.2	531	35	236
		SMALL (S) - 600 Cos.	*Group*				**x600 (S)**	**x600 (S)** *Sort*	**x600 (S)**
		Building Materials Industry							
		VERY LARGE (V) - 300 Cos.	*Group*				**x300 (V)**	**x300 (V)** *Sort*	**x300 (V)**
V	MAS	MASCO CORP	B	B	6.7	10.9	109	46	119
		LARGE (L) - 500 Cos.	*Group*				**x500 (L)**	**x500 (L)** *Sort*	**x500 (L)**
L	USG	USG CORP	A	D	14.0	21.7	11	11	390
L	ACK	ARMSTRONG WORLD INDS INC	D	D	6.4	7.7	320	24	307
L	FLR	FLUOR CORP	D	D	7.6	6.3	370	12	382
L	JM	JOHNS MANVILLE CP	D	D	4.4	7.6	330	12	384
L	MLM	MARTIN MARIETTA MATERIALS	D	E	5.5	6.5	367	3	424
L	OWC	OWENS CORNING	E	E	5.1	4.6	439	1	431
		MEDIUM (M) - 600 Cos.	*Group*				**x600 (M)**	**x600 (M)** *Sort*	**x600 (M)**
M	TRIP	TRIANGLE PACIFIC CORP	B	D	9.3	10.4	230	10	442
M	DTL	DAL-TILE INTERNATIONAL INC	C	C	11.6	9.6	275	24	329
M	JEC	JACOBS ENGINEERING GROUP	C	D	8.1	8.3	345	13	414
M	TJCO	TJ INTERNATIONAL INC	C	E	4.6	9.1	304	-58	597
M	MK	MORRISON KNUDSEN	E	D	2.5	4.0	561	14	405

SMALL (S) - 600 Cos.

			Group				x600 (S)	Sort	x600 (S)
S	WIRE	ENCORE WIRE CORP	A	B	12.7	23.2	21	42	150
S	RHH	ROBERTSON CECO CORP	A	D	1.0	14.2	106	14	370
S	BLDG	NCI BUILDING SYSTEMS INC	A	D	17.1	15.6	81	2	458
S	SSD	SIMPSON MANUFACTURING INC	B	B	11.1	13.7	121	33	216
S	TII	THOMAS INDUSTRIES INC	C	D	4.2	8.1	353	13	382
S	UFPI	UNIVERSAL FOREST PRODS INC	C	D	9.7	10.1	242	3	448
S	CABP	CAMERON ASHLEY BLDG PROD	C	E	11.1	9.5	271	-4	495
S	APOG	APOGEE ENTERPRISES INC	C	E	5.0	8.4	341	-6	501
S	ABTC	ABT BUILDING PRODUCTS CORP	C	E	12.3	9.4	281	-9	508
S	INSUA	INSITUFORM TECNOL INC -CL A	C	E	9.5	9.2	295	-12	525
S	ELK	ELCOR CORP	D	C	5.8	7.7	368	24	291
S	BBR	BUTLER MFG CO	D	E	5.1	6.0	477	-18	546
S	GVA	GRANITE CONSTRUCTION INC	D	E	4.3	6.7	441	-30	576
S	ZRN	ZURN INDUSTRIES INC	E	C	2.9	5.4	509	24	289
S	AMN	AMERON INTERNATIONAL INC	E	E	4.2	4.7	533	-2	485
S	JSTN	JUSTIN INDUSTRIES	E	E	7.6	5.3	513	-17	544

Cement & Aggregates Industry

VERY LARGE (V) - 300 Cos.
LARGE (L) - 500 Cos.

			Group	Group			x300 (V) x500 (L)	Sort Sort	x300 (V) x500 (L)
L	VMC	VULCAN MATERIALS CO	C	D	4.3	8.1	298	20	328
L	SDW	SOUTHDOWN INC	C	D	5.3	9.0	257	14	369
L	LAF	LAFARGE CORP	D	E	5.7	7.9	308	-15	464

MEDIUM (M) - 600 Cos.

			Group				x600 (M)	Sort	x600 (M)
M	CXP	CENTEX CONSTRN PRODS INC	B	D	5.7	10.5	229	10	449
M	LCE	LONE STAR INDUSTRIES	B	D	-0.5	13.4	137	7	464
M	MSA	MEDUSA CORP	C	E	8.0	9.7	267	-12	555
M	TXI	TEXAS INDUSTRIES INC	D	E	5.3	7.5	391	-21	575
M	CZM	CALMAT CO	E	C	0.1	1.0	597	32	261
M	FRK	FLORIDA ROCK INDS	E	E	3.7	5.6	508	-25	583

SMALL (S) - 600 Cos.

			Group				x600 (S)	Sort	x600 (S)
S	GCHI	GIANT CEMENT HOLDING INC	C	D	6.6	9.3	287	0	473
S	DRV	DRAVO CORP	D	E	4.4	7.0	416	-11	520

(continued overleaf)

HOLT USA2000 Universe
Size / #cos / mkt cap
Very large / 300 / $3.93B+
Large / 500 / $1.03–3.93B
Medium / 600 / $.42–1.03B
Small / 600 / $154–425M

Grouped by Forecast +1 year CFROI Grade (Near Term)
which is then sorted high-to-low on numerical % Future

Chemical (Diversified) Industry

		HOLT DualGrade® Performance		CFROI Cash Flow Return on Investment			% of Total Market Value Attributed to Future Investments		
		#1 Near Term Fcst +1-year CFROI Grade	#2 Long Term % Future Grade	Past 5-year Median CFROI	Forecast +1-year CFROI	Forecast +1-year CFROI Rank	% Future	Sort	% Future Rank
VERY LARGE (V) - 300 Cos.		*Group*				**x300 (V)**		**Sort**	**x300 (V)**
V MMM	MINNESOTA MINING & MFG CO	B	C	9.4	11.3	96	40	142
V PPG	PPG INDUSTRIES INC	C	D	7.2	9.1	152	14	235
V GRA	GRACE (W R) & CO	D	B	4.2	6.6	219	52	92
V APD	AIR PRODUCTS & CHEMICALS	D	D	4.7	6.0	237	11	239
V POT	POTASH CORP SASK INC	D	E	5.1	7.5	198	5	253
V EMN	EASTMAN CHEMICAL CO	E	E	4.2	3.3	291	-3	267
LARGE (L) - 500 Cos.		*Group*				**x500 (L)**		**Sort**	**x500 (L)**
L MIL	MILLIPORE CORP	B	B	13.3	12.5	127	43	166
L PLL	PALL CORP	B	C	10.6	10.7	167	35	220
L IGL	IMC GLOBAL INC	C	E	3.8	9.0	259	-56	495
L CYT	CYTEC INDUSTRIES INC	D	C	6.2	8.1	301	26	292
L GR	GOODRICH (B F) CO	D	D	5.4	7.9	306	12	383
L CBT	CABOT CORP	D	E	5.5	7.1	348	4	419
L ALB	ALBEMARLE CORP	E	D	2.8	4.1	450	17	348
L MCH	MILLENNIUM CHEMICALS INC	E	E	4.4	4.2	449	9	401
MEDIUM (M) - 600 Cos.		*Group*				**x600 (M)**		**Sort**	**x600 (M)**
M BRCOA	BRADY (WH) CO	C	B	8.5	9.9	258	45	185
M TRA	TERRA INDUSTRIES INC	C	E	5.0	8.4	335	-21	574
M DEX	DEXTER CORP	D	D	6.2	8.0	365	8	461
M FRP	FREEPORT MCMORAN RES -LP	D	E	4.6	6.4	460	-22	579
M CEM	CHEMFIRST INC	E	D	6.0	5.2	529	12	425

Chemical (Speciality) Industry

		Name	Group				x600 (S)	Sort	x600 (S)
SMALL (S) - 600 Cos.									
S	SGK	SCHAWK INC -CL A	B	B	6.8	12.6	156	42	155
S	SEH	SPARTECH CORP	B	B	9.2	11.2	198	30	238
S	MWT	MCWHORTER TECHNOLOGIES IN	C	C	11.7	9.4	275	21	313
S	BCU	BORDEN CHEM&PLAST -LP COM	D	E	8.0	6.5	452	-21	560

		Name	Group				x300 (V)	Sort	x300 (V)
VERY LARGE (V) - 300 Cos.									
V	IFF	INTL FLAVORS & FRAGRANCES	A	B	14.6	15.0	56	55	79
V	SIAL	SIGMA-ALDRICH	B	B	12.2	11.7	85	49	104
V	AVY	AVERY DENNISON CORP	B	B	7.2	11.1	101	48	110
V	HPC	HERCULES INC	C	D	6.2	8.4	173	28	183
V	SHW	SHERWIN-WILLIAMS CO	C	D	8.8	8.8	161	20	214
V	MII	MORTON INTERNATIONAL INC	D	C	9.6	7.9	189	34	163
V	ROH	ROHM & HAAS CO	D	D	5.3	7.2	208	15	227
V	PX	PRAXAIR INC	D	E	5.8	6.5	224	2	261

		Name	Group				x500 (L)	Sort	x500 (L)
LARGE (L) - 500 Cos.									
L	VAL	VALSPAR CORP	A	B	13.3	13.7	99	45	148
L	CNK	CROMPTON & KNOWLES CORP	A	C	11.8	14.6	80	31	253
L	AGU	AGRIUM INC	A	E	9.2	14.0	92	-47	491
L	ECL	ECOLAB INC	B	B	11.9	13.3	109	50	125
L	NLC	NALCO CHEMICAL CO	B	C	10.7	11.7	144	31	251
L	BTL	BETZDEARBORN INC	B	C	10.1	10.2	196	26	285
L	GLK	GREAT LAKES CHEMICAL CORP	B	E	16.7	10.1	198	-1	437
L	RPOW	RPM INC-OHIO	C	C	8.9	8.7	273	27	276
L	WIT	WITCO CORP	C	D	5.1	9.5	228	22	317
L	MAH	HANNA (M A) CO	C	D	7.6	9.2	240	20	325
L	EC	ENGELHARD CORP	C	D	7.5	8.5	280	11	388
L	ISP	INTL SPECIALTY PRODS INC	D	D	6.7	7.6	328	19	334
L	LZ	LUBRIZOL CORP	D	E	7.1	7.7	319	2	428

		Name	Group				x600 (M)	Sort	x600 (M)
MEDIUM (M) - 600 Cos.									
M	WDFC	WD-40 CO	A	A	38.1	39.8	4	59	108
M	MACD	MACDERMID INC	A	B	7.9	14.5	106	50	150

(continued overleaf)

HOLT USA2000 Universe
Size / #cos / mkt cap
Very large / 300 / $3.93B+
Large / 500 / $1.03–3.93B
Medium / 600 / $.42–1.03B
Small / 600 / $154–425M

Grouped by Forecast +1 year CFROI Grade (Near Term)
which is then sorted high-to-low on numerical % Future

			HOLT DualGrade® Performance		CFROI Cash Flow Return on Investment			% of Total Market Value Attributed to Future Investments	
			#1 Near Term Fcst +1-year CFROI Grade	#2 Long Term % Future Grade	Past 5-year Median CFROI	Forecast +1-year CFROI	Forecast +1-year CFROI Rank	% Future	% Future Rank
M	HXL	HEXCEL CORP	B	C	0.0	13.1	145	26	311
M	LI	LILLY INDS INC -CL A	B	D	11.8	13.7	127	16	391
M	EY	ETHYL CORP	B	E	9.4	10.4	234	-10	549
M	LAW	LAWTER INTERNATIONAL INC	C	B	9.0	9.2	295	35	235
M	ACOL	AMCOL INTERNATIONAL CORP	C	C	6.5	8.4	339	24	328
M	OMP	OM GROUP INC	C	C	11.0	9.9	255	21	343
M	SHLM	SCHULMAN (A.) INC	C	C	8.3	8.8	316	20	354
M	FOE	FERRO CORP	C	C	7.0	9.8	263	19	355
M	NL	NL INDUSTRIES	C	D	4.0	8.1	354	17	382
M	TG	TREDEGAR INDUSTRIES INC	D	B	1.9	8.0	367	37	224
M	CBM	CAMBREX CORP	D	D	6.6	7.4	400	13	421
M	FULL	FULLER (H. B.) CO	D	E	6.1	6.9	437	2	494
M	SNTC	SYNETIC INC	E	B	2.7	5.3	522	50	151
M	ARG	AIRGAS INC	E	D	6.4	5.9	490	14	406
M	NCH	NCH CORP	E	D	5.8	5.7	498	10	448
M	BOA	BUSH BOAKE ALLEN INC	E	D	6.4	5.4	517	9	454
M	CCC	CALGON CARBON CORP	E	D	5.4	5.6	503	9	455
M	WLM	WELLMAN INC	E	E	7.9	4.4	554	-9	544
M	GON	GEON COMPANY	E	E	1.2	3.3	573	-19	571
SMALL (S) - 600 Cos.			**Group**		**x600 (S)**		**x600 (S)**	**Sort**	**x600 (S)**
S	ALCD	ALCIDE CORP	A	A	14.9	29.8	8	76	15
S	LRI	LEARONAL INC	A	C	9.8	14.4	101	25	281
S	LDL	LYDALL INC	B	C	11.7	10.8	215	22	307
S	FMXI	FOAMEX INTERNATIONAL INC	C	C	8.2	9.4	274	22	308
S	FCY	FURON CO	D	B	7.5	7.3	398	35	205
S	PKE	PARK ELECTROCHEMICAL CORP	D	C	5.6	6.8	433	17	343

			Group				Sort	
S	LSCO	LESCO INC	D	6.1	6.9	424	14	367
S	KWR	QUAKER CHEMICAL CORP	D	4.9	7.6	381	8	412
S	CGGI	CARBIDE/GRAPHITE GROUP INC	D	4.7	7.2	406	5	437
S	TUSC	TUSCARORA INC	D	5.7	6.9	428	1	463
S	AEPI	AEP INDUSTRIES INC	C	7.9	0.1	600	26	275
S	PENX	PENFORD CORP	C	3.9	4.5	541	21	317
S	MSC	MATERIAL SCIENCES CORP	E	5.6	5.3	515	-5	500

Chemicals (Basic) Industry

			Group			x300 (V)	Sort	x300 (V)
		VERY LARGE (V) - 300 Cos.						
V	MTC	MONSANTO CO	B	6.4	8.8	156	53	88
V	DD	DU PONT (E I) DE NEMOURS	D	5.6	7.3	202	16	224
V	UK	UNION CARBIDE CORP	E	5.3	6.0	239	-26	296
V	RCM	ARCO CHEMICAL CO	D	7.4	5.7	242	11	240
V	DOW	DOW CHEMICAL	E	4.3	5.6	243	-4	269

			Group			x500 (L)	Sort	x500 (L)
		LARGE (L) - 500 Cos.						
L	LYO	LYONDELL PETROCHEMICAL	E	2.3	6.2	373	-10	456
L	SOI	SOLUTIA INC	C	5.1	4.7	434	27	277
L	OLN	OLIN CORP	E	3.4	5.5	403	8	405

			Group			x600 (M)	Sort	x600 (M)
		MEDIUM (M) - 600 Cos.						
M	GCG	GENERAL CHEMICAL GRP INC	D	18.5	17.4	58	7	467
M	GGC	GEORGIA GULF CORP	B	19.9	11.0	208	37	220
M	GRO	MISSISSIPPI CHEMICAL CORP	E	7.2	4.5	553	-27	585

			Group			x600 (S)	Sort	x600 (S)
		SMALL (S) - 600 Cos.						
S	SYC	SYBRON CHEMICALS INC	C	10.3	8.6	330	25	288
S	PGH	POLYMER GROUP INC	D	4.0	7.5	388	-3	489

Computer & Peripherals Industry

			Group			x300 (V)	Sort	x300 (V)
		VERY LARGE (V) - 300 Cos.						
V	DELL	DELL COMPUTER CORP	A	19.3	32.0	2	83	6
V	CSCO	CISCO SYSTEMS INC	A	30.5	26.9	3	79	12

(continued overleaf)

HOLT USA2000 Universe
Size / #cos / mkt cap
Very large / 300 / $3.93B+
Large / 500 / $1.03–3.93B
Medium / 600 / $.42–1.03B
Small / 600 / $154–425M
Grouped by Forecast +1 year CFROI Grade (Near Term)
which is then sorted high-to-low on numerical % Future

			HOLT DualGrade® Performance		CFROI — Cash Flow Return on Investment			% of Total Market Value Attributed to Future Investments	
			#1 Near Term Fcst +1-year CFROI Grade	#2 Long Term % Future Grade	Past 5-year Median CFROI	Forecast +1-year CFROI	Forecast +1-year CFROI Rank	% Future	% Future Rank
V	NN	NEWBRIDGE NETWORKS CORP	A	A	19.0	17.8	37	69	27
V	EMC	EMC CORP/MA	A	A	21.0	19.8	26	66	33
V	ASND	ASCEND COMMUNICATIONS INC	A	A	14.7	18.8	33	65	37
V	GTW	GATEWAY 2000 INC	A	B	28.0	24.2	6	58	61
V	ADPT	ADAPTEC INC	A	B	17.3	18.8	32	57	66
V	CPQ	COMPAQ COMPUTER CORP	A	B	15.9	18.4	35	57	70
V	SUNW	SUN MICROSYSTEMS INC	A	B	14.9	20.3	20	54	82
V	BAY	BAY NETWORKS INC	A	B	18.6	17.5	41	51	98
V	COMS	3COM CORP	B	A	16.8	13.5	65	62	48
V	HWP	HEWLETT-PACKARD CO	B	B	11.4	13.2	67	52	93
V	IBM	INTL BUSINESS MACHINES CORP	B	C	6.2	7.6	195	33	165
V	SEG	SEAGATE TECHNOLOGY	D	E	10.9	4.1	275	5	252
V	DEC	DIGITAL EQUIPMENT	E	E	0.3	4.9	261	0	265
LARGE (L) - 500 Cos.			Group				x500 (L)	Sort	x500 (L)
L	TSAI	TRNSACTN SYS ARCHTCTS -CL	A	A	12.0	18.5	31	80	26
L	IOM	IOMEGA CORP	A	A	3.9	23.7	7	69	41
L	APCC	AMERICAN PWR CNVRSION	A	B	31.1	19.9	21	53	106
L	QNTM	QUANTUM CORP	A	D	12.5	16.6	51	13	373
L	SCI	SCI SYSTEMS INC	B	B	10.1	12.3	133	41	177
L	STK	STORAGE TECHNOLOGY CP -CL	B	C	3.6	12.7	121	36	207
L	TECD	TECH DATA CORP	B	C	7.4	10.2	193	32	245
L	SGI	SILICON GRAPHICS INC	B	E	12.8	13.5	105	-36	490
L	FORE	FORE SYSTEMS INC	C	A	11.1	8.9	265	56	91
L	CS	CABLETRON SYSTEMS	C	D	24.3	9.8	214	23	312
L	UIS	UNISYS CORP	D	C	4.5	7.3	340	36	209
L	WDC	WESTERN DIGITAL CORP	E	C	17.4	5.2	418	26	289

Size	Ticker	Company	Group				x600 (M)	Sort	x600 (M)
L	NCR	NCR CORP	E	D	-5.4	1.2	497	13	376
L	AAPL	APPLE COMPUTER INC	E	E	1.0	2.2	488	1	432
MEDIUM (M) - 600 Cos.									
M	SMOD	SMART MODULAR TECHNOLGS	A	A	31.6	28.1	11	63	80
M	INTL	INTER-TEL INC -SER A	A	A	8.1	14.4	112	59	111
M	SNDK	SANDISK CORP	A	B	10.2	14.3	115	54	128
M	ZBRA	ZEBRA TECHNOLOGIES CP -CL	A	B	21.8	17.9	52	54	129
M	WANG	WANG LABS INC	A	D	12.6	14.7	101	8	459
M	MRVC	MRV COMMUNICATIONS INC	B	B	11.9	13.8	125	51	144
M	TTRR	TRACOR INC	B	C	7.4	11.6	194	27	303
M	MUEI	MICRON ELECTRONICS INC	C	B	20.5	9.9	254	37	227
M	GRB	GERBER SCIENTIFIC INC	C	C	4.2	8.8	315	32	265
M	SQNT	SEQUENT COMPUTER SYSTEMS	C	D	7.8	8.4	340	5	478
M	RDRT	READ-RITE CORP	C	E	5.3	9.7	266	-28	587
M	SRA	STRATUS COMPUTER INC	D	D	6.4	7.5	393	4	480
M	DGN	DATA GENERAL CORP	D	E	-8.4	6.2	471	-1	512
M	INGR	INTERGRAPH CORP	E	E	-7.8	1.1	595	3	489
M	KMAG	KOMAG INC	E	E	9.0	4.6	545	-19	570
SMALL (S) - 600 Cos.			Group				x600 (S)	Sort	x600 (S)
S	IDX	IDENTIX INC	A	A	-2.3	18.0	45	80	5
S	SPLH	SPLASH TECHNOLOGY HLDGS	A	A	59.3	31.0	7	74	18
S	SCUR	SECURE COMPUTING CORP	A	A	-1.7	17.1	57	73	22
S	MTIC	MTI TECHNOLOGY CORP	A	A	2.1	23.0	22	67	40
S	RSYS	RADISYS CORP	A	A	12.5	19.1	40	55	87
S	MCRS	MICROS SYSTEMS INC	A	B	15.3	17.4	55	54	93
S	VTCH	VITECH AMERICA INC	A	B	48.5	20.5	30	42	152
S	INFS	IN FOCUS SYSTEMS INC	A	B	10.3	14.8	87	39	176
S	NMBS	NIMBUS CD INTERNATIONAL INC	A	B	17.5	13.8	115	35	204
S	ACTL	ACTEL CORP	A	B	11.8	14.3	104	33	217
S	DGII	DIGI INTERNATIONAL INC	A	C	16.2	13.8	119	28	262
S	RNBO	RAINBOW TECHNOLOGIES INC	B	B	12.7	12.9	143	43	142
S	XIRC	XIRCOM INC	B	B	11.8	10.2	238	31	233
S	ASPX	AUSPEX SYSTEMS INC	B	D	13.5	11.8	181	10	397
S	CMPC	COMPUCOM SYSTEMS INC	B	D	10.3	11.5	189	7	414

(continued overleaf)

HOLT USA2000 Universe
Size / #cos / mkt cap

Very large / 300 / $3.93B+
Large / 500 / $1.03–3.93B
Medium / 600 / $.42–1.03B
Small / 600 / $154–425M

Grouped by Forecast +1 year CFROI Grade (Near Term) which is then sorted high-to-low on numerical % Future

			HOLT DualGrade® Performance		CFROI Cash Flow Return on Investment			% of Total Market Value Attributed to Future Investments	
			#1 Near Term Fcst +1-year CFROI Grade	#2 Long Term % Future Grade	Past 5-year Median CFROI	Forecast +1-year CFROI	Forecast +1-year CFROI Rank	% Future	Future Rank
S	PCLE	PINNACLE SYSTEMS INC	C	A	-2.4	10.1	243	47	120
S	MYLX	MYLEX CORP	D	B	14.9	6.6	450	35	199
S	OAKT	OAK TECHNOLOGY INC	D	E	13.4	7.6	376	-12	524
S	MADGF	MADGE NETWORKS NV	D	E	24.5	6.9	420	-41	585
S	DIMD	DIAMOND MULTIMEDIA SYS INC	E	B	7.0	5.8	484	34	209
S	ESCC	EVANS & SUTHERLAND CMP	E	D	3.1	5.3	514	10	403
S	ALSC	ALLIANCE SEMICONDUCTOR	E	E	20.4	4.0	555	-24	569

Computer Software & Services Industry

VERY LARGE (V) - 300 Cos.			Group		Past 5-year Median CFROI	Forecast +1-year CFROI	x300 (V)	Sort	x300 (V)
V	PSFT	PEOPLESOFT INC	A	A	13.0	25.4	4	90	1
V	PAYX	PAYCHEX INC	A	A	17.1	20.8	18	86	2
V	MSFT	MICROSOFT CORP	A	A	24.5	23.9	7	82	7
V	CPWR	COMPUWARE CORP	A	A	19.5	21.9	12	76	13
V	BMCS	BMC SOFTWARE INC	A	A	19.1	23.0	8	76	14
V	PMTC	PARAMETRIC TECHNOLOGY	A	A	22.7	25.0	5	75	17
V	CA	COMPUTER ASSOCIATES INTL	A	A	14.4	17.6	40	72	21
V	CDN	CADENCE DESIGN SYS INC	A	A	13.5	20.1	22	72	24
V	ORCL	ORACLE CORP	A	A	21.6	19.5	27	71	26
V	AOL	AMERICA ONLINE INC	B	A	5.3	13.1	68	83	5
V	AUD	AUTOMATIC DATA PROCESSING	B	A	11.5	11.7	83	65	39
V	FDC	FIRST DATA CORP	B	C	6.2	11.1	100	36	155
V	CSC	COMPUTER SCIENCES CORP	D	B	6.1	7.5	200	48	112
V	EDS	ELECTRONIC DATA SYSTEMS	D	C	8.1	7.6	194	39	143

LARGE (L) - 500 Cos.		Group				x500 (L)	Sort	x500 (L)
L	ITWO	I2 TECHNOLOGIES INC	A	A	23.9	20.5	18	89	4
L	VRTS	VERITAS SOFTWARE CO	A	A	12.0	21.1	15	89	5
L	SEBL	SIEBEL SYSTEMS INC	A	A	4.1	18.5	29	88	7
L	NTAP	NETWORK APPLIANCE INC	A	A	15.7	27.1	3	87	8
L	CATP	CAMBRIDGE TECHNOLOGY PART	A	A	20.3	22.1	10	84	10
L	VSIO	VISIO CORP	A	A	21.5	26.2	5	84	11
L	KEA	KEANE INC	A	A	12.7	18.6	27	84	12
L	CBR	CIBER INC	A	A	13.4	18.6	28	83	13
L	SDTI	SECURITY DYNAMICS TECH INC	A	A	9.4	19.4	23	83	16
L	CTXS	CITRIX SYSTEMS INC	A	A	7.4	16.9	46	82	18
L	GART	GARTNER GROUP INC -CL A	A	A	16.8	20.8	17	81	19
L	CEN	CERIDIAN CORP	A	A	12.6	15.4	65	79	28
L	NETA	NETWORKS ASSOCIATES INC	A	A	29.7	30.8	2	72	33
L	NSCP	NETSCAPE COMMUNICATIONS	A	A	1.3	14.6	82	69	43
L	CDWC	CDW COMPUTER CENTERS INC	A	A	21.8	21.6	13	69	48
L	ADSK	AUTODESK INC	A	A	15.0	17.5	39	58	82
L	SNPS	SYNOPSYS INC	A	A	15.8	17.0	44	55	82
L	SYMC	SYMANTEC CORP	A	B	7.6	18.1	35	52	96
L	ADBE	ADOBE SYSTEMS INC	A	B	15.1	15.5	63	49	113
L	CHRZ	COMPUTER HORIZONS CORP	B	A	11.9	12.2	134	79	128
L	PLAT	PLATINUM TECHNOLOGY INC	B	A	6.6	11.7	145	72	27
L	SE	STERLING COMMERCE INC	B	A	27.0	13.1	112	71	34
L	YHOO	YAHOO INC	C	A	-7.6	9.5	226	95	36
L	MANU	MANUGISTICS GROUP INC	C	A	6.6	9.3	238	82	1
L	SDS	SUNGARD DATA SYSTEMS INC	C	A	7.1	9.8	216	65	17
L	SSW	STERLING SOFTWARE INC	C	B	10.8	8.4	288	40	59
L	INTU	INTUIT INC	D	A	-5.1	6.2	374	69	190
L	PMS	POLICY MANAGEMENT SYSTEMS	D	B	5.4	8.0	303	45	47
L	SYBS	SYBASE INC	D	C	15.3	5.8	385	36	146
L	CKFR	CHECKFREE CORP	E	A	-37.4	2.3	486	90	214
L	FISV	FISERV INC	E	C	3.1	3.9	455	35	3
L	CSRV	COMPUSERVE CORP	E	C	4.3	3.0	479	34	221
L	DST	DST SYSTEMS INC	E	C	2.7	4.4	446	34	231

(continued overleaf)

HOLT USA2000 Universe
Size / #cos / mkt cap
Very large / 300 / $3.93B+
Large / 500 / $1.03–3.93B
Medium / 600 / $.42–1.03B
Small / 600 / $154–425M

Grouped by Forecast +1 year CFROI Grade (Near Term) which is then sorted high-to-low on numerical % Future

		HOLT DualGrade® Performance		CFROI — Cash Flow Return on Investment			% of Total Market Value Attributed to Future Investments	
		#1 Near Term Fcst +1-year CFROI Grade	#2 Long Term % Future Grade	Past 5-year Median CFROI	Forecast +1-year CFROI	Forecast +1-year CFROI Rank x600 (M)	% Future — Sort	% Future Rank x600 (M)
MEDIUM [M] – 600 Cos.	*Group*							
M ASDV	ASPECT DEVELOPMENT INC	A	A	13.0	15.1	86	87	2
M ARSW	ARBOR SOFTWARE CORP	A	A	5.4	14.3	116	83	5
M HNCS	HNC SOFTWARE INC	A	A	8.8	15.0	93	82	9
M LGTO	LEGATO SYSTEMS INC	A	A	10.6	17.7	54	82	10
M VNTV	VANTIVE CORP	A	A	6.4	22.9	18	81	11
M VIAS	VIASOFT INC	A	A	18.4	15.2	85	80	13
M DSLGF	DISCREET LOGIC INC	A	A	13.5	41.9	2	80	16
M SAPE	SAPIENT CORP	A	A	19.2	14.3	114	79	17
M ANLY	ANALYSTS INTERNATIONAL	A	A	16.2	19.5	37	79	19
M HRBC	HARBINGER CORP	A	A	-1.7	17.5	57	78	20
M CCCG	CCC INFORMATION SVCS GRP	A	A	31.9	29.1	10	77	24
M MAST	MASTECH CORP	A	A	58.6	26.8	12	77	26
M TSK	COMPUTER TASK GROUP INC	A	A	1.4	15.5	81	75	36
M IDTC	IDT CORP	A	A	-50.7	32.4	6	73	40
M JDAS	JDA SOFTWARE GROUP INC	A	A	18.7	16.8	64	72	41
M HYSW	HYPERION SOFTWARE CORP	A	A	9.8	17.4	59	71	47
M PEGA	PEGASYSTEMS INC	A	A	12.1	14.4	108	69	57
M TSCC	TECHNOLOGY SOLUTIONS CO	A	A	9.7	14.3	113	69	58
M NATI	NATIONAL INSTRUMENTS CORP	A	A	15.6	15.5	79	67	63
M ISLI	INTERSOLV	A	A	-1.1	17.2	61	67	64
M JKHY	HENRY (JACK) & ASSOCIATES	A	A	28.2	29.2	9	67	65
M TLC	LEARNING COMPANY INC	A	A	-18.1	14.0	120	66	67
M AZPN	ASPEN TECHNOLOGY INC	A	A	8.1	14.8	100	65	70
M COGNF	COGNOS INC	A	A	7.2	19.0	41	65	71
M RMDY	REMEDY CORP	A	A	15.4	20.8	26	59	110
M ABIIB	AMER BUSINESS INFO -CL B	A	B	17.4	14.9	96	52	141

	Ticker	Company	Group				x600 (S)	Sort	x600 (S)
M	SDRC	STRUCTURAL DYNAMICS RES	A	B	5.9	15.0	95	50	152
M	FIC	FAIR ISAAC & COMPANY INC	A	B	17.3	18.0	51	41	200
M	WIND	WIND RIVER SYSTEMS INC	A	B	8.7	40.6	3	38	218
M	GTIS	GT INTERACTIVE SOFTWARE	A	B	15.3	15.0	91	37	222
M	AVNT	AVANT CORP	A	C	8.6	16.0	72	29	280
M	DCTM	DOCUMENTUM INC	B	A	10.2	13.2	142	83	6
M	IMRS	INFORMATION MGMT RES INC	B	A	20.2	10.9	210	76	31
M	SCTC	SYSTEMS & COMPUTER TECH	B	A	5.7	12.5	159	72	46
M	MERQ	MERCURY INTERACTIVE CORP	B	A	3.5	11.3	201	68	59
M	VIEW	VIEWLOGIC SYSTEMS INC	B	A	9.6	11.9	184	66	68
M	RATL	RATIONAL SOFTWARE CORP	B	A	6.4	11.1	206	62	93
M	ACXM	ACXIOM CORP	B	A	8.5	10.9	212	61	95
M	BSYS	BISYS GROUP INC	B	A	9.3	12.7	156	59	106
M	SYKE	SYKES ENTERPRISES INC	B	A	7.2	12.0	176	58	113
M	XYLN	XYLAN CORP	B	A	-31.4	13.0	149	53	140
M	AMSY	AMERICAN MANAGEMENT SYST	B	B	8.8	14.0	121	40	208
M	EFII	ELECTRONICS FOR IMAGING INC	B	C	16.7	13.4	139	34	244
M	HMTT	HMT TECHNOLOGY CORP	B	C	13.9	13.5	133	29	287
M	BHW	BELL & HOWELL COMPANY	B	C	15.4	12.3	163	22	332
M	WHIT	WHITTMAN HART INC	C	A	10.2	10.1	252	76	32
M	BROD	BRODERBUND SOFTWARE INC	C	A	18.6	9.9	257	60	100
M	BOOL	BOOLE & BABBAGE INC	C	A	6.7	9.5	281	60	105
M	CMVT	COMVERSE TECHNOLOGY INC	C	B	8.0	10.2	242	55	125
M	NDC	NATIONAL DATA CORP	C	B	6.1	9.2	299	45	182
M	BTC	BANCTEC INC	C	C	6.4	9.0	309	28	295
M	VST	VANSTAR CORP	C	D	7.3	8.4	332	8	458
M	CHSE	CHS ELECTRONICS INC	C	E	7.5	9.1	303	-11	553
M	FILE	FILENET CORP	D	A	4.9	8.0	361	58	114
M	MEDA	MEDAPHIS CORP	D	E	-7.6	7.0	427	-1	511
M	LCOS	LYCOS INC	E	A	-11.6	4.5	552	92	1
M	PIXR	PIXAR	E	A	7.3	2.4	586	74	38
M	AFA	AFFILIATED COMP SVCS -CL A	E	B	4.7	4.5	549	44	188
M	MENT	MENTOR GRAPHICS CORP	E	B	2.1	5.2	527	38	219
SMALL (S)-600 Cos.			**Group**				**x600 (S)**	**Sort**	**x600 (S)**
S	HPRI	HPR INC	A	A	15.5	17.9	48	83	2
S	ODIS	OBJECT DESIGN INC	A	A	4.2	14.8	88	77	12

(continued overleaf)

			HOLT DualGrade® Performance		CFROI — Cash Flow Return on Investment			% of Total Market Value Attributed to Future Investments	
		HOLT USA2000 Universe Size / #cos / mkt cap Very large / 300 / $3.93B+ Large / 500 / $1.03–3.93B Medium / 600 / $.42–1.03B Small / 600 / $154–425M *Grouped by Forecast +1 year CFROI Grade (Near Term) which is then sorted high-to-low on numerical % Future*	#1 Near Term Fcst +1-year CFROI Grade	#2 Long Term % Future Grade	Past 5-year Median CFROI	Forecast +1-year CFROI	Forecast +1-year CFROI Rank	% Future	% Future Rank
S	ANLT	ANALYTICAL SURVEYS INC	A	A	10.7	19.6	36	76	14
S	FDS	FACTSET RESEARCH SYSTEMS	A	A	13.8	17.7	50	73	21
S	MECK	MECKLERMEDIA CORP	A	A	-10.2	36.1	4	71	27
S	TSIX	TRANSITION SYSTEMS INC/MA	A	A	20.1	14.7	94	71	29
S	APEX	APEX PC SOLUTIONS INC	A	A	51.4	15.7	79	70	30
S	ADVS	ADVENT SOFTWARE INC	A	A	6.7	13.8	116	69	33
S	AKLM	ACCLAIM ENMNT INC	A	A	25.0	25.3	15	66	41
S	DDIM	DATA DIMENSIONS INC	A	A	69.8	46.2	1	66	44
S	CMSX	COMPUTER MGMT SCIENCES	A	A	12.1	15.9	75	66	45
S	PSQL	PLATINUM SOFTWARE CORP	A	A	-17.0	41.7	2	66	47
S	DDDDF	NEW DIMENSION SOFTWARE	A	A	4.3	21.7	25	63	51
S	BARZ	BARRA INC	A	A	13.7	16.4	67	56	83
S	MCRE	METACREATIONS CORP	A	A	-0.6	15.7	80	50	108
S	SPSS	SPSS INC	A	B	22.1	19.3	39	46	126
S	TNSI	TRANSACTION NETWORK SVCS	A	B	13.1	14.9	84	40	165
S	PMRY	POMEROY COMPUTER RES INC	A	B	14.7	20.2	33	37	185
S	INFN	INFINITY FINL TECHNOLOGY INC	B	A	22.3	13.0	142	81	4
S	ONDI	ONTRACK DATA INTL INC	B	A	16.0	12.8	151	77	10
S	EAII	ENGINEERING ANIMATION INC	B	A	8.3	10.3	231	68	35
S	FORMF	JETFORM CORP	B	A	5.0	13.1	137	67	38
S	INTS	INTEGRATED SYSTEMS INC	B	A	9.5	11.0	205	59	71
S	SOTA	STATE OF THE ART INC	B	A	10.4	12.5	158	58	77
S	SYSF	SYSTEMSOFT CORP	B	A	7.1	12.1	167	57	78
S	CYLK	CYLINK CORP	B	A	-1.5	10.9	210	53	98
S	PSDI	PROJECT SOFTWARE & DEV INC	B	B	7.8	11.8	176	45	132
S	WNDR	WONDERWARE CORP	B	B	8.6	13.2	131	42	154
S	PCNI	PHYSICIAN COMPUTER NETWK	B	D	15.7	13.5	126	9	406

	Ticker	Company	Group	Grade			x300 (V)	Sort	x300 (V)
S	EDFY	EDIFY CORP	C	A	-0.8	8.2	351	77	8
S	CLFY	CLARIFY INC	C	A	4.6	9.6	268	67	39
S	ATVI	ACTIVISION INC	C	A	-6.3	10.1	244	62	54
S	RAPT	RAPTOR SYSTEMS INC	C	A	2.9	9.0	309	59	64
S	VSVR	VIDEOSERVER INC	C	A	15.3	8.9	317	57	82
S	INFM	INFINIUM SOFTWARE INC	C	A	9.5	9.3	283	52	101
S	CDSI	COMPUTER DATA SYSTEMS INC	C	A	9.4	9.4	277	50	107
S	AMSWA	AMERICAN SOFTWARE -CL A	C	B	-5.9	9.0	312	44	139
S	CACI	CACI INTL INC -CL A	C	B	8.4	9.0	307	40	167
S	USCS	USCS INTL INC	C	B	6.7	9.1	303	38	181
S	SSAX	SYSTEM SOFTWARE ASSOC INC	C	B	10.7	9.1	296	32	226
S	PTEC	PHOENIX TECHNOLOGIES LTD	C	C	7.7	9.9	252	24	294
S	WALK	WALKER INTERACTIVE SYSTEMS	D	A	2.7	6.9	421	56	86
S	SCOP	SCOPUS TECHNOLOGY INC	D	A	8.0	7.6	382	49	113
S	PRGS	PROGRESS SOFTWARE CORP	D	B	12.2	7.5	384	44	137
S	INSO	INSO CORP	D	C	15.0	6.7	444	19	328
S	NWK	NETWORK EQUIPMENT TECH	D	E	7.2	6.8	435	-6	503
S	ML	METROMAIL CORP	D	E	6.7	7.6	377	-19	554
S	AWRE	AWARE INC	E	A	-3.2	2.0	589	79	6
S	SCBI	SCB COMPUTER TECHNOLOGY	E	A	12.2	3.6	562	62	55
S	IMNT	IMNET SYSTEMS INC	E	A	-0.3	4.3	548	55	89
S	MACR	MACROMEDIA INC	E	A	8.3	3.3	567	53	99
S	BORL	BORLAND INTERNATIONAL	E	B	-24.8	0.2	598	40	166
S	SHVA	SHIVA CORP	E	B	9.0	2.9	573	35	203
S	SIII	S3 INCORPORATED	E	E	15.2	2.8	578	-10	514

Diversified Company Industry

VERY LARGE (V) - 300 Cos.			Group				x300 (V)	Sort	x300 (V)
V	TYC	TYCO INTERNATIONAL LTD	B	B	7.2	11.0	106	58	62
V	ALT	ALLEGHENY TELEDYNE INC	B	C	6.5	11.6	87	32	168
V	ALD	ALLIEDSIGNAL INC	C	C	7.2	8.8	160	33	166
V	TXT	TEXTRON INC	C	C	10.5	10.2	122	33	167
V	UTX	UNITED TECHNOLOGIES CORP	C	D	5.4	8.6	167	24	198
V	SRV	SERVICE CORP INTERNATIONAL	D	C	5.9	6.5	221	42	132

(continued overleaf)

HOLT USA2000 Universe
Size / #cos / mkt cap

Very large / 300 / $3.93B+
Large / 500 / $1.03–3.93B
Medium / 600 / $.42–1.03B
Small / 600 / $154–425M

Grouped by Forecast +1 year CFROI Grade (Near Term) which is then sorted high-to-low on numerical % Future

			HOLT DualGrade® Performance		CFROI Cash Flow Return on Investment			% of Total Market Value Attributed to Future Investments	
			#1 Near Term Fcst +1-year CFROI Grade	#2 Long Term % Future Grade	Past 5-year Median CFROI	Forecast +1-year CFROI	Forecast +1-year CFROI Rank	% Future	% Future Rank
V	TRW	TRW INC	D	D	6.5	6.2	233	13	236
V	FO	FORTUNE BRANDS INC	E	C	7.8	2.6	296	45	124
LARGE (L) - 500 Cos.			**Group**				**x500 (L)**	**Sort**	**x500 (L)**
L	ASD	AMERN STANDARD CO INC	A	B	7.5	13.7	100	45	147
L	PZB	PITTSTON CO-BRINKS GROUP	B	B	8.4	10.8	166	43	170
L	HB	HILLENBRAND INDUSTRIES	B	B	12.2	10.2	195	42	172
L	RYC	RAYCHEM CORP	B	B	1.9	12.3	132	40	188
L	DHR	DANAHER CORP	C	A	8.3	9.2	246	57	86
L	NSI	NATIONAL SERVICE INDS INC	C	B	6.6	8.3	290	46	142
L	CR	CRANE CO	C	B	7.4	9.6	225	38	200
L	TFX	TELEFLEX INC	C	C	7.9	8.2	294	33	238
L	WH	WHITMAN CORP	C	C	8.4	8.2	296	28	273
L	PNR	PENTAIR INC	C	D	6.2	8.2	297	22	316
L	VVI	VIAD CORP	D	B	8.7	7.8	317	40	186
L	STEI	STEWART ENTERPRISES -CL A	D	C	5.4	7.0	351	30	261
L	PMI	PREMARK INTERNATIONAL INC	D	D	5.3	6.5	368	13	377
L	IV	MARK IV INDUSTRIES INC	D	D	8.5	7.9	309	12	378
L	LWN	LOEWEN GROUP INC	D	E	6.3	5.5	398	4	422
L	VHI	VALHI INC	E	C	2.7	3.9	454	26	286
L	OG	OGDEN CORP	E	E	5.0	5.0	424	7	410
L	WSC	WESCO FINANCIAL CORP	E	E	1.7	2.2	489	6	414
MEDIUM (M) - 600 Cos.			**Group**				**x600 (M)**	**Sort**	**x600 (M)**
M	JOS	JOSTENS INC	A	B	12.5	18.7	43	43	191
M	OO	OAKLEY INC	B	A	29.6	10.3	237	57	119
M	BLT.A	BLOUNT INTL INC -CL A	B	B	10.1	10.5	223	39	211
M	AME	AMETEK INC	C	C	10.4	9.4	287	32	260

	Ticker	Company	Group				Sort	
M	GFF	GRIFFON CORP	C	D	9.6	9.1	302	18	364
M	VALM	VALMONT INDUSTRIES	C	D	6.5	10.2	241	17	379
M	B	BARNESS GROUP INC	C	D	5.8	8.7	319	10	447
M	TFT	THERMO FIBERTEK INC	D	B	8.1	7.0	429	49	160
M	SXI	STANDEX INTERNATIONAL CORP	D	C	6.1	6.6	450	29	282
M	TMD	THERMEDICS INC	D	C	3.3	6.4	464	26	312
M	AXE	ANIXTER INTL INC	D	D	4.3	6.9	433	11	436
M	EQU	EQUITY CORP INTERNATIONAL	E	C	2.5	3.6	566	33	258
M	NC	NACCO INDUSTRIES -CL A	E	C	6.3	5.4	519	20	350
M	FRTZ	FRITZ COS INC	E	D	9.2	5.9	493	18	368
M	AOS	SMITH (A O) CORP	E	D	3.2	5.5	509	15	396
M	GY	GENCORP INC	E	D	3.3	5.7	497	11	428
M	SQA.A	SEQUA CORP -CL A	E	D	1.2	2.2	589	11	433

SMALL (S) - 600 Cos.

	Ticker	Company	Group				x600 (S)	Sort	x600 (S)
S	FIGIA	FIGGIE INTERNATIONAL -CL A	C	C	3.8	8.1	354	21	316
S	APR	AMERICAN PRECISION INDS	C	C	5.7	8.8	321	13	381
S	MYE	MYERS INDUSTRIES INC	C	D	8.2	9.1	298	7	419
S	FLDR	FLANDERS CORP	D	B	3.5	7.4	397	46	124
S	VRLN	VARLEN CORP	D	D	8.6	7.6	378	13	377
S	CHE	CHEMED CORP	E	B	5.0	4.6	540	33	221
S	PKOH	PARK-OHIO INDUSTRIES	E	D	5.8	4.6	538	11	392
S	KAMNA	KAMAN CORP -CL A	E	D	4.0	5.8	488	7	423
S	NTK	NORTEK INC	E	D	5.5	3.9	557	3	446
S	KT	KATY INDUSTRIES	E	E	1.8	4.3	547	-7	504

Drug Industry

VERY LARGE (V) - 300 Cos.

	Ticker	Company	Group				x300 (V)	Sort	x300 (V)
V	LLY	LILLY (ELI) & CO	A	A	12.3	17.6	39	80	10
V	PFE	PFIZER INC	A	A	14.4	17.4	42	74	18
V	SGP	SCHERING-PLOUGH	A	A	21.8	21.4	14	72	20
V	BMY	BRISTOL MYERS SQUIBB	A	A	19.8	22.5	9	71	25
V	WLA	WARNER-LAMBERT CO	A	A	14.3	15.3	53	62	45
V	AMGN	AMGEN INC	A	A	24.7	19.5	28	62	49
V	MRK	MERCK & CO	A	A	18.9	20.7	19	60	55

(continued overleaf)

HOLT USA2000 Universe
Size / #cos / mkt cap
Very large / 300 / $3.93B+
Large / 500 / $1.03–3.93B
Medium / 600 / $.42–1.03B
Small / 600 / $154–425M
Grouped by Forecast +1 year CFROI Grade (Near Term) which is then sorted high-to-low on numerical % Future

			HOLT DualGrade® Performance		CFROI Cash Flow Return on Investment			% of Total Market Value Attributed to Future Investments	
			#1 Near Term Fcst +1-year CFROI Grade	#2 Long Term % Future Grade	Past 5-year Median CFROI	Forecast +1-year CFROI	Forecast +1-year CFROI Rank	% Future	% Future Rank
V	AHP	AMERICAN HOME PRODUCTS	B	B	13.4	14.4	61	50	103
V	PNU	PHARMACIA & UPJOHN INC	D	B	9.6	6.6	218	52	91
V	GNE	GENENTECH INC	E	A	3.7	4.3	273	68	31
LARGE (L) - 500 Cos.			*Group*				*x500 (L)*	*Sort*	*x500 (L)*
L	JMED	JONES MEDICAL INDS INC	A	A	12.5	16.9	48	70	40
L	BGEN	BIOGEN INC	A	A	5.3	14.1	89	62	69
L	MYL	MYLAN LABORATORIES	A	B	17.6	14.1	90	54	102
L	ICN	ICN PHARMACEUTICALS INC	A	C	14.0	14.6	77	28	274
L	INCY	INCYTE PHARMACEUTICALS INC	B	A	−28.1	13.3	108	81	20
L	QTRN	QUINTILES TRANSNATIONAL	B	A	5.6	12.3	131	71	37
L	WPI	WATSON PHARMACEUTICALS	B	A	13.8	13.5	101	55	98
L	AZA	ALZA CORP	B	B	8.9	11.1	158	42	171
L	SHR	SCHERER (R P)/DE	B	C	11.2	10.6	177	37	203
L	CHIR	CHIRON CORP	C	B	2.8	9.9	209	44	159
L	GENZ	GENZYME CORP	C	B	1.2	9.8	215	40	191
L	FRX	FOREST LABORATORIES -CL A	D	A	11.7	7.9	305	62	64
L	DURA	DURA PHARMACEUTICALS INC	D	A	−10.5	6.3	371	62	66
L	IMNX	IMMUNEX CORP	E	A	−29.8	1.1	498	91	2
L	MEDI	MEDIMMUNE INC	E	A	−24.3	5.1	419	88	6
MEDIUM (M) - 600 Cos.			*Group*				*x600 (M)*	*Sort*	*x600 (M)*
M	BVF	BIOVAIL CORP INTERNATIONAL	A	A	22.3	29.5	8	76	33
M	BRL	BARR LABORATORIES INC	A	A	2.8	17.2	60	68	61
M	BTGC	BIO TECHNOLOGY GENERAL	A	A	−36.6	18.1	48	65	74
M	NVX	NORTH AMERICAN VACCINE INC	A	A	−17.7	45.5	1	61	96
M	THRX	THERAGENICS CORP	B	A	8.7	12.8	154	81	12
M	AGPH	AGOURON PHARMACEUTICALS	B	A	−21.9	13.6	129	62	88

	Symbol	Company	Group				x600 (S)	Sort	x600 (S)
M	SANG	SANGSTAT MEDICAL CORP	C	A	−35.0	9.9	253	78	21
M	MDRX	MEDICIS PHARMACEUT CP -CL	C	A	22.0	10.2	244	74	37
M	PRGO	PERRIGO COMPANY	C	C	9.5	8.3	343	24	321
M	NBTY	NBTY INC	C	D	9.5	9.4	284	18	365
M	BLOCA	BLOCK DRUG -CL A	D	E	6.7	7.7	387	2	498
M	IDPH	IDEC PHARMACEUTICALS CORP	E	A	−20.9	4.4	556	84	4
M	MLNM	MILLENNIUM PHARMACTCLS INC	E	A	2.0	3.4	568	75	34
M	GNSA	GENSIA SICOR INC	E	C	−52.6	5.6	507	27	301
SMALL (S) - 600 Cos.			**Group**				**x600 (S)**	**Sort**	**x600 (S)**
S	CURE	CURATIVE HEALTH SERVICES	A	A	−8.3	14.8	89	66	46
S	FAUL	FAULDING INC	A	A	4.2	13.7	120	49	109
S	VVUS	VIVUS INC	A	C	−35.2	25.9	12	22	301
S	THRT	THERATECH INC UTAH	B	A	−19.9	13.1	134	51	105
S	SERO	SEROLOGICALS CORP	C	A	9.6	9.2	293	59	65
S	CHRX	CHIREX INC	C	B	−3.2	10.0	248	47	122
S	NXTR	NEXSTAR PHARMACEUTICALS	E	A	−22.6	5.6	497	58	75
S	RPC	ROBERTS PHARMACEUTICAL	E	C	−2.6	1.6	591	18	340

Drugstore Industry

	Symbol	Company	Group					Sort	
VERY LARGE (V) - 300 Cos.			**Group**				**x300 (V)**	**Sort**	**x300 (V)**
V	WAG	WALGREEN CO	C	B	8.2	8.8	159	53	86
V	CVS	CVS CORP	D	B	6.7	7.0	211	52	94
V	RAD	RITE AID CORP	D	D	5.4	5.8	240	27	185
LARGE (L) - 500 Cos.			**Group**				**x500 (L)**	**Sort**	**x500 (L)**
L	ARBR	ARBOR DRUGS INC	C	B	8.6	9.5	229	52	116
L	LDG	LONGS DRUG STORES INC	D	D	5.7	5.7	390	14	366
MEDIUM (M) - 600 Cos.			**Group**				**x600 (M)**	**Sort**	**x600 (M)**
SMALL (S) - 600 Cos.			**Group**				**x600 (S)**	**Sort**	**x600 (S)**
S	GDX.A	GENOVESE DRUG STORES -CL	E	D	5.4	5.7	496	12	384

Electrical Equipment Industry

	Symbol	Company	Group					Sort	
VERY LARGE (V) - 300 Cos.			**Group**				**x300 (V)**	**Sort**	**x300 (V)**
V	GE	GENERAL ELECTRIC CO	B	A	10.1	11.6	86	61	52

(continued overleaf)

HOLT USA2000 Universe
Size / #cos / mkt cap

Very large / 300 / $3.93B+
Large / 500 / $1.03–3.93B
Medium / 600 / $.42–1.03B
Small / 600 / $154–425M

Grouped by Forecast +1 year CFROI Grade (Near Term) which is then sorted high-to-low on numerical % Future

		HOLT DualGrade® Performance		CFROI — Cash Flow Return on Investment			% of Total Market Value Attributed to Future Investments	
		#1 Near Term Fcst +1-year CFROI Grade	#2 Long Term % Future Grade	Past 5-year Median CFROI	Forecast +1-year CFROI	Forecast +1-year CFROI Rank	% Future	% Future Rank
V	EMR EMERSON ELECTRIC CO	B	B	10.2	11.2	98	47	117
V	GWW GRAINGER (W W) INC	B	C	10.2	11.0	107	40	140
V	GLW CORNING INC	B	C	7.9	10.5	114	38	148
V	HON HONEYWELL INC	C	C	9.3	9.5	144	29	178
V	ROK ROCKWELL INTL CORP	C	D	7.5	9.9	134	22	201
V	JCI JOHNSON CONTROLS INC	C	D	7.3	8.5	170	15	229
V	CBE COOPER INDUSTRIES INC	D	C	7.0	6.8	214	39	146
LARGE (L) - 500 Cos.		**Group**				**x500 (L)**	**Sort**	**x500 (L)**
L	JBIL JABIL CIRCUIT INC	A	A	9.5	21.2	14	66	54
L	VICR VICOR CORP	B	A	12.1	10.4	187	74	32
L	HUB.B HUBBELL INC -CL B	B	B	10.5	12.2	136	49	129
L	UCR UCAR INTERNATIONAL INC	B	D	9.1	10.8	164	22	313
L	AVX AVX CORP	B	E	10.3	10.3	191	6	415
L	GSX GENERAL SIGNAL CORP	C	C	5.2	8.8	269	35	229
L	TNB THOMAS & BETTS CORP	C	D	6.7	9.4	232	24	305
MEDIUM (M) - 600 Cos.		**Group**				**x600 (M)**	**Sort**	**x600 (M)**
M	ETEC ETEC SYSTEMS INC	A	B	14.7	18.1	49	54	133
M	LFUS LITTELFUSE INC	A	B	13.8	15.0	90	41	202
M	FSS FEDERAL SIGNAL CORP	B	B	11.0	10.6	221	45	183
M	TNL TECHNITROL INC	B	B	6.6	12.5	161	41	204
M	BWC BELDEN INC	B	C	12.2	11.4	197	22	337
M	SIPX SIPEX CORP	C	A	0.5	8.1	355	76	30
M	KUH KUHLMAN CORP	C	B	3.7	8.8	313	38	216
M	BEZ BALDOR ELECTRIC	C	B	8.3	10.1	246	37	221
M	MAG MAGNETEK INC	C	D	5.5	9.3	291	18	372

SMALL (S) - 600 Cos.

	Ticker	Company	Group	Group			x600 (S)	Sort	x600 (S)
S	TRII	TRANSCRYPT INTERNATIONAL	A	A	-6.7	24.8	17	76	13
S	SMTC	SEMTECH CORP	A	A	4.3	22.1	23	59	66
S	FELE	FRANKLIN ELECTRIC CO	B	B	9.6	10.2	240	34	207
S	LYTS	LSI INDS INC	B	B	11.0	12.3	163	32	224
S	CHP	C&D TECHNOLOGIES INC	B	B	8.7	10.2	235	30	235
S	WDHD	WOODHEAD INDUSTRIES INC	B	C	10.1	10.8	213	29	246
S	ADLT	ADVANCED LIGHTING TECH INC	D	B	8.9	7.1	413	39	177
S	KOPN	KOPIN CORP	E	A	-12.9	5.8	485	74	19

Electronics Industry

VERY LARGE (V) - 300 Cos.

	Ticker	Company	Group	Group			x300 (V)	Sort	x300 (V)
V	SLR	SOLECTRON CORP	B	B	12.5	12.9	71	56	72
V	MOLX	MOLEX INC	C	B	6.8	10.1	125	53	85
V	AMP	AMP INC	C	C	8.0	9.1	151	30	176

LARGE (L) - 500 Cos.

	Ticker	Company	Group	Group			x500 (L)	Sort	x500 (L)
L	UNPH	UNIPHASE CORP	A	A	6.1	16.6	50	81	21
L	SANM	SANMINA CORP	A	A	10.4	17.2	42	64	61
L	MCHP	MICROCHIP TECHNOLOGY INC	A	A	16.0	16.3	55	57	89
L	LXK	LEXMARK INTL GRP INC -CL A	A	B	10.5	15.6	61	55	100
L	SBL	SYMBOL TECHNOLOGIES	A	B	8.8	13.8	95	52	119
L	CREAF	CREATIVE TECHNOLOGY	A	B	33.6	22.8	8	45	154
L	VAR	VARIAN ASSOCIATES INC	B	D	9.7	12.1	139	24	303
L	ARW	ARROW ELECTRONICS INC	C	D	11.3	9.0	263	20	323
L	SRM	SENSORMATIC ELECTRONICS	C	D	7.9	8.5	283	14	367
L	PRY.A	PITTWAY CORP/DE -CL A	D	B	5.5	7.7	325	40	192
L	AVT	AVNET INC	D	C	5.9	6.7	361	26	291
L	HRS	HARRIS CORP	D	D	6.4	6.9	354	15	362
L	VSH	VISHAY INTRTECHNOLOGY	D	D	6.7	5.6	394	13	371

MEDIUM (M) - 600 Cos.

	Ticker	Company	Group	Group			x600 (M)	Sort	x600 (M)
M	MCRL	MICREL INC	A	A	9.8	19.9	30	71	51
M	PLT	PLANTRONICS INC	A	A	33.6	23.2	17	63	84
M	DYT	DYNATECH CORP	A	B	12.9	17.7	53	50	154
M	ESIO	ELECTRO SCIENTIFIC INDS INC	A	C	8.7	14.6	104	31	275

(continued overleaf)

HOLT USA2000 Universe
Size / #cos / mkt cap
Very large / 300 / $3.93B+
Large / 500 / $1.03–3.93B
Medium / 600 / $.42–1.03B
Small / 600 / $154–425M
*Grouped by Forecast +1 year CFROI Grade (Near Term)
which is then sorted high-to-low on numerical % Future*

			HOLT DualGrade® Performance		CFROI Cash Flow Return on Investment			% of Total Market Value Attributed to Future Investments	
			#1 Near Term Fcst +1-year CFROI Grade	#2 Long Term % Future Grade	Past 5-year Median CFROI	Forecast +1-year CFROI	Forecast +1-year CFROI Rank	% Future	% Future Rank
M	CPRD	COMPUTER PRODUCTS INC	B	B	8.1	13.5	134	53	136
M	FLEXF	FLEXTRONICS INTERNATIONAL	B	B	4.7	10.3	238	38	215
M	AVID	AVID TECHNOLOGY INC	B	B	8.5	13.8	124	35	239
M	CDT	CABLE DESIGN TECH CP -CL A	B	C	13.4	10.8	214	31	270
M	METHA	METHODE ELECTRONICS -CL A	B	C	12.0	13.0	148	24	323
M	TRMB	TRIMBLE NAVIGATION LTD	C	B	5.7	9.4	286	47	171
M	ANAD	ANADIGICS INC	C	B	8.6	8.2	350	44	189
M	DIIG	DII GROUP INC	C	B	6.6	9.8	262	36	230
M	KMET	KEMET CORP	C	C	9.4	9.6	273	26	306
M	FLK	FLUKE CORP	C	C	5.7	8.1	360	23	331
M	BMC	BMC INDUSTRIES INC/MN	C	D	9.6	10.1	248	12	427
M	SFE	SAFEGUARD SCIENTIFICS INC	D	B	9.8	7.4	403	46	175
M	KNT	KENT ELECTRONICS CORP	D	C	9.1	6.5	454	31	273
M	HAR	HARMAN INTERNATIONAL INDS	D	D	7.2	6.4	459	10	445
M	MI	MARSHALL INDUSTRIES	D	E	10.2	7.2	411	1	503
SMALL (S) - 600 Cos.			**Group**				**x600 (S)**	**Sort**	**x600 (S)**
S	LOJN	LO-JACK CORPORATION	A	A	8.8	21.7	24	67	37
S	GILTF	GILAT SATELLITE NETWORKS	A	A	11.9	14.0	110	55	88
S	GSCN	GENERAL SCANNING INC	A	C	7.4	14.0	112	22	299
S	QKTN	QUICKTURN DESIGN SYSTEMS	A	C	15.8	14.2	105	16	352
S	COHU	COHU INC	A	D	16.3	20.2	34	13	375
S	AGI	ALPINE GROUP INC	A	D	3.8	15.8	78	12	387
S	CREE	CREE RESEARCH INC	B	A	-2.2	11.0	202	72	24
S	FEI	FREQUENCY ELECTRONICS INC	B	B	-7.4	13.1	135	43	148
S	HLPH	HOLOPHANE CORP	B	B	12.7	11.4	192	41	159
S	HRMN	HARMON INDUSTRIES INC	B	B	11.6	11.3	195	33	222

	Ticker	Company						Sort	
S	BHE	BENCHMARK ELECTRONICS INC	B	C	11.0	12.8	148	28	255
S	PLXS	PLEXUS CORP	B	C	6.8	10.4	229	21	310
S	SG	SCIENTIFIC GAMES HLDGS	B	D	20.6	13.0	139	10	404
S	SPCT	SPECTRIAN CORP	B	D	3.2	11.8	175	4	440
S	AHA	ALPHA INDS	C	B	-8.5	9.1	301	35	198
S	ROG	ROGERS CORP	C	B	9.2	9.1	305	35	202
S	ZRO	ZERO CORP/DE	C	B	6.8	9.9	250	31	228
S	TLXN	TELXON CORP	C	C	1.3	8.5	339	25	284
S	ALRN	ALTRON INC	C	D	11.7	9.3	290	8	409
S	PIOS	PIONEER STANDARD ELECTRON	C	D	12.6	8.8	322	6	427
S	ITI	ITI TECHNOLOGIES INC	D	B	9.6	7.6	373	45	130
S	EXAR	EXAR CORP	D	D	8.7	7.1	411	6	428
S	CMIC	CALIFORNIA MICROWAVE	E	B	6.0	5.4	510	45	131
S	ELMG	ELECTROMAGNETIC SCIENCES	E	C	1.3	5.7	494	18	337
S	CUB	CUBIC CORP	E	C	2.4	5.6	500	16	349
S	CMW	CANADIAN MARCONI CO	E	D	1.9	3.8	559	1	465

Entertainment Industry

	Ticker	Company	Group				x300 (V)	Sort	x300 (V)
VERY LARGE (V) - 300 Cos.									
V	DIS	DISNEY (WALT) COMPANY	D	C	9.1	8.1	183	45	122
V	CCU	CLEAR CHANNEL COMMUN	E	A	6.3	1.3	299	75	15
V	TWX	TIME WARNER INC	E	A	2.5	0.6	300	61	53

	Ticker	Company	Group				x500 (L)	Sort	x500 (L)
LARGE (L) - 500 Cos.									
L	WONE	WESTWOOD ONE INC	A	A	4.3	15.1	72	81	24
L	LNTV	LIN TELEVISION CORP	B	A	10.1	11.0	159	62	70
L	KWP	KING WORLD PRODUCTIONS	B	B	17.2	12.7	123	40	193
L	CXR	COX RADIO INC -CL A	E	A	5.9	1.5	494	60	75
L	SBGI	SINCLAIR BROADCAST GP -CL A	E	A	2.1	2.8	484	56	93
L	BLC	BELO (AH) CORP -SER A COM	E	B	6.7	2.8	482	44	161
L	BHC	BHC COMMUNICATIONS -CL A	E	B	4.2	2.4	485	39	197
L	GET	GAYLORD ENTERTAINMENT	E	D	6.2	3.2	474	15	360

	Ticker	Company	Group				x600 (M)	Sort	x600 (M)
MEDIUM (M) - 600 Cos.									
M	EMMS	EMMIS BROADCASTING CP -CL A	C	A	11.4	8.2	353	58	112
M	UTVI	UNITED TELEVISION INC	C	B	10.4	9.4	283	49	162

(continued overleaf)

HOLT USA2000 Universe
Size / #cos / mkt cap
Very large / 300 / $3.93B+
Large / 500 / $1.03–3.93B
Medium / 600 / $.42–1.03B
Small / 600 / $.154–425M

Grouped by Forecast +1 year CFROI Grade (Near Term) which is then sorted high-to-low on numerical % Future

			HOLT DualGrade® Performance		CFROI — Cash Flow Return on Investment			% of Total Market Value Attributed to Future Investments	
			#1 Near Term Fcst +1-year CFROI Grade	#2 Long Term % Future Grade	Past 5-year Median CFROI	Forecast +1-year CFROI	Forecast +1-year CFROI Rank	% Future	Future Rank
M	REGL	REGAL CINEMAS INC	D	D	7.0	8.0	364	18	369
M	SFXBA	SFX BROADCASTING INC -CL A	D	D	5.4	7.1	419	15	392
M	SP	SPELLING ENTERTNMT GRP INC	D	D	3.7	6.5	458	14	408
M	CINRF	CINAR FILMS INC -CL B	E	A	8.7	4.4	555	77	23
SMALL (S) - 600 Cos.			*Group*				*x600 (S)*	*Sort*	*x600 (S)*
S	MBE	MALIBU ENTMT WORLDWIDE INC	A	E	2.7	25.1	16	-18	547
S	TLMD	TELEMUNDO GROUP INC -CL A	E	A	6.7	1.6	592	71	26
S	GCX	GC COMPANIES INC	E	C	3.1	2.8	576	16	354
S	AEN	AMC ENTERTAINMENT INC	E	D	6.5	5.2	520	4	441
S	CPX	CINEPLEX ODEON	E	D	0.2	2.9	575	0	469
S	CKE	CARMIKE CINEMAS INC -CL A	E	E	5.5	5.7	490	-4	493

Environmental Industry

VERY LARGE (V) - 300 Cos.			*Group*				*x300 (V)*	*Sort*	*x300 (V)*
V	UW	USA WASTE SERVICES INC	B	D	9.7	11.4	90	21	208
V	BFI	BROWNING-FERRIS INDS	D	C	5.6	7.2	209	30	175
V	RII	REPUBLIC INDUSTRIES INC	D	D	5.4	6.5	220	23	199
V	WMX	WASTE MANAGEMENT INC	E	D	6.5	5.0	258	19	219
LARGE (L) - 500 Cos.			*Group*				*x500 (L)*	*Sort*	*x500 (L)*
L	CUL	CULLIGAN WATER TECH INC	A	B	10.2	16.8	49	53	109
L	SK	SAFETY-KLEEN CORP	D	C	5.8	6.2	375	29	263
L	PHV	PHILIP SERVICES CORP	D	E	7.2	6.5	364	8	406
L	WTI	WHEELABRATOR TECHNOL	D	E	6.3	5.6	397	7	409
L	AWIN	ALLIED WASTE INDS INC	E	B	3.3	1.6	493	54	105
L	USF	U S FILTER CORP	E	B	3.1	2.3	487	50	124

	Ticker	Company	Group				x600 (M)	Sort	x600 (M)
MEDIUM (M) - 600 Cos.									
M	EESI	EASTN ENVIRONMENT SVC	D	A	-7.8	7.6	390	60	102
M	ION	IONICS INC	D	C	4.6	6.6	446	29	284
M	CTAL	CATALYTICA INC	E	B	-32.4	1.3	594	37	226

	Ticker	Company	Group				x600 (S)	Sort	x600 (S)
SMALL (S) - 600 Cos.									
S	LDR	LANDAUER INC	A	A	33.8	34.9	5	66	43
S	TTI	TETRA TECHNOLOGIES INC/DE	C	D	5.7	9.7	256	14	369
S	OHM	OHM CORP	C	E	5.4	8.8	320	-10	513
S	WATR	TETRA TECH INC	D	B	10.6	7.9	364	45	128
S	MTLM	METAL MANAGEMENT INC	D	C	-1.3	6.9	427	27	269
S	DM	DAMES & MOORE GROUP	E	C	5.8	4.8	531	22	304
S	LLE	LAIDLAW ENVIRONMENTAL SVCS	E	C	-1.3	4.1	550	16	358

Food Processing Industry

	Ticker	Company	Group				x300 (V)	Sort	x300 (V)
VERY LARGE (V) - 300 Cos.									
V	WWY	WRIGLEY (WM) JR CO	A	A	17.3	16.6	46	68	29
V	PHB	PIONEER HI-BRED INT	A	A	14.1	15.7	49	68	30
V	CPB	CAMPBELL SOUP CO	A	A	14.6	16.9	45	65	36
V	OAT	QUAKER OATS CO	A	A	10.6	14.5	60	59	58
V	GIS	GENERAL MILLS INC	A	B	14.3	15.2	54	56	73
V	K	KELLOGG CO	B	A	15.6	12.9	70	62	50
V	HSY	HERSHEY FOODS CORP	B	B	9.4	11.0	105	52	90
V	SLE	SARA LEE CORP	B	B	10.4	11.3	93	49	107
V	HNZ	HEINZ (H J) CO	B	C	11.1	12.4	75	44	127
V	CAG	CONAGRA INC	B	C	9.8	11.7	84	40	141
V	CPC	CPC INTERNATIONAL INC	C	B	9.5	10.2	123	46	120
V	NA	NABISCO HLDGS CORP -CL A	D	B	2.4	6.1	235	49	106
V	ADM	ARCHER-DANIELS-MIDLAND CO	D	E	6.2	6.4	225	-6	274

	Ticker	Company	Group				x500 (L)	Sort	x500 (L)
LARGE (L) - 500 Cos.									
L	TR	TOOTSIE ROLL INDS	B	A	11.3	10.2	194	56	90
L	MCCRK	MCCORMICK & CO	B	B	9.8	10.9	161	43	165
L	IBC	INTERSTATE BAKERIES CP	C	B	5.7	10.0	205	43	164
L	FLO	FLOWERS INDUSTRIES INC	C	C	5.4	9.1	252	38	201
L	HRL	HORMEL FOODS CORP	C	C	9.8	9.2	248	34	233

(continued overleaf)

HOLT USA2000 Universe
Size / #cos / mkt cap

Very large / 300 / $3.93B+
Large / 500 / $1.03–3.93B
Medium / 600 / $.42–1.03B
Small / 600 / $154–425M

Grouped by Forecast +1 year CFROI Grade (Near Term)
which is then sorted high-to-low on numerical % Future

		HOLT DualGrade® Performance		CFROI Cash Flow Return on Investment			% of Total Market Value Attributed to Future Investments	
		#1 Near Term Fcst +1-year CFROI Grade	#2 Long Term % Future Grade	Past 5-year Median CFROI	Forecast +1-year CFROI	Forecast +1-year CFROI Rank	% Future	% Future Rank
L	SFDS	SMITHFIELD FOODS INC	C	C	6.4	8.5	285	25	297
L	DOL	DOLE FOOD CO INC	C	D	4.8	8.2	295	21	319
L	DKB	DEKALB GENETICS CORP -CL B	D	A	3.6	7.4	338	56	95
L	DF	DEAN FOODS CO	D	B	7.0	7.8	316	40	187
L	UFC	UNIVERSAL FOODS CORP	D	C	8.5	8.1	302	28	275
L	IBP	IBP INC	D	E	8.8	3.9	453	-2	439
MEDIUM (M) - 600 Cos.		Group		x600 (M)			Sort	x600 (M)	
M	SZA	SUIZA FOODS CORP	B	D	12.5	10.5	224	18	367
M	LNCE	LANCE INC	D	B	5.6	7.9	368	50	156
M	SJM.A	SMUCKER (JM) CO -CL A	D	C	6.8	7.2	410	25	316
M	MIKL	MICHAEL FOODS INC	D	D	3.7	7.2	416	15	395
M	CHX	PILGRIMS PRIDE CORP	D	E	8.7	7.5	398	-2	516
M	DRYR	DREYER'S GRAND ICE CREAM	E	B	2.6	5.5	511	42	194
M	RAH	RALCORP HOLDINGS INC	E	C	9.2	5.6	505	24	320
M	IMC	INTL MULTIFOODS CORP	E	C	6.5	5.6	506	21	345
M	EGR	EARTHGRAINS CO	E	C	-1.6	2.5	584	19	360
M	HFI	HUDSON FOODS INC -CL A	E	D	4.4	4.9	535	13	417
M	CQB	CHIQUITA BRANDS INTL	E	E	4.3	5.5	510	-3	521
SMALL (S) - 600 Cos.		Group		x600 (S)			Sort	x600 (S)	
S	RVFD	RIVIANA FOODS INC	B	C	9.9	10.4	228	21	309
S	WFDS	WORTHINGTON FOODS INC	C	C	7.5	9.6	265	28	254
S	CBRYA	NORTHLAND CRANBERRIES -CL	C	C	4.8	8.4	343	17	346
S	SAFM	SANDERSON FARMS INC	D	E	5.6	7.6	380	-11	522

Food Wholesalers Industry

	Ticker	Company	Group				x300(V)/x500(L)/x600(M)/x600(S)	Sort	x300(V)/x500(L)/x600(M)/x600(S)
VERY LARGE (V) - 300 Cos.									
V	SYY	SYSCO CORP	B	B	9.4	10.5	113	51	95
LARGE (L) - 500 Cos.									
L	RFH	RICHFOOD HOLDINGS INC	B		11.1	13.3	107	43	162
L	SVU	SUPERVALU INC	D		7.6	7.7	326	10	393
MEDIUM (M) - 600 Cos.									
M	JPF	JP FOODSERVICE INC	C	B	7.4	8.7	318	40	205
M	RYK	RYKOFF-SEXTON INC	C	D	3.1	9.2	293	9	453
M	FLM	FLEMING COMPANIES INC	E	E	5.2	4.9	533	-16	568
SMALL (S) - 600 Cos.									
S	PFGC	PERFORMANCE FOOD GROUP	E	C	6.4	5.4	508	23	296
S	NAFC	NASH FINCH CO	E	E	4.2	4.1	551	-16	537

Furniture/Home Furnishings Industry

	Ticker	Company	Group				x300(V)/x500(L)/x600(M)/x600(S)	Sort	x300(V)/x500(L)/x600(M)/x600(S)
VERY LARGE (V) - 300 Cos.									
V	LEG	LEGGETT & PLATT INC	C		9.6	11.8	82	31	171
LARGE (L) - 500 Cos.									
L	MLHR	MILLER (HERMAN) INC	B	A	6.3	13.5	102	59	81
L	HONI	HON INDUSTRIES	B	B	12.0	13.1	111	48	133
L	ETH	ETHAN ALLEN INTERIORS INC	B	B	7.6	10.7	168	46	138
L	FBN	FURNITURE BRANDS INTL INC	D	C	6.7	7.4	339	35	227
L	SHX	SHAW INDUSTRIES INC	E	E	7.0	5.3	410	7	413
MEDIUM (M) - 600 Cos.									
M	CHML	CHICAGO MINATURE LAMP INC	B	B	6.3	11.9	185	54	130
M	CBZ	CORT BUSINESS SERVICES	B	B	10.0	10.9	211	42	198
M	DFS	DEPARTMENT 56 INC -SER A	B	C	18.8	12.9	150	33	249
M	LZB	LA-Z-BOY INC	C	C	6.9	8.2	349	19	357
M	KBALB	KIMBALL INTERNATIONAL -CL B	C	E	6.1	8.5	328	2	500

(continued overleaf)

HOLT USA2000 Universe
Size / #cos / mkt cap

Very large / 300 / $3.93B+
Large / 500 / $1.03–3.93B
Medium / 600 / $.42–1.03B
Small / 600 / $154–425M

Grouped by Forecast +1 year CFROI Grade (Near Term) which is then sorted high-to-low on numerical % Future

		HOLT DualGrade® Performance		CFROI Cash Flow Return on Investment			% of Total Market Value Attributed to Future Investments	
		#1 Near Term Fcst +1-year CFROI Grade	#2 Long Term % Future Grade	Past 5-year Median CFROI	Forecast +1-year CFROI	Forecast +1-year CFROI Rank	% Future	% Future Rank
							Sort	
						x600 (S)	x600 (S)	
SMALL (S) - 600 Cos.		**Group**						
S	VIR VIRCO MANUFACTURING	B	C	5.0	10.4	227	29	249
S	BSH BUSH INDUSTRIES -CL A	C	C	10.7	10.0	249	28	259
S	JUNO JUNO LIGHTING INC	C	C	12.2	10.2	241	25	287
S	AMWD AMERICAN WOODMARK CORP	C	C	4.4	9.7	257	23	298
S	CRC CHROMCRAFT REVINGTON INC	C	C	12.4	8.8	326	20	321
S	SY SHELBY WILLIAMS INDS INC	C	D	4.8	8.7	328	14	374
S	OSU O'SULLIVAN INDS HLDGS INC	D	E	7.0	6.5	454	-26	573
S	BSET BASSETT FURNITURE INDS	E	D	4.2	2.7	579	5	434

Grocery Store Industry

						x300 (V)	x300 (V)	
VERY LARGE (V) - 300 Cos.		**Group**						
V	ABS ALBERTSONS INC	B	C	11.3	10.5	116	43	131
V	SWY SAFEWAY INC	C	C	8.3	8.5	171	41	136
V	KR KROGER CO	C	C	9.4	9.8	138	37	154
V	FDLNA FOOD LION INC -CL A	C	D	7.8	8.3	177	15	232
V	WIN WINN-DIXIE STORES INC	D	C	7.1	7.1	210	35	158
V	ASC AMERICAN STORES CO	E	D	5.6	4.2	274	23	200
V	TSN TYSON FOODS INC -CL A	E	D	4.3	5.6	244	22	203

						x500 (L)	x500 (L)	
LARGE (L) - 500 Cos.		**Group**						
L	HRD HANNAFORD BROTHERS CO	C	C	8.8	8.6	277	27	281
L	XQ QUALITY FOOD CENTERS INC	D	C	10.9	5.9	384	35	224
L	GFS.A GIANT FOOD INC -CL A	E	D	6.2	5.0	425	21	320
L	WMK WEIS MARKETS INC	E	D	5.5	5.3	413	11	389
L	GAP GREAT ATLANTIC & PAC TEA CO	E	E	3.3	4.8	433	-15	462

			Group			x600 (M)	Sort	x600 (M)
MEDIUM (M) - 600 Cos.								
M	DFF	DOMINICKS SUPERMKTS	B	6.9	12.1	174	45	179
M	WFMI	WHOLE FOODS MARKET INC	C	4.1	8.7	320	51	147
M	SLCM	SOUTHLAND CORP	D	6.5	6.2	476	17	380
M	CASY	CASEYS GENERAL STORES INC	D	7.4	7.8	383	16	385
M	RDK	RUDDICK CORP	D	6.1	6.6	452	5	479
			Group			**x600 (S)**	**Sort**	**x600 (S)**
SMALL (S) - 600 Cos.								
S	SMF	SMART & FINAL INC	D	8.0	7.1	412	12	386
S	IMKTA	INGLES MARKETS INC -CL A	E	4.9	5.9	480	-9	509

Healthcare Information Systems Industry

			Group			x300 (V)	Sort	x300 (V)
VERY LARGE (V) - 300 Cos.								
V	HBOC	HBO & CO	A	13.8	19.9	25	84	3
V	CZT	COGNIZANT CORP	A	16.9	21.1	16	69	28
			Group			**x500 (L)**	**Sort**	**x500 (L)**
LARGE (L) - 500 Cos.								
L	SMS	SHARED MEDICAL SYSTEMS	B	7.9	10.4	190	59	78
			Group			**x600 (M)**	**Sort**	**x600 (M)**
MEDIUM (M) - 600 Cos.								
M	ACCS	ACCESS HEALTH MARKETING	A	8.5	20.8	25	68	60
M	ABRX	ABR INFORMATION SVCS INC	A	8.3	7.1	423	61	94
M	CERN	CERNER CORP	B	15.6	6.2	474	56	124
M	NCSS	NCS HEALTHCARE INC -CL A	B	1.3	0.4	599	54	132
			Group			**x600 (S)**	**Sort**	**x600 (S)**
SMALL (S) - 600 Cos.								
S	MMGR	MEDICAL MANAGER CORP	A	110.1	16.4	68	68	36

Home Appliance Industry

			Group			x300 (V)	Sort	x300 (V)
VERY LARGE (V) - 300 Cos.								
V	WHR	WHIRLPOOL CORP	E	5.0	5.6	245	7	248
			Group			**x500 (L)**	**Sort**	**x500 (L)**
LARGE (L) - 500 Cos.								
L	MYG	MAYTAG CORP	C	6.8	8.9	264	39	196
L	BDK	BLACK & DECKER CORP	D	6.0	5.8	386	32	249

(continued overleaf)

HOLT USA2000 Universe
Size / #cos / mkt cap

Very large / 300 / $3.93B+
Large / 500 / $1.03–3.93B
Medium / 600 / $.42–1.03B
Small / 600 / $154–425M

Grouped by Forecast +1 year CFROI Grade (Near Term) which is then sorted high-to-low on numerical % Future

		HOLT DualGrade® Performance		*CFROI Cash Flow Return on Investment*			*% of Total Market Value Attributed to Future Investments*	
		#1 Near Term Fcst +1-year CFROI Grade	#2 Long Term % Future Grade	Past 5-year Median CFROI	Forecast +1-year CFROI	Forecast +1-year CFROI Rank	% Future	% Future Rank
MEDIUM (M) - 600 Cos.		*Group*		**x600 (M)**		**x600 (M)**	*Sort*	**x600 (M)**
M	TTC TORO CO	D	E	8.6	7.0	426	-12	559
SMALL (S) - 600 Cos.		*Group*		**x600 (S)**		**x600 (S)**	*Sort*	**x600 (S)**
S	RCOT RECOTON CORP	D	D	8.0	7.2	410	2	459
S	NPK NATIONAL PRESTO INDS INC	D	D	6.6	6.8	431	1	464

Homebuilding Industry

		#1 Near Term Fcst +1-year CFROI Grade	#2 Long Term % Future Grade	Past 5-year Median CFROI	Forecast +1-year CFROI	Forecast +1-year CFROI Rank	% Future	% Future Rank
VERY LARGE (V) - 300 Cos.		*Group*		**x300 (V)**		**x300 (V)**	*Sort*	**x300 (V)**
V	HMT HOST MARRIOTT CORP	E	E	2.9	5.3	250	4	256
LARGE (L) - 500 Cos.		*Group*		**x500 (L)**		**x500 (L)**	*Sort*	**x500 (L)**
L	NHL NEWHALL LAND & FARM -LP	B	B	7.1	11.3	153	43	168
L	CDX CATELLUS DEVELOPMENT	D	C	2.6	6.0	379	36	216
MEDIUM (M) - 600 Cos.		*Group*		**x600 (M)**		**x600 (M)**	*Sort*	**x600 (M)**
M	FFD FAIRFIELD COMMUNITIES INC	B	A	6.4	10.8	215	60	98
SMALL (S) - 600 Cos.		*Group*		**x600 (S)**		**x600 (S)**	*Sort*	**x600 (S)**
S	MODT MODTECH INC	A	A	6.6	25.8	13	57	81
S	CROS CROSSMANN COMMUNITIES INC	B	B	14.4	13.0	140	40	163
S	HSTR AMERICAN HOMESTAR CORP	B	C	11.9	12.4	161	26	280
S	NVR NVR INC -LP	C	D	8.2	9.4	278	6	432
S	CON CONTINENTAL HOMES HOLDING	D	C	8.4	7.4	394	16	359
S	MDC MDC HOLDINGS INC	E	D	7.9	5.3	512	10	402

Hotel/Gaming Industry

VERY LARGE (V) - 300 Cos.

	Ticker	Company	Group	Group			x300 (V)	Sort	x300 (V)
V	MAR	MARRIOTT INTL INC	C	C	5.7	9.2	148	37	151
V	ITT	ITT CORPORATION	D	C	6.1	6.5	223	30	174
V	MIR	MIRAGE RESORTS INC	D	D	7.9	6.4	227	26	188
V	HLT	HILTON HOTELS CORP	E	D	5.7	4.5	267	28	182

LARGE (L) - 500 Cos.

	Ticker	Company	Group	Group			x500 (L)	Sort	x500 (L)
L	PRH	PROMUS HOTEL CORP	B	A	13.8	13.8	94	52	115
L	IGT	INTL GAME TECHNOLOGY	B	A	15.2	14.6	79	49	132
L	MGG	MGM GRAND INC	D	B	10.1	10.4	186	19	332
L	LQI	LA QUINTA INNS INC	D	C	7.4	8.8	270	11	386
L	HET	HARRAHS ENTERTAINMENT INC	E	C	9.1	8.5	284	0	435
L	SIH	SUN INTERNATIONAL HOTELS	D	D	3.2	6.2	372	10	395
L	BH	BRISTOL HOTEL CO	E	D	3.6	6.8	359	7	411
L	ESA	EXTENDED STAY AMERICA INC	C	E	-1.3	1.5	495	30	255
L	GTK	GTECH HOLDINGS CORP	D	E	7.7	5.2	414	24	304
L	TREE	DOUBLETREE CORP	D	E	10.2	2.9	480	21	318
L	CIR	CIRCUS CIRCUS ENTERPR INC	E	E	8.7	5.3	412	4	421

MEDIUM (M) - 600 Cos.

	Ticker	Company	Group	Group			x600 (M)	Sort	x600 (M)
M	SLOT	ANCHOR GAMING	A	C	14.2	20.3	27	31	266
M	WYN	WYNDHAM HOTEL CORP	C	B	12.4	9.3	288	37	223
M	RHC	RIO HOTEL & CASINO INC	D	C	5.2	7.3	409	22	338
M	SBO	SHOWBOAT INC	D	D	6.0	6.2	478	13	412
M	PRMA	PRIMADONNA RESORTS INC	D	D	8.3	7.1	420	12	426
M	PDQ	PRIME HOSPITALITY CORP	D	D	5.3	7.5	392	8	456
M	MCS	MARCUS CORP	D	E	5.8	6.9	436	4	483
M	RRI	RED ROOF INNS INC	D	E	7.4	7.1	421	-9	545
M	GND	GRAND CASINOS INC	D	E	6.2	7.9	371	-11	552
M	HPK	HOLLYWOOD PARK INC	E	D	1.9	3.0	576	15	393

SMALL (S) - 600 Cos.

	Ticker	Company	Group	Group			x600 (S)	Sort	x600 (S)
S	AMCV	AMERICAN CLASSIC VOYAGES C	B	B	0.2	10.5	224	30	241
S	ALLY	ALLIANCE GAMING CORP	C	B	1.2	10.5	222	19	327
S	BYD	BOYD GAMING CORP	E	C	7.4	8.5	338	-12	527

(continued overleaf)

HOLT USA2000 Universe
Size / #cos / mkt cap
Very large / 300 / $3.93B+
Large / 500 / $1.03–3.93B
Medium / 600 / $.42–1.03B
Small / 600 / $.154–425M

Grouped by Forecast +1 year CFROI Grade (Near Term) which is then sorted high-to-low on numerical % Future

			HOLT DualGrade® Performance		CFROI Cash Flow Return on Investment			% of Total Market Value Attributed to Future Investment	
			#1 Near Term Fcst +1-year CFROI Grade	#2 Long Term % Future Grade	Past 5-year Median CFROI	Forecast +1-year CFROI	Forecast +1-year CFROI Rank	% Future	% Future Rank
S	SER	SERVICO INC	C	E	6.9	9.4	279	-16	541
S	SLAM	SUBURBAN LODGES AMER INC	D	D	6.2	6.1	473	13	376
S	HVY	HARVEYS CASINO RESORTS	D	E	3.3	6.8	434	-23	565
S	STN	STATION CASINOS INC	E	D	4.1	5.2	521	11	390
S	AZR	AZTAR CORP	E	E	4.3	5.2	516	-31	578

Household Products Industry

			Group		x300 (V)	x300 (V)	x300 (V)	Sort	x300 (V)
VERY LARGE (V) - 300 Cos.									
V	PG	PROCTER & GAMBLE CO	A	A	12.3	14.7	59	65	35
V	CLX	CLOROX CO/DE	B	B	12.7	12.4	76	57	68
V	CL	COLGATE-PALMOLIVE CO	B	B	10.8	12.7	73	56	74
V	KMB	KIMBERLY-CLARK CORP	B	C	8.4	11.4	89	37	152
V	RAL	RALSTON PURINA CO	C	B	11.5	10.0	128	51	97
V	NWL	NEWELL COMPANIES	C	C	9.7	8.6	169	44	125
LARGE (L) - 500 Cos.			Group		x500 (L)	x500 (L)	x500 (L)	Sort	x500 (L)
L	SOC	SUNBEAM CORPORATION	A	A	6.2	15.4	68	67	52
L	DL	DIAL CORPORATION	A	A	11.8	13.8	97	60	76
L	BTH	BLYTH INDUSTRIES INC	A	A	14.5	14.4	85	57	87
L	LANC	LANCASTER COLONY CORP	A	B	13.9	13.9	93	39	195
L	TUP	TUPPERWARE CORP	B	C	13.5	10.4	185	27	283
L	RBD	RUBBERMAID INC	C	B	12.3	9.4	233	45	150
L	FBR	FIRST BRANDS CORP	D	C	8.8	6.8	360	26	293
MEDIUM (M) - 600 Cos.			Group		x600 (M)	x600 (M)	x600 (M)	Sort	x600 (M)
M	RCII	RENTERS CHOICE INC	A	C	22.8	19.8	32	31	269
M	SAMC	SAMSONITE CORP	A	C	7.6	16.0	71	22	336

	Ticker	Company	Group				x600 (S)	Sort	x600 (S)
M	LBY	LIBBEY INC	B	C	15.2	10.7	219	33	255
M	SMG	SCOTTS COMPANY	C	D	8.3	8.4	337	11	434
M	OCQ	ONEIDA LTD	D	C	4.8	6.9	432	31	274
M	CHD	CHURCH & DWIGHT INC	D	C	6.8	7.7	384	29	281
M	WSO	WATSCO INC	D	C	7.6	6.7	441	20	351
M	CENT	CENTRAL GARDEN & PET CO	E	C	5.4	6.0	485	31	272

SMALL (S) - 600 Cos.

Industrial Services Industry

	Ticker	Company	Group				x300 (V)	Sort	x300 (V)
V	EFX	EQUIFAX INC	A	A	12.7	14.9	58	74	19
V	SVM	SERVICEMASTER CO	C	A	14.0	8.9	155	65	38
V	LDW	LAIDLAW INC	E	D	4.0	3.6	290	22	204

VERY LARGE (V) - 300 Cos.

	Ticker	Company	Group				x500 (L)	Sort	x500 (L)
L	APOL	APOLLO GROUP INC -CL A	A	A	12.8	15.9	57	84	9
L	RHI	ROBERT HALF INTL INC	A	A	7.6	14.3	87	83	14
L	CXC	CORRECTIONS CORP OF AM	A	A	8.6	15.4	67	71	35
L	CTAS	CINTAS CORP	B	A	12.4	13.2	110	69	44
L	MSM	MSC INDUSTRIAL DIRECT -CL A	B	A	13.5	12.2	137	66	56
L	DV	DEVRY INC	B	A	10.4	11.3	152	65	58
L	TSG	SABRE GROUP HLDGS INC -CL	B	B	19.1	12.2	135	47	136
L	MAN	MANPOWER INC/WI	B	B	11.0	11.5	148	46	145
L	KELYA	KELLY SERVICES INC -CL A	B	C	9.4	10.6	180	29	268
L	ASI	ACCUSTAFF INC	D	A	3.8	5.8	387	56	94
L	ART	ACNIELSEN CORP	D	B	-5.9	5.7	393	40	182
L	USI	U S INDUSTRIES INC	D	B	6.5	7.3	343	40	185
L	PK	CENTRAL PARKING CORP	E	B	6.7	4.7	436	44	157
L	OLS	OLSTEN CORP	E	D	8.3	4.7	435	22	314

LARGE (L) - 500 Cos.

	Ticker	Company	Group				x600 (M)	Sort	x600 (M)
M	METZ	METZLER GROUP INC	A	A	-7.0	22.6	19	83	7
M	STRA	STRAYER EDUCATION INC	A	A	25.4	15.3	83	71	48
M	ROMC	ROMAC INTERNATIONAL INC	A	A	6.7	14.6	102	71	50
M	NIS	NOVA CORP/GA	A	A	13.7	22.5	20	70	52

MEDIUM (M) - 600 Cos.

(continued overleaf)

HOLT USA2000 Universe Size / #cos / mkt cap Very large / 300 / $3.93B+ Large / 500 / $1.03–3.93B Medium / 600 / $.42–1.03B Small / 600 / $154–425M Grouped by Forecast +1 year CFROI Grade (Near Term) which is then sorted high-to-low on numerical % Future	HOLT DualGrade® Performance		CFROI — Cash Flow Return on Investment			% of Total Market Value Attributed to Future Investments	
	#1 Near Term Fcst +1-year CFROI Grade	#2 Long Term % Future Grade	Past 5-year Median CFROI	Forecast +1-year CFROI	Forecast +1-year CFROI Rank	% Future	% Future Rank
M EDMC EDUCATION MANAGEMENT	A	A	10.2	16.6	68	70	53
M POS CATALINA MARKETING CORP	A	A	21.8	21.8	22	66	66
M VOL VOLT INFO SCIENCES INC	A	B	6.5	14.2	117	55	126
M TTEC TELETECH HOLDINGS INC	A	B	11.4	16.1	70	50	155
M APAC APAC TELESERVICES INC	A	B	26.9	19.9	31	40	209
M CLCX COMPUTER LEARNING CTRS	B	A	8.3	10.6	222	72	42
M LTRE LEARNING TREE INTL INC	B	A	18.0	12.5	160	72	43
M WHC WACKENHUT CORRECTIONS	B	A	8.8	13.7	126	72	44
M STAF STAFFMARK INC	B	B	8.3	11.3	198	56	121
M CDI CDI CORP	B	B	7.4	12.3	165	53	139
M NLCS NATIONAL COMPUTER SYS INC	B	C	8.6	11.5	196	27	297
M SFL SANTA FE PAC PIPELINE PRTNRS	B	E	12.2	11.8	186	1	504
M CWC CARIBINER INTERNATIONAL INC	C	A	10.8	9.7	265	71	49
M ESI ITT EDUCATIONAL SVCS INC	C	A	8.5	10.1	250	60	101
M SUPR SUPERIOR SERVICES INC	C	B	9.2	9.1	301	42	196
M NRL NORRELL CORP	C	C	11.0	9.2	296	26	308
M UNF UNIFIRST CORP	C	C	8.0	8.8	314	22	334
M BPL BUCKEYE PARTNERS -LP	D	D	7.4	7.4	401	13	415
M TCK THERMO ECOTEK CORP	D	D	5.7	7.0	428	10	443
M FC FRANKLIN COVEY CO	D	D	13.1	6.8	440	7	468
M CSTF CORESTAFF INC	E	A	-3.4	2.1	590	64	77
M ROL ROLLINS INC	E	B	10.9	5.5	513	56	122
M SW STONE & WEBSTER INC	E	B	-5.3	1.0	596	47	172
M GKSRA G&K SERVICES INC -CL A	E	B	8.8	4.8	538	40	206
M ABM ABM INDUSTRIES INC	E	C	4.4	5.3	523	34	242
M EBY ELSAG BAILEY PROCS AUTOMAT	E	E	8.0	5.3	526	-25	582

SMALL (S) - 600 Cos.		Group				x600 (S)	Sort	x600 (S)
S	ACRT	ACTRADE INTERNATIONAL LTD	A	A	10.4	21.0	27	84	1
S	VCAM	VINCAM GROUP INC	A	A	10.3	17.4	54	82	3
S	ASGN	ON ASSIGNMENT INC	A	A	17.7	16.8	62	75	17
S	QRSI	QUICKRESPONSE SERVICES	A	A	11.8	14.6	96	73	20
S	PRGX	PROFIT RECOVERY GRP INTL	A	A	23.8	19.0	41	69	31
S	BNTT	BARNETT INC	A	A	14.8	14.1	108	66	42
S	ALRC	ALTERNATIVE RESOURCES	A	A	22.5	16.8	60	61	56
S	SESI	SUPERIOR ENERGY SERVICES	A	A	0.5	21.4	26	60	62
S	BTN	BALLANTYNE OF OMAHA INC	A	A	19.1	20.2	32	58	76
S	INT	WORLD FUEL SERVICES CORP	A	B	11.9	14.6	95	43	140
S	ARON	AARON RENTS INC	A	C	18.5	18.0	44	17	342
S	BACU	BACOU USA INC	A	C	22.6	18.7	42	17	345
S	ASF	ADMINISTAFF INC	B	A	10.9	11.6	187	72	23
S	LBOR	LABOR READY INC	B	A	5.4	11.9	173	72	25
S	SRSV	SOURCE SERVICES CORP	B	A	10.9	13.1	136	61	57
S	WSTF	WESTERN STAFF SERVICES INC	B	B	8.2	10.3	232	39	170
S	YRKG	YORK GROUP INC	B	B	14.5	11.0	203	37	191
S	MATW	MATTHEWS INTL CORP -CL A	B	B	11.5	13.6	124	35	201
S	PRRC	PRECISION RESPONSE CORP	B	C	15.0	12.4	162	28	264
S	PKT	PINKERTONS INC	B	C	10.5	12.2	164	20	324
S	MXWL	MAXWELL TECHNOLOGIES INC	C	A	-2.2	9.0	313	61	58
S	DRTK	GTS DURATEK INC	C	B	1.6	9.0	308	43	147
S	URS	URS CORP	C	C	9.0	9.3	288	26	270
S	BOR	BORG-WARNER SECURITY CP	C	C	8.0	9.6	267	20	325
S	EMCG	EMCOR GROUP INC	C	D	-18.2	9.4	280	12	385
S	FA	FAIRCHILD CORP -CL A	C	D	4.5	9.4	282	-1	475
S	FYI	FYI INC	D	A	6.5	6.6	451	54	94
S	SPEH	MAY & SPEH INC	D	B	8.9	7.2	408	43	144
S	WAK	WACKENHUT CORP -SER A	D	C	7.3	7.2	409	19	333
S	UTOG	UNITOG COMPANY	D	D	7.0	7.6	375	5	435
S	CRSV	CARRIAGE SERVICES INC -CL A	E	A	-3.0	4.7	532	48	115
S	IRIC	INFORMATION RESOURCES INC	E	E	-0.2	4.9	529	11	395
S	AGL	ANGELICA CORP	E	D	3.9	3.8	560	0	470

(continued overleaf)

HOLT USA2000 Universe
Size / #cos / mkt cap
Very large / 300 / $3.93B+
Large / 500 / $1.03–3.93B
Medium / 600 / $.42–1.03B
Small / 600 / $154–425M

Grouped by Forecast +1 year CFROI Grade (Near Term)
which is then sorted high-to-low on numerical % Future

Machinery Industry

		HOLT DualGrade® Performance		CFROI Cash Flow Return on Investment			% of Total Market Value Attributed to Future Investments	
		#1 Near Term Fcst +1-year CFROI Grade	#2 Long Term % Future Grade	Past 5-year Median CFROI	Forecast +1-year CFROI	Forecast +1-year CFROI Rank	% Future	% Future Rank

VERY LARGE (V) - 300 Cos. (Group / x300 (V) / Sort / x300 (V))

		Grade	Grade	Median	+1yr	x300 (V)	Sort	x300 (V)
V	DOV DOVER CORP	B	B	10.9	11.2	97	48	111
V	DE DEERE & CO	B	D	9.3	11.4	91	19	218
V	SWK STANLEY WORKS	C	B	6.0	9.9	133	47	116
V	IR INGERSOLL-RAND CO	C	D	7.3	10.1	127	25	194
V	PH PARKER-HANNIFIN CORP	C	D	8.1	9.8	139	22	206
V	CSE CASE CORP	C	E	8.5	9.8	135	5	251
V	CAT CATERPILLAR INC	C	E	9.6	9.6	142	4	254

LARGE (L) - 500 Cos. (Group / x500 (L) / Sort / x500 (L))

		Grade	Grade	Median	+1yr	x500 (L)	Sort	x500 (L)
L	KDN KAYDON CORP	A	B	10.6	14.5	84	48	134
L	DCI DONALDSON CO INC	B	B	8.6	10.7	172	45	152
L	AG AGCO CORP	B	E	14.7	12.3	130	2	426
L	TMS TRIMAS CORP	C	C	9.4	9.3	239	35	226
L	SNA SNAP-ON INC	C	C	7.5	9.6	223	28	272
L	BGG BRIGGS & STRATTON	C	D	8.4	9.2	243	16	356
L	FLS FLOWSERVE CORP	C	D	5.9	8.9	267	13	372
L	ANV AEROQUIP-VICKERS INC	C	D	7.4	8.7	272	11	392
L	HPH HARNISCHFEGER INDUSTRIES	C	E	5.3	9.1	253	-6	450
L	YRK YORK INTL	D	D	7.7	7.7	318	18	342
L	CUM CUMMINS ENGINE	D	E	6.5	6.5	365	-17	468
L	FWC FOSTER WHEELER CORP	E	D	5.5	5.1	420	15	361
L	FMC FMC CORP	E	E	5.6	4.9	428	-6	448
L	TECUA TECUMSEH PRODUCTS CO -CL	E	E	6.7	5.4	406	-33	486

MEDIUM (M) - 600 Cos.

			Group				x600 [M]	Sort	x600 [M]
M	PRIA	PRI AUTOMATION INC	A	A	10.0	14.4	111	57	120
M	JLG	JLG INDUSTRIES INC	A	B	20.3	14.4	107	51	148
M	ROP	ROPER INDUSTRIES INC/DE	A	B	16.9	15.8	73	48	169
M	TEX	TEREX CORP	A	C	3.2	20.3	28	34	246
M	ZOLT	ZOLTEK COS INC	B	A	7.3	13.4	138	58	117
M	APW	APPLIED POWER -CL A	B	B	8.5	10.7	220	42	193
M	MTW	MANITOWOC CO	B	B	2.6	10.3	239	38	217
M	GGG	GRACO INC	B	B	6.7	12.6	157	36	229
M	NDSN	NORDSON CORP	B	B	12.9	11.2	203	35	238
M	MLR	MILLER INDUSTRIES INC/TN	B	C	10.4	13.5	135	34	243
M	IEX	IDEX CORP	B	C	10.4	12.1	173	32	264
M	RBC	REGAL BELOIT	C	D	12.5	9.0	308	15	394
M	CMZ	CINCINNATI MILACRON INC	C	D	5.3	8.4	333	6	470
M	WTS	WATTS INDUSTRIES -CL A	D	C	6.6	7.5	399	28	294
M	AIN	ALBANY INTL CORP -CL A	D	E	5.4	7.4	405	4	481
M	SSSS	STEWART & STEVENSON SERV.	D	E	10.0	7.5	394	2	491
M	DDC	DETROIT DIESEL CORP	E	D	7.4	5.4	518	15	398
M	APZ	APPLIED INDUSTRIAL TECH INC	E	D	5.8	6.0	481	9	450

SMALL (S) - 600 Cos.

			Group				x600 [S]	Sort	x600 [S]
S	AEIS	ADVANCED ENERGY INDS INC	A	A	27.3	20.8	29	59	69
S	CTI	CHART INDUSTRIES INC	A	A	23.4	19.7	35	58	74
S	HELX	HELX TECHNOLOGY CORP	A	A	16.1	24.3	18	51	104
S	LNN	LINDSAY MANUFACTURING CO	A	A	14.0	16.7	63	48	118
S	HRSH	HIRSCH INTL CORP -CL A	A	B	21.7	14.7	92	37	190
S	ITEQ	ITEQ INC	B	A	-3.5	10.2	239	54	97
S	ICP	INTL COMFORT PRODUCTS	B	C	3.3	13.6	125	16	351
S	ALG	ALAMO GROUP INC	B	D	10.5	11.4	191	10	396
S	RSV	RENTAL SERVICE CORP	B	D	6.4	11.8	177	2	455
S	MPO	MOTIVEPOWER INDUSTRIES INC	C	B	0.4	8.3	348	36	196
S	GDI	GARDNER DENVER MACHINERY	C	C	6.5	9.2	294	28	253
S	TANT	TENNANT CO	C	C	8.1	8.9	315	28	261
S	CMCO	COLUMBUS MCKINNON CORP	C	C	8.7	8.2	350	26	271
S	GRC	GORMAN-RUPP CO	C	C	7.0	8.0	360	16	355

(continued overleaf)

HOLT USA2000 Universe
Size / #cos / mkt cap

Very large / 300 / $3.93B+
Large / 500 / $1.03–3.93B
Medium / 600 / $.42–1.03B
Small / 600 / $154–425M

Grouped by Forecast +1 year CFROI Grade (Near Term) which is then sorted high-to-low on numerical % Future

		HOLT DualGrade® Performance		CFROI Cash Flow Return on Investment			% of Total Market Value Attributed to Future Investments	
		#1 Near Term Fcst +1-year CFROI Grade	#2 Long Term % Future Grade	Past 5-year Median CFROI	Forecast +1-year CFROI	Forecast +1-year CFROI Rank	% Future	% Future Rank
S	POWL POWELL INDUSTRIES INC	C	D	5.7	9.7	262	15	362
S	TEC COMMERCIAL INTERTECH	C	D	7.4	9.8	254	12	383
S	DTII DT INDUSTRIES INC	C	D	9.0	10.0	247	11	394
S	OSM OSMONICS INC	D	C	8.7	6.4	455	26	272
S	ABCR ABC RAIL PRODUCTS CORP	D	C	10.9	7.5	393	18	338
S	ASTE ASTEC INDUSTRIES INC	D	D	12.3	6.4	459	9	405
S	HDNG HARDINGE BROTHERS INC	D	D	4.4	6.7	439	3	447
S	FSI FSI INTL INC	D	D	10.7	6.7	447	1	467
S	JASN JASON INC	D	D	7.9	6.4	456	–1	477
S	CW CURTISS-WRIGHT CORP	E	C	2.4	2.6	580	23	295
S	SCT SCOTSMAN INDUSTRIES INC	E	D	8.7	5.8	489	15	363
S	CAE CASCADE CORP	E	E	6.1	5.6	503	–12	526
S	GLE GLEASON CORP	E	E	0.6	5.6	498	–16	540
S	MINES MINE SAFETY APPLIANCES CO	E	E	1.8	2.1	588	–19	553
S	GIX GLOBAL INDUSTRIAL TECH INC	E	E	2.9	5.6	501	–43	586

Manufactured Housing/Recreational Vehicles Industry

							Sort x300 (V)	x300 (V)
VERY LARGE (V) - 300 Cos.	Group						Sort	
LARGE (L) - 500 Cos.	Group					x500 (L)	x500 (L)	
L	OH OAKWOOD HOMES	A	B	10.2	17.2	41	46	139
L	FLE FLEETWOOD ENTERPRISES	B	C	8.0	10.4	189	35	225
L	CMH CLAYTON HOMES INC	B	C	12.2	12.3	129	32	246
MEDIUM (M) - 600 Cos.	Group					x600 (M) Sort	x600 (M)	
M	PII POLARIS INDS INC	A	B	49.2	24.9	13	35	237
M	CHB CHAMPION ENTERPRISES INC	A	C	22.6	19.5	36	33	256

SMALL (S) - 600 Cos.

			Group				x600 (S)	Sort	x600 (S)
S	THO	THOR INDUSTRIES INC	B	C	13.3	12.9	145	21	315
S	COA	COACHMEN INDUSTRIES INC	B	D	12.2	11.3	196	14	371
S	WGO	WINNEBAGO INDUSTRIES	E	D	6.9	4.0	553	14	372

Maritime Industry

VERY LARGE (V) - 300 Cos.
LARGE (L) - 500 Cos.

			Group				x300 (V) / x500 (L)	Sort	x300 (V) / x500 (L)
L	STLTF	STOLT-NIELSEN SA	D	E	4.8	6.0	380	-20	475
L	ALEX	ALEXANDER & BALDWIN INC	E	E	3.6	3.3	466	-16	465

MEDIUM (M) - 600 Cos.

			Group				x600 (M)	Sort	x600 (M)
M	TMAR	TRICO MARINE SERVICES INC	A	C	7.1	18.6	45	29	288
M	HLX	HALTER MARINE GROUP INC	B	A	13.3	13.0	147	63	86
M	KEX	KIRBY CORP	D	E	5.4	6.6	447	4	482
M	AVDL	AVONDALE INDUSTRIES INC	E	D	5.1	5.7	502	13	413
M	SCR.A	SEA CONTAINERS LTD -CL A	E	E	4.8	4.8	536	-6	534
M	OSG	OVERSEAS SHIPHOLDING GR	E	E	1.1	2.7	581	-11	554

SMALL (S) - 600 Cos.

			Group				x600 (S)	Sort	x600 (S)
S	HMAR	HVIDE MARINE INC -CL A	B	E	8.0	13.2	133	-23	563
S	CRCL	CIRCLE INTERNATIONAL GRP	C	D	7.2	8.4	345	15	366
S	OMM	OMI CORP	D	E	1.9	6.1	468	-10	515

Medical Services Industry

VERY LARGE (V) - 300 Cos.

			Group				x300 (V)	Sort	x300 (V)
V	HMA	HEALTH MANAGEMENT ASSC	B	A	11.9	13.1	69	64	41
V	HRC	HEALTHSOUTH CORP	B	C	9.0	12.6	74	38	147
V	UNH	UNITED HEALTHCARE CORP	C	D	10.4	8.4	174	22	202
V	THC	TENET HEALTHCARE CORP	C	D	6.7	8.3	175	15	228
V	MDM	MEDPARTNERS INC	D	B	0.3	7.6	191	52	89
V	COL	COLUMBIA/HCA HLTHCR -VTG	D	E	9.1	6.7	215	1	262

(continued overleaf)

HOLT USA2000 Universe
Size / #cos / mkt cap
Very large / 300 / $3.93B+
Large / 500 / $1.03–3.93B
Medium / 600 / $.42–1.03B
Small / 600 / $154–425M

Grouped by Forecast +1 year CFROI Grade (Near Term) which is then sorted high-to-low on numerical % Future

			HOLT DualGrade® Performance		CFROI Cash Flow Return on Investment			% of Total Market Value Attributed to Future Investments	
			#1 Near Term Fcst +1-year CFROI Grade	#2 Long Term % Future Grade	Past 5-year Median CFROI	Forecast +1-year CFROI	Forecast +1-year CFROI Rank	% Future	% Future Rank
			Group				x500 (L)	Sort	x500 (L)
LARGE (L) - 500 Cos.									
L	RXSD	REXALL SUNDOWN INC	A	A	20.1	18.7	26	81	25
L	HCCC	HEALTHCARE COMPARE CORP	A	A	20.8	15.2	71	56	92
L	LNCR	LINCARE HOLDINGS INC	A	B	20.0	14.8	76	46	144
L	TRL	TOTAL RENAL CARE HLDG -CL	B	B	13.2	13.0	117	45	156
L	QHGI	QUORUM HEALTH GROUP INC	B	C	10.3	10.5	181	26	290
L	TCA	THERMO CARDIOSYSTEMS	C	A	2.6	8.5	279	81	22
L	CCMC	CONCENTRA MANAGED CARE	C	A	2.9	9.0	260	64	60
L	HCR	HEALTH CARE & RETIREMENT/DE	C	B	8.0	9.5	230	38	198
L	WLP	WELLPOINT HLTH NETWRK -CL	C	C	14.3	9.2	250	36	217
L	UHS	UNIVERSAL HEALTH SVCS -CL	C	C	6.0	8.1	300	36	218
L	MNR	MANOR CARE INC	C	C	7.3	8.6	276	25	299
L	PHYC	PHYCOR INC	D	C	4.5	5.7	392	33	235
L	PGN	PARAGON HEALTH NETWORK	D	C	5.6	7.1	350	25	294
L	OCR	OMNICARE INC	E	A	3.2	3.9	457	65	57
L	HUM	HUMANA INC	E	C	8.3	4.7	437	35	222
L	OXHP	OXFORD HEALTH PLANS INC	E	C	15.5	5.1	421	32	243
L	BEV	BEVERLY ENTERPRISES	E	E	3.9	4.3	448	1	430
L	VC	VENCOR INC	E	E	7.4	5.5	401	-2	440
			Group				x600 (M)	Sort	x600 (M)
MEDIUM (M) - 600 Cos.									
M	WJCO	WESLEY JESSEN VISIONCARE	A	A	-21.7	24.5	14	74	39
M	PDX	PEDIATRIX MEDICAL GROUP INC	A	A	9.6	14.9	97	58	115
M	RCGI	RENAL CARE GROUP INC	A	B	17.3	16.6	67	55	127
M	RXT	RENAL TREATMENT CTRS INC	A	B	14.2	15.6	76	35	240
M	IDXC	IDX SYSTEMS CORP	B	A	10.9	12.0	179	69	55
M	OCA	ORTHODONTIC CENTERS OF AM	B	A	10.2	12.4	162	60	103

	Ticker	Company		Group			x600 (S)	Sort	x600 (S)
M	CVTY	COVENTRY CORPORATION	B	B	11.8	13.4	140	48	166
M	PRXL	PAREXEL INTERNATIONAL CORP	C	A	5.2	8.6	324	70	54
M	PSSI	PHYSICIAN SALES & SERVICE INC	C	A	4.6	8.8	317	58	116
M	NHC	NATIONAL HEALTHCARE -LP	C	D	7.8	9.3	292	19	361
M	MGL	MAGELLAN HEALTH SVCS	C	D	11.4	10.1	247	17	374
M	MRNR	MARINER HEALTH GROUP INC	C	E	4.8	8.4	338	-10	547
M	AHG	APRIA HEALTHCARE GROUP	D	E	10.9	10.1	249	-11	551
M	SNRZ	SUNRISE ASSISTED LIVING INC	D	B	2.9	7.9	372	42	195
M	AORI	AMERICAN ONCOLOGY RES INC	D	C	1.3	6.2	477	32	262
M	NOV	NOVACARE INC	D	C	5.7	6.4	462	20	353
M	PHYN	PHYSICIAN RELIANCE NETWORK	D	D	6.7	8.0	363	14	411
M	IHS	INTEGRATED HEALTH SVCS INC	E	E	4.7	6.5	455	-7	539
M	VTK	VITALINK PHARMACY SVCS INC	E	B	15.0	2.3	587	48	164
M	RURL	RURAL/METRO CORP	E	B	3.7	4.8	537	47	174
M	PHMX	PHYMATRIX CORP	E	B	-2.7	5.9	491	39	210
M	SHG	SUN HEALTHCARE GROUP INC	E	D	3.0	5.2	528	13	419
M	DGX	QUEST DIAGNOSTICS INC	E	D	-5.6	4.0	562	8	457
SMALL (S) - 600 Cos.			**Group**				**x600 (S)**	**Sort**	**x600 (S)**
S	ATRX	ATRIX LABS INC	A	A	-25.8	15.9	73	77	11
S	OSTE	OSTEOTECH INC	A	A	5.3	17.5	52	71	28
S	PMSI	PRIME MEDICAL SVCS INC	A	D	13.7	26.4	10	5	436
S	MATR	MATRIA HEALTHCARE INC	A	E	-2.3	23.8	19	-57	597
S	IMPH	IMPATH INC	B	A	14.6	12.0	170	58	72
S	HH	HOOPER HOLMES INC	B	B	4.4	12.1	166	47	121
S	AHOM	AMERICAN HOMEPATIENT INC	C	D	8.5	8.6	331	4	439
S	MRII	MEDICAL RESOURCES INC	C	E	9.3	9.7	259	-13	528
S	RSCR	RES-CARE INC	D	B	9.1	7.3	400	37	188
S	DOSE	PHARMERICA INC	D	C	-3.4	6.3	460	29	248
S	HBR	HARBORSIDE HEALTHCARE	D	C	11.8	6.7	445	19	329
S	MCTH	MEDCATH INC	D	D	7.9	5.9	479	2	453
S	HGR	HANGER ORTHOPEDIC GRP	E	B	2.5	4.6	535	45	129
S	MAM	MAXXIM MEDICAL INC	E	C	5.1	5.2	519	20	319
S	LH	LABORATORY CP OF AMER HLD	E	E	7.6	0.1	599	-19	551

(continued overleaf)

HOLT USA2000 Universe
Size / #cos / mkt cap

Very large / 300 / $3.93B+
Large / 500 / $1.03–3.93B
Medium / 600 / $.42–1.03B
Small / 600 / $154–425M

Grouped by Forecast +1 year CFROI Grade (Near Term) which is then sorted high-to-low on numerical % Future

		HOLT DualGrade® Performance		CFROI — Cash Flow Return on Investment			% of Total Market Value Attributed to Future Investments	
		#1 Near Term Fcst +1-year CFROI Grade	#2 Long Term Future Grade	Past 5-year Median CFROI	Forecast +1-year CFROI	Forecast +1-year CFROI Rank x300 (V)	% Future (Sort)	% Future Rank x300 (V)
VERY LARGE (V) - 300 Cos.		**Group**				**x300 (V)**	**Sort**	**x300 (V)**
V	GDT	GUIDANT CORP	A	A	13.3	19.4	29	84	4
V	MDT	MEDTRONIC INC	A	A	17.3	21.1	15	81	8
V	BSX	BOSTON SCIENTIFIC CORP	A	A	18.2	20.0	24	66	34
V	JNJ	JOHNSON & JOHNSON	A	A	14.4	16.1	48	64	43
V	ABT	ABBOTT LABORATORIES	A	A	18.2	17.7	38	61	54
V	CAH	CARDINAL HEALTH INC	B	A	12.4	13.7	62	62	46
V	BDX	BECTON DICKINSON & CO	B	D	9.1	10.5	115	28	184
V	BAX	BAXTER INTERNATIONAL INC	C	B	8.9	10.0	129	46	118
V	MCK	MCKESSON CORP	D	C	7.3	8.1	182	42	133
LARGE (L) - 500 Cos.		**Group**				**x500 (L)**	**Sort**	**x500 (L)**
L	AVEI	ARTERIAL VASCULAR ENGR INC	A	A	18.2	26.4	4	83	15
L	SFSK	SAFESKIN CORP	A	A	23.8	25.3	6	79	29
L	SDG	SOFAMOR/DANEK GROUP INC	A	A	23.1	17.7	37	69	46
L	BMET	BIOMET INC	A	A	16.5	16.2	56	60	73
L	STRL	STERIS CORP	A	B	12.3	14.5	83	43	163
L	AAS	AMERISOURCE HEALTH CP -CL	A	B	16.3	13.8	96	40	184
L	CNTO	CENTOCOR INC	B	A	-19.2	12.9	119	76	31
L	SYK	STRYKER CORP	B	A	12.0	12.8	120	60	74
L	DPU	DEPUY INC	B	A	14.6	10.4	184	57	85
L	XRAY	DENTSPLY INTERNATL INC	B	B	11.2	10.6	175	52	117
L	STJ	ST JUDE MEDICAL INC	B	B	17.2	11.1	157	45	151
L	AGN	ALLERGAN INC	B	C	13.7	10.6	179	35	228
L	BCR	BARD (C.R.) INC	C	B	10.3	9.1	256	41	181
L	BBC	BERGEN BRUNSWIG CORP -CL	C	C	7.5	9.3	236	36	213

Medical Supplies Industry

			Group				x600	Sort	x600
L	BEC	BECKMAN INSTRUMENTS INC	C	D	9.3	8.5	282	19	333
L	USS	U S SURGICAL CORP	D	C	7.6	7.4	336	28	269
L	MKG	MALLINCKRODT INC	D	D	8.7	7.0	352	20	324
L	BOL	BAUSCH & LOMB INC	D	E	7.1	7.8	310	4	420
MEDIUM (M) - 600 Cos.				**Group**			**x600 (M)**	**Sort**	**x600 (M)**
M	MNTR	MENTOR CORP	A	A	15.8	16.4	69	69	56
M	COO	COOPER COMPANIES INC	A	A	0.6	17.6	55	60	99
M	PDCO	PATTERSON DENTAL CO	A	A	15.7	15.6	75	60	104
M	BMP	BALLARD MEDICAL PRODUCTS	A	A	16.0	15.1	87	57	118
M	MNMD	MINIMED INC	B	A	2.4	10.5	225	77	27
M	LTEK	LIFE TECHNOLOGIES INC	B	B	10.5	12.1	170	51	145
M	RESP	RESPIRONICS INC	B	B	15.3	11.8	188	47	173
M	ARRO	ARROW INTERNATIONAL	B	B	13.8	12.0	178	43	192
M	GSMS	GULF SOUTH MED SUPPLY INC	C	A	17.3	9.9	259	64	76
M	ATLI	ATL ULTRASOUND INC	C	B	3.4	9.3	290	49	161
M	SOL	SOLA INTL INC	C	B	9.6	8.7	321	41	203
M	IVCR	INVACARE CORP	C	B	8.5	9.4	285	36	233
M	IDXX	IDEXX LABS INC	D	C	9.5	7.8	382	30	278
M	MARQ	MARQUETTE MEDICAL SYS	D	C	8.8	7.9	374	28	290
M	FSH	FISHER SCIENTIFIC INTL INC	D	C	6.3	6.8	438	28	291
M	ACN	ACUSON CORP	D	C	6.5	6.7	442	25	315
M	OMI	OWENS & MINOR INC	D	C	7.4	7.9	376	22	340
M	BDY	BINDLEY WESTERN INDS	D	D	6.6	7.5	397	16	384
M	GHV	GENESIS HEALTH VENTURES	D	D	5.7	6.6	449	13	416
M	CYTC	CYTYC CORP	E	A	-50.4	2.7	580	76	29
M	ALO	ALPHARMA INC -CL A	E	C	2.5	5.5	514	21	341
SMALL (S) - 600 Cos.				**Group**			**x600 (S)**	**Sort**	**x600 (S)**
S	STAA	STAAR SURGICAL CO	A	A	13.7	14.5	97	62	53
S	TECH	TECHNE CORP	A	A	16.9	16.6	64	61	60
S	HDTC	HEALTHDYNE TECHNOLOGIES	A	A	10.8	13.8	118	59	63
S	RESM	RESMED INC	A	A	13.4	16.8	61	59	70
S	PHYS	PHYSIO-CONTROL INTL CORP	A	A	21.8	15.4	82	58	73
S	VISX	VISX INC/DE	A	A	-13.5	14.0	111	53	100
S	PBIO	PERSEPTIVE BIOSYSTEMS INC	A	A	-15.5	13.8	114	52	103

(continued overleaf)

HOLT USA2000 Universe
Size / #cos / mkt cap

Very large / 300 / $3.93B+
Large / 500 / $1.03–3.93B
Medium / 600 / $.42–1.03B
Small / 600 / $154–425M

Grouped by Forecast +1 year CFROI Grade (Near Term) which is then sorted high-to-low on numerical % Future

			HOLT DualGrade® Performance		CFROI Cash Flow Return on Investment			% of Total Market Value Attributed to Future Investments	
			#1 Near Term Fcst +1-year CFROI Grade	#2 Long Term % Future Grade	Past 5-year Median CFROI	Forecast +1-year CFROI	Forecast +1-year CFROI Rank	% Future	% Future Rank
S	EMPI	EMPI INC	A	B	15.0	15.1	83	37	183
S	LUNR	LUNAR CORPORATION	A	B	13.2	14.0	113	36	193
S	ADAC	ADAC LABORATORIES	A	B	18.9	16.8	59	31	227
S	LASRF	LASER INDUSTRIES LTD -ORD	B	A	8.6	13.6	122	54	96
S	CNMD	CONMED CORP	B	B	8.8	10.5	225	40	164
S	TCNL	TECNOL MEDICAL PRODUCTS	B	B	11.5	11.1	201	37	184
S	HOLX	HOLOGIC INC	B	B	10.2	11.8	174	33	215
S	MURXF	INTL MUREX TECH CORP	B	B	4.9	12.5	157	33	219
S	VITL	VITAL SIGNS INC	B	C	13.6	11.7	185	22	305
S	DP	DIAGNOSTIC PRODUCTS CORP	B	C	11.3	10.6	221	20	318
S	ESON	ENDOSONICS CORP	C	A	-19.0	8.8	319	54	92
S	MED	MEDIQ INC	C	C	6.2	8.4	342	25	286
S	GFI	GRAHAM FIELD HEALTH PDS	D	A	-1.5	6.7	448	49	111
S	DSCP	DATASCOPE CORP	D	B	7.7	7.9	365	35	200
S	REGN	REGENERON PHARMACEUT	D	C	-25.7	7.7	370	29	252
S	BIO.A	BIO-RAD LABS -CL A	D	E	8.6	7.7	367	-9	510
S	LCBM	LIFECORE BIOMEDICAL INC	E	A	-5.6	3.4	563	77	9
S	CCON	CIRCON CORP	E	C	4.7	5.9	482	27	267
S	CGEN	COLLAGEN CORP	E	D	5.9	3.4	565	11	393
S	HAE	HAEMONETICS CORPORATION	E	D	11.7	3.4	564	7	416
S	SLMD	SPACELABS MED INC	E	E	7.5	3.6	561	-8	506

Metal Fabricating Industry

			Group				x300 (V)	Sort	x300 (V)
VERY LARGE (V) - 300 Cos.			B	B	10.0	10.7	111	55	75
V	ITW	ILLINOIS TOOL WORKS							

	Ticker	Company	Group			x-val	Sort	x-val
LARGE (L) - 500 Cos.						**x500 (L)**	**Sort**	**x500 (L)**
L	MLI	MUELLER INDUSTRIES	B	8.0	10.9	163	19	337
L	TRN	TRINITY INDUSTRIES	B	7.2	10.7	169	17	349
L	HSC	HARSCO CORP	C	9.3	10.0	204	10	394
L	KMT	KENNAMETAL INC	D	6.6	7.1	349	21	321
L	TKR	TIMKEN CO	E	2.8	5.7	391	0	436
MEDIUM (M) - 600 Cos.						**x600 (M)**	**Sort**	**x600 (M)**
M	LSS	LONE STAR TECHNOLOGIES	E	2.6	10.4	232	-3	523
M	ST	SPS TECHNOLOGIES INC	C	2.5	8.6	323	20	346
M	OREM	OREGON METALLURGICAL	E	-2.2	9.7	269	3	484
M	RS	RELIANCE STEEL & ALUMINUM	E	6.6	7.7	385	2	492
M	RT	RYERSON TULL INC -CL A	E	6.4	6.5	457	-31	589
SMALL (S) - 600 Cos.						**x600 (S)**	**Sort**	**x600 (S)**
S	MAVK	MAVERICK TUBE CORP	A	7.1	20.9	28	45	133
S	CSI	CHASE INDUSTRIES INC	A	20.0	14.2	107	8	410
S	LAWS	LAWSON PRODUCTS	B	10.4	10.2	237	31	229
S	SGR	SHAW GROUP INC	B	7.1	11.8	180	20	326
S	ADP	ALLIED PRODUCTS	B	10.8	10.9	207	18	336
S	RESC	ROANOKE ELECTRIC STEEL	C	6.2	9.0	306	2	460
S	PNN.A	PENN ENGR & MFG CORP -CL A	C	7.6	8.8	327	-2	483
S	CAST	CITATION CORP/AL	C	8.1	9.3	286	-18	550
S	HNH	HANDY & HARMAN	E	4.1	2.4	583	33	218
S	AIZ	AMCAST INDL CORP	D	5.2	3.2	569	6	426

Metals & Mining (Diversified) Industry

	Ticker	Company	Group			x-val	Sort	x-val
VERY LARGE (V) - 300 Cos.						**x300 (V)**	**Sort**	**x300 (V)**
V	RLM	REYNOLDS METALS CO	D	2.0	6.4	226	-17	285
V	AA	ALUMINUM CO OF AMERICA	E	2.6	7.2	207	-32	298
V	AL	ALCAN ALUMINIUM LTD	E	0.9	4.0	282	-59	300
LARGE (L) - 500 Cos.						**x500 (L)**	**Sort**	**x500 (L)**
L	FCX	FREEPRT MCMOR COP&GLD	B	8.3	11.1	156	-22	477
L	AMX	ALUMAX INC	E	2.4	6.0	381	-27	482
L	PD	PHELPS DODGE CORP	D	6.4	6.9	353	-57	496

(continued overleaf)

HOLT USA2000 Universe
Size / #cos / mkt cap
Very large / 300 / $3.93B+
Large / 500 / $1.03–3.93B
Medium / 600 / $.42–1.03B
Small / 600 / $154–425M

Grouped by Forecast +1 year CFROI Grade (Near Term) which is then sorted high-to-low on numerical % Future

	Company	HOLT DualGrade® Performance		CFROI Cash Flow Return on Investment			% of Total Market Value Attributed to Future Investments	
		#1 Near Term Fcst +1-year CFROI Grade	#2 Long Term % Future Grade	Past 5-year Median CFROI	Forecast +1-year CFROI	Forecast +1-year CFROI Rank	% Future	Future Rank
L	CYM CYPRUS AMAX MINERALS CO	E	E	2.2	2.8	483	-33	487
L	N INCO LTD	E	E	0.9	0.3	500	-47	492
L	PCU SOUTHERN PERU COPPER	E	E	5.5	5.2	416	-159	500
MEDIUM (M) - 600 Cos.		*Group*				*x600 (M)*	*Sort*	*x600 (M)*
M	TIMT TITANIUM METALS CORP	A	E	8.8	15.3	84	-4	529
M	WLV WOLVERINE TUBE INC	B	E	12.4	11.0	207	-8	542
M	KLU KAISER ALUMINUM CORP	C	E	3.8	8.3	342	-4	525
M	MTX MINERALS TECHNOLOGIES INC	D	D	4.9	6.1	479	15	400
M	FTX FREEPORT MCMORAN INC	D	E	5.9	7.9	375	-14	565
M	ROM RIO ALGOM LTD	E	E	1.7	5.9	486	-9	543
M	AR ASARCO INC	E	E	0.7	2.1	591	-133	600
SMALL (S) - 600 Cos.		*Group*				*x600 (S)*	*Sort*	*x600 (S)*
S	RTI RMI TITANIUM CO	A	E	-5.2	14.0	109	-23	568
S	IMR IMCO RECYCLING INC	B	E	11.9	11.1	200	-26	571
S	CENX CENTURY ALUMINUM CO	B	E	10.5	12.8	147	-48	591
S	SWC STILLWATER MINING CO	E	B	-2.4	3.9	556	30	234
S	KGC KINROSS GOLD CORP	E	E	4.8	2.3	584	-14	531
S	BW BRUSH WELLMAN INC	E	E	3.3	4.3	546	-20	558
S	CMIN COMMONWEALTH INDUSTRIES	E	E	4.5	4.7	534	-47	590
Natural Gas (Diversified) Industry								
VERY LARGE (V) - 300 Cos.		*Group*				*x300 (V)*	*Sort*	*x300 (V)*
V	UPR UNION PACIFIC RESOURCES GR	C	E	7.8	8.8	163	-22	292
V	WMB WILLIAMS COS INC	D	E	4.9	6.3	229	4	255
V	SNT SONAT INC	E	E	3.6	5.2	255	-5	272

Size	Symbol	Company	Group	Group				Sort	
							x500 (L)	**Sort**	**x500 (L)**
V	CNG	CONSOLIDATED NATURAL GAS	E	E	1.0	2.9	294	-6	275
V	CG	COLUMBIA GAS SYSTEM	E	E	0.5	3.2	292	-10	278
V	CGP	COASTAL CORP	E	E	4.7	5.7	241	-12	281
V	ENE	ENRON CORP	E	E	4.3	5.2	252	-28	297
LARGE (L) - 500 Cos.			**Group**				**x500 (L)**	**Sort**	**x500 (L)**
L	TEJ	TEJAS GAS CORP/DE	D	D	6.5	7.3	342	12	380
L	NGL	NGC CORP	D	D	5.1	6.8	358	12	385
L	DVN	DEVON ENERGY CORPORATION	E	D	3.2	7.6	331	9	402
L	SGO	SEAGULL ENERGY CORP	E	D	7.2	7.8	315	-27	480
L	EOG	ENRON OIL & GAS	D	E	5.0	4.9	430	12	379
L	MDA	MAPCO INC	D	E	6.1	5.4	404	12	381
L	KNE	K N ENERGY INC	D	E	2.1	5.2	415	11	391
L	EQT	EQUITABLE RESOURCES INC	E	E	3.4	3.1	475	-4	442
L	NFG	NATIONAL FUEL GAS CO	E	E	3.0	5.2	417	-5	445
L	STR	QUESTAR CORP	E	E	4.0	4.7	438	-8	453
L	TTG	TRANSTEXAS GAS CORP	E	E	4.6	3.8	460	-19	472
MEDIUM (M) - 600 Cos.			**Group**				**x600 (M)**	**Sort**	**x600 (M)**
M	KCS	KCS ENERGY INC	B	D	12.8	10.3	240	10	441
M	VPI	VINTAGE PETROLEUM INC	B	E	6.8	10.4	236	2	490
M	SNY	SNYDER OIL CORP	C	E	6.6	9.2	298	-10	550
M	XTO	CROSS TIMBERS OIL CO	D	C	2.9	6.1	480	24	327
M	LD	LOUIS DREYFUS NAT GAS CORP	E	D	5.5	5.5	516	6	472
M	EFU	EASTERN ENTERPRISES	E	E	3.8	4.5	551	1	505
M	COG	CABOT OIL & GAS CORP -CL A	E	E	1.2	3.2	575	-4	524
M	SUG	SOUTHERN UNION CO	E	E	4.9	4.7	542	-28	588
SMALL (S) - 600 Cos.			**Group**				**x600 (S)**	**Sort**	**x600 (S)**
S	KOGC	KELLEY OIL & GAS CORP	B	E	0.4	11.7	184	-26	572
S	PLX	PLAINS RESOURCES INC	E	D	1.3	5.7	492	9	407
S	DGP	USX-DELHI GROUP	E	E	-0.6	0.4	597	-33	579
S	SWN	SOUTHWESTERN ENERGY CO	E	E	4.8	4.0	554	-37	582

Newspaper Industry

Size	Symbol	Company	Group	Group			x300 (V)	Sort	x300 (V)
VERY LARGE (V) - 300 Cos.			**Group**				**x300 (V)**	**Sort**	**x300 (V)**
V	GCI	GANNETT CO	B	B	8.9	10.8	110	54	84

(continued overleaf)

HOLT USA2000 Universe
Size / #cos / mkt cap

Very large / 300 / $3.93B+
Large / 500 / $1.03–3.93B
Medium / 600 / $.42–1.03B
Small / 600 / $154–425M

Grouped by Forecast +1 year CFROI Grade (Near Term) which is then sorted high-to-low on numerical % Future

		HOLT DualGrade® Performance		CFROI Cash Flow Return on Investment			% of Total Market Value Attributed to Future Investments	
		#1 Near Term Fcst +1-year CFROI Grade	#2 Long Term % Future Grade	Past 5-year Median CFROI	Forecast +1-year CFROI	Forecast +1-year CFROI Rank	% Future	% Future Rank
LARGE (L) - 500 Cos.		**Group**				**x500 (L)**	**Sort**	**x500 (L)**
V	SSP EW SCRIPPS -CL A	C	B	5.8	8.3	179	56	71
V	TMC TIMES MIRROR COMPANY -SER	C	B	4.9	8.7	166	51	99
V	WPO WASHINGTON POST -CL B	C	B	8.2	9.7	141	50	100
V	NYT NEW YORK TIMES CO -CL A	D	B	3.7	8.0	185	49	108
V	KRI KNIGHT-RIDDER INC	D	D	7.1	7.0	212	17	222
V	TRB TRIBUNE CO	E	B	6.3	5.2	254	54	81
V	DJ DOW JONES & CO INC	E	B	4.0	2.7	295	51	96
MEDIUM (M) - 600 Cos.		**Group**				**x600 (M)**	**Sort**	**x600 (M)**
L	PTZ PULITZER PUBLISHING	B	B	11.5	12.0	141	53	110
L	ECP CENTRAL NEWSPAPERS -CL A	B	B	7.4	13.5	106	49	130
L	LEE LEE ENTERPRISES	B	B	11.7	11.9	143	46	143
L	MNI MCCLATCHY NEWSPAPERS -CL	E	B	5.8	2.0	491	46	141
L	MEG.A MEDIA GENERAL -CL A	E	D	3.6	2.8	481	9	399
SMALL (S) - 600 Cos.		**Group**				**x600 (S)**	**Sort**	**x600 (S)**
S	ENQ AMERICAN MEDIA INC -CL A	B	A	7.6	11.2	199	51	106

Office Equipment & Supplies Industry

		#1 CFROI Grade	#2 Future Grade	Past 5-year Median CFROI	Forecast +1-year CFROI	Forecast +1-year CFROI Rank	% Future	% Future Rank
VERY LARGE (V) - 300 Cos.		**Group**				**x300 (V)**	**Sort**	**x300 (V)**
V	XRX XEROX CORP	B	C	7.9	13.7	63	45	121
V	SPLS STAPLES INC	C	B	5.7	8.5	172	49	105
V	PBI PITNEY BOWES INC	C	C	8.7	9.7	140	45	123
LARGE (L) - 500 Cos.		**Group**				**x500 (L)**	**Sort**	**x500 (L)**
L	VKNG VIKING OFFICE PRODS INC	A	A	16.6	15.2	70	62	65

Class	Ticker	Company	Group	Grade			x	Sort	x
L	DBD	DIEBOLD INC	A	A	10.0	14.3	88	62	68
L	WCS	WALLACE COMPUTER SVCS INC	B	C	6.8	10.1	200	36	212
L	REY	REYNOLDS & REYNOLDS -CL A	B	C	13.2	12.7	124	28	270
L	OFIS	U S OFFICE PRODUCTS CO	B	D	3.0	10.5	183	20	331
L	CEXP	CORPORATE EXPRESS INC	C	D	4.9	8.6	278	20	327
L	ODP	OFFICE DEPOT INC	D	C	6.1	7.3	344	30	257
L	IKN	IKON OFFICE SOLUTIONS	D	C	5.5	7.3	341	27	279
L	OMX	OFFICEMAX INC	E	D	3.0	5.3	408	17	350
L	MCL	MOORE CORP LTD	E	E	4.1	3.7	462	-18	470

MEDIUM (M) - 600 Cos. — Group — x600 (M) — Sort — x600 (M)

Class	Ticker	Company	Group	Grade			x600 (M)	Sort	x600 (M)
M	NEB	NEW ENGLAND BUSINESS SVC	B	B	10.3	13.6	131	52	142
M	USTR	UNITED STATIONERS INC	B	C	5.5	12.1	169	27	298
M	GML	GLOBAL DIRECTMAIL CORP	B	C	14.3	11.8	189	21	342
M	GBND	GENERAL BINDING CORP	E	C	6.9	5.7	499	19	359

SMALL (S) - 600 Cos. — Group — x600 (S) — Sort — x600 (S)

Class	Ticker	Company	Group	Grade			x600 (S)	Sort	x600 (S)
S	DAYR	DAY RUNNER INC	A	B	13.7	17.6	51	40	168
S	HUN	HUNT CORP	B	C	8.3	10.7	217	28	260
S	ABP	AMERICAN BUSINESS PRODS/GA	C	D	9.3	9.7	255	7	422
S	ATX.A	CROSS (A.T.) & CO -CL A	D	E	4.6	6.0	474	-2	481
S	BTF	BT OFFICE PRODS INTL INC	E	D	3.8	5.0	527	3	450

Oilfield Services Industry

VERY LARGE (V) - 300 Cos. — Group — x300 (V) — Sort — x300 (V)

Class	Ticker	Company	Group	Grade			x300 (V)	Sort	x300 (V)
V	ESV	ENSCO INTERNATIONAL INC	A	B	7.1	20.0	23	48	113
V	NE	NOBLE DRILLING CORP	A	C	0.9	15.0	55	44	128
V	GLM	GLOBAL MARINE INC	A	C	5.2	18.9	31	37	150
V	DO	DIAMOND OFFSHORE DRILLING	A	B	2.2	18.7	34	37	153
V	SLB	SCHLUMBERGER LTD	B	B	5.2	10.5	112	57	67
V	HAL	HALLIBURTON CO	C	B	0.9	8.6	168	54	83
V	RIG	TRANSOCEAN OFFSHORE INC	C	C	-1.7	8.9	154	38	149
V	BHI	BAKER-HUGHES INC	C	C	5.6	9.4	146	34	162
V	DI	DRESSER INDUSTRIES INC	C	C	7.3	9.8	137	32	169
V	WAI	WESTERN ATLAS INC	D	C	6.7	7.2	206	41	138

(continued overleaf)

HOLT USA2000 Universe
Size / #cos / mkt cap
Very large / 300 / $3.93B+
Large / 500 / $1.03–3.93B
Medium / 600 / $.42–1.03B
Small / 600 / $154–425M
Grouped by Forecast +1 year CFROI Grade (Near Term)
which is then sorted high-to-low on numerical % Future

			HOLT DualGrade® Performance		CFROI — Cash Flow Return on Investment			% of Total Market Value Attributed to Future Investments		
			#1 Near Term Fcst +1-year CFROI Grade	#2 Long Term % Future Grade	Past 5-year Median CFROI	Forecast +1-year CFROI	Forecast +1-year CFROI Rank x500 (L) / x600 (M)	% Future / Sort		% Future Rank x500 (L) / x600 (M)
LARGE (L) - 500 Cos.		**Group**								
L	VRC	VARCO INTERNATIONAL	A	A	3.8	15.4	66	63	63	63
L	NR	NEWPARK RESOURCES	A	B	7.9	14.1	91	54	54	104
L	EVI	EVI INC	A	B	5.1	16.9	47	50	50	122
L	MDCO	MARINE DRILLING CO INC	A	B	4.7	20.4	19	49	49	131
L	NBR	NABORS INDUSTRIES	A	C	8.2	15.7	60	37	37	204
L	GLBL	GLOBAL INDUSTRIES LTD	B	A	10.2	12.7	122	55	55	97
L	RON	COOPER CAMERON CORP	B	A	-6.4	10.7	171	55	55	99
L	SII	SMITH INTERNATIONAL INC	B	B	8.5	13.5	104	42	42	175
L	RB	READING & BATES CORP	B	B	-0.1	12.6	125	41	41	176
L	TBI	TUBOSCOPE INC	B	C	4.5	11.5	150	36	36	208
L	CAM	CAMCO INTERNATIONAL INC	C	B	3.6	10.0	203	47	47	135
L	BJS	BJ SERVICES CO	C	C	1.9	9.9	206	32	32	244
L	RDC	ROWAN COS INC	C	D	-1.7	10.0	201	19	19	335
L	TDW	TIDEWATER INC	C	E	2.1	8.4	287	1	1	434
L	PDE	PRIDE INTERNATIONAL INC	C	E	1.4	8.7	271	-5	-5	446
L	WII	WEATHERFORD ENTERRA INC	D	D	4.2	7.7	324	23	23	308
L	HP	HELMERICH & PAYNE	D	E	0.8	6.7	363	7	7	412
L	MEOHF	METHANEX CORP	D	E	3.3	5.5	399	-34	-34	488
L	MDR	MCDERMOTT INTL INC	E	D	1.8	3.8	458	23	23	310
MEDIUM (M) - 600 Cos.		**Group**								
M	CRBO	CARBO CERAMICS INC	A	A	34.9	21.6	23	62	62	89
M	ATW	ATWOOD OCEANICS	A	B	1.1	14.1	119	46	46	177
M	CDG	CLIFFS DRILLING CO	A	C	4.2	15.6	78	19	19	358
M	VTS	VERITAS DGC INC	A	D	4.3	15.0	94	17	17	376
M	GW	GREY WOLF INC	B	B	-13.4	12.8	152	51	51	146

Size	Symbol	Company	Group	Gr			x600(S)	Sort	x600(S)
M	SCSWF	STOLT COMEX SEAWAY SA	B	B	5.7	11.7	192	43	190
M	PKD	PARKER DRILLING CO	B	E	-3.1	10.4	233	1	502
M	BOG	BELCO OIL & GAS CORP	B	E	24.0	13.3	141	-36	593
M	PESC	POOL ENERGY SERVICES CO	C	D	2.8	8.5	330	7	469
M	CKH	SEACOR SMIT INC	C	E	6.2	8.9	310	3	488
M	THX	HOUSTON EXPLORATION CO	D	E	2.2	6.3	470	-1	514
M	BRR	BARRETT RESOURCES CORP	E	D	4.7	5.7	501	18	373
M	OIL	OCEANEERING INTERNATIONAL	E	D	5.4	5.9	492	7	463
M	OLOG	OFFSHORE LOGISTICS	E	E	7.3	2.8	579	-35	592

SMALL (S) - 600 Cos. — Group | | | x600(S) | Sort | x600(S)

Size	Symbol	Company	Group	Gr			x600(S)	Sort	x600(S)
S	UTI	UTI ENERGY CORP	A	B	3.0	14.4	100	39	174
S	KAB	KANEB SERVICES INC	B	E	8.8	10.6	220	-56	596
S	KEG	KEY ENERGY GROUP INC	C	D	8.0	9.6	266	6	433
S	SEI	SEITEL INC	C	E	9.8	8.8	325	-14	530
S	DAN	DANIEL INDUSTRIES	D	B	2.2	7.6	372	31	230
S	DPSI	DAWSON PRODTN SVCS INC	E	C	7.6	4.9	530	25	285

Packaging & Container Industry

VERY LARGE (V) - 300 Cos. — Group | | | x300(V) | Sort | x300(V)

Size	Symbol	Company	Group	Gr			x300(V)	Sort	x300(V)
V	OI	OWENS-ILLINOIS INC	C	D	7.8	8.7	165	20	211
V	CCK	CROWN CORK & SEAL CO INC	E	D	4.8	4.1	279	27	186

LARGE (L) - 500 Cos. — Group | | | x500(L) | Sort | x500(L)

Size	Symbol	Company	Group	Gr			x500(L)	Sort	x500(L)
L	SEE	SEALED AIR CORP	A	A	16.4	15.3	69	69	42
L	BMS	BEMIS CO	C	C	8.0	9.4	234	36	210
L	SON	SONOCO PRODUCTS CO	C	C	7.8	8.3	289	30	254
L	AGREA	AMERICAN GREETINGS -CL A	D	D	7.3	7.9	304	17	347
L	BLL	BALL CORP	E	D	5.5	3.7	461	10	397

MEDIUM (M) - 600 Cos. — Group | | | x600(M) | Sort | x600(M)

Size	Symbol	Company	Group	Gr			x600(M)	Sort	x600(M)
M	CLC	CLARCOR INC	B	C	9.2	10.5	226	26	304
M	SHOR	SHOREWOOD PACKAGING CORP	C	C	11.2	9.6	274	34	247
M	ATR	APTARGROUP INC	C	C	6.9	8.1	357	33	257
M	ACX	ACX TECHNOLOGIES INC	D	E	2.4	7.9	369	3	485

(continued overleaf)

HOLT USA2000 Universe
Size / #cos / mkt cap
Very large / 300 / $3.93B+
Large / 500 / $1.03–3.93B
Medium / 600 / $.42–1.03B
Small / 600 / $.154–425M
Grouped by Forecast +1 year CFROI Grade (Near Term) which is then sorted high-to-low on numerical % Future

			HOLT DualGrade® Performance		CFROI — Cash Flow Return on Investment			% of Total Market Value Attributed to Future Investments	
			#1 Near Term Fcst +1-year CFROI Grade	#2 Long Term % Future Grade	Past 5-year Median CFROI	Forecast +1-year CFROI	Forecast +1-year CFROI Rank	% Future	% Future Rank
M	GBCOA	GREIF BROS CORP -CL A	E	C	4.6	0.2	600	22	333
M	WST	WEST CO INC	E	E	5.1	5.7	500	-3	522
SMALL (S) - 600 Cos.			**Group**				**x600 (S)**	**Sort**	**x600 (S)**
S	BY	BWAY CORP	B	D	9.7	11.7	183	3	445
S	USC	U S CAN CORP	C	E	10.7	8.6	332	-7	505
S	JARS	ALLTRISTA CORP	D	D	7.3	7.9	363	3	444
S	GCR	GAYLORD CONTAINER CP	D	E	-0.4	7.3	402	-5	499
S	GIBG	GIBSON GREETINGS INC	E	D	0.8	2.3	585	13	378

Paper & Forest Products Industry

VERY LARGE (V) - 300 Cos.			**Group**				**x300 (V)**	**Sort**	**x300 (V)**
V	FJ	FORT JAMES CORP	C	D	1.7	9.9	132	24	197
V	GP	GEORGIA-PACIFIC CORP	E	E	3.2	4.7	264	9	245
V	WY	WEYERHAEUSER CO	E	E	3.9	4.3	272	1	263
V	IP	INTL PAPER CO	E	E	2.0	3.8	287	-22	291
V	CHA	CHAMPION INTERNATIONAL	E	E	1.4	3.0	293	-26	294
LARGE (L) - 500 Cos.			**Group**				**x500 (L)**	**Sort**	**x500 (L)**
L	DLP	DELTA & PINE LAND CO	A	A	16.5	21.6	12	78	30
L	PCL	PLUM CREEK TIMBER CO -LP	B	C	18.7	10.1	199	31	252
L	JJSC	JEFFERSON SMURFIT CP	C	D	9.1	8.6	275	17	352
L	RYN	RAYONIER INC	D	E	7.6	7.5	333	1	433
L	ABY	ABITIBI CONSOLIDATED INC	D	E	-1.9	5.7	389	-64	498
L	SJP	ST JOE CORP	E	C	0.3	1.1	499	32	247
L	WLL	WILLAMETTE INDUSTRIES	E	E	4.2	5.0	426	-3	441
L	STO	STONE CONTAINER CORP	E	E	3.5	4.9	431	-5	444

			Group			x600 [M]	Sort	x600 [M]
L	BCC	BOISE CASCADE CORP	E	0.0	3.3	470	-6	449
L	TIN	TEMPLE-INLAND INC	E	3.8	3.8	459	-9	454
L	CDP	CONSOLIDATED PAPERS INC	E	3.4	5.4	407	-13	460
L	PCH	POTLATCH CORP	E	2.3	2.1	490	-16	466
L	W	WESTVACO CORP	E	1.9	3.3	468	-20	474
L	BOW	BOWATER INC	E	1.4	4.9	427	-28	483
L	UCC	UNION CAMP CORP	E	1.9	3.0	477	-29	484
L	MEA	MEAD CORP	E	3.0	3.0	478	-34	489
L	DTC	DOMTAR INC	E	1.8	4.1	451	-54	494

MEDIUM [M] - 600 Cos.			**Group**			**x600 [M]**	**Sort**	**x600 [M]**
M	BKI	BUCKEYE TECHNOLOGIES INC	B	15.9	13.0	146	33	259
M	CRO	CROWN PACIFIC PARTNERS -LP	C	11.1	13.1	143	31	271
M	MWL	MAIL-WELL INC	C	7.7	12.9	151	28	296
M	CSAR	CARAUSTAR INDUSTRIES INC	D	11.9	12.0	180	14	407
M	IPT	IP TIMBERLANDS -LP-CL A	B	19.7	12.1	172	-83	599
M	SR	STANDARD REGISTER CO	D	7.2	9.6	272	18	370
M	SWM	SCHWEITZER-MAUDUIT INTL INC	D	10.4	10.2	243	11	438
M	WSAU	WAUSAU-MOSINEE PAPER CORP	C	8.6	8.9	312	0	507
M	MOSI	MOSINEE PAPER CORP	C	4.2	8.3	346	-2	520
M	CSK	CHESAPEAKE CORP	E	2.8	4.6	546	-6	533
M	LFB	LONGVIEW FIBRE CO	E	3.3	2.5	583	-8	541
M	RKT	ROCK-TENN COMPANY	E	7.1	5.9	488	-17	569
M	GLT	GLATFELTER (P H) CO	E	3.9	4.3	557	-25	581

SMALL [S] - 600 Cos.			**Group**			**x600 [S]**	**Sort**	**x600 [S]**
S	RGC	REPUBLIC GROUP INC	E	8.3	14.4	99	-4	492
S	LOG	RAYONIER TIMBERLANDS -LP	E	24.8	36.9	3	-162	600
S	AGP	AMERICAN PAD & PAPER CO	B	10.2	11.8	178	-23	566
S	CSS	CSS INDS INC	C	7.2	9.7	261	7	415
S	POP	POPE & TALBOT INC	D	1.3	2.5	582	-15	536
S	ARH	ASIA PAC RES INTL HLD -CL A	E	1.0	5.0	528	-44	588

Petroleum (Integrated) Industry

VERY LARGE [V] - 300 Cos.			**Group**			**x300 [V]**	**Sort**	**x300 [V]**
V	TOS	TOSCO CORP	C	7.0	8.8	162	-2	266

(continued overleaf)

HOLT USA2000 Universe
Size / #cos / mkt cap

Very large / 300 / $3.93B+
Large / 500 / $1.03–3.93B
Medium / 600 / $.42–1.03B
Small / 600 / $154–425M

Grouped by Forecast +1 year CFROI Grade (Near Term) which is then sorted high-to-low on numerical % Future

			HOLT DualGrade® Performance		CFROI Cash Flow Return on Investment			% of Total Market Value Attributed to Future Investments	
			#1 Near Term Fcst +1-year CFROI Grade	#2 Long Term % Future Grade	Past 5-year Median CFROI	Forecast +1-year CFROI	Forecast +1-year CFROI Rank	% Future	% Future Rank
V	ASH	ASHLAND INC	D	E	3.7	6.3	230	−14	282
V	MOB	MOBIL CORP	E	D	3.3	5.0	257	15	230
V	XON	EXXON CORP	E	D	4.2	4.9	259	14	234
V	CHV	CHEVRON CORP	E	D	2.9	4.8	262	12	238
V	UCL	UNOCAL CORP	E	E	1.7	4.1	276	5	250
V	TX	TEXACO INC	E	E	3.9	4.1	277	3	257
V	ARC	ATLANTIC RICHFIELD CO	E	E	4.2	4.9	260	−5	273
V	AN	AMOCO CORP	E	E	3.4	4.3	270	−8	277
V	OXY	OCCIDENTAL PETROLEUM CORP	E	E	1.2	3.9	283	−11	279
V	P	PHILLIPS PETROLEUM CO	E	E	2.3	4.3	271	−19	289
V	MRO	USX-MARATHON GROUP	E	E	3.6	4.4	268	−23	293
V	AHC	AMERADA HESS CORP	E	E	1.7	2.1	297	−26	295
LARGE (L) - 500 Cos.			*Group*				x500 (L)	Sort	x500 (L)
L	LHP	LAKEHEAD PIPE LINE PTNS-LP	B	D	8.6	10.8	165	15	357
L	UDS	ULTRAMAR DIAMOND SHAMROC	C	E	5.5	9.0	258	−25	478
L	VLO	VALERO ENERGY CORP	D	E	4.4	7.6	329	−14	461
L	PZL	PENNZOIL CO	E	E	2.7	3.6	464	−1	438
L	MUR	MURPHY OIL CORP	E	E	0.1	1.3	496	−7	451
L	KMG	KERR-MCGEE CORP	E	E	1.0	4.4	445	−10	455
L	SUN	SUN CO INC	E	E	1.6	5.5	402	−18	469
MEDIUM (M) - 600 Cos.			*Group*				x600 (M)	Sort	x600 (M)
M	NFX	NEWFIELD EXPLORATION CO	B	E	13.3	11.9	183	−2	519
M	ENP	KINDER MORGAN ENERGY -LP	C	C	5.1	8.4	334	33	253
M	TPP	TEPPCO PARTNERS -LP	C	D	8.5	9.5	279	8	460

	Code	Company	Group				x600 (S)	Sort	x600 (S)
M	HEC	HARKEN ENERGY CORP	E	A	-4.7	3.2	574	75	35
M	KSF	QUAKER STATE CORP	E	D	1.8	4.6	544	14	404

SMALL (S) - 600 Cos.

	Code	Company	Group				x600 (S)	Sort	x600 (S)
S	GTY	GETTY REALTY CORP	B	C	5.4	10.6	219	26	278
S	GI	GIANT INDUSTRIES INC	C	E	3.4	8.1	359	-33	580
S	HOC	HOLLY CORP	C	E	9.7	9.6	264	-37	584
S	TSO	TESORO PETROLEUM CORP	D	E	6.7	6.0	475	-29	574

Petroleum (Producing) Industry

VERY LARGE (V) - 300 Cos.

	Code	Company	Group				x300 (V)	Sort	x300 (V)
V	BR	BURLINGTON RESOURCES INC	E	E	4.2	5.4	247	9	243
V	PCZ	PETRO-CANADA INC	E	E	0.8	3.8	285	-15	283

LARGE (L) - 500 Cos.

	Code	Company	Group				x500 (L)	Sort	x500 (L)
L	FLC	FALCON DRILLING COMPANY INC	A	B	7.3	18.9	25	45	153
L	NBL	NOBLE AFFILIATES INC	B	E	5.3	10.3	192	-15	463
L	SFR	SANTA FE ENERGY RESOURCES	C	D	2.6	8.5	281	13	375
L	VRI	VASTAR RESORUCES INC	D	E	4.9	6.9	355	-17	467
L	OIL	TRITON ENERGY LTD	E	B	-1.7	3.9	456	42	174
L	EEX	EEX CORP	E	D	-1.7	3.0	476	18	343
L	APC	ANADARKO PETROLEUM CORP	E	E	0.8	3.2	471	9	403
L	APA	APACHE CORP	E	E	4.1	5.3	411	-18	471
L	ORX	ORYX ENERGY CO	E	E	5.0	3.6	463	-22	476
L	UTH	UNION TEXAS PETRO HLDGS	E	E	6.0	5.4	405	-32	485
L	PXD	PIONEER NATURAL RESOURCES	E	E	8.0	4.9	429	-58	497

MEDIUM (M) - 600 Cos.

	Code	Company	Group				x600 (M)	Sort	x600 (M)
M	OEI	OCEAN ENERGY INC	A	D	12.5	19.4	39	6	473
M	FEN	FORCENERGY INC	C	E	4.1	9.5	282	-2	515
M	NEV	NUEVO ENERGY CO	C	E	5.2	9.9	260	-9	546
M	RJL	RIGEL ENERGY CORP	C	E	3.3	8.6	327	-24	580
M	CHK	CHESAPEAKE ENERGY CORP	C	E	6.5	8.6	326	-28	586
M	SGY	STONE ENERGY CORP	D	C	4.9	7.1	422	20	349
M	UMC	UNITED MERIDIAN CORP	D	D	3.9	7.2	414	7	462
M	TMBR	BROWN (TOM) INC	E	C	-3.8	2.9	578	26	310

(continued overleaf)

HOLT USA2000 Universe
Size / #cos / mkt cap
Very large / 300 / $3.93B+
Large / 500 / $1.03–3.93B
Medium / 600 / $.42–1.03B
Small / 600 / $154–425M

Grouped by Forecast +1 year CFROI Grade (Near Term) which is then sorted high-to-low on numerical % Future

		HOLT DualGrade® Performance		CFROI Cash Flow Return on Investment			% of Total Market Value Attributed to Future Investments	
		#1 Near Term Fcst +1-year CFROI Grade	#2 Long Term % Future Grade	Past 5-year Median CFROI	Forecast +1-year CFROI	Forecast +1-year CFROI Rank	% Future	% Future Rank
M	PPP POGO PRODUCING CO	E	E	2.4	4.2	559	0	508
M	FST FOREST OIL CORP	E	E	-0.9	1.6	592	-34	590
SMALL (S) - 600 Cos.		**Group**		**x600 (S)**		**x600 (S)**	**Sort**	**x600 (S)**
S	TMG TRANSMONTAIGNE OIL CO	A	D	5.1	16.0	72	13	379
S	CRK COMSTOCK RESOURCES INC	A	D	2.4	16.1	71	10	399
S	BNO BENTON OIL & GAS CO	A	E	8.2	14.8	86	-17	545
S	BRY BERRY PETROLEUM -CL A	C	B	5.3	8.5	337	34	208
S	WOL WAINOCO OIL CORP	C	C	2.2	9.1	302	23	297
S	SFY SWIFT ENERGY CO	C	D	5.5	9.1	297	15	365
S	MARY ST MARY LAND & EXPLOR CO	D	C	3.8	6.7	442	22	303
S	ECA ENCAL ENERGY LTD	D	D	3.8	6.3	463	0	468
S	LOM LOMAK PETROLEUM INC	D	E	5.1	7.7	366	-15	535
S	COHO COHO ENERGY INC	D	E	4.3	6.1	472	-17	542
S	HSE HS RESOURCES INC	D	E	6.3	6.1	470	-20	559
S	BSNX BASIN EXPL INC	E	C	7.1	2.1	587	29	250
S	HUGO HUGOTON ENERGY CORP	E	D	1.6	3.1	572	12	388
S	UNT UNIT CORP	E	E	1.6	5.9	481	-19	552
S	CID CHIEFTAIN INTL INC	E	E	1.3	3.2	568	-29	575

Precision Instrument Industry

		Group		x300 (V)		x300 (V)	Sort	x300 (V)
VERY LARGE (V) - 300 Cos.								
V	EK EASTMAN KODAK CO	C	D	5.4	8.8	157	26	189
LARGE (L) - 500 Cos.		**Group**		**x500 (L)**		**x500 (L)**	**Sort**	**x500 (L)**
L	CGNX COGNEX CORP	A	A	16.2	17.4	40	62	67
L	PKN PERKIN-ELMER CORP	A	A	12.6	15.7	59	57	88

	Symbol	Company	Group				x600 (M)	Sort	x600 (M)
L	WAT	WATERS CORP	A	B	15.5	17.2	43	52	112
L	KLAC	KLA-TENCOR CORP	A	C	14.6	17.6	38	33	240
L	IO	INPUT/OUTPUT INC	B	A	12.4	13.0	115	58	84
L	SYB	SYBRON INTL CORP	C	B	9.9	9.7	221	51	121
L	TEK	TEKTRONIX INC	C	C	6.2	9.9	208	26	288
L	PRD	POLAROID CORP	E	D	1.9	3.3	469	20	330
MEDIUM (M) - 600 Cos.			**Group**				**x600 (M)**	**Sort**	**x600 (M)**
M	DNEX	DIONEX CORP	A	A	13.2	19.6	35	66	69
M	TMQ	THERMOQUEST CORP	D	B	5.2	6.9	431	50	153
M	OAK	OAK INDUSTRIES INC	D	B	7.5	6.6	445	40	207
M	EGG	EG&G INC	D	C	6.2	7.1	418	31	267
M	CKP	CHECKPOINT SYSTEMS INC	D	C	6.1	6.9	435	29	286
M	VWRX	VWR SCIENTIFIC PRODUCTS	E	B	3.9	4.2	558	48	170
M	TKN	THERMOTREX CORP	E	C	4.2	2.3	588	33	250
M	HTCH	HUTCHINSON TECH	E	E	4.8	4.1	560	2	496
M	SCIXF	SCITEX CORP LTD -ORD	E	E	6.6	2.6	582	-12	557
M	SEW	SINGER CO N V	E	E	10.6	4.8	540	-27	584
SMALL (S) - 600 Cos.			**Group**				**x600 (S)**	**Sort**	**x600 (S)**
S	XRIT	X-RITE INC	A	A	17.5	17.2	56	60	61
S	ENCD	ENCAD INC	A	A	25.5	25.4	14	57	80
S	MDYN	MOLECULAR DYNAMICS INC	A	A	8.8	13.8	117	54	91
S	INVX	INNOVEX INC	A	A	13.4	26.7	9	48	116
S	PRCP	PERCEPTRON INC	B	A	19.2	17.9	46	40	162
S	ROBV	ROBOTIC VISION SYSTEMS INC	B	A	27.2	16.5	66	36	192
S	ORBKF	ORBOTECH LTD	B	A	12.4	18.3	43	36	194
S	ZIGO	ZYGO CORP	B	A	6.3	19.4	38	34	212
S	OXE	OEC MED SYS INC	B	B	12.5	10.2	234	47	123
S	LCRY	LECROY CORP	B	B	7.6	12.8	150	44	138
S	IVI	II-VI INC	B	B	8.1	12.6	155	43	145
S	KRON	KRONOS INC	B	B	10.4	11.7	182	41	160
S	MTSC	MTS SYSTEMS CORP	B	B	5.7	10.5	223	39	175
S	TOK	TOKHEIM CORP	B	B	2.9	11.4	193	38	179
S	TGI	TRIUMPH GROUP INC	B	B	11.6	11.8	179	30	237
S	SYMM	SYMMETRICOM INC	C	C	9.4	11.0	204	16	357
S	COHR	COHERENT INC	D	D	5.1	10.9	209	3	451

(continued overleaf)

HOLT USA2000 Universe
Size / #cos / mkt cap
Very large / 300 / $3.93B+
Large / 500 / $1.03–3.93B
Medium / 600 / $.42–1.03B
Small / 600 / $154–425M

Grouped by Forecast +1 year CFROI Grade (Near Term) which is then sorted high-to-low on numerical % Future

	Company	HOLT DualGrade® Performance #1 Near Term Fcst +1-year CFROI Grade	#2 Long Term % Future Grade	CFROI Past 5-year Median CFROI	Forecast +1-year CFROI	Forecast +1-year CFROI Rank	% of Total Market Value Attributed to Future Investments % Future	% Future Rank
S	MOVA MOVADO GROUP INC	C	C	7.9	8.7	329	29	245
S	UTEK ULTRATECH STEPPER INC	C	D	10.5	9.1	304	14	368
S	ESL ESTERLINE TECHNOLOGIES	C	D	6.9	9.2	292	13	380
S	PSX PACIFIC SCIENTIFIC CO	D	B	6.2	6.8	430	35	197
S	KOL KOLLMORGEN CORP	D	B	2.8	6.9	426	34	206
S	LTXX LTX CORP	D	E	-1.2	6.2	467	-18	548
S	THS THERMOSPECTRA CORP	E	C	2.0	3.2	570	19	330
S	TAL TALLEY INDUSTRIES INC	E	D	7.8	5.2	517	6	431

Publishing Industry

	Company	Group					Sort	x300 (V)
VERY LARGE (V) - 300 Cos.								
V	DNB DUN & BRADSTREET CORP	A	A	13.0	20.9	17	62	44
V	MHP MCGRAW-HILL COMPANIES	C	B	8.3	10.1	126	57	64
V	DNY DONNELLEY (R R) & SONS CO	E	C	5.0	4.5	266	33	164

	Company	Group					Sort	x500 (L)
LARGE (L) - 500 Cos.								
L	VCI VALASSIS COMMUNICATIONS	A	A	33.4	33.4	1	68	50
L	DLX DELUXE CORP	A	B	12.7	15.5	64	41	179
L	PRM PRIMEDIA INC	B	C	8.8	10.4	188	33	239
L	HTN HOUGHTON MIFFLIN CO	B	C	12.8	11.4	151	30	259
L	RDA READERS DIGEST ASSN -CL A	C	A	18.6	9.7	218	60	72
L	H HARCOURT GENERAL INC	C	D	9.0	9.8	212	16	353
L	HLR HOLLINGER INTL INC -CL A	C	E	4.8	8.4	286	-10	457
L	PQB QUEBECOR INC -CL A	C	E	6.9	9.2	241	-107	499
L	SLVN SYLVAN LEARNING SYSTEMS	E	A	-0.6	4.5	443	69	45
L	MDP MEREDITH CORP	E	A	4.8	4.8	432	66	55

MEDIUM (M) - 600 Cos.

				Group			x600 (M)	Sort	x600 (M)
M	PRST	PRESSTEK INC	A	A	9.6	18.3	47	83	8
M	CGX	CONSOLIDATED GRAPHICS INC	B	A	11.0	13.9	123	62	90
M	JW.A	WILEY (JOHN) & SONS -CL A	B	B	13.3	10.8	213	53	135
M	JH	HARLAND (JOHN H.) CO	B	C	13.0	13.1	144	25	317
M	AGTX	APPLIED GRAPHICS TECHNGS	C	A	4.1	8.9	311	72	45
M	BNE	BOWNE & CO INC	C	C	9.5	8.3	348	21	344
M	SCHL	SCHOLASTIC CORP	D	D	10.2	6.9	434	17	375
M	BNTA	BANTA CORP	D	D	7.5	7.0	425	5	476
M	WRC	WORLD COLOR PRESS INC	D	E	4.2	6.3	469	-12	556

SMALL (S) - 600 Cos.

				Group			x600 (S)	Sort	x600 (S)
S	PLA	PLAYBOY ENTERPRISES -CL B	B	B	17.6	16.6	65	30	236
S	MRLL	MERRILL CORPORATION	C	A	14.7	14.8	85	20	322
S	WAVR	WAVERLY INC	A	A	7.3	13.3	129	76	16
S	STEK	STECK-VAUGHN PUBLISHING CP	B	B	11.0	12.6	153	44	136
S	DEVN	DEVON GROUP INC	C	C	9.4	9.7	260	21	312
S	TNM	NELSON (THOMAS) INC	D	D	5.3	6.0	476	7	418
S	GBFE	GOLDEN BOOKS FAMILY ENTMT	E	A	-3.4	1.6	593	69	32
S	GCS	GRAY COMMUNICATIONS	E	B	4.3	5.2	518	42	151
S	CDMS	CADMUS COMMUNICATIONS	E	D	4.6	5.5	505	-1	474

Railroad Industry

VERY LARGE (V) - 300 Cos.

				Group			x300 (V)	Sort	x300 (V)
V	CSX	CSX CORP	E	E	4.0	4.1	278	-12	280
V	BNI	BRLNGTN NTHRN SANTA FE	E	E	3.0	4.8	263	-16	284
V	CP	CANADIAN PACIFIC LTD	E	E	3.8	5.6	246	-18	287
V	UNP	UNION PACIFIC CORP	E	E	5.0	4.0	280	-18	288
V	NSC	NORFOLK SOUTHERN CORP	E	E	4.0	4.0	281	-45	299

LARGE (L) - 500 Cos.

				Group			x500 (L)	Sort	x500 (L)
L	WCLX	WISCONSIN CENTRAL TRANSP	C	E	8.3	8.3	291	5	416
L	IC	ILLINOIS CENTRAL CORP	C	E	9.4	9.9	207	-4	443
L	KSU	KANSAS CITY SOUTHERN INDS	D	D	5.7	7.9	307	18	344

(continued overleaf)

HOLT USA2000 Universe
Size / #cos / mkt cap

Very large / 300 / $3.93B+
Large / 500 / $1.03–3.93B
Medium / 600 / $.42–1.03B
Small / 600 / $.154–425M

Grouped by Forecast +1 year CFROI Grade (Near Term) which is then sorted high-to-low on numerical % Future

			HOLT DualGrade® Performance		CFROI Cash Flow Return on Investment			% of Total Market Value Attributed to Future Investments	
			#1 Near Term Fcst +1-year CFROI Grade	#2 Long Term % Future Grade	Past 5-year Median CFROI	Forecast +1-year CFROI	Forecast +1-year CFROI Rank	% Future Sort	% Future Rank
MEDIUM (M) - 600 Cos.			*Group*				**x600 (M)**	*Sort*	**x600 (M)**
SMALL (S) - 600 Cos.			*Group*				**x600 (S)**	*Sort*	**x600 (S)**
S	GBX	GREENBRIER COMPANIES INC	C	D	9.4	8.3	347	10	398
Recreation Industry									
VERY LARGE (V) - 300 Cos.			*Group*				**x300 (V)**	*Sort*	**x300 (V)**
V	MAT	MATTEL INC	A	A	18.4	16.3	47	64	40
V	HDI	HARLEY-DAVIDSON INC	B	B	12.7	12.8	72	58	63
V	CCL	CARNIVAL CORP	B	C	11.9	12.1	79	39	144
V	HAS	HASBRO INC	D	B	6.6	7.5	197	55	80
LARGE (L) - 500 Cos.			*Group*				**x500 (L)**	*Sort*	**x500 (L)**
L	ELY	CALLAWAY GOLF CO	A	B	30.7	22.4	9	53	108
L	FUN	CEDAR FAIR -LP	A	C	20.7	19.5	22	33	236
L	ERTS	ELECTRONIC ARTS INC	B	A	16.9	13.0	118	66	53
L	RCL	ROYAL CARIBBEAN CRUISES	C	D	10.0	9.2	249	15	363
L	BC	BRUNSWICK CORP	C	D	8.1	8.9	268	9	398
MEDIUM (M) - 600 Cos.			*Group*				**x600 (M)**	*Sort*	**x600 (M)**
M	ACTN	ACTION PERFORMANCE COS	A	A	13.8	20.2	29	59	109
M	IMAXF	IMAX CORP	A	B	10.1	14.8	99	56	123
M	RGR	STURM RUGER & CO INC	B	C	13.0	11.8	187	25	314
M	CLN	COLEMAN CO INC	C	C	7.9	8.6	325	32	263
M	TRK	SPEEDWAY MOTORSPORTS INC	D	B	14.2	7.2	415	45	181
M	WMS	WMS INDUSTRIES INC	D	B	7.3	7.5	396	42	199
M	BFIT	BALLY TOTAL FITNESS HLDG CP	E	D	1.4	4.7	543	15	402

SMALL (S) - 600 Cos.

	Ticker	Company	Group			x600 (S)	Sort	x600 (S)
S	FOTO	SEATTLE FILMWORKS INC	A	21.0	19.4	37	44	135
S	QUIK	QUIKSILVER INC	B	10.6	10.8	211	29	242
S	BIKE	CANNONDALE CORP	C	11.3	11.9	171	24	290
S	LVB	STEINWAY MUSICAL INSTRS INC	C	10.6	10.9	208	20	320
S	ACAT	ARCTIC CAT INC	B	16.6	12.9	144	-8	507
S	TBZ	TOY BIZ INC -CL A	E	28.2	9.6	269	27	265
S	KTO	K2 INC	C	5.0	8.6	333	4	442
S	FGCI	FAMILY GOLF CENTERS INC	D	1.4	6.3	462	34	210
S	CPY	CPI CORP	B	5.4	6.2	465	15	364
S	SPWY	PENSKE MOTORSPORTS INC	D	8.9	6.5	453	2	456
S	ESSF	ESSEF CORP	D	8.3	6.8	429	-2	478
S	HDL	HANDLEMAN CO	D	8.1	6.4	458	-48	592
S	GAL	GALOOB TOYS INC	E	9.6	2.9	574	19	331
S	HUF	HUFFY CORP	E	5.9	5.7	493	-4	494

Restaurant Industry

VERY LARGE (V) - 300 Cos.

	Ticker	Company	Group			x300 (V)	Sort	x300 (V)
V	YUM	TRICON GLOBAL RESTAURANTS	D	5.2	6.6	217	26	190
V	MCD	MCDONALDS CORP	D	8.1	7.6	193	18	221

LARGE (L) - 500 Cos.

	Ticker	Company	Group			x500 (L)	Sort	x500 (L)
L	PHL	PLANET HOLLYWOOD INTL INC	B	13.0	14.6	81	44	158
L	OSSI	OUTBACK STEAKHOUSE INC	A	17.1	14.9	74	23	309
L	CBRL	CRACKER BARREL OLD CTRY	C	9.9	10.1	197	33	237
L	SBUX	STARBUCKS CORP	B	5.9	9.4	231	54	103
L	WEN	WENDY'S INTERNATIONAL INC	E	7.3	8.2	293	5	418
L	EAT	BRINKER INTL INC	D	7.8	5.7	388	14	370
L	CKR	CKE RESTAURANTS INC	D	3.8	4.5	441	17	346
L	DRI	DARDEN RESTAURANTS INC	E	6.4	4.6	440	7	408

MEDIUM (M) - 600 Cos.

	Ticker	Company	Group			x600 (M)	Sort	x600 (M)
M	PZZA	PAPA JOHNS INTERNATIONAL	A	10.6	12.6	158	63	82
M	INDQA	INTL DAIRY QUEEN -CL A	C	15.8	13.6	132	33	251
M	APPB	APPLEBEES INTL INC	E	11.0	12.1	171	2	495
M	STAR	LONE STAR STEAKHOUSE SALOON	E	12.9	11.1	205	-14	564

(continued overleaf)

HOLT USA2000 Universe
Size / #cos / mkt cap

Very large / 300 / $3.93B+
Large / 500 / $1.03–3.93B
Medium / 600 / $.42–1.03B
Small / 600 / $.154–425M

Grouped by Forecast +1 year CFROI Grade (Near Term) which is then sorted high-to-low on numerical % Future

			HOLT DualGrade® Performance		CFROI Cash Flow Return on Investment			% of Total Market Value Attributed to Future Investments	
			#1 Near Term Fcst +1-year CFROI Grade	#2 Long Term % Future Grade	Past 5-year Median CFROI	Forecast +1-year CFROI	Forecast +1-year CFROI Rank	% Future	% Future Rank
M	LDRY	LANDRYS SEAFOOD RESTAURANT	C	C	6.9	9.8	264	24	324
M	SHBZ	SHOWBIZ PIZZA TIME INC	C	D	5.3	8.2	352	18	371
M	BOCB	BUFFETS INC	C	E	9.1	8.5	329	–10	548
M	RAIN	RAINFOREST CAFE INC	D	B	3.4	7.8	378	39	214
M	BOBE	BOB EVANS FARMS	D	D	8.9	6.3	466	18	362
M	FM	FOODMAKER INC	D	D	4.1	7.8	377	15	399
M	SBA	SBARRO INC	D	D	7.9	7.7	386	12	423
M	APSO	APPLE SOUTH INC	D	E	8.0	7.0	430	2	493
M	HMS	HOST MARRIOTT SVCS CORP	E	D	3.8	4.9	534	16	387
M	RI	RUBY TUESDAY INC	E	D	5.2	5.8	496	11	432
M	BOST	BOSTON CHICKEN INC	E	E	4.3	0.7	598	–55	596
SMALL (S) - 600 Cos.			**Group**				**x600 (S)**	**Sort**	**x600 (S)**
S	SONC	SONIC CORP	A	C	16.0	14.8	90	22	300
S	CAKE	CHEESECAKE FACTORY INC	C	B	8.4	9.8	253	39	169
S	COP	CONSOLIDATED PRODUCTS INC	C	C	8.4	9.3	284	25	283
S	RYAN	RYAN'S FAMILY STK HOUSES INC	C	E	8.2	8.5	340	–36	581
S	DANB	DAVE & BUSTERS INC	D	B	6.0	6.9	423	31	231
S	TBY	TCBY ENTERPRISES INC	D	C	5.1	7.7	369	29	247
S	LUB	LUBYS CAFETERIAS INC	D	E	8.7	6.9	422	–11	519
S	SHN	SHONEY'S INC	D	E	12.7	7.5	386	–19	555
S	NPCI	NPC INTERNATIONAL INC	E	C	5.7	5.1	524	26	274
S	VRES	VICORP RESTAURANTS INC	E	E	3.7	3.1	571	–3	488

Retail (Special Lines) Industry

VERY LARGE (V) - 300 Cos.			**Group**				**x300 (V)**	**Sort**	**x300 (V)**
V	IBI	INTIMATE BRANDS INC -CL A	A	B	17.3	18.1	36	48	114

	Ticker	Company	Group				x500 (L)	Sort	x500 (L)
V	GPS	GAP INC	B	B	11.6	11.4	92	53	87
V	AZO	AUTOZONE INC	B	C	15.4	13.3	66	43	130
V	TJX	TJX COMPANIES INC	B	C	9.7	11.3	95	36	156
V	TAN	TANDY CORP	C	C	6.9	9.3	147	30	177
V	LTD	LIMITED INC	D	D	7.8	7.3	204	16	223
V	TOY	TOYS R US INC	D	E	9.4	7.5	199	9	246
LARGE (L) - 500 Cos.			**Group**				**x500 (L)**	**Sort**	**x500 (L)**
L	CPU	COMPUSA INC	A	A	10.3	15.0	73	59	80
L	DLTR	DOLLAR TREE STORES INC	A	B	15.6	16.5	52	51	120
L	BBBY	BED BATH & BEYOND INC	B	A	12.4	12.4	128	64	62
L	GNCI	GENERAL NUTRITION COS -CL A	B	B	7.3	10.9	160	52	118
L	LE	LANDS END INC	B	B	13.9	13.5	103	46	140
L	ROST	ROSS STORES INC	B	C	7.5	12.1	138	37	206
L	WSGC	WILLIAMS-SONOMA INC	C	B	6.5	9.1	251	46	137
L	TIF	TIFFANY & CO	C	C	7.4	9.5	227	32	248
L	BBY	BEST BUY CO INC	C	D	7.9	8.7	274	18	340
L	PIR	PIER 1 IMPORTS INC/DE	D	C	5.9	7.5	332	36	211
L	BGP	BORDERS GROUP INC	D	C	0.9	6.5	366	30	256
L	BKS	BARNES & NOBLE INC	D	C	5.7	7.4	335	30	258
L	PSS	PAYLESS SHOESOURCE INC	D	C	7.1	7.5	334	25	295
L	CC	CIRCUIT CITY STR CRCT CTY GP	D	C	9.3	5.5	400	25	298
L	PBY	PEP BOYS-MANNY MOE & JACK	D	E	7.4	6.8	357	-5	447
MEDIUM (M) - 600 Cos.			**Group**				**x600 (M)**	**Sort**	**x600 (M)**
M	HNV	HANOVER DIRECT INC	A	A	11.2	19.8	33	65	73
M	NATR	NATURES SUNSHINE PRODS INC	A	A	17.3	19.3	40	63	81
M	CELL	BRIGHTPOINT INC	B	B	13.6	11.7	191	48	165
M	BYL	BRYLANE INC	B	B	15.8	11.0	209	45	180
M	GYMB	GYMBOREE CORP	B	C	11.7	10.4	231	31	268
M	SUIT	MENS WEARHOUSE INC	B	B	8.7	9.3	289	37	225
M	CLE	CLAIRES STORES INC	C	C	8.4	9.9	256	29	285
M	RUS	RUSS BERRIE & CO INC	C	C	5.2	10.2	245	28	292
M	GDYS	GOODYS FAMILY CLOTHING INC	C	D	6.7	8.3	347	15	401
M	BCF	BURLINGTON COAT FACTORY W	C	D	7.3	9.7	268	10	446
M	STH	STANHOME INC	D	C	10.6	7.9	373	25	313
M	DBRN	DRESS BARN INC	D	C	5.5	6.3	468	22	339

(continued overleaf)

HOLT USA2000 Universe
Size / #cos / mkt cap
Very large / 300 / $3.93B+
Large / 500 / $1.03–3.93B
Medium / 600 / $.42–1.03B
Small / 600 / $.154–425M
Grouped by Forecast +1 year CFROI Grade (Near Term)
which is then sorted high-to-low on numerical % Future

| | | HOLT DualGrade® Performance | | CFROI Cash Flow Return on Investment | | | % of Total Market Value Attributed to Future Investments | |
		#1 Near Term Fcst +1-year CFROI Grade	#2 Long Term % Future Grade	Past 5-year Median CFROI	Forecast +1-year CFROI	Forecast +1-year CFROI Rank	% Future	% Future Rank
M	PETC	PETCO ANIMAL SUPPLIES INC	D	D	6.9	7.8	381	18	363
M	FHT	FINGERHUT COMPANIES INC	D	D	8.9	6.7	443	10	444
M	BOP	BOISE CASCADE OFFICE PDS CP	D	D	7.2	7.8	379	7	465
M	TSA	SPORTS AUTHORITY INC	D	E	5.2	6.2	475	-2	517
M	FTS	FOOTSTAR INC	D	E	8.0	7.2	417	-4	527
M	PETM	PETSMART INC	E	C	5.4	4.8	539	23	330
M	MIKE	MICHAELS STORES INC	E	C	6.5	5.8	495	20	347
M	CNJ	COLE NATL CORP -CL A	E	D	6.8	6.0	484	14	410
M	MWHS	MICRO WAREHOUSE INC	E	D	10.0	5.3	524	7	466
M	TLB	TALBOTS INC	E	D	9.2	5.1	532	5	477
M	ZLC	ZALE CORP	E	E	4.7	5.9	487	3	487
M	SPGLA	SPIEGEL INC -CL A	E	E	3.7	4.6	548	2	497
M	HMY	HEILIG-MEYERS CO	E	E	6.8	3.7	565	0	506
M	CHRS	CHARMING SHOPPES	E	E	4.9	3.3	571	-7	538
SMALL (S) - 600 Cos.			Group				x600 (S)	Sort	x600 (S)
S	FOSL	FOSSIL INC	A	A	23.8	14.4	103	49	114
S	MENS	K&G MENS CENTER INC	B	A	19.7	13.2	132	65	48
S	NSIT	INSIGHT ENTERPRISES INC	B	A	11.1	11.6	186	62	52
S	DZTK	DAISYTEK INTL CORP	B	C	11.9	12.6	154	28	256
S	MXG	MAXIM GROUP INC	B	D	4.8	11.3	197	4	443
S	ICO	INACOM CORP	B	E	11.1	13.0	138	-18	549
S	UGLY	UGLY DUCKLING CORP	B	E	1.8	10.8	214	-50	593
S	MICA	MICROAGE INC	B	E	8.8	12.1	169	-56	595
S	WLMR	WILMAR INDUSTRIES INC	C	A	18.8	9.3	285	54	90
S	GADZ	GADZOOKS INC	C	C	8.8	9.3	289	27	266
S	WMAR	WEST MARINE INC	C	C	9.5	8.4	344	26	279

S	MLG	MUSICLAND STORES CORP	C	4.6	8.3	346	17	344
S	CPRT	COPART INC	C	8.9	9.4	276	10	401
S	FINL	FINISH LINE INC -CL A	C	8.0	8.9	316	8	413
S	ANIC	ANICOM INC	A	1.2	6.7	437	59	67
S	PCAI	PCA INTERNATIONAL INC	B	11.9	6.1	471	39	171
S	GRDG	GARDEN RIDGE CORP	C	8.9	7.5	389	28	257
S	AEOS	AMERN EAGLE OUTFITTERS INC	C	6.2	7.0	415	27	268
S	PGDA	PIERCING PAGODA	C	7.8	7.9	362	18	339
S	WTSLA	WET SEAL INC -CL A	C	5.0	6.6	449	16	347
S	HKF	HANCOCK FABRICS INC	C	4.9	6.4	457	16	356
S	FEET	JUST FOR FEET INC	D	3.4	6.2	466	10	400
S	LVC	LILLIAN VERNON CORP	D	9.0	6.8	436	8	411
S	FNLY	FINLAY ENTERPRISES INC	D	7.5	7.7	371	2	457
S	RAYS	SUNGLASS HUT INTL INC	D	8.7	7.0	418	1	462
S	MKS	MIKASA INC	D	8.8	6.2	464	0	471
S	FCA.A	FABRI-CENTERS OF AMER -CL A	D	5.2	7.5	387	-2	479
S	DAP	DISCOUNT AUTO PARTS INC	E	8.9	7.6	379	-11	521
S	FRDM	FRIEDMANS INC -CL A	E	12.0	7.2	405	-23	567
S	CML	CML GROUP	B	8.5	0.6	596	37	186
S	JC	CRAIG (JENNY) INC	B	7.6	2.2	586	30	240
S	CACOA	CATO CORP -CL A	D	6.8	5.6	502	9	408
S	ANN	ANNTAYLOR STORES CORP	D	3.8	4.3	545	7	424
S	BBA	BOMBAY CO INC	E	7.6	3.9	558	-2	484
S	HAVT	HAVERTY FURNITURE	E	4.7	5.6	499	-17	543
S	BL	BLAIR CORP	E	12.5	1.9	590	-46	589

Retail Building Supply Industry

			Group		x300 (V)	Sort	x300 (V)
VERY LARGE (V) - 300 Cos.							
V	HD	HOME DEPOT INC	B	A	10.3	12.1	78	60	56
V	LOW	LOWES COS	B	C	9.3	10.3	119	35	159

			Group	x500 (L)	Sort	x500 (L)
LARGE (L) - 500 Cos.						
L	FAST	FASTENAL CO	A	18.5	19.2	24	68	51

			Group	x600 (M)	Sort	x600 (M)
MEDIUM (M) - 600 Cos.						
M	HUG	HUGHES SUPPLY INC	C	5.1	9.2	294	20	348

(continued overleaf)

HOLT USA2000 Universe
Size / #cos / mkt cap
Very large / 300 / $3.93B+
Large / 500 / $1.03–3.93B
Medium / 600 / $.42–1.03B
Small / 600 / $154–425M

Grouped by Forecast +1 year CFROI Grade (Near Term) which is then sorted high-to-low on numerical % Future

		HOLT DualGrade® Performance		CFROI Cash Flow Return on Investment			% of Total Market Value Attributed to Future Investments	
		#1 Near Term Fcst +1-year CFROI Grade	#2 Long Term % Future Grade	Past 5-year Median CFROI	Forecast +1-year CFROI	Forecast +1-year CFROI Rank	% Future	% Future Rank
M	EAGL EAGLE HARDWARE & GARDEN	E	D	3.8	5.8	494	17	377
SMALL (S) - 600 Cos.	*Group*				**x600 (S)**	*Sort*	**x600 (S)**	
S	HOMEBASE INC	E	E	6.7	5.1	523	–25	570

Retail Store Industry

VERY LARGE (V) - 300 Cos.	*Group*				**x300 (V)**	*Sort*	**x300 (V)**	
V	DG DOLLAR GENERAL	B	A	11.7	13.6	64	62	47
V	KSS KOHLS CORP	B	A	11.6	10.3	120	59	57
V	WMT WAL-MART STORES	B	C	12.1	11.0	103	41	137
V	COST COSTCO COMPANIES INC	C	B	8.4	9.2	149	47	115
V	DH DAYTON HUDSON CORP	C	D	8.3	9.5	145	27	187
V	MAY MAY DEPARTMENT STORES CO	C	D	9.4	10.0	130	25	196
V	S SEARS ROEBUCK & CO	C	D	9.8	10.1	124	14	233
V	NOBE NORDSTROM INC	D	C	7.0	7.2	205	36	157
V	FD FEDERATED DEPT STORES	D	E	6.0	7.9	188	7	247
V	JCP PENNEY (J C) CO	E	D	6.5	5.1	256	15	226
V	KM K MART CORP	E	E	3.9	4.7	265	–20	290
LARGE (L) - 500 Cos.	*Group*				**x500 (L)**	*Sort*	**x500 (L)**	
L	CNS CONSOLIDATED STORES CORP	B	C	9.1	10.6	178	29	267
L	FDO FAMILY DOLLAR STORES	C	B	8.2	9.2	242	49	127
L	MFI MACFRUGALS BARGAINS	C	C	8.3	8.3	292	30	260
L	BJ BJS WHOLESALE CLUB INC	C	C	10.0	9.9	211	27	282
L	STGE STAGE STORES INC	C	C	10.4	10.0	202	25	300
L	NMG NEIMAN-MARCUS GROUP INC	C	D	8.8	9.3	235	20	329

			Group				x600 (M)	Sort	x600 (M)
L	PFT	PROFFITTS INC	D	D	6.0	7.7	322	20	326
L	SKS	SAKS HOLDINGS INC	D	D	6.2	7.8	312	11	387
L	Z	WOOLWORTH CORP	D	E	4.1	5.6	396	3	425
L	DDS	DILLARDS INC -CL A	D	E	7.3	6.1	376	−11	459
L	MST	MERCANTILE STORES CO INC	E	D	5.0	5.1	422	15	365
L	FMY	MEYER (FRED) INC	E	E	5.6	4.5	442	8	407

MEDIUM (M) - 600 Cos.			Group				x600 (M)	Sort	x600 (M)
M	NDN	99 CENTS ONLY STORES	B	A	11.9	13.9	122	63	85
M	BKE	BUCKLE INC	B	B	9.5	11.3	200	49	157
M	SMRT	STEIN MART INC	B	C	11.5	12.3	166	24	326
M	CRP	CARSON PIRIE SCOTT & CO/IL	C	C	7.2	8.1	358	30	279
M	SKO	SHOPKO STORES INC	D	E	6.3	7.3	407	−22	577

SMALL (S) - 600 Cos.			Group				x600 (S)	Sort	x600 (S)
S	HLYW	HOLLYWOOD ENTMT CORP	A	E	12.8	14.4	102	−55	594
S	PCTY	PARTY CITY CORP	C	B	10.3	9.0	311	43	143
S	PSUN	PACIFIC SUNWEAR CALIF INC	C	B	5.6	8.1	355	33	214
S	AMES	AMES DEPT STORES INC	C	D	9.0	9.9	251	3	449
S	CPWM	COST PLUS INC	D	C	6.8	7.3	399	29	243
S	TWMC	TRANS WORLD ENTMT CORP	D	C	5.1	6.9	419	19	335
S	BONT	BON-TON STORES INC	D	E	5.5	7.0	414	−3	490
S	VCD	VALUE CITY DEPT STORES INC	D	E	6.8	6.7	438	−20	556
S	SME	SERVICE MERCHANDISE CO	D	E	7.4	5.9	478	−37	583
S	FRED	FREDS INC	E	C	3.7	4.6	536	22	306

Semiconductor (Capital Equipment) Industry

VERY LARGE (V) - 300 Cos.			Group				x300 (V)	Sort	x300 (V)
V	AMAT	APPLIED MATERIALS INC	A	C	16.0	17.1	44	43	129

LARGE (L) - 500 Cos.			Group				x500 (L)	Sort	x500 (L)
L	ALTR	ALTERA CORP	A	A	14.8	14.9	75	58	83
L	XLNX	XILINX INC	A	B	19.6	14.4	86	53	107
L	NVLS	NOVELLUS SYSTEMS INC	A	C	17.7	18.5	30	34	230
L	TER	TERADYNE INC	A	C	9.2	15.7	58	30	262
L	VTSS	VITESSE SEMICONDUCTOR	B	A	1.5	11.7	146	70	39

(continued overleaf)

HOLT USA2000 Universe
Size / #cos / mkt cap
Very large / 300 / $3.93B+
Large / 500 / $1.03–3.93B
Medium / 600 / $.42–1.03B
Small / 600 / $.154–425M

Grouped by Forecast +1 year CFROI Grade (Near Term)
which is then sorted high-to-low on numerical % Future

			HOLT DualGrade® Performance		CFROI Cash Flow Return on Investment			% of Total Market Value Attributed to Future Investments	
			#1 Near Term Fcst +1-year CFROI Grade	#2 Long Term % Future Grade	Past 5-year Median CFROI	Forecast +1-year CFROI	Forecast +1-year CFROI Rank	% Future	Future Rank
MEDIUM (M) - 600 Cos.			*Group*				**x600 [M]**	*Sort*	**x600 [M]**
M	KLIC	KULICKE & SOFFA INDUSTRIES	B	E	10.0	12.3	164	–1	510
SMALL (S) - 600 Cos.			*Group*				**x600 [S]**	*Sort*	**x600 [S]**
S	WJ	WATKINS–JOHNSON	E	E	2.8	1.4	594	–11	518

Semiconductor Industry

			#1 Near Term Fcst +1-year CFROI Grade	#2 Long Term % Future Grade	Past 5-year Median CFROI	Forecast +1-year CFROI	Forecast +1-year CFROI Rank	% Future	Future Rank
VERY LARGE (V) - 300 Cos.			*Group*				**x300 [V]**	*Sort*	**x300 [V]**
V	LLTC	LINEAR TECHNOLOGY CORP	A	A	20.4	20.1	21	68	32
V	MXIM	MAXIM INTEGRATED PRODUCTS	A	A	23.0	22.5	10	72	23
V	INTC	INTEL CORP	A	A	20.6	19.3	30	59	60
V	ADI	ANALOG DEVICES	B	B	7.7	11.2	99	49	109
V	TXN	TEXAS INSTRUMENTS INC	C	C	8.7	9.8	136	41	135
V	MOT	MOTOROLA INC	D	D	9.1	7.9	190	19	216
V	MU	MICRON TECHNOLOGY INC	E	C	17.0	1.7	298	28	180
LARGE (L) - 500 Cos.			*Group*				**x500 [L]**	*Sort*	**x500 [L]**
L	DS	DALLAS SEMICONDUCTOR CORP	A	B	10.4	15.5	62	40	183
L	LSCC	LATTICE SEMICONDUCTOR	B	B	14.2	11.2	154	45	149
L	VLSI	VLSI TECHNOLOGY INC	B	D	4.5	10.6	174	15	364
L	ATML	ATMEL CORP	B	D	12.4	10.7	170	10	396
L	NSM	NATIONAL SEMICONDUCTOR	C	D	6.8	8.1	299	23	311
L	LRCX	LAM RESEARCH CORP	D	D	15.8	6.0	382	15	358
L	LSI	LSI LOGIC CORP	D	D	6.3	6.1	377	17	351
L	AMD	ADVANCED MICRO DEVICES	E	E	8.2	3.2	472	–10	458

MEDIUM (M) - 600 Cos.

	Ticker	Company	Group				x600 (M)	Sort	x600 (M)
M	PMCS	PMC-SIERRA INC	A	A	5.7	18.8	42	77	28
M	CMOS	CREDENCE SYSTEMS CORP	A	C	17.1	16.9	63	30	277
M	GEN	GENRAD INC	A	A	5.2	14.2	118	59	107
M	UTR	UNITRODE CORP	A	B	11.7	15.6	77	41	201
M	BBRC	BURR-BROWN CORP	B	B	4.0	10.8	216	48	167
M	CRUS	CIRRUS LOGIC INC	B	E	8.7	10.7	218	-1	513
M	CUBE	C-CUBE MICROSYSTEMS INC	B	B	4.0	11.2	204	49	158
M	PLAB	PHOTRONICS INC	C	C	8.8	8.1	359	29	283
M	SVGI	SILICON VALLEY GROUP INC	D	E	6.4	6.7	444	-5	530
M	DPMI	DUPONT PHOTOMASKS INC	D	D	8.3	7.3	406	16	390
M	IDTI	INTEGRATED DEVICE TECH INC	D	E	9.2	7.4	404	-12	558
M	IRF	INTL RECTIFIER CORP	E	D	2.9	5.6	504	14	409
M	CY	CYPRESS SEMICONDUCTOR	E	E	7.2	5.5	515	-13	562

SMALL (S) - 600 Cos.

	Ticker	Company	Group				x600 (S)	Sort	x600 (S)
S	ICST	INTEGRATED CIRCUIT SYSTEMS	A	A	18.0	23.8	20	57	79
S	ATMI	ATMI INC	A	A	-0.5	16.1	70	63	49
S	ASYT	ASYST TECHNOLOGIES INC	A	B	9.2	17.8	49	46	127
S	ADEX	ADE CORP/MA	A	C	10.7	17.1	58	16	353
S	SMTL	SEMITOOL INC	B	C	18.7	12.7	152	21	314
S	SDLI	SDL INC	B	B	5.4	11.5	190	38	178
S	QLGC	QLOGIC CORP	C	B	6.8	9.6	263	41	157
S	EGLS	ELECTROGLAS INC	C	D	17.0	8.8	323	6	430
S	IPEC	INTEGRATED PROCESS EQ	C	C	4.3	9.5	270	19	332
S	CHPS	CHIPS & TECHNOLOGIES INC	C	B	13.8	8.1	357	38	182
S	ESST	ESS TECHNOLOGY INC	C	C	27.9	9.0	310	24	293
S	TQNT	TRIQUINT SEMICONDUCTOR INC	D	C	1.5	6.1	469	21	311
S	ZLG	ZILOG INC	D	E	12.3	7.5	392	-30	577

Shoe Industry

VERY LARGE (V) - 300 Cos.

	Ticker	Company	Group				x300 (V)	Sort	x300 (V)
V	NKE	NIKE INC -CL B	B	C	17.0	11.0	104	44	126

LARGE (L) - 500 Cos.

	Ticker	Company	Group				x500 (L)	Sort	x500 (L)
L	RBK	REEBOK INTERNATIONAL LTD	B	D	19.1	10.7	173	19	339

(continued overleaf)

HOLT USA2000 Universe
Size / #cos / mkt cap
Very large / 300 / $3.93B+
Large / 500 / $1.03–3.93B
Medium / 600 / $.42–1.03B
Small / 600 / $154–425M

Grouped by Forecast +1 year CFROI Grade (Near Term) which is then sorted high-to-low on numerical % Future

		HOLT DualGrade® Performance		CFROI Cash Flow Return on Investment			% of Total Market Value Attributed to Future Investments	
		#1 Near Term Fcst +1-year CFROI Grade	#2 Long Term % Future Grade	Past 5-year Median CFROI	Forecast +1-year CFROI	Forecast +1-year CFROI Rank	% Future	% Future Rank
MEDIUM (M) - 600 Cos.		**Group**				**x600 (M)**	**Sort**	**x600 (M)**
M TBL	TIMBERLAND CO -CL A	B	C	8.9	10.5	227	34	245
M NIN	NINE WEST GROUP INC	C	D	15.6	8.3	344	6	471
M WWW	WOLVERINE WORLD WIDE	D	B	5.4	6.6	451	51	149
M SRR	STRIDE RITE CORP	D	B	5.9	6.8	439	36	232
SMALL (S) - 600 Cos.		**Group**				**x600 (S)**	**Sort**	**x600 (S)**
S KCP	COLE KENNETH PROD INC -CL A	B	B	20.2	13.0	141	43	141
S VANS	VANS INC	C	B	4.8	9.1	299	30	239
S GCO	GENESCO INC	C	C	4.5	9.7	258	19	334
S BG	BROWN GROUP INC	E	E	4.2	5.7	495	-10	511

Steel (General) Industry

		HOLT DualGrade® Performance		CFROI Cash Flow Return on Investment			% of Total Market Value Attributed to Future Investments	
VERY LARGE (V) - 300 Cos.		**Group**				**x300 (V)**	**Sort**	**x300 (V)**
V NUE	NUCOR CORP	B	E	9.9	10.4	117	3	258
LARGE (L) - 500 Cos.		**Group**				**x500 (L)**	**Sort**	**x500 (L)**
L WTHG	WORTHINGTON INDUSTRIES	D	D	9.1	7.2	347	9	400
L IPS	IPSCO INC	D	E	4.5	6.9	356	9	404
MEDIUM (M) - 600 Cos.		**Group**				**x600 (M)**	**Sort**	**x600 (M)**
M STLD	STEEL DYNAMICS INC	A	E	3.6	14.4	110	-4	526
M CLF	CLEVELAND-CLIFFS INC	D	E	6.9	7.0	424	-47	595
M LUC	LUKENS INC	E	D	3.7	3.3	570	14	403
M OS	OREGON STEEL MILLS INC	E	D	3.1	4.6	547	12	424

	Symbol	Company	Group				x600 (S)	Sort	x300 (S)
M	BIR	BIRMINGHAM STEEL CORP	E	E	2.6	2.9	577	0	509
M	CRS	CARPENTER TECHNOLOGY	E	E	3.6	5.5	512	-13	563
M	CMC	COMMERCIAL METALS	E	E	4.9	5.2	530	-22	576
M	NS	NATIONAL STEEL CORP -CL B	E	E	1.8	3.3	569	-66	598

SMALL (S) - 600 Cos. — Group | x600 (S) | Sort | x300 (S)

	Symbol	Company	Group				x600 (S)	Sort	x300 (S)
S	NSS	NS GROUP INC	B	B	4.2	12.8	149	-4	491
S	CAS	CASTLE (A M) & CO	D	E	6.4	6.7	446	-4	496
S	SCHN	SCHNITZER STEEL INDS -CL A	D	E	6.1	7.3	401	-43	587
S	JL	J & L SPECIALTY STEEL	E	B	9.8	1.1	595	31	232
S	ZEUS	OLYMPIC STEEL INC	E	D	7.3	5.0	526	5	438
S	AP	AMPCO-PITTSBURGH CORP	E	E	4.1	4.6	539	-2	482
S	NX	QUANEX CORP	E	E	3.6	5.1	525	-10	512

Steel (Integrated) Industry

VERY LARGE (V) - 300 Cos. — Group | x300 (V)
LARGE (L) - 500 Cos. — Group | x500 (L) | Sort | x500 (L)

	Symbol	Company	Group				x500 (L)	Sort	x500 (L)
L	X	USX-U S STEEL GROUP	E	E	2.9	3.2	473	-53	493

MEDIUM (M) - 600 Cos. — Group | x600 (M) | Sort | x600 (S)

	Symbol	Company	Group				x600 (M)	Sort	x600 (S)
M	LTV	LTV CORP	D	E	6.1	6.2	472	-15	566
M	AKS	AK STEEL HOLDING CORP	D	E	12.5	7.3	408	-20	573
M	BS	BETHLEHEM STEEL CORP	E	E	0.6	2.5	585	-15	567
M	IAD	INLAND STEEL INDUSTRIES INC	E	E	0.7	1.4	593	-20	572
M	CSM	CHAPARRAL STEEL COMPANY	E	E	4.1	5.9	489	-35	591

SMALL (S) - 600 Cos. — Group | x600 (S) | Sort | x600 (S)

	Symbol	Company	Group				x600 (S)	Sort	x600 (S)
S	SHLO	SHILOH INDUSTRIES INC	D	D	6.6	6.7	443	7	421
S	ROCK	GIBRALTAR STEEL CORP	E	D	7.6	8.0	361	-5	498
S	ROU	ROUGE INDUSTRIES INC	D	E	23.0	6.7	440	-68	598
S	WHX	WHX CORP	D	D	3.2	4.2	549	12	389

Telecommunication Equipment Industry

VERY LARGE (V) - 300 Cos. — Group | x300 (V) | Sort | x300 (V)

	Symbol	Company	Group				x300 (V)	Sort	x300 (V)
V	TLAB	TELLABS INC	A	A	20.4	21.9	11	80	11

(continued overleaf)

HOLT USA2000 Universe
Size / #cos / mkt cap

Very large / 300 / $3.93B+
Large / 500 / $1.03–3.93B
Medium / 600 / $.42–1.03B
Small / 600 / $154–425M

Grouped by Forecast +1 year CFROI Grade (Near Term) which is then sorted high-to-low on numerical % Future

			HOLT DualGrade® Performance		CFROI Cash Flow Return on Investment			% of Total Market Value Attributed to Future Investments	
			#1 Near Term Fcst +1-year CFROI Grade	#2 Long Term % Future Grade	Past 5-year Median CFROI	Forecast +1-year CFROI	Forecast +1-year CFROI Rank	% Future	% Future Rank
V	ADCT	ADC TELECOMMUNICATIONS INC	A	A	10.8	15.4	52	75	16
V	LU	LUCENT TECHNOLOGIES INC	C	A	3.8	8.3	176	64	42
	LARGE (L) - 500 Cos.		*Group*				*x500 (L)*	*Sort x500 (L)*	
L	AFCI	ADVANCED FIBRE COMM INC	A	A	11.3	18.5	32	81	23
L	PAIR	PAIRGAIN TECHNOLOGIES INC	A	A	11.6	20.8	16	70	38
L	ADTN	ADTRAN INC	A	A	22.0	14.6	78	62	71
L	ASPT	ASPECT TELECOMMUNICATIONS	A	B	12.3	16.5	53	54	101
L	ANDW	ANDREW CORP	A	B	10.9	16.3	54	38	199
L	ECILF	ECI TELECOMMUNICATIONS -OR	A	C	18.8	18.1	34	36	219
L	QCOM	QUALCOMM INC	B	B	3.0	11.2	155	43	169
L	SFA	SCIENTIFIC-ATLANTA INC	B	C	8.9	13.1	114	32	242
L	DIGI	DSC COMMUNICATIONS CORP	D	C	8.0	7.4	337	29	265
	MEDIUM (M) - 600 Cos.		*Group*				*x600 (M)*	*Sort x600 (M)*	
M	NMSS	NATURAL MICROSYSTEMS CORP	A	A	14.3	14.8	98	80	15
M	CCSC	COHERENT COMMUNICATIONS	A	A	31.6	24.1	15	78	22
M	TKLC	TEKELEC	A	A	2.4	15.0	89	77	25
M	BBOX	BLACK BOX CORP	A	A	12.4	16.8	65	67	62
M	BSN	BOSTON TECHNOLOGY INC	A	A	13.0	19.6	34	64	75
M	CLST	CELLSTAR CORP	A	B	11.2	22.2	21	37	228
M	MTZ	MASTEC INC	A	C	12.3	24.0	16	26	307
M	DLGC	DIALOGIC CORP	B	A	16.3	13.6	130	64	78
M	DMIC	DIGITAL MICROWAVE CORP	B	B	-1.8	11.8	190	52	143
M	MLT	MITEL CORP	B	C	5.5	12.0	181	34	241
M	ALN	ALLEN TELECOM INC	B	D	9.9	12.0	182	9	452
M	LEVL	LEVEL ONE COMMUNICATIONS	C	B	10.7	8.2	351	53	137

M	GEMS	GLENAYRE TECHNOLOGIES INC	D	D	11.2	6.4	463	5	474
			Group	D			x600 (S)	Sort	x600 (S)
	SMALL (S) - 600 Cos.								
S	DAVX	DAVOX CORP	A	A	8.6	25.9	11	77	7
S	OCCF	OPTICAL CABLE CORP	A	A	38.5	32.1	6	63	50
S	OLCMF	OLICOM A/S	A	A	12.9	16.1	69	52	102
S	DSPG	DSP GROUP INC	A	A	8.0	14.5	98	49	110
S	CDCO	CIDCO INC	B	B	17.8	10.4	230	32	225
S	CSII	COMMUNICATIONS SYSTEMS	B	C	11.5	11.9	172	29	244
S	AFCX	AFC CABLE SYSTEMS INC	B	C	12.3	10.7	216	25	282
S	ORTL	ORTEL CORP	D	B	7.6	7.4	396	41	158
S	STII	STANFORD TELECOMMUNICATION	D	B	2.0	7.0	417	39	173
S	PC	PRICELLULAR CORP -CL A	D	B	-1.5	7.5	385	32	223
S	TCSI	TCSI CORP	E	A	12.3	2.5	581	54	95
S	PCTL	PICTURETEL CORP	E	E	6.1	3.4	566	-22	562

Telecommunications Services Industry

M	GEMS	VERY LARGE (V) - 300 Cos.	Group	D	11.2	6.4	x300 (V)	Sort	x300 (V)
V	CSN	CINCINNATI BELL INC	B	B	6.0	11.1	102	55	78
V	ATI	AIRTOUCH COMMUNICATIONS	D	B	3.0	6.4	228	57	69
V	T	AT&T CORP	D	B	7.7	6.9	213	50	102
V	AIT	AMERITECH CORP	D	C	5.9	7.3	203	29	179
V	FRO	FRONTIER CORP	D	D	5.4	6.5	222	26	191
V	AT	ALLTEL CORP	D	D	8.1	8.0	184	25	192
V	SBC	SBC COMMUNICATIONS INC	D	D	6.6	7.5	196	25	193
V	BLS	BELLSOUTH CORP	D	D	5.3	6.3	231	22	205
V	GTE	GTE CORP	D	D	6.3	6.3	232	21	207
V	BEL	BELL ATLANTIC CORP	D	D	6.6	6.7	216	19	217
V	MCIC	MCI COMMUNICATIONS	E	C	5.8	3.7	289	39	145
V	FON	SPRINT CORP	E	D	5.6	3.8	288	28	181
V	USW	U S WEST COMMUNICATIONS	E	D	4.7	5.4	249	19	215

M	GEMS	LARGE (L) - 500 Cos.	Group	D	11.2	6.4	x500 (L)	Sort	x500 (L)
L	UVSGA	UNITED VIDEO SATEL -CL A	A	A	16.2	19.9	20	69	49
L	LCI	LCI INTERNATIONAL INC	B	B	7.6	12.0	142	50	123
L	TALK	TEL-SAVE HOLDINGS INC	C	B	18.0	9.2	244	44	160

(continued overleaf)

HOLT USA2000 Universe
Size / #cos / mkt cap

Very large / 300 / $3.93B+
Large / 500 / $1.03–3.93B
Medium / 600 / $.42–1.03B
Small / 600 / $154–425M

Grouped by Forecast +1 year CFROI Grade (Near Term) which is then sorted high-to-low on numerical % Future

			HOLT DualGrade® Performance		CFROI Cash Flow Return on Investment			% of Total Market Value Attributed to Future Investments	
			#1 Near Term Fcst +1-year CFROI Grade	#2 Long Term % Future Grade	Past 5-year Median CFROI	Forecast +1-year CFROI	Forecast +1-year CFROI Rank	% Future	% Future Rank
L	PAGE	PAGING NETWORK INC	C	C	12.4	9.0	262	27	284
L	TGO	TELEGLOBE INC	C	D	4.7	9.2	247	19	338
L	ALNT	ALIANT COMMUNICATIONS INC	D	B	6.3	7.7	323	43	167
L	CTL	CENTURY TELEPHONE ENTERPR	D	C	8.0	7.7	321	26	287
L	XO	360 COMMUNICATIONS CO	D	D	5.8	7.3	345	25	301
L	MTEL	MOBILE TELECOMMUNICATIONS TEC	E	A	-4.4	4.3	447	60	77
L	USM	US CELLULAR CORP	E	C	-0.5	5.3	409	29	264
L	SNG	SOUTHERN NEW ENG TELECOM	E	D	4.9	3.3	467	24	302
L	TDS	TELEPHONE & DATA	E	D	2.5	1.9	492	16	355
L	CZN	CITIZENS UTILITIES -SER B	E	E	5.8	5.0	423	-27	481
MEDIUM (M) - 600 Cos.			Group				x600 (M)	Sort	x600 (M)
M	PGEX	PACIFIC GATEWAY EXCHANGE	A	A	16.3	21.2	24	85	3
M	BILL	BILLING INFORMATION CONCEPT	A	A	64.2	30.9	7	80	14
M	PCMS	P-COM INC	A	A	8.7	19.4	38	63	79
M	WAXS	WORLD ACCESS INC	A	A	-11.4	15.8	74	63	83
M	ACCC	ACC CORP	A	B	8.6	15.0	92	54	134
M	PRMS	PREMISYS COMMUNICATIONS	B	A	8.8	11.7	193	79	18
M	PTEK	PREMIERE TECHNOLOGIES INC	B	A	9.5	12.0	175	62	91
M	CELS	COMMNET CELLULAR INC	B	B	0.7	12.7	155	39	212
M	SWW	SITEL CORP	B	C	10.6	13.5	136	28	289
M	CTCO	COMMONWLTH TELE ENTER	C	C	6.3	9.8	261	33	252
M	VCELA	VANGUARD CELLULAR SYS -CL	C	C	3.7	9.5	278	25	319
M	NTLI	NTL INC	C	D	-6.0	9.0	306	13	418
M	RCN	ROGERS CANTEL MOB COM -CL	D	C	-4.4	6.2	473	28	293
M	RG	ROGERS COMMUNICATION -CL	E	C	2.0	3.9	563	20	352

SMALL (S) - 600 Cos.

	Code	Company	Group	Group			x600 (S)	Sort	x600 (S)
S	XPED	XPEDITE SYSTEMS INC	A	A	15.4	20.4	31	49	112
S	TLDCF	TELEDATA COMMUNICATION LTD	A	B	10.6	17.9	47	45	134
S	USLD	USLD COMMUNICATIONS CORP	B	A	13.9	12.1	168	56	85
S	DY	DYCOM INDUSTRIES INC	B	B	10.8	13.3	130	39	172
S	SMTK	SMARTALK TELESERVICES INC	B	C	-6.6	10.2	233	18	341
S	PLDI	PLD TELEKOM INC	B	E	-9.9	13.4	128	-20	557
S	CFWC	CFW COMMUNICATIONS CO	C	B	6.0	8.1	356	43	149
S	NRRD	NORSTAN INC	C	D	8.3	9.2	291	6	425
S	SGA	SAGA COMMUNICATIONS -CL A	D	A	4.9	7.6	374	48	119
S	CKSG	CKS GROUP INC	D	C	11.8	7.3	404	24	292
S	ITRI	ITRON INC	E	B	4.2	5.4	511	36	195

Textile Industry

VERY LARGE (V) - 300 Cos. / LARGE (L) - 500 Cos.

	Code	Company	Group	Group			x300 (V) / x500 (L)	Sort	x300 (V) / x500 (L)
L	WPSN	WESTPOINT STEVENS INC	B	B	11.9	13.0	116	39	194
L	UFI	UNIFI INC	C	C	9.7	9.7	220	37	202
L	SMI	SPRINGS INDUSTRIES -CL A	E	E	4.0	4.5	444	-26	479

MEDIUM (M) - 600 Cos.

	Code	Company	Group	Group			x600 (M)	Sort	x600 (M)
M	IFSIA	INTERFACE INC -CL A	C	D	3.2	6.6	448	27	299
M	PXR	PAXAR CORP	D	D	10.8	7.7	388	18	366
M	GFD	GUILFORD MILLS INC	E	E	5.3	6.6	453	-7	540
M	BUR	BURLINGTON INDS INC	E	E	8.3	7.5	395	-22	578

SMALL (S) - 600 Cos.

	Code	Company	Group	Group			x600 (S)	Sort	x600 (S)
S	CFA	CHEMFAB CORPORATION	B	B	6.9	10.5	226	34	211
S	PTX	PILLOWTEX CORP	C	C	8.3	9.1	300	26	273
S	GNL	GALEY & LORD INC	C	E	8.2	8.5	336	-3	487
S	FQE	FUQUA ENTERPRISES INC	D	C	6.5	7.5	391	16	350
S	CFI	CULP INC	E	C	5.2	5.8	486	16	348
S	FIT	FAB INDUSTRIES INC	E	E	6.4	2.8	577	-14	532
S	COE	CONE MILLS CORP	E	E	6.6	4.1	552	-16	539

(continued overleaf)

HOLT USA2000 Universe
Size / #cos / mkt cap
Very large / 300 / $3.93B+
Large / 500 / $1.03–3.93B
Medium / 600 / $.42–1.03B
Small / 600 / $154–425M
Grouped by Forecast +1 year CFROI Grade (Near Term)
which is then sorted high-to-low on numerical % Future

			HOLT DualGrade® Performance		CFROI Cash Flow Return on Investment			% of Total Market Value Attributed to Future Investments	
			#1 Near Term Fcst +1-year CFROI Grade	#2 Long Term % Future Grade	Past 5-year Median CFROI	Forecast +1-year CFROI	Forecast +1-year CFROI Rank	% Future	% Future Rank
					Tire & Rubber Industry				
	VERY LARGE (V) - 300 Cos.		**Group**				**x300 (V)**	**Sort**	**x300 (V)**
V	GT	GOODYEAR TIRE & RUBBER CO	C	E	7.3	8.1	180	−4	270
	LARGE (L) - 500 Cos.		**Group**				**x500 (L)**	**Sort**	**x500 (L)**
L	CLS	CARLISLE COS INC	C	C	6.5	9.3	237	31	250
L	BDG	BANDAG INC	C	D	15.4	9.6	224	15	359
L	CTB	COOPER TIRE & RUBBER	C	E	10.6	9.2	245	3	423
	MEDIUM (M) - 600 Cos.		**Group**				**x600 (M)**	**Sort**	**x600 (M)**
	SMALL (S) - 600 Cos.		**Group**				**x600 (S)**	**Sort**	**x600 (S)**
S	TBCC	TBC CORP	C	D	12.9	9.5	273	6	429
					Tobacco Industry				
	VERY LARGE (V) - 300 Cos.		**Group**				**x300 (V)**	**Sort**	**x300 (V)**
V	UST	UST INC	A	B	48.3	38.5	1	55	76
V	MO	PHILIP MORRIS COS INC	A	C	13.5	15.6	50	41	134
V	RN	RJR NABISCO HLDGS CORP	E	D	4.8	5.4	248	15	231
	LARGE (L) - 500 Cos.		**Group**				**x500 (L)**	**Sort**	**x500 (L)**
L	DMN	DIMON INC	C	D	5.9	9.1	255	19	336
L	UVV	UNIVERSAL CORP/VA	C	D	8.1	9.7	219	14	368
	MEDIUM (M) - 600 Cos.		**Group**				**x600 (M)**	**Sort**	**x600 (M)**
M	CIG	CONS CIGAR HLDGS INC -CL A	A	C	19.9	34.9	5	27	300

SMALL (S) - 600 Cos.

			Group				x600 (S)	Sort	x600 (S)
S	STW	STANDARD COMMERCIAL CORP	E	D	1.2	4.4	544	-2	480

Toiletries/Cosmetics Industry

VERY LARGE (V) - 300 Cos.

			Group				x300 (V)	Sort	x300 (V)
V	G	GILLETTE CO	A	A	13.6	15.5	51	72	22
V	AVP	AVON PRODUCTS	A	B	15.2	17.1	43	50	101
V	EL	LAUDER ESTEE COS INC -CL A	B	A	9.6	12.0	80	62	51

LARGE (L) - 500 Cos.

			Group				x500 (L)	Sort	x500 (L)
L	REV	REVLON INC -CL A	B	C	9.0	13.1	113	33	241
L	ACV	ALBERTO-CULVER CO -CL B	D	C	7.2	7.8	311	36	215

MEDIUM (M) - 600 Cos.

			Group				x600 (M)	Sort	x600 (M)
M	PYX	PLAYTEX PRODUCTS INC	A	B	14.5	14.4	109	44	186
M	HELE	HELEN OF TROY CORP LTD	B	B	9.2	11.5	195	48	168
M	HSIC	SCHEIN HENRY INC	D	B	-1.4	7.9	370	42	197
M	RGIS	REGIS CORP/MN	D	C	5.4	7.2	413	22	335
M	CAR	CARTER-WALLACE INC	E	C	6.1	6.0	482	30	276

SMALL (S) - 600 Cos.

			Group				x600 (S)	Sort	x600 (S)
S	RAZR	AMERICAN SAFETY RAZOR	B	C	10.7	10.2	236	20	323
S	PTB	PARAGON TRADE BRANDS INC	B	E	12.9	10.9	206	-152	599
S	TLZ	THERMOLASE CORP	D	A	-1.7	7.2	407	59	68

Trucking & Transport Leasing Industry

VERY LARGE (V) - 300 Cos.
LARGE (L) - 500 Cos.

			Group				x300 (V) / x500 (L)	Sort	x300 (V) / x500 (L)
L	CBB	CALIBER SYSTEMS INC	C	C	4.4	9.6	222	35	223
L	CNF	CNF TRANSPORTATION INC	D	D	2.6	5.9	383	21	322
L	R	RYDER SYSTEM INC	D	E	4.2	6.7	362	-8	452

(continued overleaf)

HOLT USA2000 Universe
Size / #cos / mkt cap
Very large / 300 / $3.93B+
Large / 500 / $1.03–3.93B
Medium / 600 / $.42–1.03B
Small / 600 / $154–425M

Grouped by Forecast +1 year CFROI Grade (Near Term)
which is then sorted high-to-low on numerical % Future

| | | HOLT DualGrade® Performance | | CFROI Cash Flow Return on Investment | | | % of Total Market Value Attributed to Future Investments | |
		#1 Near Term Fcst +1-year CFROI Grade	#2 Long Term % Future Grade	Past 5-year Median CFROI	Forecast +1-year CFROI	Forecast +1-year CFROI Rank	% Future	% Future Rank
	MEDIUM (M) - 600 Cos.	**Group**				**x600 (M)**	**Sort**	**x600 (M)**
M	HTLD HEARTLAND EXPRESS INC	A	A	18.4	14.5	105	62	87
M	CUI COACH USA INC	B	D	7.3	12.8	153	13	420
M	BD BUDGET GROUP INC -CL A	B	E	4.2	10.4	235	-6	532
M	SWFT SWIFT TRANSPORTATION CO	C	B	9.1	10.1	251	44	187
M	WERN WERNER ENTERPRISES INC	C	D	9.4	9.1	305	17	381
M	AIND ARNOLD INDUSTRIES INC	C	D	11.1	9.2	297	11	429
M	USFC USFREIGHTWAYS CORP	C	D	6.2	9.0	307	10	440
M	RLC ROLLINS TRUCK LEASING	D	D	6.2	7.2	412	5	475
M	XTR XTRA CORP	D	E	6.1	6.3	467	3	486
M	JBHT HUNT (JB) TRANSPRT SVCS INC	E	D	6.4	3.8	564	11	431
M	UHAL AMERCO	E	E	3.0	3.3	572	-13	560
M	YELL YELLOW CORP	E	E	0.0	3.6	567	-40	594
	SMALL (S) - 600 Cos.	**Group**				**x600 (S)**	**Sort**	**x600 (S)**

Estimating retirements

Recall from Appendix B the gross plant identity (using current dollars):

BEG PLANT + CAPX − RETIREMENT = END PLANT

Under the assumption of a constant, real historic growth rate (g), then

RETIREMENT = CAPX$/[1 + g]^L$

where L is gross plant life. Appendix B contains the following expression for CAPX in terms of END PLANT (note that g needs to be non-zero):

$$\text{CAPX} = \frac{\text{END PLANT}\left[1 - \dfrac{1}{1+g}\right]}{\left[1 - \dfrac{1}{(1+g)^L}\right]}$$

Substituting for CAPX in the RETIREMENT expression gives

$$\text{RETIREMENT} = \frac{\text{END PLANT}\left[1 - \dfrac{1}{1+g}\right]}{[1+g]^L\left[1 - \dfrac{1}{(1+g)^L}\right]}$$

$$\text{RETIREMENT} = \frac{\text{END PLANT}\left[\dfrac{1+g-1}{1+g}\right]}{[1+g]^L - \dfrac{[1+g]^L}{[1+g]^L}}$$

$$\text{RETIREMENT} = \frac{\text{END PLANT }(g)}{[1+g][(1+g)^L - 1]}$$

When dealing not just with gross plant but also total gross operating assets, released non-depreciating assets are treated as retirements.

Glossary

Assumptions

To emphasize the importance of continually seeking and needing feedback information in order to test and judge the reliability of conceptual beliefs and to correct erroneous beliefs, we use 'assumptions' as a synonym for 'knowledge' when discussing what knowledge is and how it improves. In other contexts, 'assumption' has its usual meaning—purported facts or causal descriptions accepted as reliable with little or no supporting empirical evidence for such.

Assets, operating assets

The firm's assets are divided into operating assets used in the firm's businesses and non-operating assets. CFROIs and net cash receipts are based on operating assets. Many accounting and inflation adjustments are made to standard financial-statement data in calculating an amount of CFROI-operating assets.

CAPM and CAPM/beta

CAPM is shorthand for 'capital asset pricing model.' The CAPM specifies the expected return on a specific stock as the expected return on a risk-free asset plus a risk premium which is the product of 'beta' multiplied by the estimated *excess* return for the general stock market over the risk-free rate. 'Beta' is a measure of the sensitivity of a specific stock's price to movements in the general stock market. Betas greater than 1.0 indicate greater sensitivity than the market, and betas less than 1.0 indicate the opposite.

CFROI

CFROI is an abbreviation for 'cash flow return on investment' and is used to refer to both (1) the complete CFROI *valuation model* and (2) the CFROI *performance metric*, which is a key component of the model. The CFROI performance metric is an approximation of the average *real* internal rate of return earned by a firm on all its operating assets.

Company-specific risk differentials

In the CFROI model, a real risk differential—positive, negative, or zero—is added to the real market discount rate to determine a company-specific real discount rate. Risk differentials are related to the company's size and financial leverage. The company-specific real discount rate is used to calculate a present value of the firm's forecasted net cash receipts stream.

Competitive life cycle and fade

A well-accepted proposition in economics is that competition, over the long term, *tends to* force returns toward the average. The CFROI model incorporates this effect of competition in the form of baseline forecasts for above-average CFROIs to fade downward over time and below-average CFROIs to fade upward over time; and similarly for above-average growth and below-average growth. Fade rates for CFROIs and growth are key determinants of NCRs.

Constant dollars

Dollar (or other monetary unit) amounts for different years are expressed in dollars (or other monetary unit) having the same purchasing power.

Cost of capital, or discount rate

'Cost of capital' is the rate of return investors demand from companies for the use of their capital. As such, cost of capital also is the discount rate used for calculating the present value of a stream of future receipts. Types of cost-of-capital rates include weighted-average cost of capital, equity cost of capital, and debt cost of capital. In the CFROI model, the cost of capital, or discount rate, is a real rate and is the weighted average of a real debt rate and a real equity rate.

Current dollars

Dollar (or other monetary unit) amounts for different years have the purchasing power of the dollar (or other monetary unit) for the year for which the amount is recorded.

Discount rate

See Cost of capital.

DualGrade®, DualGrade® performance scorecard

DualGrade® is a two-grade summary grading system for companies which is based on the CFROI model. One grade is for expected near-term CFROI economic performance level and the other is for the percentage of a company's total value attributable to future investments. The DualGrade® Performance Scorecard presents selected other measures along with dual grades. DualGrade® is a trademarked product of HOLT Value Associates.

Fade

See Competitive life cycle.

Growth/sustainable growth

The CFROI valuation model uses a competitive life-cycle perspective in which NCRs forecasted to come from future investments are driven by forecasted ROIs on incremental projects and forecasted amounts invested in them. For valuation purposes, 'growth' is the year-by-year amounts invested in these future projects. The *rate* of such growth over the long run closely approximates rate of growth in the firm's operating assets. With a given CFROI level, *sustainable growth* can be calculated by assuming no change in dividend payout or capital structure, and this can be used to estimate the year-by-year amounts invested in future projects.

Historical dollars

Dollar (or other monetary unit) amounts for a given year are the summation of different-year current-dollar amounts; thus they are amounts of mixed-purchasing-power dollars (or other monetary unit).

Inflation-adjusted, or real, magnitudes

Inflation is a rise in the general level of prices, and indicates a decrease in the value of the monetary unit. We make adjustments to all quantities measured as monetary amounts in order to eliminate recorded changes owing solely to inflation. Measurements adjusted for changes in the values of monetary units are called *inflation-adjusted*, or *real*, magnitudes. We use the terms interchangeably. Similar adjustments would be made if deflation were to occur.

Internal rate of return (IRR)

An IRR is the discount rate that equates the cost for an investment with the subsequent net cash receipts over a number of years that result from the investment.

Managerial skill

Skill is observable as performance. A firm's managerial skill is revealed by the extent *over a longer term* that: (1) customers believe they have received high value from the firm's products or services, (2) the average competitor in the industry is unable to reproduce what the firm delivers to customers, and/or to achieve its level of resource efficiency, and (3) larger investments are made while the firm continues to earn returns on those investments well above its cost of capital.

Market-derived discount rate, or market rate

In the CFROI model, the 'market rate' is a real rate *derived* by a procedure consistent with the model and incorporating the market's valuation of an *aggregate* of firms. Since valuation at any given time is based on expectations of receiving a stream of *future* receipts, the market-derived discount rate is *forward looking*.

Model

'Model' is synonymous with 'conceptual framework' in our usage. By these terms we mean a posited causal description of the key components to valuation and the relationships among them. We do *not* use model in the sense of a set of mathematical equations for calculating the 'right' price of individual common stocks.

Net cash receipts (NCRs)

On an intuitive level, a firm's net cash receipt for a time period is the cash inflow less the cash outflow. Outflows are needed to make the investments and conduct the operations which will eventually provide additional inflows. Hence, the value of the firm is the present value of this *net* cash receipt stream. Also, the CFROI model separates the forecasted NCR stream into two components: NCRs from *existing assets* and NCRs from *future investments*.

NCRs are payments to both debt and equity capital suppliers. They are in constant dollars and have included the payment of corporate taxes and the benefit of interest payments being tax deductible. Hence, they should be discounted with a real weighted-average discount rate which does *not* require an adjustment to the real debt rate to capture the tax-deductibility-of-interest benefit.

Present value factor

To calculate the present value of a future sum, the sum is divided by $(1 + \text{discount rate})$ raised to a power equal to the number of periods between the period of the future sum and the period for which the present value is calculated. To illustrate, if the discount rate is 10 per cent and the sum to be present-valued is 3 years into the future, the divisor would be $(1.10)^3$, which is 1.331. To convert a divisor into a multiplier factor, take its reciprocal: in the illustration, 1/1.331, which is 0.751. Any sum to be present-valued at 10 per cent for a 3-year period would be multiplied by this factor.

Real magnitudes

See Inflation-adjusted magnitudes.

Relative wealth index

Trends in the Relative Wealth Index indicate how a firm's total share-holder return (dividends plus price change) compares to the total return from the general market (the S&P 500 in the United States). A flat trend in the Index implies total shareholder return matching the market. Upward or downward trends indicate outperforming or underperforming the market.

Residual income (RI)/residual income model

RI is what a firm earns in excess of that required to compensate owners for the cost of using their capital. In the standard academic 'residual income model', a firm's RI for any period is calculated as the product of the 'spread' between the firm's return-on-equity and its equity-cost-of-capital multiplied by the firm's accounting-equity-value at the beginning of the period. The firm's warranted equity at a point in time, is the sum of accounting equity value plus the present value of the stream of forecasted annual RI amounts for a selected number of years. At the end of the selected period, the RI for the final year is typically assumed to continue in perpetuity, which permits an easy present-value calculation of the assumed perpetuity RI. EVA® (economic value added) is a version of RI which uses total capital instead of equity capital, a variety of accounting adjustments, and a nominal weighted average cost of capital via CAPM/beta.

ROI

Whereas the CFROI metric is an approximation of the average real internal rate of return earned by a firm on all its operating assets, ROI is the real internal rate of return earned on incremental investments, or projects.

Setting the line

With an actual price of a company's stock and a forecasted company CFROI level for one year in the future, the CFROI model can be used to infer the market's expectation for the company's CFROI performance at year 5 in the future. In a graphical display of CFROIs, a line can be drawn connecting the +1-year and +5-year CFROIs. This is called 'setting the line'. If the firm delivers CFROIs higher or lower than the line, its stock price will likely outperform or underperform the market.

Sustainable growth

See Growth.

Total system, total system approach

Total system approach, as used in the book's sub-title, refers to the need to understand how variables key to firms' values are related, including how non-accounting variables produce the results reflected in accounting statements. This approach provides, in the form of the CFROI model, a template for nurturing critical thinking about measuring firms' economic performance, making forecasts of future economic performance, and calculating warranted values.

Warranted equity value per share

A firm's warranted equity value per share is based on subtracting the estimated market value of debt, preferred stock, and minority interest from the total-firm's warranted value and dividing that sum by common shares outstanding, adjusted for dilution.

Warranted value

In general, a 'warranted value' is a value of a company calculated from use of a valuation model. A warranted value should *not* be uncritically interpreted as the *right* value. In the case of the CFROI model, a firm's warranted value is the sum of (1) the net present value of forecasted NCR streams attributable to the firm's existing operating assets and to expected future investments in operating assets, both discounted by the company's real discount rate and (2) the realizable after-tax value of the firm's non-operating assets.

Index